Stranger in Our Midst

Also by Harold B. Segel—

The Literature of Eighteenth-Century Russia

The Death of Tarelkin and Other Plays by Alexander Sukhovo-Kobylin

The Major Comedies of Alexander Fredro

The Baroque Poem

Polish Romantic Drama

Twentieth-Century Russian Drama from Gorky to the Present

Turn-of-the-Century Cabaret: Paris, Barcelona, Berlin, Munich, Vienna, Cracow, Moscow, St. Petersburg, Zurich

Renaissance Culture in Poland: The Rise of Humanism, 1470–1543

The Vienna Coffeehouse Wits 1890–1938

Pinocchio's Progeny: Puppets, Marionettes, Automatons, and Robots in Modernist and Avant-Garde Drama

Stranger in Our Midst

Images of the Jew in Polish Literature

Edited with an Introduction by

■ **Harold B. Segel**

Cornell University Press / Ithaca & London

First published 1996 by Cornell University Press.

Text design by Carrie Nelson House.

Printed in the United States of America

⊗ The paper in this book meets the minimum requirements
of the American National Standard for Information Sciences—
Permanence of Paper for Printed Library Materials, ANSI Z39.48-1984.

Library of Congress Cataloging-in-Publication Data

Stranger in our midst : images of the Jew in Polish literature / edited with
    an introduction by Harold B. Segel.
        p.   cm.
    Includes bibliographical references.
    ISBN 0-8014-2865-3 (cl. : alk. paper). — ISBN 0-8014-8104-x (pbk. : alk.
paper)
    1. Polish literature—Translations into English.   2. Jews—Poland—
Literary collections.   I. Segel, Harold B., 1930-   .
PG7445.E1S77   1996
891.8'50935203924—dc20   95-50480

To the memory of my mother, who knew both worlds and saw the best in them.

I gazed astounded at those pages [the novel *The Inn* by Julian Stryjkowski], which had yellowed and darkened during those fourteen years, and I thought about that world, great and splendid, majestic and romantic, funny and laughable, moving and tragic, the unforgettable and already forgotten world and universe of the Polish Jews.

A planet died. A globe incinerated by a cosmic disaster. A black hole. Antimatter.

Oh, God, how did it happen? Anti-Semitism, philo-Semitism, Zionism, nationalism, converts and Hasids, hatreds and rivalries, moments of solidarity and community, good days, bad days, humanity, inhumanity, all of it mixed and whirled together in one land, divided and united, two civilizations and two cultures. Then, suddenly, during the brief night of the occupation, something was amputated. Some part of the landscape, the flora, the fauna, the architecture, the sound track was forever severed and borne away into the icy darkness of the universe which is our heaven and our hell.

—TADEUSZ KONWICKI, *Moonrise, Moonset*

Contents

Illustrations

Preface

Polish literature is a literature of Jewish experience; indeed, it is the greatest European literature of Jewish experience, a proposition that seems unlikely at best. Widely regarded as notoriously anti-Semitic, the Poles seem hardly likely to have encompassed Jewish experience in their literature in any but the most negative terms. But this is not the case.

Poland has the richest Jewish history of any country in Europe, and one of the richest in the world. Jewish habitation, which can be traced back as early as the late tenth century, expanded in time to such an extent that on the eve of the German invasion of Poland in September 1939, Jews constituted over 10 percent of the total population of the country. But dry statistics can scarcely do justice to the impact of the Jewish presence on the Polish consciousness. Whatever their relations with the Poles, which changed as Polish fortunes changed in the course of history, whatever the estrangement of the majority of the Jews from mainstream Polish society, no significant Jewish emigration from Poland occurred until the twentieth century. Poland in fact had achieved its sizable Jewish community because of Jewish migration into the country in past centuries. And even with the increasing emigration to Palestine and elsewhere in the period between the two world wars, the Jewish community still numbered some three and a half million in 1939. Whatever preconceived notions may exist concerning the Poles' treatment of their huge Jewish population, the fact remains that that population, as indeed all of European Jewry, was targeted for extinction by the Germans, who invaded Poland in September 1939 and occupied the country until 1945. Polish-Jewish relations at their worst cannot even remotely approximate the magnitude, and horror, of that genocide.

This book is an attempt to look at Polish-Jewish relations from the perspective of Polish literature. Or to be more specific, from the viewpoint of that Polish imaginative literature written by Poles who were not, or are not, Jews. Assimilated Jews who spoke and wrote Polish began contributing to Polish literary culture only in the twentieth century, mainly in the interwar period. Their number includes some of the finest literary talents in the Polish language in this century — the poets Julian Tuwim and Aleksander Wat, the prose writers Bruno Schulz and Kazimierz Brandys, and the playwright and director Tadeusz Kantor — but so complete has been their identification with Polish culture, and so strong their desire to be regarded as *Polish* writers, that very few Jewish writers in Polish have turned to Jewish subjects or relations between Poles and Jews in their works. Ethnic Polish writers, however, free of the constraints and inhibitions of Jewish assimilation, and representative of the host culture, have attempted to come to grips with the huge but largely alien Jewish community in their midst for centuries.

In the virtual absence of a living Jewish culture in Poland today, historiography and other forms of recovery of the past collaborate on at least a documentary and iconographic reconstitution of the lost Jewish community. In so doing the Poles are attempting to recover a now extinct dimension of their own past. Their efforts are paralleled by the extraordinary scholarship on virtually every facet of the history of the Jews of Poland which has occurred in both the English-speaking world and Israel in recent years.

With this book I seek to make a modest contribution to the ever-growing literature on the Jews of Poland and the history of Polish-Jewish relations. Through a carefully selected collection of texts, the great majority from works of imaginative literature, Polish literature has been called upon to disclose its own shifting perspective on the Jewish community in Poland. The importance of literary culture in Poland and the immense presence of the Jew in that culture enhance the value of such an endeavor.

The huge body of texts available for an anthology of Polish literature on the Jew could easily fill more than a single volume. Limited, however, by practical considerations, I have tried to choose texts that are generally regarded as of major significance in Polish literary culture yet representative of Polish literary treatment of the Jew in any given period. For texts from the sixteenth and eighteenth centuries and for a cross-section of the anti-Semitic popular press of the period 1915–1929, I incorporated political and social commentary where it seemed useful to complement, or to compensate for a paucity of, appropriate imaginative literature.

Since it was impossible to include entire novels, novellas, plays, and lengthy poems, excerpts had to be chosen with an eye to their interest and typicality for the individual text. Each selection is preceded by its own concise introduction whose purpose is to provide basic information on the author and the text from which it comes so that the reader has a helpful frame of reference. In some instances, for example, novels, I have interpolated brief summaries of the narrative at key junctures.

No selection of texts such as this one, to say nothing of the process of excerpting itself, will please everyone familiar with the material. I would have much preferred to include whole texts, but that was out of the question if the book was to materialize in what I regard as its most useful form. I also deeply regret not being able to include every author I would have liked, from Asnyk to Żeromski; but the line had to be drawn somewhere. In view of the scope of the book, however, I regard omissions as regrettable but not grievous.

Since the purpose of the book is to illuminate non-Jewish Polish attitudes toward the Jews of Poland and patterns of Polish-Jewish relations through the ages, Polish writers of Jewish origin have been omitted. The sole exception is

Antoni Słonimski, who had an impressive Jewish pedigree but was raised as a Catholic. Perhaps that is why Słonimski felt more comfortable writing about Jews than a fellow writer of Jewish origin such as Julian Tuwim, at least until the Holocaust revived Tuwim's sense of Jewishness. Until the interwar period there was no significant Jewish contribution to Polish literary culture except for the literary and art criticism of the nineteenth-century writer Julian Klaczko, who began writing in Hebrew and then switched to Polish and French. When writers of Jewish origin began making their presence felt in Polish literature they rarely wrote on Jewish subjects, notwithstanding efforts by some scholars to identify patterns of subliminal and subtextual Jewishness, as, for example, in the case of Bruno Schulz. For obvious reasons, the impressive Yiddish literature that blossomed in interwar Poland was similarly excluded from consideration. The works of a Yiddish writer such as Isaac Bashevis Singer, which conjure up their own world of old Polish Jewry, make splendid reading for comparative purposes but have no integral place in the present anthology.

All translations from the Polish are my own except where indicated otherwise in the notes. Information on the original texts used for translations also appears in the notes. All Polish and Jewish names appear as they do in the original except for Jewish first names, which have been transliterated from the Polish spelling of the Yiddish and Hebrew originals. Thus Mosze appears as Moshe, Szloma as Shloma, Jankiel as Yankel, Cipa as Tsipa, and so on. For the sake of avoiding undue Anglicization and in order to preserve the Polish flavor of the original, Polish terms of address have been retained. Hence: *pan* ("mister," "sir"), *pani* ("mrs.," "madam"), *panna* ("miss"), *panowie* ("sirs," "gentlemen"). The sole exception is the character Irma Seidenman in Andrzej Szczypiorski's novel *Początek*. Since my excerpts have been taken from the published translation, *The Beautiful Mrs. Seidenman,* I thought it best not to change "Mrs. Seidenman" back into "Pani Seidenman." Finally, Yiddish and Hebrew terms occurring in Polish texts have generally been left as they appear in the originals as a way of showing the greater or lesser familiarity of the authors with these terms.

The concept for this book grew out of an international conference on Polish-Jewish relations through the ages which I organized in 1983 in my capacity as director of the Institute on East Central Europe of Columbia University's School of International and Public Affairs. The lecture I delivered at the conference, on images of the Jew in Polish literature, was repeated subsequently on other public occasions in somewhat altered versions. The response to these lectures, and the comments I received at other forums, encouraged me to proceed with the anthology and to attempt to realize it in its present form.

For permission to translate from the Polish or to reprint excerpts from translations in print, grateful acknowledgment is made to the holders of copyright, publishers, or representatives listed below.

Farrar, Straus & Giroux, Inc. Excerpts from Jarosław M. Rymkiewicz, *The Final Station: Umschlagplatz.* Translated by Nina Taylor. Translation copyright © 1994 by Farrar, Straus & Giroux. Copyright © by Éditions Robert Laffont, S. A., Paris. Excerpt from Tadeusz Konwicki, *Moonrise, Moonset.* Translated by Richard Lourie. Translation copyright © 1987 by Farrar, Straus & Giroux, Inc. First Polish edition published by Index on Censorship, London, in Zapis 21, copyright © 1982 by Tadeusz Konwicki.

Grove/Atlantic, Inc. Excerpts from Andrzej Szczypiorski, *The Beautiful Mrs. Seidenman.* Translated by Klara Glowczewska. Copyright © 1989 by Grove Press. Copyright © 1988 by Diogenes Verlag, A. G.

Giesenheyner & Crone (Stuttgart). Permission to translate Tadeusz Borowski, "Człowiek z paczką."

Hippocrene Books, Inc. Excerpts from Adam Mickiewicz, *Pan Tadeusz.* Translated by Kenneth R. Mackenzie. Copyright © Polish Cultural Foundation, 1986.

Sterling Lord Literistic, Inc. Excerpts from Czesław Miłosz, *Native Realm: A Search for Self-Definition.* Translated by Catherine S. Leach. Published by Doubleday. Copyright © 1968 by Czesław Miłosz Royalties, Inc. Reprint "A Poor Christian Looks at the Ghetto" from Czesław Miłosz, *Collected Poems, 1931–1987.* Translated by Czesław Miłosz. Published by Ecco Press. Copyright © 1988 by Czesław Miłosz Royalties, Inc. I also express my sincere thanks to Czesław Miłosz for his gracious personal permission to include material from his works in this book.

Pan Andrzej Mierzejewski of the Dział Literacki of the Agencja Autorska Fundacja (Warsaw) for his generous assistance in securing permissions to translate Marian Piechał's "Ostatni koncert Jankiela," from the volume *Moje Imperium,* Tadeusz Różewicz's *Gałąź,* and excerpts from Jerzy Andrzejewski's *Wielki tydzień.*

Professor Piotr Słonimski (CNRS, Gif Sur Yvette) for his kind permission to translate two poems by Antoni Słonimski.

Prof. dr hab. Daniel Grinberg, Director, Żydowski Instytut Historyczny (Warsaw), for his kind permission to reprint copies of pictures in the collection of the ŻIH.

Muzeum Narodowe (Warsaw) for their kind permission to reprint copies of pictures in their collection.

Muzeum Narodowe (Wrocław) for their kind permission to reprint the copy of Juliusz Kossak's painting *Jarmark pod Warszawą* from their collection.

Robert L. Kirkland III of the Warsaw office of the Kosciuszko Foundation, for his time and effort in helping me track down pictorial material in Poland.

Special thanks are also due my editors, Andrew Lewis and Carol Betsch of Cornell University Press, for their equanimity throughout the arduous process of ensuring that the book enters the world as unblemished as possible. For any errors or infelicities that may yet have made their way into print, I alone bear full responsibility.

HAROLD B. SEGEL
New York City and Tucson, Arizona

Stranger in Our Midst

Introduction

The centuries-old history of the Jews in Poland is at an end.[1] What the Germans failed to destroy between 1939 and 1945 has been scattered by the winds of postwar politics. So little of Jewry and Jewishness survives in Poland today that one can hardly speak of a meaningful Jewish presence there anymore. The "state within a state," as the huge Jewish community in Poland was often referred to, has evaporated. For Jews, the abiding sense of loss of one of the greatest and most vibrant communities of world Jewry underscores the efforts at preservation in whatever form. For the Poles, the legacy of the German genocide of Polish and European Jewry on Polish soil, combined with the expediency and cynicism of postwar Polish communism, has created its own imperative. Ignoring the Jewish past in Poland, cultivating forgetfulness—in the presence of Jewish absence—is widely regarded as unacceptable.

Adversity has long imposed on Poland a reverence for history. It was obliterated as a state by the partitions of the late eighteenth century, subjected to Germanization and Russianization throughout the nineteenth century, and turned into a killing field for Jews in World War II. Themselves physically and culturally assaulted in the same period more grievously than at any time in the past, the Poles cannot morally tolerate empty pages in their history as a nation. Hence the ongoing postcommunist archaeology of the Jewish past in Poland.

History entwined the fates of the Poles and the Jews to such an extent that the two peoples have become dimensions of each other. There are surely painful memories on both sides, but for different reasons. The Jewish soul is seared forever by the recollection of systematic mass slaughter and the violent end of the once formidable Jewish presence in Poland. The Polish recollection of the Jewish past is accompanied by its own torments. Not only was Polish Jewry exterminated in Poland, but the country became a slaughterhouse for many Jews transported there from elsewhere in Europe. The sense of moral involvement, if not responsibility, is inescapable. And if Poles cannot help but ask themselves the inevitable questions—Could we have done more to help? Did we really want to help?—the questions are also asked for them, and of them. And as they are asked, the Poles find themselves newly victimized. Despite the magnitude of their own losses in the war, the Poles have had to live the later nightmare of suspicion of collusion

---

1. The Selected Bibliography contains an extensive list of publications in English on the history of the Jews in Poland. For a general history of Poland, see the two-volume work by Norman Davies, *God's Playground: A History of Poland* (New York: Columbia University Press, 1982).

in the Holocaust, of their moral failure in abandoning the Jews in their most desperate hour of need, of even betraying many of them. This second victimization, as it were, of the Poles fails to confront the realities of the German occupation for the Poles themselves. These realities shrank the potential for heroism while at the same time bringing out the worst and the best in human response to grave danger. There were Poles who felt morally compelled to help Jews, despite the risks, and they have been duly acknowledged, and honored. Their number is not small. There were many more Poles who were so numbed by fear of what could happen to them that even had they had the desire to help, they did not. Then there were the masses of Poles for whom the world had become so constricted by the imperative of survival that the plight of the Jews was ignored, shrugged off, or at best passively lamented.

In light of the much greater prewar Jewish population of Poland compared to Germany, and the deterioration of Polish-Jewish relations in the interwar period, particularly after the death of Marshal Józef Piłsudski in 1935, attempts to find a "final solution" to the "Jewish question" might have seemed more plausible in the Polish context. The Jewish population of Poland was the largest in Europe in 1939, when World War II erupted, and the largest in the world after that of the United States. It numbered some three and a half million souls and represented over ten percent of the total population of Poland. By contrast, the number of Jews in prewar Germany was substantially less than a million in a country nearly twice as populous as Poland. Statistics tell only part of the story. So large was the concentration of Jews in major Polish cities that they numbered a third or more of the population of Warsaw and were similarly disproportionately represented in other urban centers. The *shtetl,* the small provincial community usually no larger than a village that was wholly, or nearly wholly, Jewish, had no counterpart in Western Europe. German Jews not only did not live in their own districts in cities, in ghettos, if you will, or cluster together in their own little towns and villages scattered throughout the countryside, they were—with few exceptions—thoroughly secularized and culturally assimilated. Their everyday language was German, and they took pride in German culture and their ability to participate in it. The Yiddish language was rare and mocked, and German Jews, like their Viennese brethren, regarded the masses of Yiddish-speaking Polish Jews with as much a sense of alienation as most Poles.

By contrast, the majority of the Jews of Poland were neither secularized nor assimilated. Acculturation picked up speed after World War I during the twenty years of independent interwar Poland. That progress (if one chooses to view it as such) notwithstanding, most Polish Jews were still Orthodox in their religious beliefs and practices, traditional in garb, Yiddish in speech, and aloof from mainstream Polish social and cultural life.

The resentment that this "otherness" bred among the Poles should be understandable. Ethnic minorities always attract prejudice and social tension. Once this regrettable but basic fact of human nature is acknowledged, it follows logically that the larger, the more visible, the ethnic minority, the greater the prejudice against it. In this respect, the Poles are no different from any other people. Yet in certain respects the Poles have been remarkably different.

Religious tolerance is an established fact of Polish history. Indeed, it can be argued that Protestantism fared worse in Poland than Judaism, particularly in light of the serious threat to the privileged position of the Roman Catholic Church posed by the inroads of Lutheranism and Calvinism in the sixteenth century. Yet Poland never experienced the Protestant-Catholic strife of Western Europe. The peculiar accommodation of religious difference on the part of the Polish nobility, who dominated the internal politics of the Polish state from the sixteenth to eighteenth centuries, extended as well to the Jews. When religious bigotry, persecution, and expulsion in the West wrote new chapters in the long history of their diaspora, the Jews migrated in large numbers to a Poland they celebrated as a haven. Whatever the barriers they faced, Poland never ceased being a haven for the Jews as long as there was a Poland. When the Poles were the masters of their own state up to the third partition in 1795, and again between 1918 and 1939, the Poles never instigated any mass Jewish exodus from the country, to say nothing of far more drastic measures to resolve any "Jewish question." No significant emigration of Jews from Polish lands occurred until the interwar period and the intense Zionist campaign to resettle as many Jews in Palestine as possible. That Polish nationalists were only too glad to see large numbers of Jews leave could only have been regarded as fortuitous by the Zionists, who had their own agenda to promote regardless of the actual state of Polish-Jewish relations. Even without the enthusiastic encouragement of the Polish right wing, and the intensifying anti-Semitism especially of the 1930s, the Zionists would still have worked tirelessly to resettle Polish Jews in Palestine.

In the history of the Polish-Lithuanian Commonwealth (the *Rzeczpospolita*—the Polish equivalent of *res publica*—as it was known), the political structure of the state, with its decentralization and powerful noble class, acted as a virtual guarantee of Jewish security. Jews were allowed into the country in ever greater numbers in the wake of the Inquisition in Spain, the plague (which many blamed on them), and the frenzy of religious conflict in the German world. Not only were the Jews given legal protection, as evidenced, for example, in the sixteenth-century compilation of laws of Grand Hetman of the Crown Jan Tarnowski, but they were permitted the free exercise of their faith and the free conduct of their own affairs. What this meant, in effect, was that the Jews were allowed to live as Jews in a Jewish environment.

This Jewish autonomy in Poland can be viewed in two ways. From an assimilationist Jewish perspective, the autonomy of the Jewish community was a de facto form of segregation. The Jews were really forced to live apart, were not allowed to enter the mainstream of Polish social and cultural life, and so developed their own patterns of communal existence. From the Polish perspective—and the Polish literary tradition bears this out—the majority of Polish Jews were Orthodox and traditionalist and evolved a way of life that accorded with, and accommodated, their outlook and desires. Two consistent, recurring themes in the Polish writing on Jews, belletristic and otherwise, are the preference of the masses of Jews to live their own lives by and large apart from Poles, the better to be able to fulfill themselves spiritually as Jews, and the complicity, if you will, of the Poles in the realization of that goal. Much of Polish literature dealing with Jews isolates the self-centeredness and shortsightedness of the Polish noble class as the leading causes of the emergence of the Jewish "state within a state" in Poland. A tradition of religious tolerance among the Polish gentry indeed kept them from interfering in the spiritual affairs of the Jewish community. They also tolerated the Jewish faith and Jewish ways because they were essentially indifferent to them. They saw the Jews primarily as a tool with which to further their own economic goals and so they used Jews as middlemen, agents, tax collectors, and as a means of exploiting peasants in villages without having to bear direct responsibility themselves. But in order to forestall future competition, they hobbled Jewish economic advancement in much the same way as they impeded the economic progress of other classes. However much Jews may have resented any curtailments of their pursuit of economic self-betterment, the majority were not ungrateful for a society that did not interfere with their religious observances, manner of dress, schooling, and language preference, and indeed allowed them their own courts and a fair measure of autonomy in the administration of their own communities.

Even allowing for the growth of an assimilationist movement among Jews in the nineteenth century, particularly in the second half of the century, and the emergence of a Jewish monied class, the basic patterns of life of the traditional Jewish community continued undisturbed until the reestablishment of an independent Polish state following World War I. The return of Poland to the political map of Europe was a mixed blessing to the Polish Jews. The interwar period accelerated Jewish secularization and acculturation. Apart from the numerically significant entry of Jews into the professions, even including the military, a secular Jewish culture asserted itself in both Polish and Yiddish. A vibrant Jewish press, in both languages, came into existence, and secular Jewish writers using Polish as their primary language stood out on the Polish literary landscape. One need go no further by way of example than Julian Tuwim, one of the outstanding Polish-language poets of the twentieth century. In "My, Żydzi polscy . . ." ("We, Polish Jews . . ."), a moving declaration of himself as a Pole and as a Jew written in April 1944, within a year after the Warsaw Ghetto Uprising, Tuwim speaks of his Polishness in words that most assimilationist Jews would have easily understood:

> If it came to defining my nationality, or rather my sense of national belonging, then I am a Pole for the most simple, almost primitive reasons, mostly

rational, partly irrational, but without any "mystical" embellishment. To be a Pole is neither an honor, nor a glory, nor a privilege. The same as breathing. I have not yet met a person who is proud of the fact that he breathes.

A Pole, because it was in Poland that I was born, raised, and educated; because it was in Poland that I was happy and unhappy; because from exile I want to return to Poland, even though I was promised the joys of paradise elsewhere. . . .

A Pole, because I was told so in my own home in Polish; because from infancy I was nourished on Polish speech; because my mother taught me Polish songs and verses; because when the first tremor of poetry gripped me, it was in Polish words that it burst forth; because what became the most important thing in my life — poetic creativity — is unthinkable in any other language no matter how fluent I might be in it.[2]

Yet in precisely the same period that Jews were beginning to make their presence felt in the Polish literary world, Yiddish literature in Poland achieved its greatest florescence, represented, above all, by the celebrated figure of Isaac Bashevis Singer.

But the political and economic instabilities of interwar Poland, worsened by the ever more strident demands of the large ethnic minorities (Ukrainians, Lithuanians, Jews, Belorussians, Germans) for greater autonomy, put severe strains on the new state. Its weaknesses were difficult to paper over or minimize. Frustration and the search for easy solutions to complex problems encouraged the growth of nationalism, much as it did in post–World War I Germany. Compromise and tolerance soon lost their appeal among those who regarded centrist positions as blemishes on the national character. Long-standing grievances against the Jews for their numbers, their separateness, and their alleged parasitism, aggravated by the greater prominence of Jews in the professions and trades, erupted in the form of often virulent anti-Semitism and a de facto quota system aimed at heading off the Jewish domination of the professions by limiting the enrollment of Jewish students in the universities and professional schools. There were also voices demanding the expulsion of the Jews from Poland, but nothing really was done to implement these demands. The inherent paradox of the more strident anti-Semitism of many Poles in the interwar period is that it came at a time when the Jews were in fact doing what Poles, well meaning and otherwise, had been urging them to do for centuries — becoming secularized and Polonized. The more the Jews acculturated, the more their presence was felt in the professions, the trades, and the economic life of the country as a whole. Economic considerations again became an important determinant of Polish-Jewish relations. In the good old days of the "noble republic," as the Commonwealth was often re-

2. Julian Tuwim, *My, Żydzi polscy . . . / We, Polish Jews . . .* , ed. Ch. Shmeruk (Jerusalem: Magnes Press, Hebrew University, 1984), 27–28.

ferred to, the gentry shaped the economy of the country largely to satisfy their own needs and aspirations and in so doing shaped the place of the majority of Jews in Polish society. The day of noble hegemony had long since waned before the creation of an independent interwar Poland; while still a numerous class, and certainly not without influence, the gentry were no longer in a position to maintain a stranglehold on the Polish economy any more than they could on Polish political life. In the new realities of the Second Republic, the Jews soon discovered that theirs was essentially a no-win situation. The more Polish they became, the more they were regarded as an intolerable economic threat and the more they were resented. The more Jewish they remained, the more they were perceived as an unbearable burden on the strained resources of the financially shaky Polish state.

In *The Un-Divine Comedy* (*Nie-boska komedia*, 1834), one of the outstanding plays of nineteenth-century Polish romanticism, Count Henryk Krasiński, a conservative Catholic nobleman, dramatized his profound fear of social upheaval in an era of political revolutionary fervor. Shaped by Hegelian dialectics, the play conjures up the menacing vision of the last decisive battle between the old order of privilege and the new order of godless materialism. Krasiński assigned an important role in his work to crypto-Jews, Jewish converts to Christianity who secretly practice Judaism but pretend to be Christians in order to use the revolution as the means to achieve their own goal of world domination.

Interwar Polish nationalists tended to cast the Jews of their own time in a similarly sinister light. With the notorious *Protocols of the Elders of Zion* serving as a more immediate source of inspiration than Count Krasiński's romantic drama, the crypto-Jews of interwar Poland were now identified as crypto-assimilationists, Jews pretending to assimilate in order to subvert Polish society and dominate its institutions.

Since it is well understood by now that nationalism begets nationalism, so too in interwar Poland did the intensifying Polish nationalism of the period beget a parallel Jewish nationalism. If Zionism was born in Vienna, it reached its political maturity in interwar Poland, where it became a leading expression, and vehicle, of Jewish nationalism.

As the pace of Jewish emigration to Palestine quickened in the late 1920s and early 1930s, Polish curiosity about that land grew. Some Poles who could manage the trip visited the Holy Land as if to reassure themselves and others that the Jews were really better off there, just as Poland would be better off in their absence. Others approached a visit to Palestine with a sense of objective interest. Both attitudes, possibly sharing a common if curious nostalgia, are reflected in interwar Polish literature. As early as 1922, the poet Antoni Słonimski wrote an account of a visit to Palestine titled *Podróż na Wschód* (*A Journey to the East*) as well as a few poems, which are included in this book, in which he emphasized certain superficial similarities between Palestine and Poland and the nostalgia of Jewish émigrés for the land they left behind. Słonimski's message seems to be that the bonds between Poles and Polish Jews were such that, despite their grievances, they missed one another and could not help waxing nostalgic over the long shared past with all its vicissitudes. There is some of that feeling prevalent today in Poland, despite the mass destruction of the Jewish community and the absence of meaningful Polish-Jewish interaction.

The prominent novelist Maria Kuncewiczowa, who observed Jews at close range in her native Kazimierz-on-the-Vistula, brought to her *Miasto Heroda: Notatkie palestyńskie (The City of Herod: Palestinian Notes)* — an account of a trip to Palestine in 1939 at the invitation of the poet Yehuda Warszawiak on behalf of the Hebrew P.E.N. Club — the same unbiased and dignified treatment of Jews exhibited in her fiction. But the sharp-witted satirist Adolf Nowaczyński, whose political and ideological sympathies lay with the Polish nationalists, had sought out Palestine a few years before Kuncewiczowa and in *Moja podróż po Palestynie (My Trip through Palestine,* 1934) delivered himself of a travel book full of snideness and derision.

The peculiar Polish fascination with Palestine, and later Israel, even before the relocation of General Władysław Anders's army there during World War II, has continued to the present. In his story about émigré Polish Jews in Chile, "Kwartet Mendelssohna" ("The Mendelssohn Quartet," 1954), the immensely prolific and highly respected writer Jarosław Iwaszkiewicz introduced the unsympathetic portrait of the Polish Jew Friedenssohn's son, who emigrated to Israel primarily to fight Arabs. The more recent novelist Andrzej Szczypiorski, whose writing — like Iwaszkiewicz's — betrays certain ambivalent feelings toward Jews, could not resist the temptation to conclude his novel about a Jewish woman in occupied Warsaw, *Początek* ("Beginning," translated under the title *The Beautiful Mrs. Seidenman,* 1986), on a similar note. A Jewish girl who escapes death in Poland migrates to Israel, recovers a sense of Jewish identity and purpose, but her elation at being in Israel turns to loathing as she observes Israeli soldiers terrorizing Palestinian fedayeen. The once extremely popular postwar writer Marek Hłasko, sometimes referred to as the James Dean of Poland because of his cynicism and rebelliousness, went to Israel in 1959 and stayed there for two years after being denied a Polish return visa while on a trip to France. Although not a Jew, Hłasko felt a certain kinship with the Jews he met in Israel and made his experiences and observations there the subject of such stories as "The Day of His Death" ("W dzień jego śmierci"), "All Were Turned Aside" ("Wszyscy byli odwróceni"), "Dirty Deeds" ("Brudne czyny"), "Converted in Jaffa" ("Nawrócony w Jaffie"), and "Killing the Dog a Second Time" ("Drugie zabicie psa"). Unlike Iwaszkiewicz or Szczypiorski, Hłasko had no ambivalent feelings toward Jews. Attracted to Israel because of its large number of Polish Jews, with whom he shared a common language in more than just the linguistic sense, Hłasko spent two years traveling around the small country and made his experiences the subject of his stories.

So clamorous were nationalism and anti-Semitism in the Poland of the 1930s that they tended to drown out the voices of protest against bigotry and the debasement of Polish democratic traditions. These voices came mostly from the leftist intelligentsia. Articles denouncing Polish fascism and exclusionary measures against Jews appeared from time to time in the press. But in 1937 several of the most cogent of such articles were collected in a single volume and published under the title *Poles about Jews: A Collection of Articles from the Press.* Two pieces are excerpted in this book. The first, by the Marxist novelist and dramatist Leon Kruczkowski, addresses the issue of cultural anti-Semitism; the second, by Zygmunt Szymanowski, a socialist, was a response to the *numerus clausus,* which sought to limit the number of Jews admitted to Polish institutions of higher learning and then segregated those who were admitted. Even allowing for the Marxist orientation of the collection, the book reminds us that opposition to racism was not a muted voice in Poland, and that the polarization of politics and opinion had become an accomplished fact of Polish public life in the 1930s, above all in the period between the death of Marshal Piłsudski in 1935 and the German invasion in September 1939.

In his contribution to *Poles and Jews,* "Cultural Anti-Semitism," Kruczkowski recalls the "Judeophilic" traditions of Polish literature:

> Out of fairness, it must be said that the advocates of "cultural" anti-Semitism among us (with very few exceptions) are predominantly mediocre, weak, and third-rate talents. They lament most vocally the would-be "Jewification" of Polish cultural life for the purpose of presenting their own lack of talent, or spiritual infirmity, as an oppressed virtue, as a sacrifice to hostile Jewish competition. But a considerable majority of the more or less outstanding, or of the most outstanding, creators, writers, and artists of bourgeois "Aryan" origin do not nurture, or at least do not manifest, anti-Semitic feelings. Perhaps this is because the "Judeophilic" traditions of Polish literature of the period of servitude . . . are in some measure still active.[3]

It is time to consider these "Judeophilic," or "philo-Semitic," traditions of Polish literature since they were impressive and have no parallels elsewhere in Europe.

Literature has long held a privileged position in Polish society. In the nearly three centuries of the Polish-Lithuanian Commonwealth, beginning with late-fifteenth-century Renaissance humanism, it was through literature that Poland became an integral part of Western culture. The noble domination of Polish society and culture, at least up to the late nineteenth century, also put its stamp on literature. The gentry's acquisition of effective political power in the course of the

---

3. Leon Kruczkowski, "Antysemityzm kulturalny," in *Polacy o żydach: Zbiór artykułów z prasy* (Warsaw: Wydawnictwo Polskiej Unii Zgody Narodów, 1937), 32–33.

sixteenth century, and the political institutions they developed to accommodate the outlook and aspirations of their class, turned literature into a kind of debating society for the supporters and opponents of gentry privilege. Consequently, Poland developed one of the most politically vibrant literatures in all Europe.

Until the appearance in 1821 of Julian Ursyn Niemcewicz's novel *Lejbe i Sióra* (*Levi and Sarah*), Polish literary interest in the Jewish community developed within the context of the political tradition. This is evident, for example, in the selections from Grand Hetman of the Crown Jan Tarnowski's mid–sixteenth century compilation of Polish laws. The principal exception is the first piece included in this book, Jan Dantyszek's Latin-language "Poem about Jews" ("Carmen de Iudaeis"), a typical or, better said, stereotypical inventory of the Jew's moral failings by a high-ranking Catholic clergyman. Once one of the most illustrious Polish diplomats of the Renaissance, Dantyszek might be expected to have been above such a diatribe against Jews; indeed his own moral lapses were themselves the stuff of pungent rumor.

The paucity of Polish writing about Jews in the sixteenth and seventeenth centuries is in a way a testimony to the political hegemony of the gentry. The place of Jews in the society and economy of the Commonwealth having been determined by the gentry, patterns of Jewish life — and Polish attitudes toward Jews — were fixed for a very long period of time and admitted relatively few deviations. Jews thereafter commanded little or no literary interest.

There was, however, a curious adumbration of later-eighteenth-century uses of the Jew in Polish political literature in a not widely known late-sixteenth-century comedy of small artistic significance. The work is titled *The Jewish Expedition to the War* (*Wyprawa żydowska na wojnę*), the war in question being one then taking place in Livonia. The author is anonymous, and the unsophisticated little work belongs to late-sixteenth- and early-seventeenth-century "burgher literature" (*literatura mieszczańska*), so called because it did not originate among the culturally dominant gentry but was the product of literate townspeople, mostly in Cracow and its environs. This literature was primarily one of social protest, since the small Polish middle class of the time was much discomforted by the gentry, who had the political and legislative clout necessary to prevent it from becoming serious economic competition. A subspecies of the burgher literature was a type of rudimentary comedy known as "komedia rybałtowska," the adjectival "rybałtowska" deriving from the word "rybałt," which has nothing to do with "ribald" and refers here to mostly anonymous, mostly itinerant writers of burgher origin. The *rybałts*, who were probably parochial school teachers until economic hardship in the late sixteenth and early seventeenth centuries cost many of them their jobs, tried to make a living at popular comedy. Little is known of their actual performances. While interesting historically as a possible reflection of the influence of Italian commedia dell'arte troupes that toured Poland, and Russia, during this period, "rybałt" comedy was overwhelmingly satirical, its satire aimed at both the Roman Catholic clergy and the gentry, whom the authors of the plays held responsible for their misery.

At first glance, *The Jewish Expedition to the War* seems to be mocking the Jews, but the comedy is really a satire on the gentry's preoccupation with trade and commerce to the neglect of their traditional role as the defender of the state. The Polish word for nobility, or gentry, is *szlachta*. It comes from the German *schlachten*, "to do battle" (*Schlacht* in German means "battle"), and refers to the duty, and privilege, of the Polish gentry to bear arms. But in *The Jewish Expedition to the War*, the gentry cannot wage war against Poland's enemies because they are too busy pursuing profit, and the defense of the state falls to the Jews, who were not only prohibited from bearing arms since they were not members of the nobility but traditionally regarded as cowards. The point of the comedy is this reversal of roles.

This use of the Jew as a weapon against the gentry, or at least those elements within the gentry opposed to political and social change, reappeared in the writings of the Enlightenment reformers, who wanted to build a new, stronger Poland in the wake of the first partition of 1772. This is the spirit in which the writings of such prominent figures as Franciszek Salezy Jezierski, Stanisław Staszic, and Julian Ursyn Niemcewicz have to be taken. Jezierski's *Katechizm o tajemnicach rządu polskiego* (*Catechism of the Secrets of the Polish Government,* 1790) is first and foremost an indictment of the Polish nobility for their traditional aloofness from trade and commerce. While harsh in his condemnation of Jewish business practices, above all the exploitation of peasants through control of the sale of spirits in rural areas, Jezierski, in the entry under "Jew" in his *Niektóre wyrazy porządkiem abecadła zebrane . . . (Some Terms Collected in Alphabetical Order . . . ,* 1791), is consistent in his faulting of the nobility for a state of affairs only the nobility can correct. In *Przestrogi dla Polski* (*Admonishments for Poland,* 1790), Staszic similarly lays the responsibility for most of Poland's social and economic woes at the doorstep of the nobility (he himself was of burgher origin); but he is far more vituperative in his treatment of the Jews than Jezierski or, for that matter, any other writer of Enlightenment Poland.

Serious Polish literary interest in the Jews begins with Niemcewicz's epistolary novel *Levi and Sarah* of 1821. However antiquarian it may strike the reader today, the work must be seen as paradigmatic of the Polish Enlightenment approach to the Jews. Niemcewicz, like Jezierski, Staszic, and Hugo Kołłątaj, was a prominent member of the reform camp that had emerged after the calamity of the partition of 1772. Shocked by this first partial dismemberment of their country, the reformers, backed by the last king of Poland, Stanisław August Poniatowski, sought to liberalize Polish society and politics in order to strengthen the country against possible further encroachments on its territory. The partition of 1772 was looked upon as evidence of Poland's internal weaknesses, which neighboring countries were only too happy to exploit for their own advantage. The lack of a strong central authority, the slow growth of a Polish bourgeois class, and the consequent deficiencies in the Polish economy, the low state of the peasantry, costly foreign policy decisions, and even the separateness of the Jewish community were collectively viewed as the fault of a noble class too used to its privileges, too resistant to change, and too conservative to understand the urgent need for change. The success of the reformers can be measured by the relatively liberal Polish constitution of May 3, 1791, the most progressive in Europe at the time. But the Russians, who had already insinuated themselves into Polish internal affairs, responded to the document like a bull to a red flag and moved to block its implementation for fear the contagion of liberalism might spread to autocratic Russia itself. The promulgation of the constitution led to the second partition of 1793, Kościuszko's rebellion the following year, its suppression, and the third partition of Poland in 1795. By the time Niemcewicz came to write *Levi and Sarah*, the Polish-Lithuanian Commonwealth no longer existed. Further undermining Polish self-esteem and national dignity, the alliance with Napoleon, which many Poles believed would culminate in the defeat of Russia and the return to Poland of lands seized in the partitions, failed to materialize. Napoleon was defeated and humiliated, and Polish hopes of national regeneration went down with him.

Niemcewicz's approach to the Jews in *Levi and Sarah* was wholly consistent with Polish Enlightenment social philosophy; with various modifications it would recur through much of the subsequent Polish literature on the Jews, as for example in the works of Józef Korzeniowski, Bolesław Prus, Eliza Orzeszkowa, and Klemens Junosza. To Niemcewicz, Jewish separateness, the Jewish "state within a state," represented an intolerable division of Polish society. The nobility was again held ultimately responsible for the prevailing state of affairs. But Niemcewicz projected onto the Jewish community the struggle between progressive and conservative forces that beset Polish society itself. The dominance of the gentry in the old Polish-Lithuanian Commonwealth thus had its counterpart among the Jews in the power and authority of ultraconservative rabbis fanatically opposed to secularization and anything else that threatened the traditional structure of their communities. Niemcewicz could easily relate to the Jewish Enlightenment, the Haskala, which was fought tooth and nail by the dominant Orthodox Jewish rabbinate in Poland. In the spirit both of this Enlightenment, and that of Europe in general, Niemcewicz portrayed in his novel the yearning for change and secular learning of a young man, clearly intended as a model for Jewish youth, whose defiance leads to his banishment from his community by its traditionalist elders.

What distinguishes Niemcewicz's novel from previous Polish literature on the Jew is its religious dimension, an innovation emulated many times thereafter. As a typical Enlightenment thinker, Niemcewicz vigorously opposed clericalism in a caftan as well as in a cassock. Thus, armed with Enlightenment philosophy, on the one hand, and the discomfort of Polish social and political reformers with the de facto Jewish "state within a state," on the other, Niemcewicz set out to discredit what he came to regard as the principal obstacle to Jewish reform — the Talmud. So obviously proud was Niemcewicz of his layman's knowledge of the Talmud that he makes a point of it in his introduction to *Levi and Sarah*. Moreover, he makes his purpose plain: to quote chapter and verse from the Talmud in order to prove his contention that it underlay Jewish ignorance, fanaticism, superstition, separateness, and hatred of Christians. And quote he does. Talmudic scholars can better address the matter of the accuracy of his quotations and the distortions caused by quotation out of context. But it would be reasonably safe to assume that for Polish readers in the nineteenth century, who knew little or nothing about Judaism, Niemcewicz's apparent familiarity with the Talmud made his case for its pernicious influence on the Jews, and on Jewish relations with Poles, eminently convincing. Once the influence of the Talmud was overcome, presumably through secularized education, the Jews would be more easily assimilated and the "Jewish question" finally resolved. Although he shies away from explicitly recommending that eventual Jewish acceptance of Christianity would be best for Poles and Jews alike, Niemcewicz's writings lend themselves to such an inference. Again, his attitude should best be viewed as a reflection of Enlightenment thought. The fewer the differences between peoples, the safer and, presumably, the more governable societies, and the world, would be. And, in the same spirit of the Enlightenment, Niemcewicz's Christianity was highly secularized, free of any traces of medieval superstition and fanaticism. So the more like Poles the Jews became, the better off Polish society as a whole would be, and if the Jews became Christians as well, then the more happily homogeneous the society.

This Polish brief, as it were, against "Talmudism" was filed by other Polish writers after Niemcewicz and probably under the influence of *Levi and Sarah*. Once Hasidism developed among the Jews of Poland in the eighteenth century, it too was added to "Talmudism" as a major obstacle in the way of Jewish assimilation. Those Poles (Orzeszkowa would be a good example) who read extensively on Jewish beliefs and customs in order to portray Jews in their writings as faithfully as possible, attributed to Hasidism a blending of the Cabala and the Talmud. The combination made for a very dangerous brew. The countless rules and injunctions governing virtually every aspect of Jewish behavior, and their multifarious rabbinical interpretations through the centuries, were now augmented by the major text of Hasidic belief, the Cabala, which the Poles regarded as a mind-boggling combination of mysticism, superstition, and fantasy. Orzeszkowa's treatment of the twin dangers of "Talmudism" and Hasidism in her major novel of Jewish life in provincial Poland, *Meir Ezofowicz*, attests not only to her knowledge, which is unquestionable, but to the similarity of her outlook to Niemcewicz's. Still, Orzeszkowa was clearly the more sympathetic of the two writers where Jews were concerned. It seems highly unlikely that Orzeszkowa could ever have written a work so derisive, however amusing it must have been to his contemporaries, as Niemcewicz's *Rok 3333* (*The Year 3333*) in which he projects a vision of a distant future when Warsaw will have become a primarily Jewish city and renamed Mosz-kopolis (Moshkopolis, Moshko being the nickname for Moshe). The tenacity of Polish fear of an ever-rising Jewish birthrate and the belief that "Talmudism" and Hasidism were the main impedimenta to Jewish assimilation and better Polish-Jewish understanding are evidenced in the blatantly anti-Semitic texts from the period 1915–1929 included in this book.

Philosophical and social orientation obviously had a considerable bearing on the Polish literary portraiture of the Jew. For writers imbued with Enlightenment ideals, masses of Polish Jews still lived in the darkness of religious fanaticism and had to be brought into the light, which implied secularization through assimi-lation. To someone like Orzeszkowa, whose outlook was shaped by the Polish version of European positivism, assimilation was again the answer to the "Jewish Question." But Orzeszkowa's advocacy of assimilation was motivated less by her loathing for religious fanaticism than her belief that a modern Polish society could be achieved only if the divisions of the past were finally overcome. This meant bringing marginalized or disenfranchised communities — peasants, women, and Jews — into the mainstream of Polish society and giving them the opportunity to contribute to national, social, and economic progress.

The variety of determinants in the literary treatment of the Jew in Poland is demonstrated, for example, by the case of Stanisław Vincenz, a writer from the Hutzul (Hucul, in Polish) region of the Carpathian Mountains. Vincenz carried on a lifelong romance with the peoples and cultures of the area. His major lit-erary achievement, begun in 1936 but never actually completed because of the outbreak of World War II, was the multivolume work *Na wysokie połoninie* (*On the High Uplands*). A curious blend of fiction, anthropology, and cultural his-tory, the collection is notable for its stories about the Jews of the Hutzul region, many of whom were Hasidim. The Hasidic roots of the Jews there went deep; the founder of Hasidism, the Baal-Shem-Tov, had once lived among them and propa-gated his beliefs in the small Jewish villages that dotted the Hutzul. For Vincenz, the Hasidic Jews were part of the Hutzul world and could not be omitted from any group portrait. Unconcerned about "Talmudism" and Hasidism, and free of the baggage of positivist social commitment and didacticism, Vincenz set about creating a literary record of the beliefs and customs of the Hasidic Jews as an inte-gral part of the Hutzul landscape. His affectionately crafted stories — "Bałaguła," for example, which is included here — throb with the life and lore of the Jews he knew from firsthand experience and provide an engaging (and valuable) comple-ment to the scholarly studies on Hasidism in Poland.

How historical circumstance could alter the perception of the Jew, at least on the literary level, is exemplified by Polish romanticism. The suppression of the November Insurrection of 1830–31 resulted in the emigration to the West of thou-sands of Poles, among them many luminaries of Polish political, artistic, and intellectual life. The center of the Great Emigration, as it was called, was Paris, and it was there that a new Polish culture arose. For the Poles this was their first experience of a diaspora, and parallels with the much longer and more oppressive diaspora of the Jews were soon found. The Jewish diaspora could also be regarded as an object lesson for the Poles, mired in despair and frustration over the disastrous outcome of their first armed revolt against foreign rule on the territory of the Russian partition. Through their centuries of exile and wandering, the Jews managed to preserve their faith, their identity as a people, their traditions and culture, and their hope in the inevitability of return to the ancestral homeland. Thus the Poles could learn from Jewish experience how to preserve their own traditions, their "Polishness," and how to resist assimilation into a foreign culture. After all, it was the obstinate resistance of the Jews to assimilation that was at the root, historically, of most of their problems with the Poles. Some of the lessons to be drawn from the Jewish diaspora were incorporated into the lectures and sermons delivered, usually on the steps of the Notre Dame Cathedral after Sunday mass, by one of the most curious and enigmatic figures in the Great Emigration, a mystagogue (as he is usually described) named Andzrej Towiański, who, like the great poet of Polish romanticism, Adam Mickiewicz, came from the former Lithuanian region of the Polish-Lithuanian Commonwealth. To some, Towiański was an unfrocked priest who believed himself to be the savior of the Polish people; to others, he was a Russian spy planted among the Polish émigrés in Paris to sow discord and prevent them from becoming an effective political force. He was eventually expelled from France by the authorities, who came to regard his activities as an embarrassment and a liability.

The Polish romantic movement, which flowered in the time of the Great Emigration, also contributed to the changing of attitudes toward the Jews. Inclined toward the spiritual and supernatural, receptive to mystical experience, contemptuous of the cognitive value of mere reason, romanticism invested its poets with unique attributes, among them prophetic power. The new interest in the Bible and in the tradition of the Prophets shaped the perception of the Jews as the biblical Hebrew people and had its appropriate literary correlatives.

In the specifically Polish romantic context, the Jews were also seen as a people of messianic tradition. In their desperate search for meaning in the calamities visited on Poland from the partitions to the defeat of the November Insurrection, some Poles turned to a messianic interpretation of Polish destiny. Poland was singled out among the Christian nations of Europe—by God, of course—to suffer a martyrdom like Christ's so that a lapsed Christendom could find its way back to true Christianity. The moral bankruptcy of European Christendom was nowhere more apparent than in the dismemberment of Poland, that erstwhile bulwark of Christianity against the infidel Turk, by nominally Christian nations—Austria, Prussia, and Russia. Thus it was rightly Poland whose political crucifixion and resurrection would eventually redeem the rest of Europe.

Polish messianism was no sideshow, or freak show, of the Great Emigration. It became the major current of Polish philosophical thought during the period, was preached by Towiański and other members of his circle, and became a hallmark of the writing of the leading Polish romantic poets Krasiński and Słowacki, for example, but above all Adam Mickiewicz. Together with diaspora and the biblical prophetic tradition, Jewish messianism understandably became another link in the chain of destiny drawing Poles and Jews together. In literary terms, apart from the parallels between the Jewish and Polish diasporas drawn by Towiański in his sermons, this convergence of the destinies of both peoples translated primarily into the remarkable figure of the Orthodox Jewish innkeeper, Jankiel (Yankel), in Mickiewicz's *Pan Tadeusz*.

Yankel is generally regarded as the ideal Polish Jew—observant, traditional, *and* at the same time an ardent Polish patriot. The Polish historical novelist Józef Ignacy Kraszewski delineates a basically similar, though far more acculturated type, in his novel *Żyd* (*The Jew*, 1866). Yankel, however, is no minor or marginal character in the acknowledged masterpiece of Polish poetry. It can be argued, in fact, that he is the real hero of the work, apart, of course, from the mostly nameless Polish officers and soldiers about to embark on the campaign against Russia under Napoleon's banners. But the Polish troops who fought with Napoleon are seen only as a group portrait; Yankel stands out as an individual, more so, to be sure, than the eponymous "hero" of the poem, Tadeusz himself, or Zosia, his eventual betrothed, or the faintly ludicrous Telimena and Count Horeszko. Mickiewicz, to begin with, assigns Yankel the very important function of presenting an inspirational musical review, as it were, of the great Polish calamities of the late eighteenth and early nineteenth centuries at a banquet honoring the Franco-Polish army about to invade Russia. Moreover, Yankel, of the major characters in *Pan Tadeusz*, is the epic poem's only selfless hero. All the other leading figures are either uninvolved in the unfolding historical drama or are involved in it for personal reasons, like Father Robak, who is expiating a deeply troubling moral lapse. Yankel is a patriot who loves Poland and is willing to act as a spy, unselfishly, slipping back and forth between hostile camps in order to bring back valuable information to the French and Poles. Although the notion that he is the true hero of *Pan Tadeusz* might raise some eyebrows, this interpretation of Yankel's role in the poem is easily supported by a careful reading of the text.

The defeat of the November Insurrection, and the eventual disappearance from the stage of history of leading figures in the Great Emigration, redirected Polish attention from the now thwarted hopes for the future embodied in the Emigration to the down-to-earth realities of the partitioned country. The ascent of Tsar Alexander II to the throne of Russia in 1855 and the subsequent emancipation of the serfs in that country gave Poles reasons to believe that a corner had been turned in their relations with the Russians, whose partition they resented the most and against whom they rebelled twice in the nineteenth century. Sensing a significant change in atmosphere in imperial Russia, the Poles began a restless clamor for long-denied rights and happily seized on virtually any public occasion to demonstrate. In order to prevent this patriotic fervor from becoming threatening, the tsar placed the civil administration of the Kingdom of Poland in the hands of a conservative aristocrat, Count Aleksander Wielopolski. Although Wielopolski sought to implement reforms intended to placate his fellow Poles, the need to impose discipline on an increasingly restive populace became his paramount concern. The more repressive Wielopolski's measures, the greater the defiance of the Poles under his jurisdiction. During a demonstration in Warsaw on February 27, 1861, five people were killed by police gunfire. A hundred civilians were similarly massacred in another demonstration in Warsaw's Castle Square on April 8, 1861. The outcome was perhaps predictable—another attempt by the Poles to regain their freedom by force of arms. But the sixteen-month-old insurrection that erupted in January 1863 was suppressed with unprecedented ruthlessness. The Russians thereafter pursued a stern policy of Russification to prevent any further such assaults on their authority.

The period from the defeat of the January Insurrection of 1863 to the turn of the century is conventionally subsumed under the rubric of positivism. While obviously indebted to Western positivist philosophy, Polish positivism had its own agenda and must be thought of primarily as a response to the specific conditions of Polish life in the aftermath of the January Insurrection. The romantic celebration of revolution lost its mystique, and indeed romanticism itself was held by some to be ultimately responsible for the grievous miscalculation of the January Insurrection. With the enthusiasm for armed struggle delivered a stunning blow by the brutality of the Russian defeat, Polish postinsurrectionary society turned inward.

Nineteenth-century positivism in the Polish context was an attempt to rebuild society from the bottom up in order to strengthen it for whatever lay ahead. The events of 1830–31 and 1863–64 stripped away the remaining veils of illusion; among the first casualties of the new sobriety were revolutionary fervor and romanticism. The new positivists decried the mystico-messianic ideas of the romantics as delusions of grandeur. Spurning the romantic cult of the hero, the positivists propagated a new heroism of the everyday and ordinary. Betrayed by the Polish romantic adulation of the poet, positivism cultivated the prosaic. And instead of the romantic belief in the power of individual will, the positivists placed their trust instead in the collective.

Positivism was as practical as it was pragmatic. The society of partitioned Poland needed a new infrastructure if economic and political strength was ever to be achieved. This meant working toward a new social cohesion by breaking down the divisions between the classes. A modern Polish society could not be created without significant improvement in the status of peasants, women, burghers, and Jews. Emphasizing the dignity of work and the necessity for collective engagement, the positivists took particular aim at the nobility's traditional contempt for labor and commerce.

By fostering a new sense of social unity and national purpose, the positivists achieved much in the areas of education, urban life, economic self-sufficiency, and, perhaps most important, a heightened social consciousness. Certainly one of the greatest achievements of positivism was its sincere effort to narrow the gap separating Poles and Jews. Imbued with a great sense of civic responsibility, Polish writers in the era of positivism strove to educate Poles about Jews, to make Jewish strangeness less strange, and to plead the case for social and cultural reform within the Jewish community itself.

In terms of its commitment to the cause of better Polish-Jewish understanding, positivism remains the single most impressive movement in the history of Polish literature. Indeed, it would not be an exaggeration to characterize the literature of Polish positivism as overwhelmingly philo-Semitic. Virtually every major literary figure of the period addressed the "Jewish Question" at one time or another: Adam Asnyk, Wiktor Gomulicki, Klemens Junosza, Maria Konopnicka, Józef Ignacy Kraszewski, Teofil Lenartowicz, Eliza Orzeszkowa, Bolesław Prus, Henryk Sienkiewicz, Aleksander Świętochowski, and Adam Szymański. The way to the positivist approach to the Jew had been prepared by the patriotic fervor of 1861, which sought to unite Pole and Jew in what was perceived to be a common struggle for Polish liberation. This patriotic inclusiveness is very much in evidence in Cyprian Kamil Norwid's impressive poem "Żydowie polscy" ("Polish Jews"), where he uses an actual incident that took place during the demonstration in Castle Square in April 1861 as a rallying point for Polish-Jewish unity. The Judeophilic bias of the poem is evident from its very title in Polish. The standard plural form of *Żyd* (Jew) is *Żydzi;* the addition of the honorific suffix *-owie* to *Żyd* creates the plural *Żydowie,* which is intended to convey esteem.

Apart from Norwid's poem, few literary works of Polish positivism dealing with the Jews have a political character. The great exception is Kraszewski's novel *The Jew.* Set in the time of the January Insurrection of 1863, the novel portrays a secular Jew who takes pride in his religion, remains faithful to it, yet as an ardent Polish patriot feels compelled to participate in the insurrection. Ideologically, Norwid's poem and Kraszewski's novel originate ultimately in the figure of Yankel in Mickiewicz's *Pan Tadeusz.*

Many of the Polish insurrectionaries of 1863 were exiled to Siberia after the Russian defeat. Adam Szymański knew such exile at first hand and built his literary career out of stories with Siberian settings notable both for their realistic descriptions of the life of the Polish exiles there and for their attention to the Siberian landscape and its indigenous population. One of his best stories, "Srul z Lubartowa" ("Srul of Lubartów," 1885), underscores the common love for a lost homeland of both the Pole and the Jew in exile.

Most Polish positivist writers who wrote about Jews did so in a spirit similar to that of their Russian contemporaries—Turgenev, for example—who took up the cause of peasants in their fiction in the time of the emancipation. The approach was one of compassion motivated by a desire to reveal the humanness of their subjects. The principal task of the Poles writing about Jews in the era of positivism was to bring the essentially alien world of the Jews closer by showing it from within in knowledgeable detail. It was as if Jewish writers were writing on familiar Jewish subjects. This fiction about Jews is often exceptionally impressive for the wealth of information it contains, mostly about small-town Jewish life. The weakness of some of this literature—apart from purely artistic considerations—derives from the inherent didacticism of positivism itself, which sought to reform by enlightening and moralizing. Orzeszkowa's writings about Jews—the story "Silny Samson" ("Mighty Samson"), for example, or the novels *Eli Makower* and *Meir Ezofowicz*—typify this tendency, with the result that the author's zeal for bridging the gap between Polish reader and Jewish subject produces a tone that is oddly, and doubtless unconsciously, paternalistic and condescending.

Like Orzeszkowa and Konopnicka, Klemens Junosza learned as much about Jewish life as he could, even going so far as to acquire a reading knowledge of Yiddish and translating the novel *Di Kliatche* (*The Nag*) by the important nineteenth-century Yiddish writer Mendele Moykher Sforim. But Junosza's desire for improved Polish-Jewish relations did not compromise an objectivity that allowed him to see his subjects' flaws as well as virtues. Although sometimes dismissed as anti-Semitic, mostly on the basis of his negative treatment of various aspects of Jewish life in Poland in his treatise *Nasi Żydzi w miasteczkach i na wsiach* (*Our Jews in Towns and Villages,* 1889), Junosza wrote too warmly about Jews in such well-known stories as "Łaciarz" ("The Tailor," 1884) and "Froim" (1889) to warrant such an accusation. The grievances against certain Jewish practices he discusses at length in *Our Jews in Towns and Villages* were held sincerely. By discussing them with his Polish readers Junosza clearly sought to confront irrational prejudice with a sober assessment of the principal obstacles to harmonious Polish-Jewish relations. But, as his writings imply, reform cannot be a one-way street; there is much the Jews themselves can do to achieve better understanding with their fellow Poles and eventually take their rightful place in Polish society.

Bolesław Prus was the great urban writer of Polish positivism; his major novel, *Lalka* (*The Doll,* 1881), sweeps broadly across contemporary Warsaw. His treatment of the crosscurrents within urbanized Jewish society carry as much conviction as Orzeszkowa's genre scenes of shtetl life. *Lalka,* as well as the journalistic "chronicles" Prus wrote through much of his career, sheds interesting light on Jews in the world of business and the resentment against them in Polish quarters. But it is in Prus more than in any other Polish writer of the time that we can see the complexities of Jewish secularization and assimilation both within the Jewish community itself and in terms of Polish-Jewish relations.

With the turn of the century, certain shifts of emphasis occur in Polish writing on Jewish subjects. Works set wholly within the Jewish community were still being written, as for example the plays *Małka Szwarcenkopf* (1897) and *Jojne Firułkes* (1899) by the dramatist and prose writer Gabriela Zapolka. But Zapolka, a zealous feminist, makes the issue of women's rights her principal focus. She neither takes up the matter of Polish-Jewish relations nor engages in the sentimentalization of Jewish shtetl life in the manner of the positivists. Her concern is with women, specifically young urbanized Jewish women who are educated but poor and who have to struggle with ignorance and backwardness within their families and community as they try to define themselves in a modern society. Although criticized for the shallowness of her characters, Zapolska's plays attracted attention in their time both for the novelty of their preoccupation with Jewish women and her obvious attempt to create a theater intended for Jewish audiences.

The "new" Jewish woman of Polish modernism makes an appearance also in the major work of the outstanding Polish dramatist of the period, Stanisław Wyspiański. In *Wesele* (*The Wedding*, 1901), a play about the tyranny of the past over the Polish consciousness, Wyspiański assigns a prominent role to Rachela, the worldly and poetically inclined daughter of a Jewish innkeeper. It is the vividness of Rachela's poetic imagination that adds a magical dimension to the village wedding celebration from which the play derives its title. Seeing a straw man (*chochoł*) covering a rosebush in a nearby garden, she whimsically invites it to the wedding party. Brought to life by the power of Rachela's imagination, the straw man becomes a key figure in the play's finale. As the people onstage dance to its fiddle playing, Wyspiański draws a grim contrast between the inanimate being who comes to life and the living people whose somnambulistic dance symbolizes their status as puppets manipulated by the power of the past.

Wyspiański made more extensive use of Jewish characters and setting in his tragedy *Sędziowie* (*Judges*, 1907). But the Jewish milieu here seems only incidental. Jews are a familiar component of the Polish provincial landscape in both *The Wedding* and *Judges*. Wyspiański demonstrates no overt interest in the matter of Polish-Jewish relations nor in the matter of the need for Jewish acculturation. He accepts his Jews as he finds them; he has no social agenda to advance. Rachela is an emancipated young woman of her time who happens to be the daughter of the local Jewish innkeeper. Wyspiański may have intended to imply that her seductive and poetic nature is rooted in her Jewishness. Turn-of-the-century artists often endowed dark-haired women, preferably of non-Western origin, with an irresistible, ultimately destructive, sensuality. Jewish women were sometimes so perceived by Polish writers at the time, as, for example, in Kazimierz Przerwa-Tetmajer's autobiographical novel *Panna Mary* (*Miss Mary*, 1899). However, there is nothing in the setting and principals of *Judges* to suggest anything other than the incidental. The play is based on an actual murder that took place in a Jewish village in Eastern Galicia in 1899. What attracted Wyspiański's interest in the incident was the trial, at which the verdict of not guilty was returned in the face of the obvious guilt of the accused.

Whatever the overriding feminist aspect of Zapolka's "Jewish" plays, or the incidental nature of the Jewish characters and settings in Wyspiański's plays, Polish modernism was hardly indifferent to the growing intolerance toward Jews in Poland and elsewhere in Europe in the late nineteenth and early twentieth centuries. The incitement of riots against Jews and assaults on Jewish property and lives in the Russian territories did not escape the attention of the Poles, since in many instances they were carried out in former territories of the Polish-Lithuanian Commonwealth. It was also in these areas that the Russian imperial authorities had historically fueled Polish resentment against Jews, especially in the economic sphere, by restricting Jewish settlement in Russia proper and crowding Jews instead into Polish-populated regions. Since the Poles were no more immune than other Europeans to the virus of this more malignant form of Judeophobia of the turn of the century, attacks on Jews and Jewish interests also occurred in predominantly Polish towns and cities. Unlike the better organized pogroms in Russia proper, these tended to be more random, much less frequent, and of considerably smaller scope. To some extent they were encouraged, however unintentionally, by the works of writers hostile to positivism and intent on portraying the evils of contemporary capitalism with which Jews were inevitably linked. These included, among others, Michał Bałucki's novels W żydowskich rękach (In Jewish Hands, 1884) and Przeklęte pieniądze (Damned Money, 1899), Teodor Jeske Choiński's Na straconym posterunku (On the Lost Outpost, 1891), Klemens Junosza's later, symbolically titled works Pająki (The Spiders, 1894), Czarnobłoto: Pająki wiejskie (Blackmud: The Rural Spiders, 1895), and W pajęczej sieci (In the Spider's Web, 1894), and the Nobel laureate (1924) Władysław Reymont's Ziemia obiecana (The Promised Land, 1899), a novel about high finance in the industrial city of Łódź, the Polish Manchester. To its credit, Polish literature of this period was equally harsh on anti-Semitism.

Maria Konopnicka's long story "Mendel Gdański" ("Mendel of Gdańsk"), despite its sentimental touches, unflinchingly portrays an anti-Jewish riot in the port city of Gdańsk. Gabriela Zapolska is similarly unsparing in her novella Antysemitnik (The Anti-Semite, 1897–98), in which her target is the emergence of the nationalistic anti-Semitic press. Although she waxes vitriolic in her portrait of a venal young Polish journalist who in order to further his career betrays his Jewish actress girlfriend, Zapolska resorts to gross stereotypes in her treatment of other Jewish characters in the story. Zapolska is not unique in this respect. Although undeniably sensitive to Jewish issues, often impressively knowledgeable about Jewish life, and obviously committed to the cause of improved Polish-Jewish relations, Polish writers of liberal persuasion sometimes reveal a curious, doubtless subconscious, bias against Jews. This assumes the form of the stereotypicality we find in Zapolska's Anti-Semite. Very many Jews in Poland were uneducated, in the secular sense, poor, and shabby. Needless to say, not all were splendidly formed. There were also unscrupulous moneylenders among them, innkeepers who plied peasants with drink for profit, shopkeepers who cheated their customers, and craftsmen who did shoddy work. But it is just such Jews who often come to the fore in Polish works of fiction and drama inspired by the desire to bridge the gap between Poles and Jews and pave the way for the eventual entry of the Jews into mainstream Polish life. That Polish writers were nevertheless able to transcend stereotypicality and find beauty and poetry in the drabness and poverty of so much Jewish life in Poland is exemplified by Orzeszkowa's splendid story "Mighty Samson" (1877) and Wiktor Gomulicki's moving poem "El mole rachmim . . ." (1879), both of which are included here.

The contagion of anti-Semitism, which spread throughout Europe in the late nineteenth century and, in its Polish form, found concrete political expression in the National Democratic Movement (popularly known as "National Democracy," or *Endecja* in Polish) founded in 1897 by Roman Dmowski (1864–1939), persisted throughout World War I and turned virulent in the twenty years of the interwar Polish state. So much attention has been focused on the mass extermination of Jews in Poland during World War II, and on the awesome destruction endured by the country as a whole, that the ravages of World War I are all too easily overlooked. But the first "world war" delivered a crushing blow to Polish resources and manpower, from which Poland never fully recovered in the interwar period.

The reconstitution of a Polish state after World War I was the fulfillment of Polish aspirations since 1795 but the legacy of the partitions, and of the war itself, cast a long shadow over the two brief decades of independence that followed. Hardly did the new Polish Second Republic come into existence than it was plunged into a series of concurrent territorial conflicts with Lithuania, the Ukraine, Germany, Czechoslovakia, and the new Soviet Union. The problems, and challenges involved in creating an integrated Polish state out of the recovered lands of the three partitions were undeniably immense. Economic instability, which plagued Poland throughout the interwar period, was compounded by the international monetary crisis of 1929–30. Political instability kept pace with the economic. The proliferation of political parties and the hobbling of the Diet resulted in the coup d'état in May 1926 led by Marshal Józef Piłsudski, a military hero who had previously rejected the presidency because of the limitations imposed on it. Although shunning direct dictatorial rule of the country, Piłsudski remained the dominant element in Polish political life until his death in 1935. The *Sanacja* (literally, "sanitation") regime he instituted achieved a degree of stability, but its growing conservatism, nationalism, and intolerance of political opposition compromised the democratic principles on which the newly independent Polish state had been founded and which were incorporated into the Polish constitution of March 17, 1921. When the reins of power passed into the hands of military officers (the regime of the "colonels") after Piłsudksi's death, the Second Republic entered its bleakest period politically. The extreme nationalism and rampant anti-Semitism of this period immediately preceding the outbreak of World War II are deeply engraved in the minds of many Jews, the more so because of the genocide of the Jews that followed from 1939 to 1945. And although that genocide was perpetrated by Germans, the decade 1935–45 looms so large as a time of trials and martyrdom for the Jews of Poland that it grotesquely distorts the larger picture of the entire history of Polish Jewry and Polish-Jewish relations.

Although a strong current of anti-Semitism was an indisputable fact of Polish life in the interwar period, it can be better understood if viewed within the proper context. Unless the internal and external weaknesses of the Second Republic are taken into account, the anti-Semitisim of the interwar period is all too easily dismissed as an innate flaw of the Polish character. That anti-Jewish prejudice can exist and, to be sure, flourish, independent of the kinds of stresses and strains endured by the Poles in the interwar period is a given for which even a cursory glance at Western Europe in the same period offers ample documentation. But the conditions of Polish life from World War I to World War II must be taken into account for the sake of a more objective assessment of the anti-Jewish sentiment of the period.

The nature of this prejudice, primarily on the popular level, and of the opposition to it from during World War I to just two years before the German invasion of Poland in September 1939 are exemplified by six prose treatises excerpted in this book. The first four are wholly anti-Semitic in nature; the last two, vehemently repudiating anti-Semitism, and of Marxist origin, have been previously discussed. The anti-Semitic treatises are an anonymous diatribe against the Jews for their alleged pro-German sympathies during the war; two treatises by J. Grabowski and Stanisław Pieńkowski, the latter especially well known for his militant anti-Semitism; and a treatise, *On the Jewish Question,* by a priest named Jan Gnatowski, which can be regarded as fairly typical of the kind of anti-Jewish literature that emanated from the ranks of the Polish Roman Catholic clergy. These anti-Semitic writings share the assumption that the Jews cannot transcend their status as eternal aliens in Poland even through assimilation, that "Jewishness" cannot be overcome by the superficial acquisition of Polish ways of dress, speech, and education, that Jews are bound to remain outside Polish society. These anti-Semitic writers reject assimilation and even conversion as little more than tactics used by Jews to permeate the entire fabric of Polish society in order to ultimately dominate it. The irony of this new Polish attitude toward Jewish assimilation is inescapable, and bitter. Precisely when Jewish assimilation — which, to repeat, had long been presented as the most reasonable solution to the "Jewish Question" — was accelerating rapidly in the time of the Second Republic, and Jews were entering the trades and professions in larger numbers than ever before, assimilation was now decried largely on the grounds of the unfair economic and even political advantages it offered Jews.

The growing resentment toward the Jews in the Second Republic may have sprung in part from a perceived threat of economic competition, but it was also part of what rightly may be considered the single greatest thorn in the side of interwar Poland—its minority problem. The Polish-Lithuanian Commonwealth had been a multiethnic, multicultural state. So, too, was the reconstituted Polish republic of the interwar years. But the difference between them in terms of multiple ethnicity was defined by the twentieth-century political and cultural aspirations of the minorities and their clamor for autonomy and in some instances statehood. If the Jews became perhaps the most problematic of the minorities both because of their numbers and their very different culture, the Poles had their hands full with millions of Lithuanians, Belorussians, Germans, and especially Ukrainians. The post–World War I break-up of the empires that had perpetrated the partitions of Poland in the late eighteenth century—Russia, Austria-Hungary, and Prussia—and the shakiness of the new Polish republic encouraged the minorities to test the limits of Polish weakness and endurance. The new statehood of the Poles fueled the political aspirations of minorities who agitated for ever-increasing autonomy or unification with their kinsmen in neighboring countries.

The difference in political outlook between the Jews and the other ethnic communities in the Second Republic was that the Jews could not think of a separate state in Europe. There were enough Belorussians, Lithuanians, and Ukrainians within and beyond the borders of Poland to rationalize such aspirations. And for the Germans and many Silesians there was, of course, the appeal of incorporation into a Greater Germany. But what historical lands could the Jews rightfully claim in Europe as the basis of an independent Jewish state? None, to be sure. Jewish cultural and political aspirations were initially limited to three principal goals: the right to practice the Jewish faith; the right to employ the Jewish languages, Yiddish and Hebrew, in a Jewish parochial school system; and the right to political representation for the Jewish community in the Sejm, or Diet, of the new Polish republic. These goals were in fact achieved and guaranteed by the framers of the Polish constitution of 1921, who, under the watchful eye of the League of Nations, could not effectively ignore the issue of minority rights. The political freedom enjoyed by the Jews in the Second Republic was manifest not only in their representation in the Diet but in the proliferation of Jewish political parties. These spanned the entire spectrum of opinion within the Jewish community, from the extreme left to the extreme right, both in the secular and religious spheres.

The Zionist movement, which took root in Poland in the late nineteenth century, represented yet another outlet for Jewish separatism and nationalism. The fragmented nature of the Jewish community in interwar Poland, and the hostility of religious groups to the secular nature and objectives of mainstream Zionism, prevented the movement from becoming the predominant expression of Jewish political aspirations. But the resettlement to and colonization of Palestine advocated by the Zionists appealed to many Jews for both religious and nationalistic reasons. When their social and economic position began deteriorating in the Second Republic as a result of discriminatory measures that flouted the Polish constitution and a more competitive, and hostile, economic environment, more and more Jews sought to emigrate from Poland, over a hundred thousand of them resettling in Palestine before the British authorities reduced the flow to a trickle in the late 1930s.

The literature of interwar Poland deviates markedly from previous Polish literature in its treatment of Jews. The philo-Semitic positivists lost their impetus as a movement with the emergence of a newly independent Polish state after World War I. The idealism of the Polish romantics was now meaningless. Jews had rights guaranteed by the new Polish constitution, and the messianism of the Polish diaspora had lost its reason for being. A new Poland had risen phoenix-like from the ashes of World War I and was open to Poles anxious to rejoin their fellow countrymen within the borders of a Polish state. The sense of kinship with another people who had preserved their national identity in diaspora had evaporated.

The broad range of problems facing the new Polish state absorbed the energies of Polish literary creativity without the need for the previous level and type of interest in the status of the Jews. Accelerated Jewish assimilation, the greater entry of Jews into Polish cultural life, and the emergence of a vibrant Jewish secular culture in the interwar period legitimized, as it were, a benign Polish literary neglect of Jewish issues. Most notably, Polish literary works set entirely in a Jewish milieu, such as those by Orzeszkowa and Zapolska, all but disappeared from view, with the extraordinary exception of Stanisław Vincenz's tales of Carpathian Hasidim. Jews writing in Polish could take up the slack, if they were so inclined. Understandably, however, the more prominent writers of Jewish origin who used Polish as their literary language—writers such as Roman Brandstaetter, Kazimierz Brandys, Marian Hemar, Mieczysław Jastrun, Bruno Jasieński, Bolesław Leśmian, Bruno Schulz, Antoni Słonimski, Julian Tuwim, Adam Ważyk, Aleksander Wat, and Józef Wittlin—rarely tapped Jewish life in Poland in their fiction and poetry.[4] Even Bruno Schulz, one of the most gifted Polish writers of this century, who never disdained or concealed his Jewishness and obviously drew inspiration for much of his phantasmagoric writing from his own family experiences, did not in fact write explicitly about Jews. By using Polish, Jewish writers identified with Polish culture and sought to avoid being stereotyped as "Jewish writers" of primarily parochial significance. By no stretch of the imagination did this mean that Jewish characters would simply disappear from the pages of Polish literature, whether that literature was created by ethnic Poles or by assimilated Jews writing in Polish. Jews appear in many works of interwar Polish fiction and

4. For a perceptive article on Jewish writers in twentieth-century Polish literature, with reference primarily to the post–World War II period, see Jan Błoński, "Is There a Jewish School of Polish Literature?" *Polin: A Journal of Polish-Jewish Studies* 1 (1989): 196–211.

drama, but they are in most instances far less dominant than they were in the past. The greater urbanization and industrialization of Polish society and culture during the Second Republic also drew attention away from provincial life with its traditional landed gentry, village peasants, and shtetl Jews. There are Jews in the novels and stories, for example, of Maria Dąbrowska, Michał Choromański, and Maria Kuncewiczowa. But they are relatively minor figures set in a traditional landscape, as in Dąbrowska's multivolume family chronicle *Noce i dni* (*Nights and Days,* 1928–34), or in an urbanized setting, as in Choromański's once popular crime novel *Zazdrość i medycyna* (*Jealousy and Medicine,* 1933).

Jews attracted to a literary career in interwar Poland had two options available to them. They could write in Polish, if they knew the language—which secularized and assimilated Jews certainly would have known—or they could write in Yiddish or Hebrew. Those assimilated Jews who hoped to establish themselves in mainstream Polish culture by writing in Polish generally shied away, as I indicated, from Jewish subjects. Apart from the understandable desire to be recognized as *Polish* writers, there was the legitimate fear in a time of mounting anti-Jewish prejudice that their works would be met with negative criticism and scorn. The Polish intelligentsia and literary community tended on the whole to be sympathetic to Jews; but the public at large was another matter.

There was, however, a community of secular Jewish writers who wrote predominantly on Jewish subjects in Polish, thereby creating a kind of Polish-Jewish literature.[5] This literature was aimed primarily, but not exclusively, at Polish-speaking Jewish readers. A curious cultural phenomenon virtually unique to interwar Poland, few talents of enduring significance arose from this Polish-Jewish literary milieu with the principal exception of Władysław Szlengel, who died in the Warsaw Ghetto Uprising of 1943 and left a moving collection of poems about the ghetto during the occupation titled *Co czytałem umarłym* (*What I Read to the Dead,* published for the first time in 1977).

For the Jew writing in Yiddish or Hebrew, it was a different story. Although secular Hebrew writing had been cultivated in both Poland and Russia in the nineteenth century, a modern Hebrew literary culture arose to all intents and purposes only with significant Jewish settlement in Palestine in the 1920s and 1930s, and especially after the creation of the State of Israel. The principal language of Jewish writers who were disinclined to develop careers in Polish was Yiddish. The secularization of significant numbers of Jews in interwar Poland, coupled with the rise of Jewish nationalism and separatism, greatly encouraged a secular Yiddish literature and press. Interwar Poland became home to a vibrant and impressive Yiddish literature, a worthy successor to the tradition of Mendele Moykher Sforim, Sholom Aleichem, and Itzhak Leib Peretz, and internationally

---

5. For a Polish study of the interwar Polish-Jewish literature, see Eugenia Prokop-Janiec, *Między-wojenna literatura polska-żydowska* (Cracow: Universitas, 1992).

recognized in the Nobel Prize for Literature awarded Isaac Bashevis Singer, the best-known twentieth-century Yiddish writer, in 1978.

The great changes that occurred in Jewish life in interwar Poland and the remarkable expansion of Yiddish literary culture effectively transferred the artistic venue of Jewish experience from Polish to Polish-Jewish and Yiddish literatures. With Jewish writers now able to give voice to the whole spectrum of Jewish life in Poland in two and even three languages (Yiddish, Polish, and Hebrew), Polish writers no longer felt any strong compulsion to bear the additional burden of Jewish concerns. The complexities and uncertainties of Polish society in the first independent Polish state in 123 years offered a surfeit of material to the literary imagination.

The rise of overt anti-Jewish prejudice and practices in the interwar years shifted the issue of Polish-Jewish relations from the fictional realm to the arena of political and social commentary. The outpouring of anti-Semitic writing from the crudely nationalistic to the quasi-scholarly was countered by voices of reason cautioning against the irrationality of anti-Jewish feeling and appealing to the best traditions of Polish tolerance and democracy. The polarization of both Polish and Jewish attitudes in the 1930s was paralleled in the political polarization of the time, with the most effective opposition to extreme Polish nationalism coming from the political left, as evidenced in the previously mentioned *Poles about Jews: A Collection of Articles from the Press* (1937).

The German invasion of Poland in September 1939 ended the existence of the two-decade-old Polish Second Republic and led to the martyrdom of Polish Jewry. The Poles themselves suffered terribly. Those not incarcerated in concentration camps or killed were forced to witness the destruction of their cities and the mindless assault on their culture. Poles and Jews acquitted themselves heroically in the two great uprisings of the war, the Warsaw Ghetto Uprising of 1943 and the Warsaw Uprising of 1944, both of which were crushed mercilessly.

So much has been written about Polish-Jewish relations during the war — and I have already touched on this subject earlier — that there is no point in covering familiar ground. Jews have felt for some time that more Poles could have helped them in their greatest hour of need but did not out of long-standing animosity. Polish scholars have gone out of their way to document the number of Poles who helped or tried to help Jews on pain of death. Such Poles have been numbered among the Righteous Gentiles in Israel and have been appropriately honored.

Questions about what the Poles might have done, or should have done, to help the Jews during the German occupation continue to be raised and probably will be until the futility of such inquiry is finally recognized. In the meantime, there is no justification for ill-founded accusations and the imposition of the heavy burden of collective guilt.[6] There are Poles who in retrospect doubtless regret that

---

6. Perhaps the most incisive Polish commentary on the matter of Polish moral complicity, or lack of any, in the destruction of Polish Jewry during World War II is Jan Błoński's essay of 1987 "The Poor

they did not do more, or imagine that they could have done more but did not do so out of fear. The penalty for aiding or hiding Jews was death; not many Poles were willing to take the risk. Constant danger and crushing oppression enfeebled all but the most courageous. And so the Jews went to the slaughter, unrescued by anyone including the majority of the Poles surrounding them, who were too numbed by fear to do much of anything. Perhaps many Poles were indifferent in light of so much common suffering. Perhaps some were glad that the "Jewish Question" was finally being resolved, horribly, pitilessly, but resolved nevertheless. Can we ever really know?

The collective experience of World War II has generated an enormous literary response in Poland as the greatest calamity in Polish history. Some of the best of this literature transcends the usual writing about war and occupation by raising profound moral and ethical questions about human behavior in inhuman circumstances. But the postwar Polish literature on the Jewish dimension of the collective experience, on the Holocaust, is not quantitatively impressive. There are plausible reasons for this shortfall, beginning with the forty-four-year postwar communist rule of Poland, which followed the Soviet policy of not distinguishing the genocide of the Jews from the slaughter of non-Jews in the German-occupied areas. Moreover, anti-Jewish incidents in the immediate aftermath of the war, most notably and notoriously the so-called Kielce pogrom of July 4, 1946, in which perhaps as many as sixty Jews lost their lives, and later the vicious anti-Jewish "anti-Zionist" campaign of 1968, after which 15,000–20,000 Jews left the country, stirred memories of prewar anti-Semitism, again raised questions about Polish behavior during the war, and in general cast such a pall over Polish-Jewish relations both within and beyond Poland that writing about the plight of the Jews during the occupation would surely not have been easy.

What then is the balance sheet of Polish imaginative writing about the plight of the Jew both during and after the war? There is, first of all, poetry—Czesław Miłosz's "Campo dei Fiori" and "A Poor Christian Looks at the Ghetto," Antoni Słonimski's "Elegy of Jewish Towns," Mieczysław Jastrun's "The Guarded Hour," which were written during the war in an effort to capture the immediacy of impact of the extermination of the Jews, and the clandestinely printed anthology on the plight of the Jews titled *Z otchłani* (*Out of the Abyss*, 1944), edited by T. Sarnecki and containing poems by the literary critic Jan Kott and the poets Jastrun and Miłosz. One of the better postwar poems inspired by the Holocaust is Marian Piechal's poignant "Ostatni koncert Jankiela" ("Yankel's Last Concert)," which evokes the memory of Mickiewicz's *Pan Tadeusz* with its unfulfilled wish for a new future for Poles and Jews living together.

Of the enormous body of postwar Polish prose fiction about World War II,

---

Poles Look at the Ghetto." Originally published in English translation in *Polin: A Journal of Polish-Jewish Studies* 2 (1987): 321–36, it was subsequently included in *Four Decades of Polish Essays*, ed. Jan Kott (Evanston, Ill.: Northwestern University Press, 1990), 222–35.

Tadeusz Borowski's concentration camp stories, written mostly in Munich after his liberation from Dachau and contained in two collections, *Pożegnanie z Marią* (*Farewell to Mary*, 1948) and *Kamienny świat* (*World of Stone*, 1948), are unsurpassed in their chilling realism and objectivity. They are beyond doubt some of the most powerful fictional accounts of concentration camp life in any language. One typical story, "The Man with the Package," appears in the present anthology. In its fidelity to the events and its impact on the reader, the only other Polish prose work on the Holocaust at all comparable to Borowski's is the huge volume of stories published in 1952 under the title *Żywe i martwe morze* (*The Dead and Living Sea*) by Adolf Rudnicki, a writer of Jewish origin. A well-established novelist before the outbreak of World War II, Rudnicki fought in the campaign of 1939 and later participated in the Warsaw Uprising of 1944. Even during the war he began a series of long stories designed to serve as a testimony to the martyrdom of the Jews and eventually incorporated into the volume *The Dead and the Living Sea*. Arguably the best of these stories, "Wielki Stefan Czarnecki" ("The Great Stefan Czarnecki"), deals with an assimilated Jew who becomes so estranged from his fellow Jews that he even gravitates to the Polish political right; but Konecki's identification with Polish culture proves to no avail during the occupation, when he is ultimately made to share the same fate as the Jews he scorned. Plunged into the depths of psychic and physical agony, Czarnecki pitifully rediscovers his Jewishness amid the horror all around him, and it is this rediscovery that costs him his life at the end. Julian Tuwim, who managed to flee Poland after the German conquest and spent the war years in Rio de Janeiro and New York, returning to Poland in 1946, similarly rediscovered his own consciously ignored Jewishness under the impress of the Holocaust. His feelings were articulated in his deeply moving manifesto "We, Polish Jews . . ." of 1944.

A story such as Rudnicki's "The Great Stefan Czarnecki" could not easily have been written by an ethnic Pole, who in all probability would not have appreciated the complexity of the issue of assimilation among Polish Jews. By the same token, the Polish writer of Jewish origin would surely have been less comfortable with the treatment of Polish-Jewish relations during and after the war characteristic of works by such writers as Jerzy Andrzejewski, Jarosław Iwaszkiewicz, Andrzej Szczypiorski, and Jarosław Marek Rymkiewicz included in this book.

With the exception of Iwaszkiewicz's story, "The Mendelssohn Quartet," which is essentially a communist propaganda piece intended to reveal the disillusionment in Israel of many Jews who left Poland to live in a Jewish homeland in Palestine in the 1920s and 1930s, the works excerpted here use the experiences of Jews in the war to expose a broad range of Polish attitudes toward the Holocaust. What Andrzejewski's *Wielki tydzień* (*Holy Week*), Szczypiorski's *Początek* (*The Beautiful Mrs. Seidenman*), and Rymkiewicz's *Umschlagplatz* (*The Final Station: Umschlagplatz*, in English translation) have in common is the desire to confront Polish attitudes, both sympathetic and hostile, toward the plight of the Jews during the war. But there is a curious balancing act in this fiction. On the surface this body of work seems sympathetic toward Jews and forthright in its depiction of Poles who were either indifferent to Jewish suffering or who contributed to it by betraying Jews. Scrutinized more closely, it becomes apparent that these writers strove to offset negative portrayals of Polish types with positive ones, and to show Jews themselves in unfavorable as well as favorable light. The German occupation brought out the best and the worst in people, Poles and Jews alike. Simply acknowledging the humanness of human behavior would have been bold enough without the compromise of symmetry.

And so we are back to the beginning of this introduction. For all practical considerations, Poland has no Jews; the lives of the few thousand remaining survivors are warmly preserved in the novels and stories of the now deceased Polish-Jewish writer Stanisław Beński.[7] Jewish culture, such as it exists in the country, is negligible. The "Jewish Question" has been resolved, though not in a manner anyone might have foreseen. It is a half century since the end of World War II and the Holocaust, and nearly a decade since the end of communist rule in Poland. The Polish-Jewish debate has become the shared recovery of a common heritage. The Jewish experience in Poland spanning ten centuries cannot be fully understood without fair consideration of the Polish context in which that experience took place. Nor can the Poles properly recover their own past by denying the stranger who was in their midst for so long. The fictional re-creation of the Polish-Jewish past has engaged the talents of a tiny number of mostly Jewish writers, chief among them Isaac Bashevis Singer, who wrote only in Yiddish, and Julian Stryjkowski (born 1905), a prewar communist whose postwar literary career in Poland rests primarily on such well-received novels about the past life of the Polish-Jewish community as *Austeria* (1966) and *Sen Azrila* (*Azril's Dream*, 1975). Imaginative literature, faced with the inescapable reality of an extinct community, has for the most part yielded to the preservation of facts and artifacts.

7. A collection of Beński's writings in English translation has been published under the title *Missing Pieces*. See Stanisław Beński, *Missing Pieces*, trans. Walter Arndt (San Diego: Harcourt Brace Jovanovich, 1990).

Part One ■ From the Renaissance to the Mid-Nineteenth Century

■ Jan Dantyszek (Ioannes Dantiscus; 1485–1543)
"Poem about Jews" (mid-1530s)

[Jan Dantyszek was an outstanding representative of the early Renaissance in Poland. He was a prominent diplomat, confidant of kings and emperors, and a highly respected humanist who wrote exclusively in Latin and counted Erasmus among his correspondents. In 1537 he was chosen over Copernicus as bishop of Warmia, one of the most prestigious and powerful ecclesiastical posts in Poland at the time. Although Protestants were the principal targets of Dantyszek's religious satire, his "Carmen de Iudaeis" ("Poem about Jews") was probably a manifestation of the anti-Jewish sentiment in Cracow, which is believed to have been incited by Queen Bona, the Italian wife of King Sigismund I. The poem was discovered among other manuscripts in his library and published only in 1621. A Polish translation of the work went through four editions in the second half of the eighteenth century under the title *Błędy talmudowe* (*Errors of the Talmud*).]

Poem about Jews

They are alien, rude, impudent, quarrelsome, brazen,
Treacherous, fawning, insolent, deceitful, uncultivated,
Deceptive, unreliable, unwilling, injurious, wild,
reprobate, fraudulent, villainous, impious, profane,
Cruel, monstrous, cunning, misshapen, prating,
Foolish, silly, unwholesome, spiteful, obstinate,
Disparaging, mendacious, invidious, barbarous, greedy,
Shrewd, inconstant, smooth-talking, raging, two-tongued,
Nimble, impatient, ambitious, slippery,
Ungrateful, domineering, drink-loving, wearisome, rebellious,
Intoxicated, sycophantic, slothful, voracious,
Garrulous, vain, menacing, imprudent, querulous, grasping,
Litigious, tenacious, impetuous, vagrant,
Repulsive and snappish, imitative, irreverent, stern,
Trifling, unjust, provincial, caustic, salacious.
Filthy, untamed and violent, inglorious, dreadful,
Vexing, bold, dilatory, indigent, cowardly,
Cunning, dark and infamous, reckless, furious,
Negligent, unteachable, needful, unsightly, unskillful.
By nature they lack desire for goodness and justice,
They lack virtue and love of honesty.
If you can add anything, dear reader,
Please do, and God will grant your just rewards.

Ioannis Dantisci Poetae Laureati, *Carmina*, ed. Stanislaus Skimina (Cracow: Sumptibus Polonicae Academiae Litterarum et Scientiarum, 1950), 166–67. The date of the poem is unknown.

■ Jan Tarnowski (1488–1561)
Principles of Law of the Polish Land (1579)

[As Grand Hetman of the Crown, the magnate Jan Tarnowski was one of the most power-ful men in sixteenth-century Poland. He was an outstanding military leader and man of state. In later life he was much concerned with civic and legal issues, a fact reflected in his popular compilation of Polish laws under the full title *Ustawy prawa ziemskiego polskiego, dla pamięci lepszej, krótko i porządnie z statutów i z konstytucyj zebrane* (*Principles of Law of the Polish Land, For Easier Memorization, Briefly and Accurately Gathered from the Stat-utes and Constitutions*). The following excerpts are from the section dealing with Jews.]

Concerning Jews

A Jew may not lend a Christian money on any account under pain of losing such money.

Jews are not allowed to collect taxes.

All goods brought to Jews in pawn, or pledged to them, must be inscribed in their books.

If something stolen is left with a Jew and he does not indicate from whom the item was obtained, such a Jew must be punished as a thief.

Jews must not conduct any business in villages; Christians who buy from them are subject to punishment.

No office can judge a Jew accused of a crime except ourselves, or our vojevoda, or his judge. And if a Jew committed a crime worthy of capital punishment, only we can judge that.

If someone wounds a Jew, then such a person must be punished as we deem suitable, and must give the wounded Jew what he gave for treatment or other-wise spent.

If someone kills a Jew, and is convicted by law, the movable and immovable property of such a person is in our power.

Jews are free to travel everywhere in our kingdom, so long as they bear the guilt of no crime. However, they are subject to the same sales taxes as the towns-people in the city in which they reside.

When a dead Jew is transported from one district to another, or from one city to another, no tax may be collected on such a corpse; and if a tax collector should exact any, he will be regarded as a pillager.

If anyone disturbs a Jewish cemetery, he should be punished in accordance with local custom; his estate then devolves upon us.

Jan Tarnowski, *Ustawy prawa ziemskiego polskiego*, ed. Kazimierz Józef Turowski (Cracow: Nakładem Wydawnictwa Biblioteki Polskiej, 1858), 125–31.

If someone attacks a Jewish school, such a person must forfeit to the vojevoda two pounds of pepper.

If a court decides against a Jew, he must deliver to the judge a pound of pepper.

If a Jew does not appear before a court in the year designated, he forfeits a pound of pepper each the first and second years; and if he does not appear the third year, he pays a similar penalty.

A Jew does not have to take an oath on a stool, except where weighty matters are involved, anything amounting to fifty *grzywny* silver, or more; where anything less is concerned, he can take an oath at a side door.

If someone kills a Jew secretly, and there is no witness to this, Jews are empowered by law to bring charges against the person they believe to be guilty and he must be taken into custody.

A Jewish judge cannot try a Jew anywhere but in a Jewish school or in some other designated place.

Jews cannot be sentenced to punishment except in a school or in some ordinary place. However, we, or our vojevoda, can bring them up on charges, or summon them.

We do not wish for a Christian to lodge with Jews.

If someone abducts or steals a Jewish child, such a person must be judged as a thief.

A Jew is free of the law on a holy day.

No one can summon a Jew by law on his holy day.

If someone takes a pledge from a Jew by force, or causes him harm in his own home, such a person must be punished as if he ravaged our royal chamber.

If a Christian child is killed, and someone accuses a Jew and proves it on the strength of witnesses, that is, by three Christians and three Jews, then the Jew must be sentenced to death. But if it should be plainly evidenced that that Christian made a false accusation against the Jew, then such a Christian must suffer the same punishment.

If a Jew suffers an attack at night and a Christian refuses to help him, he pays a penalty.

If a Jew calls out in the night that he is being harmed, and his Christian neighbor refuses to come to his aid, such a Christian must pay a penalty of thirty schillings.

Jews are free to purchase bread and other necessities of life; if someone prevents them from so doing, such a person is accountable to the vojevoda.

■ Fr. Franciszek Salezy Jezierski (1740–91)

Catechism of the Secrets of the Polish Government as Written about the Year 1735 by the Esteemed Mr. Sterne in the English Language, Later Translated into French, and Now Finally into Polish (1790)

[Fr. Franciszek Salezy Jezierski was a leading publicist of Enlightenment Poland. An inspector of the lay Commission of National Education, which assumed supervision of secondary schools in Poland after the Society of Jesus (Jesuits) was expelled in 1773, and was the first such commission in Europe, Jezierski worked closely with the principal reformer of the time, Hugo Kołłątaj (1750–1812). So closely was he identified with Kołłątaj, that he was called the "Vulcan of the Forge's Thunderbolts" ("Wulkan gromów Kuźnicy"), a reference to the circle of liberal reformers — "The Forge" ("Kuźnica") — with whom Kołłątaj sought to carry out his agenda of political and social change. Although the *Catechism* was presented as a translation from the English, the work was written by Jezierski. Political reformers at the time occasionally resorted to such stratagems to conceal their real names.]

Q: Who satisfies the principal needs of shopkeeping and trade in such a large country [Poland]?
A: The Jews, because in view of their numbers hardly a tenth of the ethnic Poles would engage in them.
Q: What is the reason for that?
A: The fact that all shopkeeping and trades are prohibited to the nobility because of the dignity of their class, just as sins are prohibited by divine and legal commandment. And since the professions of urban life are so despised, the Jews, endowed with perverse enterprise, baseness, and endurance in infamy, easily take the place of the urban class.
Q: Then the nobleman loses the honor of his class if he is useful to society through trade or shopkeeping?
A: So it is, because in Poland thievery and knavery are not as debased as shopkeeping and trade.
Q: Would it not seem that for such reasons the nobility would be the poorest class?
A: It should be the wealthiest, since the noble estate in Poland is like an absolute monarch on the throne.
Q: Explain that more clearly.
A: In Poland the nobleman is the inheritor of the land, the absolute master having no superior above him save for the law, which he himself determines and does

Franciszek Salezy Jezierski, *Wybór pism,* ed. Zdzisław Skwarczyński, introduction by Jerzy Ziomek (Warsaw: Państwowy Instytut Wydawniczy, 1952), 69–70.

not obey when it pleases him, regarding it with the intimacy reserved for a personal possession.

Q: Who sets and pays taxes?

A: The noble estate imposes the taxes, and they are paid by the peasant, the burgher, the Jew, and the priest, for how can the nobleman impose a tax on himself? If he gives something, he calls that a sacrifice, for the sake of differentiating master from subject. . . .

■ Stanisław Staszic (1755–1826)
"Jews" (1790)

[Educated at the universities of Leipzig and Göttingen, as well as at the Collège de France, Stanisław Staszic was a geologist and political thinker whose program for reform in Poland is contained in his two major treatises, *Uwagi nad życiem Jana Zamoyskiego* (*The Life of Jan Zamoyski*, 1785) and *Przestrogi dla Polski* (*Admonishments for Poland*, 1790). Staszic's ideas must be viewed in the context of the European Enlightenment and the campaign for far-reaching social and political reform animating the Four-Year Diet (1788–92) and culminating in the liberal Polish constitution of May 3, 1791, a date celebrated in Poland as a national holiday.

Of burgher origin, he advocated improvements in the conditions of burgher life in Poland leading to their full participation in Polish civic and economic life. He also deplored the status of the peasants and championed their right to personal freedom as well as ownership of the land they tilled; he stopped short, however, of calling for their full economic emancipation. Most of the social criticism in his treatises is directed at the unbridled power and privileges of the nobility, whose selfishness and arrogance he held responsible for the partial disenfranchisement of the bourgeoisie and the exploitation of the peasants. His harsh treatment of the Jews in *Admonishments for Poland* reflects both common Enlightenment attitudes and the widespread belief in Poland that the Jews, serving as middlemen for the gentry landowners, exploited the peasants in the villages and were detrimental to their moral and economic well-being.

Staszic was held in high esteem in Poland in later years. In 1808 he was elected president of the Society of the Friends of Learning in Warsaw, which became the Polish Academy of Sciences. The palace he built in Warsaw to accommodate the Society of the Friends of Learning, and the statue of Copernicus in front of it, survived World War II and are still standing today.]

Wherever the agricultural estate and the merchant estate began to develop, they were brought to ruin by the Jews, the foremost of all good-for-nothings. The Jews are the bloodsuckers of the farmer. None of them apply themselves to augmenting the country's harvests nor, apart from a small number of artisans, does this race of people assist in the renewal or processing of such harvests. All of them live just from other, industrious classes. Their consumption in Poland has the same effect on the country as if the grain, cloth, and linen, which the Jews need, were destroyed by worms or burned by fire.

Jews are the summer and winter locust plague of our country. These two species of creatures accelerate the flow of money, facilitate the transformation of wealth, impoverish industrious people, lay waste the most fertile fields, fill villages

Stanisław Staszic, "Żydzi," in *Przestrogi dla Polska,* in *Pisma filozoficzne i społeczne,* ed. Bogdan Sucho-dolski (Warsaw: Państwowe Wydawnictwo Naukowe, 1954), 298–303.

with want, and infect the air with putrefaction. The Jewish race impoverishes our villages and infects our cities with rot. . . .

Our peasant will raise himself from his poverty only with difficulty so long as the Jewish race, conditioned by its religion and upbringing to cheat, will continue to rule over that poison by which, when it wants, it can turn the heads of several million people with impunity and, depriving the peasant of his consciousness for several hours, can dispose of his property as it chooses.

Jews, the last rabble, deluded by the numerous rites of their religion aimed just at the senses — which are strongest in the person who is more inclined to acquiring habits than thought — still bear the spirit of idleness and vagabondage of their first fathers, shepherds. Similarly, the Jewish order, like the order once upon a time of our Templars, Knights of the Cross, and so on, at no time ever wanted to work but only to go on pilgrimages, wander about, pray, and plunder foreign lands.

The laws of the Jewish order do not prepare people for great work or for that work which today is necessary for societies. That is why the Jewish race cannot maintain itself among industrious people. Only in bad governments, only in those countries where idlers enjoy protection and uphold the right of lawlessness, only there do the Jews flourish, nest, and multiply. In all feudal states, a Jewish nest existed, with the Jews functioning as the intermediaries between the lord and his subjects. Prevented by his religion from overt extortion, the nobleman had here an opportune and suitable instrument for the satisfaction of his greed. What the master was unable to pluck from his subjects without pangs of conscience, he skinned from them by means of Jewish deceit with a perfectly peaceful conscience.

Every nobleman repeats incessantly that because the Polish peasant is so stupid, unindustrious, and lazy, he cannot be granted either justice or freedom.

But no nobleman realizes, or wants to realize, that he is the reason for this, or that the Polish peasant is the same human being as the German peasant, or the peasant just over the border in Silesia, Prussia, and Saxony. Why are those enlightened, industrious, and of benefit to their country? The nature of the Polish peasant is not the cause of the problem, but rather the anarchy of the nobility reigning in Poland. Our peasant in Poland will not change so long as the landed nobility itself does not change.

The nobleman will complain that the Polish peasant is a terrible drunkard, yet every nobleman will establish five or six taverns in each of his villages or towns, just like a net for trapping that peasant. He then puts them in the hands of the most competent Jews he can find, those who would pay him the most, which is to say, those who would be the most effective in deceiving the peasants and inducing them most to drinking.

Unmindful squire! Do not base the increase in your revenues on the drunkenness or impoverishment of your subjects. The cheating and skinning from the peasant of his last cent by Jews impedes his farming, so that instead of enriching the country, he destroys it and prepares your downfall. Every złoty with which the Jew increases the fee he pays you to operate a tavern is the złoty by which he impoverishes you.

So it is. Besides the unlawful slavery of our farmer, the Jews are the second great cause of his lack of industriousness, of his ignorance, of his drunkenness, and of his poverty. It is only the peasants who bear the burden of having to clothe and feed several hundreds of thousands of Jews. This disgusting race, having cheated the peasant out of his last morsel of bread, steals his money, deprives him of all industry, health, and even reason.

When the Jews were forced to work in Egypt, they robbed the country and fled, preferring to wander across wild deserts as idle vagabonds. This race of people has customs, a way of life, and morality which are incompatible with the moral code of our own religion. One reads in their holy books that for wrongs suffered at the hands of people of another religion, they can make off with various utensils and silver pieces borrowed from them. Our religion teaches the contrary: on no account, no matter what the circumstances, does it sanction theft and swindle. It teaches that no one is ever free to redress a wrong on his own. Thus, the Jew, because of his morality, will always be dangerous and false, and whenever he swindles will easily assuage his conscience by calling that a recompense for the wrongs done him.

The farmer in Poland, a northern country, needs a certain amount of warming drink. All spirits, but especially *gorzałka* [a type of whiskey], which is natural to Poland, have the terrible property of depriving a person of his reason, consciousness, and memory for several hours.

To grant Jews the provisioning of spirits of such terrible consequences is to entrust the property of our farmer to people without faith, who are inimicable to Christians, and thus to place in their hands a weapon by which they can with impunity make whatever use they please of the farmer's property.

The Jews know full well how profitable the property of such a drink can be to them, how very advantageous to their way of thinking; hence they do not betake themselves avidly to the brewing of beer, since beer, by not depriving a person of his consciousness, does not facilitate the means of cheating him.

In Poland, a northern country, it is impossible to prohibit warming drinks, but government must have the good sense in no way to allow Jews to traffic in spirits. Let the government of the country allow the Jews the same ease of earnings as every other inhabitant save for the provisioning of spirits, which, for the sake of improving the country's agriculture, should be sternly prohibited to them throughout Poland, in all villages and cities.

Of all the inhabitants of Poland subject to the ruling noble class, it is the Jews to whom the nobility grants the greatest freedoms and laws. Until the present, it has no desire to ensure justice for the Christian farmer; on the contrary, it continues to repeat these bizarre words: only when the nobleman becomes a slave will the farmer have justice. But it does not in the least offend the prejudices of this same unthinking nobleman that he must stand in court together with the Jew.

Neither Lutherans, nor Calvinists, nor Greeks, nor Armenians, nor indeed any another group of people resident in any city are permitted to have their own laws, administrations, and judges, but must submit to the laws and magistrates of the city in which they live. But the Jews, on the contrary, possess their own separate laws, their own magistrates and judges, wherever they reside.

This lawlessness is attributable to the fact that the nobility, everywhere driven only by personal gain and full of crude prejudices concerning their own free-dom, which they are never inclined to relinquish, for the ostensible good of the entire country has already placed one half of the wealthiest cities under the yoke of foreign despots, and fills the rest with Jews.[1] This lawlessness is attributable to the fact that a significant part of the remainder of the Polish nation not yet lost through lawlessness is already changing over to the Jewish. One part of the Polish people has been crushed by unmistakable slavery; a second has been degraded throughout almost all royal lands by greedy *starostas* (district officials) more than Jews. That is why the real Polish nation lacks that spirit of industriousness which we see in other countries. We have no community in our cities other than the Jewish. The burgher is indifferent to all foreign wrongs and outrages committed against the bishops and delegates [to the Diet], while in fact it is the improvi-dent rule of the nobility that bears responsibility for his loss of attachment to the country . . .

Let the old landowning nobility henceforth strengthen the nation of Poles and not the nation of Jews. Let the Jews not enjoy the special protection of provin-cial, regional, and district authorities. Rather let the Jews, just as the Lutherans, Calvinists, and others be subject to the laws, magistrates, and judges of the cities in which they reside. They should no longer be allowed to maintain any *kahal* of elders, but just a rabbi for the celebration of their religious rites.

Two laws are absolutely essential to prevent the Jews from causing further in-jury to the development of agriculture and the growth of cities.

The first: A law forbidding Jews from further trafficking in spirits.

The second: A law requiring the Jews resident in cities, just like residents who observe other religions, to become wholly subject to the magistracy and govern-ment of the city. They must no longer be permitted to maintain their own officials or separate communal administration, separate council of elders, or kahal.

Moreover, for the most effective uprooting of their spirit of assembly and sepa-rate class status, their education must be placed in the hands of the National

---

1. Staszic is referring to the majority of Protestants in many Polish cities because of whom the king of Prussia was allowed to take those cities under his legal protection, at least in the area of religious freedoms.

Commission of Education, which would then assume responsibility for assigning them teachers, prescribing morality and other elementary books.

In order to disincline the Jews from a life of idleness, the law must decree that no Jew be allowed to take a wife unless he takes up agriculture or learns a trade. And finally, since the Jews no longer speak Hebrew, do not know their native tongue, their original liturgical language, but conduct their rites in a corrupted German language from the time they were expelled from Germany and descended on Poland and live exclusively from Poland, let them henceforth speak the Polish language, receive education in the Polish language, and conduct their religious rites and learning in this language.

■ Julian Ursyn Niemcewicz (1758–1841)
Levi and Sarah (1821)

[Julian Ursyn Niemcewicz was one of the most colorful figures in late-eighteenth- and early-nineteenth-century Poland. A vigorous advocate of reform, he had the opportunity to express his views both as a deputy to the Four-Year Diet and as the author of the influential political comedy *Powrót posła* (*The Return of the Deputy*, 1790). After the second partition of Poland in 1793, Niemciewicz threw his lot in with Kościuszko in the insurrection of 1794, becoming the general's adjutant and secretary of state. The Russian defeat of the insurrection led to his two-year imprisonment, along with Kościuszko. Freed by the Emperor Paul I in 1796, Niemcewicz accompanied Kościuszko, who had previously participated in the Revolutionary War, on his return trip to America. Niemcewicz remained in America after Kościuszko's sudden, and mysterious, return to Europe. He acquired U.S. citizenship and all told spent ten years in America. His account of his extensive travels in this country, written originally in French and Polish, still make interesting reading. They were translated into English under the title *Under Their Vine and Fig Tree: Travels through America in 1797–1799, 1805.*[1]

Niemcewicz returned to Poland permanently after Napoleon created the Duchy of Warsaw in 1807. His subsequent career was devoted to political, scholarly, and literary pursuits. In the novel *Dwaj panowie Sieciechowie* (*The Two Gentlemen Sieciech*, 1815), he again took up the cause of progressive reform over the obscurantism mainly of the provincial gentry. His novel about Jewish life in Poland, *Lejbe i Sióra* (*Levi and Sarah*, 1821)—the first of its kind in Polish literature—transposes the conflict of obscurantism versus reform from a Christian to a Jewish milieu and gives it a generational character. From Niemcewicz's point of view, the only way young Jews especially could achieve the cultural emancipation that would enable them to take their place in a modern secular society was by breaking free of the yoke of the ultraconservative Orthodox rabbinate, who kept the Jewish communities mired in stultifying traditionalism.

After the suppression of the Polish insurrection of 1830–31, Niemcewicz joined the so-called Great Emigration in Paris. He died not long after completing his memoirs, which remain one of the more important literary monuments of the period.]

To the Reader

A foreign people, scattered over the entire expanse of our land, comprising one sixth of our general population and almost the whole population of smaller cities and towns; a people separate not only by faith but also by language, dress, and

---

J. U. Niemcewicz, *Lejbe i Sióra czyli Listy dwóch kochanków* (Cracow: Towarzystwo Miłosników Książki, 1931), ix–xii, 31–34, 36–37, 37–38, 44–51, 52–53, 77–84, 98–106, 112–14, 120–22.

1. Julian Ursyn Niemcewicz, *Under Their Vine and Fig Tree: Travels through America in 1797–1799, 1805,* trans. and ed. Metchie J. E. Budka (Elizabeth, N.J.: Grassmann Publishing, 1965). This is volume 14 in the Collections of The New Jersey Historical Society at Newark.

customs; a people who having abandoned the true law of Moses does not acknowledge civil laws, nor the courts of the land, nor does it acknowledge Christians as fellow men, as human beings, and who from childhood inculcates their young with hatred toward us, in short a people comprising a dangerous *status in statu* [state within a state]. No wonder that they have aroused the greatest and most concerned apprehension in other countries as well as among us. Every one of us asks what will become of the name Pole, what will become of Christianity, if this people, remaining in its separateness, in its hatred, and in its crude prejudices, will continue to multiply at today's rate.

Many citizens, struck by the sight of this danger, have sought to publish their thoughts and opinions in such a vital matter. It is pleasant for us to see that, with the exception of a very small number, all, truthful to the teaching of our Savior, far from persecution and harsh measures, return pity for hatred, and benevolent wishes for imprecations. In sketching an image of harmful Jewish prejudices, they have at the same time offered the means of averting them and of leading a people misled by its elders onto the path of good sense and their own welfare. . . .

Hence the desire on my part in some way to contribute to such an important matter gave rise to the thought that the prejudices of the Jews, the inhuman teachings and counsels of their elders, if set forth in a dramatic manner, as it were, might make them still clearer, and through their very form and the title "romance," might make the information about so many prejudices more universal. And most to be desired, in their ludicrousness they might convince the Jews themselves how contrary to the Bible, erroneous, and harmful are the talmudic teachings, teachings which the elders, for their own profit only, do not cease inculcating in the young. That was the only reason for which following so many enlightened writers, I ventured to say something in this important matter.

The thought is indeed far from me to condemn this unfortunate people to extermination or exile, but rather to reform it, to bring it to its senses, to a recognition of its own good, that is, what the Christian learning offers.

Every wise Jew who happens to read this modest work will discover that all the human prejudices and ludicrous superstitions pointed out in it are taken faithfully from the Talmud and the commentaries on it, with an indication even of the chapters and pages where they can be found. I could enlarge this modest work to several large volumes, if I wanted further to demonstrate their unfathomable tales. But out of a desire not to bore my readers, I decided that what I am now offering is ample. I was not driven by hatred if I painted in unflattering colors the figure of Yankel and the fanatics who hold a poor people in error and oppression. It was a sincere delight for me to offer in the figure of Abraham the image of an esteemed and honorable Israelite who while strictly preserving his faith managed to distinguish the words of God from the learning handed down by madmen and fanatics. The characters of Levi, Sarah, and Rachel can serve as examples for Israelite youth.

To return the Jews to the true light, to cure them of their prejudices, to point out to them that by clinging to the inhuman precepts of their elders they themselves will wallow in baseness and want and will themselves obstruct the path to all advantages in human society—that is the sole object of this modest book. I will be happy if I achieve even a part of my goal.

Letter VII / Sarah to Levi

10th of Iger
   My dear Leybele!

Why have you been silent so long? Oh, how cruel, and especially when I am being so tormented these days! Has not your absence brought me enough sadness? Why am I being persecuted and oppressed on all sides? Must one wretched girl become the object not only of the fear but even the closest attention of the rabbi of the kahal, the brotherhoods, indeed of the whole of the Hebrew elders? You are far away, and I am being persecuted by everyone; there is nobody to defend me, to offer me the slightest consolation. All I hear are scoldings and dire threats. The books you gave me have been taken away from me and have been replaced by the Talmud, the *Mishnah,* the *Gemara,* and the Cabala. They compel me to wander in this dark wilderness in which a ray of light never shines, and where all I encounter are poisonous weeds and terrible monsters. I keep my distance from them as best I can. I long for the original books of Moses, the works of *Mendelssohn, Friedländer, Ben David,* and *Kalmansohn;* a rational Hebrew never disavows these enlightened men.

Amid these humiliations, my chief comfort, besides the memory of you, has been our mutual friendship and respect, and the similarity of our feelings and way of thinking. A few days after my arrival here, I met at the synagogue my friend Rachel, the daughter of Abraham, one of the best, most rational, and I must add, one of the worthiest people who live in Israel. I will give you a brief sketch of the person, principles, and way of life of this man. Imagine a man past eighty. His aged and dignified form command both liking and veneration. When I approached him, and he greeted me amiably and blessed me, I thought I saw our patriarch Jacob as he placed a hand on the head of his son Joseph and blessed him, in the land of Egypt. Endowed with a rare intelligence, this man is fluent in whatever a true Israelite ought to know, enriched by his tireless industry, and beloved for his humanity. He would long ago have filled the highest offices in our community, but for the integrity of his morals, his spirit of tolerance, and his loathing and even contempt for all the superstitions and misdoings of the Talmud, which the present elders have taken unto themselves as holy and immutable precepts. His contempt has brought down on him countless persecutions, and he would have fallen victim to bitterness and superstition were it not for the protec-

Wincenty Smokowski (1797–1876), "Jewish Wedding" (after 1858). Courtesy Muzeum Narodowe w Warszawie.

tion of the present honorable governor of this province. Hence the kahals do not bother him because they fear him.

Heaven itself seems to have blessed the virtues and piety of Abraham, who, not by cunning, brokerage, or deceit, but by constant industry and a frugal way of life laid the foundation of the prosperity in which he now finds himself. He is a fine weaver by profession; with the growing profit of the one workshop with which he began, he now owns twenty, which are run by an equal number of young Israelites. Neither in this city, or even in its suburbs, is there a single poor Jewess to whom he has not given the means of earning an honest livelihood by spinning. His house is clean, spacious, all his weavers live in it, and are called to prayer every morning and evening. Our ancient laws are strictly observed there, but the Talmud and the Cabalistical stupidities are excluded. With children, his household staff, and servants, he employs only the language of the country. "When the Jews have forgotten how to speak Hebrew," he used to say, "it is the most natural thing for them to use the language of the nation in whose midst they were born and which took them unto its bosom in their days of persecution some six hundred years ago rather than a fractured foreign tongue." This is a great crime in the eyes of our elders, but they do not dare openly to persecute him because of the powerful protection he enjoys. . . .

New blows are being weighed against me. My father wants to give me to Yankel, the son of Hirsch, of Berdyczew. He must be the most abominable creature, and the most unbearable because of his fanaticism. But even were he the nicest of men, you know, my dear sweet Leybele, that he could never touch a heart forever devoted to you! My father has so far not said anything about his plan; but you know our customs—it will strike me all at once like a bolt of lightning. But this time they will find in me the courage of Deborah. Torment and persecution may shorten my life, but neither the rabbi, the kahal, nor all the elders will ever succeed in getting me to violate the love I have entertained for you or the oath I have sworn to you. Should this letter reach you, should you learn of the danger I remain in, should my lamentable position arouse your compassion, which I do not doubt, you will arrive to save and console your Sarah.

Farewell, my dear.

Yankel to Sarah

Berdiczew, 6th Yir
My dear dove!

My father has informed me that thou, Sarah, are to become my wife; he has also told me that thou art beautiful, O daughter of David, that thine eyes are like those of a dove between ringlets of black; that thy teeth are like a flock of sheep just as they emerge from their bath; that thy feet are beautiful in their slippers; and that both thy breasts are like a pair of young deer.

O my lovely fawn, I am, in truth, a hunchback; but even my deformity makes me in some measure the more interesting, and thou needst not regard that thy humble suitor is somewhat pallid, for I have become pale from poring over the Talmud and the Cabala, and my hair has fallen off from scratching my head in my constant meditation; but from my lips the sweet smelling oil of wisdom flows; the spikenard scented with roses and myrtles.

At the good news which my father brought, my heart began to heave toward thee. I imbibed the wine of mystery, drank deep in the mystical books, and they assured me that I should embrace thee, and that thou wouldst turn thy heart to me, and be as firm as the impression of a signet ring on sealing-wax. . . .

Letter X / Levi to Sarah

Warsaw, 31 Nissan
My dear betrothed!

. . . You must know, Sarah, that a curse has been placed on me; but when you learn the circumstances you will surely not hold me guilty. Just hear for what reasons I brought this punishment down on me. You know that my adherence to the Mosaic law causes me to feel utter contempt for all those later deviations with which fanatics have injured our religion. You know the pain I feel in my soul over the degradation of my countrymen, over the darkness in which our elders keep them, and over the extortion they practice for their own enrichment and gratification and because of which they have led our people into dire poverty.

You have often seen my uncle and benefactor Ephraim. That worthy Israelite, a faithful observer of the laws of Moses, was, throughout his whole life, the guardian angel of our poor people against the abuses and oppressions of the kahal. His zeal drew down upon him the hatred and persecution of the rabbis and of the brotherhood of elders. He was greatly tormented by them, grew ill from his woes, and ended his days not long ago. His immortal soul took flight, the perishable body of an esteemed old man grew cold, but the spirit of persecution and revenge did not grow cold in the elders.

The brotherhood of elders, in the most unjust of usurpations and abuses, has ascribed to itself the exclusive right of interring the dead. They have instilled in our ignorant people the belief that it is a great disgrace, even a hindrance to salvation, if, after a death has occurred, the deceased is not buried within a few hours. The brotherhood of elders has employed just such prejudice and usurpation against the hated Ephraim in the cruelest fashion. Despite my entreaties and endeavors, the remains of the late Ephraim lay unburied for four days.

This blind obstinacy finally exhausted my patience. I went for the last time to the brotherhood of elders, and with a voice full of grief and indignation, exclaimed: "How terrible is your cruelty! Not content with having poisoned the life of this honorable man even after his death you still deny him his peaceful rest! In what book of the law is such a right inscribed? Show it to me! You are silent, because you cannot show it to me! Our fathers and patriarchs never commanded it. Your mad superstitiousness, avarice, and pride have imposed this prejudice on an ignorant people for your own gain. So it is: you hold this people in oppression and shameful bondage worse than the Pharoahs, but you have gone beyond measure. This people is beginning to perceive and to see that the motive of all your actions is not the interests of our faith but your own personal advantage. It is you who have arrogated to yourselves the collection of the poll and recruit taxes, which you hoard for yourselves, enrich yourselves on, and build luxurious homes with while the people you mercilessly squeeze by such extortions is starving to death. Why is my uncle still unburied? If what I have already given is not enough to satisfy your avarice, I will double the amount," I said, throwing to them a purse containing a thousand thalers, "but the interment must take place immediately, or I swear by the rod of Aaron that I will disclose publicly, in the temple, before all the people, your falsehood, your wickedness, and your extortion."

At these words, which had been uttered with bold defiance, the entire brotherhood was thrown into a state of confusion. They retrieved the purse and put it away in their strong box. One of them, assuming an accommodating aspect, said: "Why are you so excited, my dear Levi? What you ask shall be done forthwith." And so my late uncle was buried a few hours later.

I assumed that the whole matter was thus ended. As much as my grief for my heavy loss allowed, I devoted myself wholly first to completing my studies and then to settling my uncle's affairs so that as soon as I was assured of independence, I could be together with my beloved bride.

In the midst of these pursuits, Chaim gave me the letter he had received from you. I read it over and over again, pressed it to my heart, and will always keep it near me. I had in mind to set out with Chaim in a few days, if possible, when on the Friday before last, as I entered the synagogue, one of the kahal thrust me from the door, and with a stern look handed me the following paper:

Ben Levi, rabbi of Głogów, together with the whole of the kahal and the brotherhood of elders, make known to all the people of Israel:

Complaints supported by proofs have been made against Levi, the son of Ben Rabi, by the rabbis, the brotherhood of elders, and the entire kahal of Warsaw to the effect that the said Levi has been guilty of obscene offenses against the law of Moses and the teachings of our sages and scholars, as evidenced by the following:

1. The aforementioned Levi has scorned the opinions of the rabbis and the learned, has scorned the Talmud, the *Mishnah,* and the *Gemara,* as well as other books, and has referred to the Cabala as incomprehensible gibberish.

2. Under pretense of his compassion for the Israelite people, he has opposed the interests of the kahal and elders by reporting that, for their own gain to the detriment of the poor, they impose and collect poll, recruitment, and other taxes.

3. The said Levi has undertaken measures to transfer the collection of these monies to someone other than the elders.

4. The said Levi, the son of Ben Rabi, has several times insisted, and does not now cease to insist, that the elders should render an account of all sums belonging to the people.

5. The said Levi, the son of Ben Rabi, has discarded almost all the ancient laws, precepts, and rites, and has turned his befouled soul to the impure goyim. He attends their schools, has shortened his garments, has changed his dress, no longer wears tsytses, and dares recite his prayers without the leathern box on his forehead. Moreover, he has been seen to eat soup made of meat, and then milk, with the same spoon.

6. He reads the offensive books of the goyim on the Sabbath, without meditating on the Talmud, the *Mishnah,* and the *Gemara;* and he has, at the time of the Feast of Tabernacles, eaten salad with vinegar, even though he knows that sours are then forbidden.

7. The aforementioned Levi has dared maintain (which we must repeat to our horror) that Christians are human beings, and have souls the same as Jews.

8. By these and similar deviations, Levi has trampled our most sacred

rights, such as the right in the book *Emelechhamelech*, fol. 67, that declares: "*You, the Israelites, are human beings, but the other nations are not, because they have originated from the adultery of Eve, and have no part of the soul.*"

9. The said Levi has trespassed against the law of the great *Yalkut Reubeni*, which declares: "*The Israelites are human beings, because their souls derive from God; but the heathens, since their souls derive from unclean spirits, are called swine. Hence each heathen is a swine in both body and soul.*" Assuming the dress and manners of the Christians, Levi has violated the law of *Menoras Haumer*, page 25, which says, "*If foreign people require us to change our ways, even to the slightest extent, be it only in the laces of our shoes, a Jew should sooner submit to death than accept this.*"

10. Levi has further trespassed on the law by studying the pernicious sciences and learning of the heathens. *Sotuch* maintains in chapter 9, volume 21: "*Cursed be he who shall raise pigs and instruct his son in the Grecian or other sciences.*"

11. Levi has, moreover, violated the law by his rebellious rising against the rabbis, the kahals, and the brotherhood of elders, inasmuch as he reproaches them with unjust taxation and demands an accounting of them which in no way is his right. As *Moses Maimonides* states clearly: "*It is not permitted to the scholar to engage in controversies with the master; he is obliged instead to consider himself his servant and to untie the laces of his shoes.*"

All these accusations having been supported by the evidence, and weighing these execrable crimes against their punishments, the Talmud, the *Mishnah*, and our other holy books prescribe herewith: That for the transgressions of the aforementioned Levi, son of Ben Rabi — each of which is worthy of being punished by stoning to death — we, the rabbis, the kahals, and the elders of the brotherhood *Mureinos, Mayuchet, Feyne Bery,* by virtue of the power invested in us by the most sacred Talmud, cast thrice on him the curses of *Niddui, Cherem,* and *Schamatha.*

Thus may this Levi, the son of Ben Rabi, be cursed in the homes of both the higher and lower judges. May terrible plagues and tormenting illnesses burden him all his days! May his house become the dwelling place of dragons and serpents, and may his star darken in heaven! May his enemies delight in his downfall, and may his gold and silver come into their hands. May he be cursed by the lips of Addiroron and Achlariel, by the lips of Sandulphion and Haudrauiel, by the lips of Anfisiel and Pathiel; may he be cursed also by the lips of Zafzafil, by the lips of Huhafil, and finally thrice by the lips of the great king of seventy names. May his race fall like that of Korah, and may his soul depart amid torments and misery. May the wrath of God smite him. May he be choked to death like Achitepel; may his leprosy be like the leprosy of Gechasi; and may he never arise from the dead. Let him not rest in the cemetery of the Israelites. We decree henceforth that Levi, the son of Ben Rabi, remain under this curse and that this be his legacy. May the peace and the blessing of God descend on us, the elders. In accordance with the provisions of these curses, we command that the said Levi not presume to shave or approach the synagogue, and that each Israelite who comes within at least four ells of him immediately flee him. Thus may he know that he has been excommunicated and cursed until such time as he regains his senses. If he should die while still under the curse, a stone must be placed on his grave as a sign that he was worthy of being stoned to death. This judgment has been executed in Warsaw by the rabbi, the kahal, and the elders of the brotherhood, and is herewith made known to all kahals.

(signed)

Ben Levi, Rabbi of Głogów
Moses Zucker, member of the kahal
Menases Bube, member of the Cabala
Jonathan Spitz, elder of the brotherhood
Izaak Federschmutz, secretary-general

Judge, my dear friend, if in the eyes not only of a Christian but of every objective and reasonable Jew, the crimes for which I have been excommunicated would not rather serve as proof of my zeal for the well-being and enlightenment of our people, and of the anguish of my heart at the oppressions of their elders that our poor Israelites endure as an eternal sacrifice. . . .

My profound grief and my often tear-filled eyes have not gone unnoticed by my old schoolmates. They are of both faiths, and I can be proud of them. I am fortunate to include in their number Count Edmund Tęczyński, a man distinguished as much by intellect and kindness as by birth. Despite the difference in our religion, a similar way of thinking and our love of the sciences have united us in mutual respect: we leave it to God to judge which of us has chosen the better. I believe that his virtues have made him surer of salvation than our elders with their persecuting spirit and their Cabala. You may perhaps wonder that a Jew, degraded by prejudice, should call one of the leading Polish lords his friend, but such are the fruits of enlightenment. We have known each other for more than two years and have together carried out experiments in chemistry. They have been Tęczyński's greatest passion. When after a while he observed my sadness, pensiveness, and distraction of mind, he showed me so much tender friendliness that I finally revealed to him the cause of my upset. The amiable and considerate young man was moved to anger when I showed him a copy of the curse pronounced on me, and when I described to him your soul and charms, my love for you, and the persecutions to which you have been exposed along with me. "Can it be," he exclaimed with the liveliness native to his age, "that in this country, where we all live under the same laws, where the law extends its protection equally to all, that a foreign official, without a hearing, arbitrarily, should be able to oppress any of our citizens? That cannot be. I have relatives in the government and the courts; I shall go to them, set before them this entire nefarious affair, and a severe punishment will befall those elders of yours." "Don't do that," I replied, "let me first try to convince them by all possible means — without going into our religious affairs or those of another faith — that their mad blindness must sooner or later lead them to misfortune." I could barely get my honorable friend to agree to a few days' delay. What result my efforts will achieve, you will soon learn; I trust that I will extricate myself from my difficulties. I implore you to keep calm. You are my only good, my only comfort in life. Jehovah will protect us from these unholy fanatics who have brought disgrace upon His commandments. Farewell, my beloved bride.

Levi

Letter XVII / Yankel, Superior of the Society of Hasidim, to Nathaniel, to Benjamin, Yosel, Rubin, and the Elders of the Brotherhood of Radziwiłłów.

15th Sivan

. . . I am resolving your important questions according to the infallible assertions of our most learned rabbis, and I command you to believe them under pain of being accursed.

As you wish first to have a representation of the greatness of God, hear what *Rabbi Ismael* says about that. "The great prince of testimony," he writes, "spoke to me thus. From the home of the capital of Almighty Jehovah to the top is one hundred and eighteen thousand times ten thousand miles, and from there another one hundred and eighteen thousand times ten thousand miles. Its height is one hundred and thirty-six times ten thousand miles. From one bottom to the other measures thirty times ten thousand miles. From His right to His left hand are seventy-seven thousand times ten thousand miles. His skull is three times ten thousand miles in length and in breadth. The crown of His head measures sixty times ten thousand miles. The soles of the feet of the King of Kings, says this same Ismael, extend thirty thousand miles. From heel to knee He measures nineteen times ten thousand and four miles, and from knee to shoulder twelve times ten thousand and four miles. From hip to neck, He measures twenty-four times ten thousand miles." Moreover, *Rabbi Akiva* relates on page 16 that "the whole of God's majesty measures twice thirty-six thousand times ten thousand miles."

Do not imagine, you ignorant creatures, that these miles are the same as ours. The miles of God are ten thousand times ten thousand ells in length, and each ell is four of God's spans.

In the book of *Osmes* we read that the court and servants of Jehovah are adapted to His size. He is attended by 360,000 angels and 10,000 seraphim; 36,000 are on duty daily. Your doubts are thus set to rest. Believe what Rabbi Ismael and Rabbi Akiva say, and be silent. I shall continue. . . .

You wish to know if the dead eat and read after death. The following passage from the Talmud provides the best answer to the question. "A certain rabbi took a walk to Tiberias, and along the way met Elias, who told him that 'God has sent me from heaven to earth and expressed an opinion concerning an important matter about which we are not able to agree in heaven. That important matter is the question whether after death the souls eat, drink, and read?' The rabbi answered him as follows: 'In the fifth Song of Solomon, verse 1, it is written: "*I met my bride in my garden and I eat my honeycomb and drink my milk. Eat, my friends, and drink abundantly.*" We read further in the Talmud, "that a Jew once passing through a graveyard at night saw with his own eyes that the dead were sitting on the tombstones and diligently reading books."

You are not the first who ask where earthquakes come from. I will therefore answer you in the words with which Rabbi *Ambras* replied to *Balat* on the same question. "When God looks down on the homes of the heathens; when He sees how peaceably and freely they enjoy this world at a time when His holy temple is overturned, and the earth is in the hands of the unbelievers, He begins to wail from grief and to shout so that the entire earth trembles from fright. At the moment that God thinks of the downfall of His people, He sheds two drops of tears into the great ocean and the roar of their falling is so terrible that it can be heard from one end of the earth to the other."

Is it permitted to cheat Christians? Do you still ask me about that; do you still have any doubts about it? Has not the question been resolved in thousands of places thousands of times by our rabbis and doctors?

Is it not written in the Talmud, in the treatise *Megilla,* page 13: "It is allowed to the Jews to cheat Christians; be pure unto the pure, and wicked unto the wicked." Further, in the book *Zoar hammor,* page 129, do not these words appear: "We know that we are in the captivity of the Edomites; but we also know that the God of Israel looks down upon the Jews and will free us from this captivity." Read further what Rabbi *Mohebar Mayemon* writes in his commentary on the Talmudist treatise *Sanchedim,* page 121: "You are obliged," he writes, "not only to cheat but also to kill all those who are uncircumcised and do not believe in our prophets. If we have the power to do so, we may eradicate them publicly; if not, we may hasten their ruin and end by cunning and trickery. If you see a goy fall into a well or pit, and a ladder is at hand, go take it and say, I have to help my son down from the roof and I'll bring the ladder right back; but do it not."

And finally, Rabbi Levi Ben Gerson, in his exposition on the fifth book of Moses, maintains that "Jews are not only free to cheat others, but it is indeed their duty to do so."

The main hope of our greatness and rule on earth lies in our extirpating the goyim by the very roots and replacing them with our own. All the countries of the earthly globe have been promised to the children of Israel, and in proportion to the increase in our population, the sooner the rule of the Jews over the whole world. With what unspeakable joy do I see, with what delight must you behold, how even in this accursed Poland our people increases in number, like the sand in the sea, and spreads over the entire earth. Look at Brody, Berdiczew, and Wilno. You will rarely see a goy there, just *peysaki*.[2]

In Warsaw, where not a single Jew was permitted to live in 1788, today, thanks to our endeavors, we now number 30,000. Look at all the cities and towns of Poland; there is hardly a wretched goy to be seen in the suburbs. The squares and all the principal streets are ours. You see how what is written in the fifth book of Moses, chapter v, is coming true: "*I shall give you great and good cities, which you did not build, and houses filled with all good things, which you did not fill, and wells dug, which you did not dig, vineyards and olive trees, which you did not plant, and you shall eat and drink your fill.*" Thus, you see how good it is to be the chosen people. If we continue to make the same progress, as I believe we shall, it will not be long before the whole earth is ours. . . .

Know then, I repeat to you a hundred times, that the Talmud is the cornerstone of the moral enlightenment of the Jews. It is our constitution, empowered by its own incomprehensibility. It is that which nourishes in us our contempt and hatred for all uncircumcised people who are rejected and disdained by God. The *Mishnah* and the *Gemara* are portions of the Talmud. . . .

Let us then hold fast to the Talmud, for without it we would already have become almost Christians and have adopted all their stupid opinions. . . .

Letter XIX / Abraham to Levi

Tenczyn, 18th Sivan

. . . Dispersed over the whole world, persecuted first by the pagans, and then by the Christians in Germany, France, Spain, and England, burned at the stake, plunged into rivers, hunted, we have found safety and protection in Poland alone. Why have we not made better use of the freedom and security offered us here? Why has not some Esdras, availing himself of the favor our beautiful Esther found in the sight of King Kazimierz the Great, restored the laws of Moses to their original purity, and adapted them to the times and to our present position? But alas, we made the erroneous opinions of men superior to the word of God.

Three hundred and eight years after the destruction of Jerusalem, Rabbi Jonathan wrote the Jerusalem Talmud, and one hundred years later Rabbi Aze published the Babylonian Talmud. Their pupils joined to these the *Mishnah* and the *Gemara*. In the beginning of the thirteenth century, Moses Maimonides extracted from them the rules governing rituals in his book *Yudhasakah*. Our supposed learned men, commentators, and Cabalists thereafter outdid one another

---

2. A reference to the Yiddish term for the long black gownlike garment traditionally worn by Orthodox Jews in Poland.

in muddling and transforming God's word, communicating their own strange dreams and visions as religious, civil, and moral principles. How far they have deviated in their books from the morality even of common sense, their works themselves make abundantly plain. How full they are of childish and unseemly fables and superstitions which are disparaging of God Himself.

Some of the writers were honestly blind in their wild opinions; others, though well aware of the absurdities of the Talmud, have found it to their own advantage to maintain the belief in them among the blind multitude. Their wish has been for this poor people to become so immersed in the incomprehensible and childish mysticisms of the Talmud that their mental powers would become both unwilling and unable to devote the time and attention necessary to acquiring that illumination and those useful sciences which would bring us close to other peoples in all social benefits.

Our more zealous elders and rabbis bring up our children in accordance with those dishonorable precepts in order keep from our people, from childhood on, a beneficial knowledge while implanting a false one in their imaginations. Even a three-year-old child hears about ghosts and apparitions. At four, they impart the idea of a God to him, while at the same time inculcating him with the notion that only the Jews are His children and that all other peoples are despicable and accursed. In his fifth year, the child is sent to a school where he studies the five books of Moses together with commentaries filled with distorted interpretations and bombastic images. He is also taught the Hebrew language, and if he is either slow or weak, he is spared neither painful blows nor the pulling of his side-locks. The child learns by rote, but he does not understand a word of anything, since even his teacher takes it all on faith. In his sixth year, bereft of the slightest knowledge of geography or other nations, the child knows only that there are Jews, who are a great people, and that there are Christians, who must be hated since they are hostile to Jews and act contrary to Jewish customs—they eat swine, do not observe the Sabbath, and are uncircumcised. In the morning, the child must wash his hands, not for the sake of cleanliness, but to drive away the unclean spirits who, during the night, seat themselves on the nails of his fingers. When he passes by a church and hears the sound of singing or of bells, the pupil must stop his ears lest these sounds pollute his soul. In this way, the child is strongly persuaded that who is not a Jew must be worse than a devil. In the seventh year, the pupil begins studying the Talmud and, though still a child, is taught about marriage, divorce, the ritual slaughtering of animals, the preparation of the Feast of the Tabernacle, and about the cleanliness and uncleanliness of women. The child exhausts himself over such splendid lectures from dawn to dusk. Scoldings and whippings descend on him in abundance. The young mind is crushed in its very infancy. As their years increase, the same pattern of education continues. The father takes on an ever more proficient teacher; his sole concern and ambition is that his son become learned in the Talmud so that he might marry well and become a rabbi.

In the twelfth year a ten-year-old girl is brought to him, whom he has never before seen, and he is ordered to marry her. After the wedding, the young husband continues his studies; eventually he becomes a rabbi, tradesman, or what is much more common, a plain idler. Except for arithmetic, everything necessary for life in society is alien to him. He has learned only prejudice, hatred, and superstition.

Such education, such formidable ignorance, such wild ideas, give rise among the masses of our people to a gullibility that zealously grasps everything astonishing, everything intelligible to their passions, everything promising unimaginable raptures and happiness. Hence our many Messiahs, miracle workers, and sanctimonious deceivers. You have heard of *Bar Kochba,* of the false Messiah of Candia in the time of the emperor Theodosius, and of David *Elroi* in the reign of the emperor Henry I. But more curious than others is the history of *Sabbatai Zevi,* who in the year 1666 declared himself to be the Messiah. Since I do not know if you are familiar with it, I am sending it to you separately. . . .

The most zealous, and also the most injurious, of our sects, bears the name Hasidim. It was founded in Podolia, about one hundred years ago, in the town of Międzyborz, by a local rabbi named Israel *Bael Achem.* He asserted that in the year 1575, in Maimonides's library in Egypt, a Jew by the name of Laryl had discovered exceptionally important knowledge, hitherto unknown truths, which led him to a better comprehension of God. Proudly announcing such major discoveries, he began to proclaim a most frivolous code of morality that flattered all human passions and permitted his followers all kinds of offences and crimes. He revealed extraordinary visions, conjured up spirits, healed the sick, made barren women fruitful, and worked miracles. He was, in short, deified in his lifetime and after his death. His dissolute and flattering teachings attracted many young people to him who to this day uphold and disseminate his harmful doctrines. . . .

The gratification of all sensual desires is both the obligation of this sect as well as its method of attracting as many devotees as possible. They often assemble with their rabbis. There tasty dishes and strong drinks excite the imagination of the votaries. Conversations are begun, one stranger than the next. Often the rabbi calls over one of those still conscious, gives him a slice of well-seasoned fish, and tells him that the soul of his dead father inhabits the fish. Many times, the rabbi falls into an ecstatic state, summons angels and spirits by name, mutters incomprehensible things, prophesies the future, and announces the coming of the Messiah. Their job is disseminating fanaticism and wallowing in idleness and debauchery. They consider it the greatest crime to use any language other than Hebrew. The number of these fanatics is on the increase. Women especially become attached to them and support them with considerable sums of money. This sect does not shrink from borrowing customs from the pagans. In the towns they build houses over the graves of rabbis, where they are accustomed to performing wild sacrifices full of unheard-of superstitions. To convince you that I am not making these things up, permit me to relate to you an incident that happened to me in my youth with one of the leading rabbis of this sect.

I was brought up, like many others, in all the incomprehensible nonsense of the Talmud, the *Mishnah,* and the *Gemara.* However, God deigned to enlighten me with sound judgment. I perceived that the impediment to the advancement of the Israelites in Poland and in the former Polish provinces comes most of all from the sect of the Hasidim, who entice our youth by their fantastic representations as well as by their debauched lives, and plunge them into an ever deeper abyss. Overcome with loathing for these seducers, and animated by the desire to save my people from further corruption and ruin, I resolved to betake myself to the highest rabbi, observe his trickery at close range, and then bring it out into the open for the good of all. I thus presented myself to him with the greatest humility, begging him to receive a sinner into his order, and in so doing to become the savior of my soul. He received me graciously, blessed me, and then initiated me into his mysteries. Oh, with what pain my heart filled at the sad state of a people devoted to the madness of these fanatics. I was then in the flower of youth, bold and cheerful. Once convinced that the rabbi was himself misled, and in fact believed that he was the lord over angels and spirits, I decided to reveal his insanity to the whole world.

With this aim in mind, I took a small book made of parchment, and in fearsome hieroglyphics wrote upon it a letter proclaiming that it was the writing of the Rabbi Israel Baal Shem, who lived a hundred years ago. The letter ordered Rabbi N.N. to undertake, in accordance with Cabalistic precepts, the preparations and ceremonies for the coming of the Messiah, since this Messiah was to appear on earth without fail the following year. I also added that the letter had been entrusted to a person who had been dead many years, and only today was being delivered to the rabbi. For the greater success of my scheme, I rubbed the parchment over with tobacco so as to make it look as if it had lain in the ground for at least fifty years. I was not sparing in the letter of the older names of angels and spirits found in the Cabala. When everything was ready, I slipped the insignificant-looking letter into a pocket of the rabbi's white silk ceremonial gown. He soon found it in his pocket, and when he noticed the seal with the awesome Hebrew letters, he was terrified and began trembling uncontrollably. With great trepidation, he finally opened the letter, but as soon as he became acquainted with its contents, his fear changed into inexpressible rapture. He leaped up from his seat, ran like a madman through the room, and ordered his confidants to be summoned to him so that he could make known to them the sacred and long-desired communication. News of it was soon received throughout the entire country with shouts of joy. Preparations for the reception of the Messiah were commenced, and a host of enthusiasts, preparing to leave for Palestine, began selling their houses. The hope of becoming masters of the world began filling ignorant people with arrogant pride. I saw with alarm that my plan had succeeded only too well; fearing violent confusion in the country, I hastened to one of my enlightened friends and revealed the secret to him, showing him irrefutable proof of the fact that the whole affair was the result of my invention. He went to the rabbi and told him the whole story. Aghast, the rabbi was overcome with grief and shame. Soon, however, his feelings changed to savage wrath. He shouted and vented his rage at me. I most certainly would have perished had I not immediately left my country and sought refuge in Berlin, where I remained for several years. This episode is well known throughout Poland, but it did not weaken the credit of the sect for long. . . .

Abraham

Letter XXI / Abraham to Levi

12th Tamuz

The principal elements of Judaism today are hatred and obstinate prejudice. So long as these venomous passions continue to occupy our hearts, no improvement in our condition, no understanding with other peoples of the world, hence no good for us can be expected. . . . I know that the elder rabbis of the kahals and brotherhoods find great personal profit in their obstinate estrangement from all the laws of the land, even in the political sense. But I also know that the masses of our people are the ultimate losers. We complain that the Polish government oppresses us, that it extends none of the rights of citizens to us, and that it bars the path to industry and self-improvement to us. But what does the government reply to our complaints and demands? If you want to enjoy equal rights of citizenship with us, must we not first recognize you as citizens, as Poles? What language do you speak? A foreign tongue, not that of this country. You write and pray in it. What of your dress? It is unlike that of any other nation on earth. Do you not yourselves declare that Poland is not your country, and that you are merely wayfarers in it? Can we recognize you as our fellow citizens by your obedience to the laws of the land? Do you not in fact excommunicate those of you who seek justice in our courts? You indeed have your own laws and your own courts. We have extended our rights and privileges to people of all faiths (except for those dogmas which God alone must judge) so long as they adhere to all the laws and decrees of the land. But even as you cling obstinately to your own contrary, separate precepts, which are harmful to society, and you wish to remain eternal strangers, yet you wish to partake of all the benefits, freedoms, and advantages of those who dwell in Poland. And even though you do not regard us as people, yet you still want us to recognize you as our fellow citizens. Preserve the purity of your faith, but repudiate, renounce forever your Talmuds, Cabalas, and all the fables and absurdities with which your elders, for their own benefit and your misfortune, continue to mislead you.

People cannot be separated from others and yet joined together with them;

people cannot escape obedience to laws and still enjoy the benefits of those laws. Show first by your language, your dress, your customs, your enlightenment, your ways, your obedience to the laws, and your love that you are like other Poles, and then we Poles will willingly acknowledge you as our countrymen. . . .

A stern law should be in effect by which every city and town, in proportion to its population, should have public schools, both for boys and girls, to which parents, under heavy financial penalties, should be obliged to send their children. In these schools, religious studies should be taught in Polish, by Jews; other studies should also be taught in the national language by Jews or Christians appointed by government commission. Moral precepts and the Polish language should hold first place in these schools.

No Jew before the age of twenty-four, and no Jewess before the age of eighteen, should be allowed to marry; marriages should be performed in the presence of notary publics. All who enter into them should show proof of the trade or business they practice, how they earn their living. They should also be examined on their ability to read and write Polish as well as on their moral principles. The foremost pupils should compose a liturgy and prayer in Polish, and in this language and no other should private and public worship be conducted. All merchants' books should be kept in the Polish language.

If these regulations are carried out accurately and faithfully, I trust that in the course of twenty years the position of the Polish Israelites will change. They will emerge from the degradation in which they find themselves today, they will occupy an appropriate place in society, and they will boldly demand and easily gain that citizenship, that equality of rights and privileges, of which they are presently unworthy and unprepared and against which they vainly remonstrate.

Let our people but read the works of our enlightened coreligionists — Mendelssohn, Wessely, Ben David, and Friedländer — or of our Polish brethren Maimon, Kalmanson, Zalkind, Hurewicz, and Wolfsohn; let them follow the lead of Hoge and Tugendhold, and abjure the fables and superstitions with which they have for too long been deluded; they will hate idleness, usury, and the pursuit of easy gain; they will come to love honesty, decency, labor, and the virtue of love for one's fellow man to which God commanded Christians and Jews alike. . . . Let us charitably grasp the hand extended to us, and we shall become happy unto ourselves and as useful to the country as we are at present harmful to it.

We must not suppose that the inhabitants of Poland harbor an unjust rancor and aversion toward us. I could cite a thousand proofs that every Israelite who has distinguished himself by his virtue, his talents, and his attachment to his country has been respected, exalted, and rewarded. One need go no further than the example of Kalmanson. [King] Stanislaus Augustus, a lover of learning, honored him with his favor and beneficence. Our present king, the emperor Alexander, has rewarded him handsomely, and the Poles have esteemed and befriended him. Have we not seen our countryman Berek, who, through his courage and dedication to his country, rose to high rank among us? Pan Stern, of Hrubieszów, who is endowed with rare intelligence—does he not hold a seat in the company of the learned, does he not enjoy the special regard of the monarch and citizens? Our truly enlightened countrymen Hogge and Tugendhold—do they not receive the esteem and respect of the Poles? Yes indeed, let us but renounce our vices and errors; let us become worthy of respect, and we shall be respected.

■ Julian Ursyn Niemcewicz
The Year 3333, or An Incredible Dream (1858)

[Niemciewicz's nightmarish vision of a future time when Warsaw had become a Jewish city and was renamed Moshkopolis (Moszkopolis, in Polish) was published for the first time in book form in 1911 by a publishing company named for Jan Jeleński, a well-known anti-Jewish writer of the second half of the nineteenth century.[1] In his short introduction to *The Year 3333*, the editor, Szczepan Jeleński, wrote, in a more serious vein than Niemce-wicz's tale itself:

> When we, who live nearly a hundred years after Niemcewicz, see how Jewry is prosper-ing everywhere, how it hangs out signs in Yiddish instead of Polish in all streets, how it establishes its Yiddish-language theaters, newspapers, and so on, I repeat that this "incredible dream" of Niemcewicz must seem truly less "incredible" and indeed very possible, and then not in the year 3333 but in perhaps a hundred years, if not sooner.]

Not long ago, when many leading papers took up the issue of the settlement of the Jews, and when in gatherings everywhere the matter of the continued existence and in time the loss of the Polish race and name was discussed, I, like others, read, listened to those more experienced than myself, and sometimes even ventured to express my own opinions.

Reading various publications, and arguing, for a long time occupied every-one's thoughts, and mine to such a degree that whether at home, or walking down the street, or in proper society—where not even half a [Jewish] side curl could be found—I began dreaming, in my excited imagination, of the figures of Orthodox Jews, and even in the elegant sanctuaries of lovely ladies, when porcelain bowls gave off the fragrance just of jasmine and roses, I caught the scent characteristic only of scoundrels.

No wonder then that these thoughts, which preoccupied me so passionately during the day, returned in my dreams, but transformed in that strange and in-credible manner only possible in the unlimited freedom of half-sleep.

It seemed to me first of all that I was in Włochy, a village about a half a mile from Warsaw.

After observing the exemplary state of agriculture there as well as the new im-plements being used, I drank a glass of excellent milk and returned to Warsaw. But you can imagine my surprise when on my approaching the capital it looked entirely different than it does today. The closer I drew to it, the more the change struck me and confused me.

Julian Ursyn Niemcewicz, *Rok 3333 czyli Sen niesłychany* (Warsaw: Biblioteka im. Jana Jeleńskiego, 1911), 5–12, 15–16, 18–31.
    1. "Moszkopolis" is a combination of a common Yiddish masculine first name, Moszko (in Polish spelling; Moshko), and "polis" ("city," in Greek).

I looked in vain for the familiar tollgates. In their place I found an unshapely gateway, actually solid barriers made of stone that had blackened with time. On the top of them there was an armorial shield supported by two leviathans. For a long time I tried to figure out the design on the shield. Finally, it dawned on me that they were *tsytses* (consecrated fringes worn by Jews on the edge of their tatters), quite skillfully carved. The cornice contained two verses in the Hebrew language and beneath them these words in Latin letters: Moshkopolis A. 3333.

Despite the privilege of dreams, in which the most bizarre things seem straightforward, I could not get over my astonishment. However, the following tale from this dream will prove that with almost every step I took, my sad wonderment grew.

Once in the city, I observed homes on both sides built in the style of today's inns, with balconies and stables. In some places there were poles sticking out. From them, from one house to the other across from it, lines were stretched as a sign that the owners of these houses were related.

Jewesses were sitting in front of the houses peddling doughnuts, challahs, and sole. There was no pavement anywhere, just an immense amount of mud. Around the houses a lot of ducks, geese, and turkeys were wallowing in the mud. On all sides, back and front, left and right, swarms of dirty Jews were hovering about.

"For God's sake!" I cried out. "Where in heaven am I? I don't see a single Christian-Pole."

Hardly did I pronounce these words when I caught sight of a small, filthy carriage and a coachman sitting in it. He was not in Jewish attire. I beckoned him, and he drove over. I got in with the express purpose of getting from this person an explanation for everything I had seen, and for what I could not understand.

Since the coach moved slowly through the extraordinary quantity of mud in the streets and the absence of pavement tended to distance all noise, I and my driver were able to hear each other quite well and converse comfortably.

"My friend," I said, "I implore you, tell me what such incomprehensible and rapid change means. Not long ago Warsaw was a Christian city, Polish; so how come today it has become so Jewified in its residents, in its homes, in short in everything?"

"Either you're dreaming, sir," the coachman answered somewhat in the Jewish style, "or you must have arrived from a foreign country. What do you mean 'not long ago'? People say that the Jews have been ruling over this once Polish land for thousands of years."

"How did it happen," I exclaimed, "that a martial people allowed themselves to be conquered by these miserable creatures?"

"Those wiser and more learned than I can explain it to you better; I know only what I learned by word of mouth from my grandfathers and great-grandfathers. They didn't conquer the Poles with weapons, but with cleverness, tricks, and bribery. I don't know exactly how it happened, but once they won the privilege of holding any office and of acquiring rural properties, nothing could resist their indefatigable cunning and subterfuges, so that through the centuries they crushed the Polish Christians, took possession of everything themselves, and when nobody wanted this dirty and bedraggled kingdom, they chose a king and renamed ancient Poland Palestine."

I was stunned by these words and would have remained numb for a long time had not the coach passed by the "blue palace." At this point my driver sighed deeply and said: "The house you see over there on the right for centuries belonged to my ancestors. It was originally the property of the Czartoryski princes and later passed to my family, the Zamoyskis."

"What are you saying?" I exclaimed. "You're a Zamoyski?"

"Indeed I am," he repeated with a sigh. "I am Zamoyski and I drive this coach. My wife is Zosia Czartoryska, a woman, people say, who is quite attractive. My brother-in-law Czartoryski has a little garden in a suburb which he tends and from which he lives."

"My God in heaven!" I cried. "What has it all come to?"

"Don't be surprised," the coachman went on, "the same happened to all the old Polish families. The Radziwiłłs are bricklayers, the Potockis and Sanguszkos deal in wagons and horses and haul wood to the Vistula, the Chodkiewiczes, Krasińskis, and Sapiehas have become carpenters. No Christians are allowed to own rural or town property unless they first become a Jew. And since many a Christian became so weighed down by poverty, so weary and degraded by oppression, he forgot what he owed to himself and to God, grew side-curls, and now rocks back and forth over the Talmud as well as the best Jew."

Hardly did he finish these words when we noticed a crowd of Jews on horses with lances in their hands, fox-fur caps on their heads, and ammunition pouches at their sides. They were riding in disorder, preceded by two trumpeters in similar garb bearing trumpets scarcely larger than the ones children play with. Suddenly they blasted so shrilly on their trumpets that the horses began getting alarmed and turning around, the riders lost their slippers, and dismounted in order to look for them in the mud. This brought to a halt not only the military retinue but my coach as well. "What does it mean?" I asked my guide.

"Those are the Royal Horse Guards," he said, "returning from the castle. There's always such a muddle when you encounter them because they're constantly losing or dropping something. It's worse even when they ride out on maneuvers; when that filth sets off at a trot, they fall all over the place like pears."

I have no idea how long that disorder would have lasted had there not appeared in the distance, in a sumptuous carriage, an old Jew with large curled side-locks and dressed in a gaberdine covered with heavy silver embroidery. Many Jews in the very flower of youth gamboled about the carriage on ponies.

As soon as the mounted retinue espied him, whether someone found his slippers or not, whether someone caught up with his horse or not, mounted or on foot, however they could, they immediately beat a retreat into a side street. My coachman, taking advantage of the cleared space in the street, moved forward, but as he rode past that grand old man, he removed his cap, bent his head to his very knees, and maintained that position for a long time. I asked who that wealthy Jew might be.

"That," he answered, "is the Prince Palatine Itsek Szmulowicz, president of the Council of State, and one of our greatest lords. Besides considerable wealth, he has a palace on the Krakowskie Przedmieście and the estate of Wilanów near the city.

"What," I exclaimed, "a Jew is master of Wilanów?"

"Where on earth are you coming from, sir?" my driver asked in astonishment.

"Rest assured, no Christian will be in possession of Wilanów now. Christians are only allowed to till the soil as corvée labor or to conduct the lowest trades in cities."

"What condition is Wilanów in today? Is it as beautiful and neat as it used to be in the days of its former owners? Are the walled village, the farm, and the new part of the garden, which Pani Potocka had installed, well maintained?"

"I don't know how it was before," the coachman answered, "but I do know that now there's a huge distillery, a brewery, and a slaughterhouse on the premises. The palace is terribly dirty, but two trees along the Vistula have been preserved since Itsek Szmulowicz observes the Feast of the Tabernacles beneath them. The king is very fond of him."

"So you have a king! And who is he, this king?"

"Who do you think? A Jew, naturally."

"And what is his name?"

"Moshko XII," my guide replied. . . .

[There follows a description of the interior of the old royal palace of the Zygmunts after which the narrator witnesses the arrival of the king himself.]

At last King Moshko himself appeared, at which all the Jews, as many of them as there were, began to genuflect in the manner of Chinese idiots. My friend, the chamberlain, said that that was the way the king was greeted. The person of the monarch struck me as very grand. He was a man of about forty years of age, unusually red, fat, and freckled. He had reddish-brown side-locks and a beard of the same color. His cloak and gaberdine were of black velvet with accessories in diamonds with the clarity of the purest water. His yarmulka was surrounded by a band of pink pearls each of which might have been fifty carats in weight. Around his neck he had a prayer shawl, as was the Jewish custom; a medal in the shape of the Golden Fleece hung from it on a gold chain. My friend told me that that was the Order of Itsek the Great. However, nothing struck my eyes more by its extraordinary brilliance than the tsytses dangling about the royal knees. They were strings of solitaires the smallest of which was the size of a large nut. The chamberlain told me that the king's father, Moshko XI, paid ten million Dutch gold pieces for those tsytses.

"Don't be surprised," the chamberlain continued. "His Majesty himself deals in precious stones and makes a great deal on them (at this point he whispered in my ear), and sometimes even sells fake ones for the real thing." . . .

[Continuing his tour of Moshkopolis, the narrator then sets out on a visit to the courts.]

Virtually the whole aspect of Warsaw, even its streets, had changed. I discerned, however, that the coach rode into a courtyard where once upon a time stood the palace of the Krasińskis, its place now taken by a huge inn.

"Where are you taking me?" I asked.

"To the courts," my driver answered.

At the entrance, despite the ticket I displayed, we encountered difficulties; they disappeared, however, as soon as I paid two thalers. Moreover, a crowd of Jews surrounded me with the true insistence of commission agents, offering me their services as guides or interpreters. I chose the most respectable of them and, in fact, chose wisely in that he was one of the most renowned Jewish attorneys.

We went up a flight of stairs full of litter and dirt and entered a huge lobby swarming with Jews. The judges were in recess. We took seats on a bench in a corner, which gave me a chance to converse with my learned attorney and to find out a great deal from him.

"Sir," I said to him, "why did you people so mercilessly raze the buildings of the city and in place of many of once splendid edifices, as I heard, erect such shabby ones?"

"We did that," the attorney answered, "on the strength of Mosaic law: 'Level to the ground,' says Moses, 'all the places wherein lived other peoples and which you now possess, and smash to pieces their altars and tear down their columns and burn their gods and wipe out their name from such places.'"

"You will grant," the attorney continued, "that the law is explicit enough. If you still find it insufficient, I shall quote further. The same Moses goes on to say: 'You shall extirpate a nation given unto you by your God; do not take your eye from it for your God will send a swarm of hornets against this nation and will wipe it away with a great grinding until it is all rooted out, and He shall deliver multitudes of them unto your hands and you shall destroy them from the face of the earth; not a one will hold his ground before you until you strike them all down. In the land that your God is giving unto you as a patrimony so that you should possess it, you shall extirpate from the earth the memory of the Amalekites. Neither shall you pity them nor intermarry with them, for God has chosen you to be a separate people. Do not forget that.'"

"I could cite a thousand similar laws and injunctions," the attorney continued.

"How," I exclaimed, "could they root out the entire tribe of ancient Polish Christians?"

"Our Talmudists," replied the lawyer, "who have even more intelligence than Moses, interpreted the words of the patriarch thus: "Exterminate all the rural and town property owners and seize their properties, but you may keep poor peasants and laborers so that they may work for you."

"How is it possible," I exclaimed, "that you could partly destroy and partly reduce to slavery such a valiant nation?"

"The way Moses ordered us, a little at a time and slowly but surely. First of all, we reasoned that it would cause no harm if they granted us the right to acquire rural and town properties. As soon as we obtained it, our chances of acquiring even more multiplied. We pushed to obtain all privileges of citizenship and the right to hold office. It cost us no little, but what can gold and perseverance not accomplish? Our wishes were fulfilled, and soon the loveliest estates were in Jewish hands. The Senate, ministries, the highest councils of the land, the foremost state dignities were held by Moshkos and Leybs. From all ends of Europe Jews began crowding into Poland in droves. For a long time no notice was taken of the fact that our religion forbids us to intermarry with other peoples, that our faith forbids us to keep the company of people of another persuasion but instead commands us to uproot them and destroy them. Christianity discerned this afterward, but it was already too late.

When the attorney had spoken these words, three raps on the door signaled that the recess was over and the door immediately opened.

"What laws, which codex do you judge by?"

"The Mosaic codex," the attorney replied.

We went into the courtroom.

In the middle of it stood a table around which eleven judges were seated. The twelfth, the highest, perhaps substituting for the Minister of Justice, sat on a somewhat higher chair from the others. He was a portly, gray-haired elder, so oppressed already by age that he could neither hear, nor see, nor even know what was going on. The young Jews who were serving as scribes and secretaries were bustling about him and the judges and probably dispensing justice as they saw fit. The first case to be heard was that of a woman and a man, both of whom were Christians. She was a huckstress about fifty years old, extraordinarily fat and reddish in complexion, and, as is commonly said, "gabby" to the highest degree. She pleaded her own case, in Yiddish, since our people have been obliged to learn that language.

"The Mosaic codex," she began, "indicates in Chapter 25 that in the event of the death of a brother without issue, the brother of her husband must marry the widow. I am in such a predicament now; I am the widow of my late husband and am without a son, but my husband's brother refuses to marry me. I am accusing him before the honorable kahal and I implore it to order him to marry me at once and to love me with his whole heart."

During her plea, the portly president of the court, his gray beard drooping on his chest, snored and heard nothing. A young scribe drew close to his ear and, as if receiving an answer, summoned the accused. He was a poorly but neatly dressed young man with a very handsome figure.

"Jakub," the scribe said, "the court asks you if it is true that you oppose the law of Moses and refuse to take your sister-in-law as a wife?"

"It is true," he answered, "because a Christian should be bound by the new law and not the law of Moses."

All the Jews present flared up at these words.

"What impudence!" they shouted. "You dare invoke the new law?"

The anger and horror of the judges passed to the spectators. Even the young Jews began rushing at Jakub and scratching him with their nails. Fortunately, the tumult awakened the shriveled president of the court. He rang for order.

Jakub spoke further.

"Apart from the reason already cited, I have no desire to take Małgorzata here as a wife: first, because she's a drunk; second, because she's homely; third, because she's old; and fourth and last, because I love another girl and am already engaged to her."

"So you definitely refuse to marry her?" the kahal inquired.

"Absolutely," answered Jakub.

At this point the kahal scribe opened up the codex and read the following law: "If a man has refused to marry his sister-in-law, and thus did not want to raise his brother's name in Israel, then his sister-in-law must approach him, in the presence of the elders, pull a shoe from his foot, spit in his face, and his home henceforth will be known as the home of a man dispossesed of his rights."

The tribunal scribe finished reading:

"Małgorzata," he called out, "do what you must do."

Małgorzata immediately removed Jakub's shoes and spat in his face. Jakub then withdrew and the case was closed.

Two Jews were then summoned who had been charged with keeping paintings and statues in their home, and the objects were placed before the court. With pleasant surprise, I noticed that the sculpture contained several beautifully chiseled antique statues, while among the paintings there were several by the most famous artists. The law was then read commanding the breaking of all idols and images; at the same moment all the objects were thrown from the windows. Jews waiting below, already armed with pickaxes and hoes, broke and smashed everything to smithereens. Taken aback by such barbarity, I did not want to listen further to such wise judgments and, giving two thalers to the attorney, I left.

Even in dreams nature observes a prescribed course. I felt a ravenous appetite, and the coachman then pointed out to me the most celebrated restaurant. I went in. Along both sides of a long, narrow room stood separate small tables; they were covered with exceptionally dirty tablecloths and had pewter flatware. Jewish boys, speaking half Yiddish and half French, immediately surrounded me, handed me the menu, and asked me what I wanted. Of the many dishes on the menu, I recall only the following: lochshen (noodles) a la Maccabee, kugel in schmalz, duck a la Jeremiah, matzohs, poppy-seed biscuits. At the bottom of the menu there was a notice, in French, to the effect that everything was kosher.

I was served many of the dishes, but all of them were so seasoned with garlic, and so frightfully dirty, that I ate just a few eggs and two pieces of matzoh without salt, paid, and left.

It was already six o'clock in the evening. On the way out of the restaurant I noticed many vehicles standing in front of a large, ugly building. My driver informed me that it was the Jewish National Theater. As a curious traveler who did not want to miss anything of interest, I went in. The upper balconies and the parterre were rather empty; but the loges were full of people. An opera under the title "Abigail Warming David" was being presented in the Yiddish language.

Some of the scenes were not the most decorous, the cymbals were the instruments heard most in the orchestra, and the voice of the first singer, although a trifle shrill, had great range. The opera had been composed by one of the actors, which is why it was being performed over and over again.

After the opera, a short farce was performed. But you can imagine my horror and deep indignation when I perceived that the play was nothing more than a mockery of the holiest mysteries of our Christian faith. I left the theater full of grief and anger, but just as I was on the verge of boarding my carriage I encountered the chamberlain.

"Why are you so flushed?" he said.

I explained to him the reason for my outrage and anger.

"Don't be surprised," he said, "the masses have to be entertained with something; besides, our policy is based on maintaining contempt for the Catholic religion. This is done for reasons of state, and you know that in such cases nobody raises the question of fairness, justice, or even sense. By the way, my aunt is giving a ball. Why don't you come to it; that will calm your furrowed brow."

I was so angered that for a long time I refused the chamberlain's invitation. But he finally overcame my objections and we went together to the festivities.

We came to a halt before the spacious inn, or rather palace, of Her Excellency, Countess Rachel. The brilliant light in the windows informed us that the ball had already begun. The chamberlain took me by the arm and conducted me into the drawing room. We entered just at the moment young Prince Itsek and Countess Shloma were dancing a national dance solo, that is to say that after taking the end of a kerchief, each jumped toward the other.

While everyone was enthusing over the grace and charm of the handsome couple, I took advantage of the occasion to take a good look at the guests gathered in the hall. The room was large and richly decorated, but the floor had not been swept and all the furniture was full of dust. I noticed even in the corners of the gilt cornices thick spiderwebs of several years duration from which a huge spider had lowered itself on its silk thread and was already sitting on the head of Princess Yoselovna. The young Count Chaim, tearing himself from his seat and rushing forward, cut the spider's thread with his fox-fur cap and crushed the awful creature with his slipper.

Applause on all sides greeted the heroic deed, and the chamberlain, my friend, told me that the count was one of the most valiant Israelite youths and that that was not the first proof of his fearless courage.

The individual battle between the count and the spider had in the meantime interrupted the dance and my friend thus had the opportunity to introduce me to his esteemed aunt.

She was a tall Jewess, about forty, still fresh and attractive. She had on a knitted dress the color of grapes; wings of large pearls protruded from beneath a red kerchief on her head covering a considerable part of her face; a large diamond pendant hung on her chest.

The lady received me with a graciousness closely bordering on what we would call coquetry.

Her nephew, the chamberlain, wanted to introduce me to other women, but Countess Rachel would not hear of it; on the contrary, requisitioning me for herself alone, she sat down with me to a side and, as if we had known each other for ages, began telling me her life's story and the habits of all the other ladies and gentlemen whom she had invited to the ball. Her conversation was truly entertaining, but I cannot say that her goodness equaled her wit.

According to Countess Rachel, there wasn't one woman there who hadn't had at least twenty romantic adventures, nor a single Jew she wouldn't make fun of a thousand times over.

"Do you know," she said, pointing out a young couple to me, "Count Lejbuś over there, who seems to be holding just that lady by the hand, at this moment, see, he's giving Countess Lejbuś hairs cut from his side-locks. Lejbuś is frightfully stupid, while she is the world's greatest coquette."

I noticed in general that the prettier the Jewess the sharper the darts of slander cast at her by the good Countess Rachel.

I am sure that more than a single reader may ask how the countess could carry on such a lengthy conversation with someone who did not know a word of Yiddish.

I should like to remind my readers first that it was all a dream, hence a fantasy full of contradictions and inconsistencies, and second, if my memory serves me correctly, that not only countesses but all Israelite ladies and even young Jewish lads gabbled preferably in French.

As proof of that, another circumstance comes to mind. I recall that the countess, as she was kindly describing to me the characters of all the people floating before our eyes, pointed out one old Jew and declared:

"There's a real original for you, always crabby and ill-tempered. A weird delusion has taken hold of his mind—he insists on Jews speaking only Yiddish and he goes on and on about it to such an extent that he's already bored everyone to death. Anyway, for other reasons as well he's an unbearable creature."

Noticing that my long conversation wasn't pleasing to several youths who were circling about the countess, I got up to see what was happening in other rooms.

And there, as everywhere else, I found clandestine conversations, whispers, and envy.

Soon vodka, mead, and cherry brandy as well as baked matzoh and poppy-seed biscuits were served. Among the confitures, I saw most of all onions in candied sugar in the shape of our chestnuts.

Defying comparison was the concern of mothers about their daughters. One whispered in her daughter's ear that she should stand straight; another forbade her daughter who was all heated up after a dance to drink beer; yet another covered her offspring with a kerchief, while one schemed for her daughter to dance a favorite dance solo (which means alone) to the lovely music of the *mayufes*.[2]

Amid the dancing and laughter, the ministers conversed about public matters while their sons whispered about love.

Waiters served cold beverages. Soon after, one of them, carrying a large tray of cups with garlic ice cream, slipped and fell sprawling on the ground with his whole load. The crash of so much shattered glass was so penetrating that it woke me up despite the fact that I was sound asleep.

I opened my eyes. Greatly deluded by deceptive images, for a long time I had no idea where I was. Only the further collection of my senses convinced me that the sad objects that disturbed me the whole night long were just an evanescent dream.

2. The song sung by Jews at Sabbath dinner.

■ Adam Mickiewicz (1799–1855)
Pan Tadeusz (1834)

[Celebrated as Poland's greatest poet, Adam Mickiewicz was the embodiment of the romantic ethos. Arrested on trumped-up charges of belonging to an anti-Russian conspiracy while a student at the University of Wilno, he was briefly imprisoned and then sent into exile in Russia for four years. These experiences inspired his innovative romantic drama, *Dziady, Część trzecia* (*Forefathers, Part Three*, 1832), in which he also traces his mystic passage from solitary poet to national bard. After the suppression of the November Insurrection of 1830–31, Mickiewicz, who was in western Europe at the time, joined the Great Emigration in Paris and sought to function as its spiritual leader. It was in fulfillment of this role that he wrote the biblical *Księgi narodu i pielgrzymstwa polskiego* (*Books of the Polish Nation and Pilgrimage*, 1832), and the work acknowledged as his masterpiece, *Pan Tadeusz, czyli ostatni zajazd na Litwie* (*Pan Tadeusz, or The Last Foray in Lithuania*, 1834). *Pan Tadeusz* is set in the Lithuanian region of the old Polish-Lithuanian Commonwealth, where Mickiewicz was born, on the eve of Napoleon's invasion of Russia. A large Polish army fought alongside the French, and hopes were high that the defeat of the Russians would lead to Polish independence. These are the events that make up the historical background of the twelve-book epic poem. But the underlying purpose of the work was to restore a sense of unity to the dispirited Polish émigrés in the West through the nostalgic evocation of the everyday life of the Polish provincial gentry at a pivotal moment in the life of the nation. The lengthy poem is a celebration of traditional Polishness viewed through the prism of an idealizing romantic nostalgia. Mickiewicz's affection for Jews comes through clearly in the poem in the figure of the Jewish innkeeper Yankel (Jankiel, in Polish), who is an observant Jew and a great Polish patriot. Through Yankel, Mickiewicz intended to demonstrate the compatibility of Jewishness and Polish patriotism. In the following passages, from books 4 and 12, Mickiewicz depicts the relations between Yankel and the Polish visitors to his inn, and, in the poem's finale, the great banquet before the Franco-Polish campaign against Russia at which Yankel, noted for his dulcimer playing, is accorded the high honor of performing a musical review of the triumphs and calamities of recent Polish history.]

'Twas Sunday and they'd come from early Mass
To drink at Yankel's and the time to pass.
Already vodka foamed in every cup,
The hostess ran around and filled them up.
The host stood in the midst in his long gown
With silver clasps, that to the floor reached down.
One hand within his black silk sash was pressed,

Adam Mickiewicz, *Pan Tadeusz*, trans. Kenneth R. Mackenzie (New York: Hippocrene Books, 1992), 164–66, 562–68.

The other gravely his gray beard caressed.
With roving glance he walked around the hall,
Commanding, serving none, but greeting all.
With some he would begin a conversation,
Of others pacify an altercation.
The Jew was old, and through the years had gained,
A name for honesty. None e'er complained,
Or gentleman or peasant, nor they should,
For everyone knew Yankel's drinks were good.
He kept a strict account, nor cheated ever,
Permitted merriment but drunkards never,
Loved every entertainment and not least
A wedding party or a christening feast.
As a musician Yankel was renowned;
Once with his dulcimer he wandered round
The country houses and much praise had gained
Both by his playing and his voice well-trained.
Though Jewish he had good pronunciation,
And specially loved the ballads of the nation.
And brought back many from his travels west,
Galician songs, mazurkas and the rest.
The rumor was, I know not whether true,
That he had introduced when it was new
Among the people of that place and time
The song that now is known in every clime,
And first was played in the Italian regions
Upon the trumpets of the Polish legions.[1]
In Lithuania the singer's art
Wins wealth and glory, and the people's heart.
So Yankel, full of fame and wealth withal,
Hung his sweet dulcimer upon the wall
And turning innkeeper had settled down
As under-rabbi in the neighboring town.
He was a welcome guest and counsel giver,
And knew the trade in grain along the river,
Which country folk hold useful information;
And was a loyal Pole by reputation. . . .
All knew that on that instrument was none
To equal him in skill or taste or tone.

1. A reference to the "March of Dąbrowski," the marching song of the Polish legions organized by General Józef Dąbrowski to fight with the French in northern Italy in 1797. The march became the Polish national anthem.

They urged him on to play, but he refused;
His hands were stiff, he said, and little used,
He dared not play before such gentlemen,
And bowing crept away; but Zosia then
Ran up; in one white hand she brought with her
The hammers used to play the dulcimer,
And with the other Yankel's beard caressed:
She curtsied: "Yankel, play for me," she pressed,
"It's my betrothal, Yankel, won't you play,
You said you'd play upon my wedding day!"

Yankel was very fond of Zosia, so
He bowed his beard his willingness to show.
They brought the dulcimer and fetched a chair,
And sat him in the middle of them. There
He sat and, taking up the instrument,
He looked at it with pride and deep content;
As when a veteran hears his country's call,
Whose grandsons take his sword down from the wall,
And laughs: it's long since he has held the blade,
But yet he feels it will not be betrayed.

Meanwhile two pupils knelt before the Jew,
And tuned the strings and tested them anew.
With half-closed eyes he sat still in his chair,
And held the hammers motionless in air.

At first he beat out a triumphal strain,
Then smote more quickly like a storm of rain.
They were amazed—but this was but a trial,
He suddenly stopped and raised the sticks awhile.

He played again: the hammers on the strings
Trembled as lightly as mosquito's wings
And made a humming sound that was so soft
'Twas hardly heard. The master looked aloft
Waiting for inspiration, then looked down
And eyed his instrument with haughty frown.

He lifts his hands, they both together fall
And smite at once, astonishing them all.
A sudden crash bursts forth from many strings
As when a band of janissaries rings
With cymbals, bells and drums. And now resounds

Maurycy Trębacz (1861–1940), "Yankel's Concert" (before 1909). Courtesy Żydowski Instytut Historyczny (Warsaw).

The Polonaise of May the Third![2] It bounds
And breathes with joy, its notes with gladness fill;
Girls long to dance and boys can scarce keep still.
But of the old men every one remembers
The Third of May, when senators and members
In the assembly hall with joy went wild,
That king and nation had been reconciled;
"Long live the King, long live the Sejm!"[3] they sang,
"Long live the Nation!" through the concourse rang. . . .

But soon they lifted up their heads again,
The master raised the pitch and changed the strain.
He, looking down once more, the strings surveyed,
And, joining hands, with both the hammers played:
Each blow was struck so deftly and so hard,
That all the strings like brazen trumpets blared,
And from the trumpets to the heavens sped
That march of triumph: *Poland is not dead!*
Dąbrowski, march to Poland! With one accord
They clapped their hands, and "March, Dąbrowski!" roared.

The player by his own song seemed amazed;
He dropped the hammers and his arms upraised;
His fox-skin hat upon his shoulders slipped;
His floating beard majestically tipped;
Upon his cheeks two strange red circles showed,
And in his eye a youthful ardor glowed.
And when at last his eyes Dąbrowski met,
He hid them in his hand, for they were wet.
"Our Lithuania has waited long for you,"
He said, "as Jews for their Messiah do.
Of you the singers long did prophesy,
Of you the portent spoke that filled the sky.
Live and wage war!" He sobbed, the honest Jew,
He loved our country like a patriot true.
Dąbrowski gave the Jew his hand to kiss,
And thanked him kindly for his courtesies.

2. A reference to the democratic Polish constitution of May 3, 1791.
3. The name of the Polish diet, or parliament.

■ Andrzej Towiański (1799–1878)
"Israel in Poland" (1840s)

[A charismatic figure, Andrzej Towiański became a leading spiritual force among the Polish émigrés in France following the defeat of the November Insurrection of 1830–31. Preaching a brand of mysticism combined with Polish national messianism, Towiański's following or "Koło" (Circle) included some of the outstanding writers of the emigration, among them Adam Mickiewicz and Juliusz Słowacki. He appeared in Paris in the early 1840s, presumably having come from Wilno, and was believed to have been an unfrocked priest. Whatever suspicion attached to his person—there were those who even regarded him as a Russian secret agent whose mission was to sow discord among the émigrés—he was for a time an undeniably powerful presence in Paris. His sermons and speeches, several of which were delivered at the Cathedral of Notre Dame, drew large numbers of auditors, and he gained the loyalty of prominent figures in the emigration who revered him as "Mistrz" (Master). Eventually, Towiański and the activities of the "Circle" attracted the attention of the French authorities, who regarded them with suspicion and expelled Towiański from the country. The following excerpts are from a letter to Feliks Niemojewski, a member of the "Circle."]

Say to Israel, these brethren of ours, who in Poland are a truer Israel than in other countries and who are accustomed to accepting ardently that which comes to them from a burning heart, that God beheld with an eye of mercy these elder children of His whom centuries ago He called "My first-born son, Israel," and that the star of Israel which for centuries now has ceased shining unto Him newly emerges for Him. Let Israel thus recognize its time and let it raise itself above the earth, which it has loved too much, to the zenith of the Israelite spirit. Easily will it grasp the summons which God in these days of compassion makes unto Israel; easily will it accept the path God designated unto it, and along which it will unite with its brothers who are today its countrymen and among whom it found hospitality ages ago. And in this partnership it will prop up its brethren-countrymen, for the good of their common fatherland, with the attributes of Israel, with faith in God, with love of God, and with the fire of the spirit.

Let those who were so faithful to the will of God, as handed down by Moses, become equally faithful to the will of God, as handed down by Him who is infinitely higher than Moses; who through love for the salvation of man descended from the supreme heights of heaven to the lowliness of earth, submitted to its laws, and patiently bore its wrongs; who extended unto man His entire path, to the very end of the world, extended the entire thought of God lying upon man, and His entire destiny; who also gave unto Israel, for its further progress, that

Andrzej Towiański, "Izrael w Polsce," in *Pisma wybrane: Kościół Chrystusowy. Izrael. Sztuki piękne. Listy. Urywki*, ed. Andrzej Boleski (Warsaw, Cracow: Wydawnictwo J. Mortkowicza, 1920), 99–103.

measure of God's way that is Christianity, a measure greater than that on which Israel stood before Moses and on which it stands to this very day, for centuries resisting progress along the path of the Lord. He who has accepted a certain measure of this path wishes to remain on it eternally; but he who offers resistance to the will of God, and to the thought of God lying upon him, rejects his own salvation. After the fulfillment of his time, he shall pass from under the law of love to the law of divine might and punishment, that the immutable will of God may become fulfilled and so that he may realize the salvation that God designated for each and every one of us.

After the repudiation by Israel of the will of God, and the Word of God, and after the crucifixion of the Word incarnate, after this terrible guilt which nineteen centuries ago set unto Israel the course of penance, Israel's endurance of penance for centuries in its resistance to the will of God, and to the Word of God, has been its great guilt, but this guilt has not yet run its course, for *Christianity has not yet been given unto Israel in the fullness of its being,* and in its clarity. Israel has been aroused to the acceptance not of Christianity so much as the form of Christianity and more by the strength of Christians than by their love. Insofar as it accepted just the form of Christianity, it has lost its ancient essence, its ancient Israelite good, without replacing this good with the far higher, Christian, good.

God today *renews his summons unto Israel* to accept His will, His Word, to accept that progress which He indicated unto man by His Word, to accept the law of Grace, to accept love and its fruit, the Christian sacrifice, which is higher than those sacrifices which Israel rendered unto God centuries ago. Summoning Israel unto that higher measure of His path, God illuminates this measure with a broader light than that which was extended by Christ and which in these times, just as at the beginning of a higher Christian epoch, becomes, by the grace of God, more understandable unto man and more applicable to his private and public life. As a result, that which had until now been an object of faith, feeling, exultation itself, is now becoming a reality on earth; it is becoming a thing that a person may recognize by his senses, and once having recognized it, can worship more and more easily fulfill. After such an outpouring, therefore, of God's grace, if Israel, its recognition of the will of God, and of the Word of God, thus facilitated, should not want to recognize it, or having recognized it, reject it, Israel's guilt before God would become complete and would consist of the full fruit of its resistance to the will of God, and even the most burning prayer of Israel would not erase its guilt, for it would not take the place of its duty, which is to proceed along the path that God indicated unto man by His Word, and above all unto Israel, His firstborn son. Such an account of Israel before God would define for it a hard course, for distant centuries, and the present generation, having spurned God's grace, would present a new obstacle for future generations of Israel and in the harrying of the spirit would have to look from the other world on the sufferings of its brothers.

Let Israel hence cease judging Christianity from Christians in whom it did not see Christianity but only its forms, and from whom in the course of centuries it experienced only their un-Christianity. Let Israel regard as *its first obligation today its recognition of Christianity,* which presents itself in more perfect truth and in its fuller heavenly brilliance. Having recognized it, let Israel not pay heed to what its forebears, the learned and those unilluminated by the divine light who see not the star of Israel, said about Christ and about Christianity. Let it not give heed unto people, but hark and fulfill without delay that unto which Israel is today summoned by the Lord and the God who led it out of the land of Egypt, out of the house of servitude, and who today, in His mercy, wants to lead it out of the slavery and darkness in which its spirit has been imprisoned for centuries.

I have gone on at some length about this subject, brother Feliks, because it lies deeply and painfully in my soul. God has summoned me to serve those brethren in their great need, at a critical juncture for them, and those brethren have heretofore opened up to me so small a field of service to them and I have served them so little for the more than twenty years that I have served my fellow men from the obligation of my calling. You know, for you yourself were troubled by how many of Israel, after receiving the summons of God in the fire of the spirit, cast it aside, as they also cast aside the responsibility they had felt to present that summons to their brethren. And so they set out onto the old earthly ways, prolonging that ancient sin of Israel, the love of earth, of mammon. And there are those among them who made pilgrimages to Jerusalem and there proclaimed the Cause and God's summons unto Israel, and later they denied those feelings that God by His Grace awakened in them for the salvation of Israel. . . .

. . . May God in His mercy not lead into temptation but save from evil those brethren of ours, and may He facilitate for them the fulfillment of their obligations the content of which is—to recognize the will of God and undertake its fulfillment, to accept the designated course and to travel on it for centuries after the star which God in His mercy again today grants unto Israel! This is what we desire and of which we ask God and for which we sacrifice ourselves, however useful our sacrifice may be. Our indifference in this regard, a sin against the love of a fellow man, would cast a weighty blemish on our Christian and Polish character; it would impede for a long time—and because of our fault—the brotherhood with our countrymen designated unto us.

It is easy to grasp how important a matter this is for Poland, and for its future— *the unification, according to God's thought, of these two parts of Poland, so close to each other in origin* and the sympathy of the spirit therefrom that manifests itself especially in the Polish people, notwithstanding their very different paths and situation on earth. It is also easy to grasp the great responsibility he takes upon himself in eternity who first raises an obstacle to this unification. Hence let our love for these brethren—who were once guests and today are our countrymen and destined, for the unity and calling of the soul, to become a homogeneous part of Poland—manifest itself in such a desire and with such sacrifice on our part, and let the debt be paid by us to the treasury of love for God and our fellow man which we assumed in the past, as Christians, with respect to these fellow men and like hosts with respect to our guests, whom God, assigning them the chief abode in our land, entrusted to our love and care.

■ Józef Korzeniowski (1797–1863)
Collocation (1848)

[Highly prominent as an educator and educational administrator both in his native Galicia and in Warsaw, Józef Korzeniowski felt an early attraction for the stage. Besides translating foreign plays, including several by Shakespeare and Schiller, he published some fifty plays of his own; the most famous of these being *Karpaccy górale* (*Carpathian Highlanders*, 1843), a melodrama based on the life of the Hucul mountaineers of southeast Poland. His comedy *Żydzi* (*The Jews*, 1843) is a social satire addressing the economic decline of Polish landowning magnates and their exploitation at the hands of Jewish moneylenders. He deals with similar issues in his novels *Spekulant* (*The Speculator*, 1846) and the artistically superior *Kollokacja* (*Collocation*, 1848; the term "collocation" was used in Poland to refer to small gentry villages resulting from the breakup, or subdivision, of a large estate). Although Korzeniowski's Jews are by and large negative portraits of cynical money manipulators, the principal goal of his novels was a realistic depiction of the self-destructive traditionalism of the provincial Polish landowning nobility, whose resistance to modern agricultural methods contributed to their economic decline and the impoverishment of entire villages. The following excerpt from *Collocation* introduces the not wholly unflattering figure of Shloma, the Jewish moneylender, who colludes with a local official (Zagartowski), possibly the director of some financial institution, in the (ultimately unsuccessful) seizure of the estate of Czaplińce from its owners, the upright gentry family of the Starzyckis. The Pożyczkowskis (a telling name in Polish; "pożyczyć" means "to borrow") are ludicrous figures representing the spendthrift owners of "collocation" villages who lived on credit.]

Closer to the door stood Shloma Krzemieniecki. Shloma was an educated Jew and a Sheyne-Moreyne.[1] He could have been about forty. Tall and well built, he had a face that was somewhat scarred by chicken pox; but his features, although roundish, with a nose a little upturned and a mouth a little too wide, were full of charm and masculine beauty. His black eyes, shaded by long lashes, radiated politeness. His mouth was almost constantly opened in a smile and revealed clean and exceptionally attractive teeth. A velvet yarmulka covered his head, and his side curls, which were not unduly long, and his beard, which was not unduly large, were meticulously groomed and shone like a raven's wings. His black cloth jacket, which was almost new, did not have a single stain on it. His large fingers tucked behind a silk sash, he held a sable cap in one hand, while the other one he exhibited, as if for display, so white and clean was it. Even Shloma's boots, with

Józef Korzeniowski, *Kollokacja,* ed. Stefan Papée (Wrocław: Wydawnictwo Zakładu Narodowego im. Ossolińskich, 1952), 47–56.

1. A Yiddish expression used in reference to a Jew who considered himself superior to the masses of ordinary Jews.

their high tops, cut in the Hungarian style, were cleaned, polished, and did not show the slightest trace of mud.

The son of a very fashionable barber in his time, Shloma was originally marked to be a doctor and until the age of sixteen had attended schools in Krzemieniec. Endowed by nature with the finest talents, he studied splendidly, and as an outstanding pupil passed the first four classes and was already two years into the first course of his higher studies. But then he was married off and the Jewish nature prevailed; he was pulled from book to ell, from algebraic calculation to the plain chalk with which złotys and grosze are written down. So he took up business and forgot about becoming a doctor. His acquaintance with young masters, his school companions of long before, made him also their banker. Out of friendship and camaraderie he lent them money at lower interest than other Jews. This way he built up a clientele without losing the respect or at times even the friendship of those young people among whom he had after all been educated. Hence, although he did not cease being a Jew, he showed that he had acquired higher forms in the way he expressed himself in a pure Polish, in politeness, and in dress. He also knew that he was a handsome male, so he added flirtatiousness and gracious courtesy to his other natural gifts and turned everything to the advantage of his pocket.

After the changes in Krzemieniec, he made the chance acquaintance of director Zagartowski.[2] They came to an understanding quickly, since they shared a common goal, despite the fact that their views of the means to achieve it were not wholly in accord. Shloma thus became an agent and expert for the director once assured of considerable income from all their dealings. He left the town and moved to Szyszkowice, where he leased a large inn along a route that permitted him to continue his business. Shloma carried everything: broadcloth, dry goods, linen, sugar, coffee, wine, meat—in short, whatever the local nobility and traveling gentlemen might have need of. For the sake of appearances, stock was kept in relatively small supply, as if purchased for personal use and given out more as a courtesy. In this way he avoided the suspicions and harassment of the local police, with whom, by the way, he managed to preserve the friendliest relations, especially by means of the wives of the officials who frequently made a carriage stop at his inn or took a night's lodging there. Shloma not only gave goods on credit but also lent money, and at a moderate interest, especially to those individual property owners whom the director brought to his attention. In this way he acquired a great reputation and had numerous customers. The inn profited from this, but if he lost something because of a debtor's inaccuracy or bankruptcy, the director covered his losses.

After convincing the Pożyczkowskis to sell off their portion of Czaplińce to

---

2. After the suppression of the Polish uprising of November 1830–31, the once-famous lyceum in Krzemieniec was closed, contributing to the decline of the town.

the director, Shloma joined the latter in coming to settle this important matter, to agree on the price and to guarantee his loan.

"You see yourself, sir," said Shloma with a smile, "that everything in my account has been scrupulously reckoned, and for less than people pay in the towns. Would you please take notice, sir, of the wine, sugar, and other products I supplied to Pani Pożyczkowska. It would all be a great deal costlier, beside the fact that my payment extends over three years."

"I really no longer see a difference. On the contrary, it seems to me that you're taking a good interest on every item," the director replied.

"That is just what my wife was saying to me," said Pan Pożyczkowski raising himself slightly on the stool and again seating himself in a straighter position.

"Sir, you are wrong," Shloma answered. "That is the usual suspicion of gentlemen such as yourselves toward people of our persuasion, that we never do a favor without great profit. No doubt in large measure we have earned this reputation, but there are exception, I mean exceptions, even among Jews."

He always pronounced pretentiously such expressions as "reputation," "honor," "morality," since they were unusual coming from a Jew's mouth; and whenever he happened to make a mistake in language he immediately corrected himself recalling those lessons in pronunciation he had taken in his first year at Krzemieniec.

Twirling his hands like a fast mill, the director bent toward Shloma and said: "Come now, Shloma! We know how well you can speak and how you manage to embellish everything!"

"What's true is true, sir," Pan Pożyczkowski hastily added, raising himself up on the stool and again dropping back. "My wife says the same too."

"And she indeed speaks the truth," replied the director. "That one's a dangerous jester who didn't go to school for nothing." Shloma smiled at these words, and again tucked his fingers into his sash and began drumming on his belly with his right hand. "Now listen, Jew!" the director added taking the bill from the table. "You're due three thousand złotys. Isn't that so, Pan Pożyczkowski?"

"Yes, sir!"

"You received grain in the amount of five hundred złotys," the mediator spoke further, "Correct?"

"Yes, sir," answered the Jew.

"Well, you see: conscience above all. A grosz given an orphan and a widow produces benefits worth a ducat; but a grosz taken from a poor person causes a quintal of sin. Everything we do is taken into account . . . up there." Having said this, the director tilted his head even more firmly; Pan Pożyczkowski, crushed, sighed deeply, while the Jew's mouth was twisted in an ironic smile. "Well now," the director continued, "considering small additions to the cost of the things you've done as well as the low prices you've put on the rye, barley, hay, received from the Pożyczkowskis . . . where can you get a bushel of rye now for four złotys? Eh? Oy, Shloma, Shloma!"

"But sir, please deign to observe . . ."

"Jesus!" the director hissed. "Do you have to tell me? Don't I buy and sell? You've got to give in, Shloma!"

"If you find, sir, that it's fair," said Shloma in a tone of resignation.

"Why unfair? It's very fair. You'll refund them five hundred złotys."

"Sir, you are our true benefactor," said Pan Pożyczkowski standing as straight as a candle. "My wife knew what she was saying when she said . . ."

"My God! Is a person to be thanked just for doing something in good conscience? What would I be if I didn't use whatever influence I had on this scoundrel here to help out my neighbors? So you will concede then?"

"What can I do?" answered the Jew. "Out of kindness. I know the position of this gentleman and lady, and the good Lord will repay, I mean to say, will reward me in another way," he added with a sly glance at the director, who sighed indifferently and again began twirling his hands since he knew that Shloma would pay the five hundred złotys.

"Then the price of the Pożyczkowski property falls by two thousand złotys," the director said in a lower voice." "But sit down, Pożyczkowski. Are there any other debts?"

"There are, sir," replied the ramrod-straight squire and then sank back on the edge of the stool.

"And those are?"

"We owe Pan Starzycki five hundred złotys."

"Well, that's just a trifle."

"That's just what my wife says, sir!"

"What else?"

"We owe the commissioner of Jampolszczyzny two thousand six hundred and sixty-six złotys. My wife says that he's a bad person and inhuman; he's ready to dispossess us."

"If a creditor demands his due it's now the fashion among us to call that inhuman," the Jew said gravely.

"Pani Pożyczkowska is right," the director interrupted. "There are circumstances in which the very demanding of one's due is an act of inhumanity. Conscience, conscience above all, Pan Shloma! I've heard that the commissioner is a hard man, so out of considerations of neighborliness and the esteem in which I hold Pan and Pani Pożyczkowski, I acquired that debt."

The Jew smiled as he drummed on his belly with his fingers a few times. Pan Pożyczkowski stood up, unsure whether he was supposed to be grateful and express his thanks or be upset and frightened.

"Sit down, Pan Pożyczkowski! You can be at ease about that debt. I still have

Pani Pożyczkowa's voucher here that I obtained from Reytsa," said the director, shaking his head. "That kindhearted Jewess took pity on you. She was persuaded to take a hundred off the thousand złotys, and I am returning them to you."

"Thank you, sir. My wife was saying . . ."

"Pani Pożyczkowska knows me well, and she can rest assured that I am always glad to be of service to her. Now then, your most important debts are: 2000 to Shloma, 500 to Pan Starzycki, 3500 to me, since I am not counting the sixty-six złotys and twenty groszy. Conscience above all, eh? All together, it comes to 6000 Polish złotys. Am I right?"

"Yes indeed, sir," said the poor squire getting up and then sitting down.

"It came out a round figure," the Jew added with a smile.

"Minor debts will doubtless come to, say, a thousand złotys. Correct? You probably don't remember all of them, my good man."

"My wife remembers all of them, sir!"

"I say! Pani Pożyczkowska is mistress of the house in the fullest sense. *Hic mulier* [quite a woman]," the Jew said, smiling.

"You still haven't forgotten your Latin," interrupted the director. "Oh you Jew you! Better to have less Latin and more conscience, conscience! Now then, I am holding those 6000 złotys plus the 1000 for small debts. The rest will be paid in cash the moment the sale is consummated."

"But my dear sir!" said the squire getting up. "My wife told me that I can't dispose of that property except by asking fifty-five ducats for each serf."

"Who do you take me for, Pan Pożyczkowski? Would I want to take advantage from the position of such worthy people? Your parcel of land suffers from the inconvenience of lying in the very middle of Czaplińce and has bad neighbors on all sides," said the director sighing and looking askance at Shloma. "But it does have water, which is of use to me. If you needed any proof of my respect for you, and my esteem for Pani Pożyczkowska, I am offering you not fifty-five but fifty-six a serf, and I will assume all expenses." The Jew shook his head, and the director continued. "Why are you surprised, Shloma? Conscience, my dear fellow, conscience above all! Does it amount to a lot for eleven serfs according to the last census?"

The Jew raised his head, his attractive eyes sparkling, and drumming on his belly with his fingers, he said: "Deducting 7,000 złotys for debts, the gentleman and the lady have 5,320 to their favor."

"Contracts are coming up soon in Dubno. For that sum of money, you can have a nice estate, and your minds can be at ease. After all, a small inheritance, Pan Pożyczkowski, can be a huge liability, isn't that so?"

"Right you are, sir! That's what my wife says too."

"Now go home, tell your wife everything, then come back either tomorrow morning or the day after in order to sign the contract. I'll submit it myself to the records. It won't cost you a cent."

The squire got up, even paler than before, bowed without moving his hands from his sides, and withdrew backward from the room. When he had already taken his place in his carriage, dressed in a threadbare overcoat with holes in it, he went over the entire conversation in his mind so that he could give his wife a good account of the matter without knowing himself if he had committed some stupidity and if he would pay for it at the hands of his better half. Meanwhile, the young coachman whipped the hungry and emaciated nags and kept tugging on the reins to spur their energy.

When he reached home and rode past the gates, he caught sight of Pani Pożyczkowska on the balcony. She was a tall, broad-shouldered, full-bodied woman, with huge red hands. Her entire face, which was regular enough, was dotted with pimples. Her gray, lashless eyes sparkled from afar. On her head she had a white chintz bonnet with a large brim which the wind kept blowing back. She was clad in an old, torn gown that was stained on the chest and wet at the elbows. She had an apron on and was holding in her hands a rolling pin with which she had just been rolling out dough to make dumplings for dinner. A girl in rags, barefoot, dirty, and untidy, ran out behind her, but her mother shoved her back into the hallway. Thus when her husband rode up beneath the balcony, he was confused by the sight before him and did not know with which foot to alight first from the carriage. Seeing him, Pani Pożyczkowska shouted down at him in a husky voice: "Hurry on in, dearest, and tell me what you did."

The poor fellow descended, no longer recalling the course of the conversation with the director. His wife grabbed "dearest" by his coat and pushed him into the hallway the doors of which soon closed with a bang behind this well-matched couple.

After Pan Pożyczkowski had left them, the director and his minister remained behind. The Jew was standing as before, holding himself by his sash and with a smile on his lips; the director was sitting as before, his hands folded on his belly. But he kept on slowly revolving his large hands, like the wheels of a windmill when the wind dies down. It was a sign of work completed, thought becalmed, and good humor. Just as once upon a time, after he ascended the Spanish throne of the Bourbons, Louis XIV declared, "The Pyrenees no longer exist," so the director, after settling in the very middle of the village for which he had long been lying in wait, thought to himself: "Czaplińce is now mine!" At that moment he glanced at the Jew, and the Jew at him, with the same look with which two Roman soothsayers beheld one another with nobody present when they were through with their prophecies and their deceit was successful.

"Why are you looking at me like that?" the director finally asked. "Was it bad?"

"Sir, you acted splendidly," Shloma replied.

"Ha! Conscience above all, my dear Shloma!"

"Czaplińce above all, my dear sir!" answered the Jew.

The director burst out laughing and hissed through the gap in his two front teeth:

"Jesus, what a rascal of a Jew you are!" He then got up, approached Shloma, extended a puffy hand to him, into which the Jew, smiling, placed his own fine, white hand. They shook hands. Then the director said: "How 'bout a glass of Malaga?"

"It's due me," answered Shloma, "and also 870 złotys."

"Five hundred, idiot!" said the director, clasping his hands and twirling them like a fast mill.

"But three percent of 12,320 złotys?"

"True, true; go on, damn you, you're skinning the hide off me."

And out they went, the director first, inclining on his short legs, and the Jew after him, dignified, elegant, and with an expression of superiority, and contempt.

■ Cyprian Kamil Norwid (1821–83)
"Polish Jews" (1861)

[Although he remained little known among his contemporaries, in part because he placed himself above the fractious politics of the Great Emigration—which circumstances made him a part of from his early twenties—and in part because of his introversive, withdrawn nature, Cyprian Kamil Norwid was one of the greatest poets of the Polish language. Extreme poverty sent him to seek his fortune in America in late 1852. He remained in the United States for two years, living alone in wretched conditions. While in the United States, he became deeply interested in the abolitionist movement and wrote two poems on John Brown. Back in Paris, he existed largely on the margins of the Emigration, ignored and indigent. In his lifetime he succeeded in publishing only a single volume of poetry, in 1863. His last years were spent in extreme poverty in a home for the aged run by Polish nuns.

Around the turn of the century, interest in Norwid began to grow, owing largely to the collection and publication of his manuscripts by the modernist poet, translator, and editor Zenon Miriam Przesmycki. Norwid's reputation since the turn of the century has grown by leaps and bounds. Virtually all his works—poetry, prose, and plays—are now available in modern editions, and a vast body of criticism and scholarship has arisen around them. Admired for his bold, sometimes elusive imagery, for his extraordinary manipulation of language, and for his universal, humane concerns, he was free to address the cynicism, commercialism, and banality all around him with an irony commanded by few of his peers.

Norwid's poem "Żydowie polscy" ("Polish Jews"), despite its occasional—and characteristic—enigmas, celebrates the antiquity, and continuity, of the Jewish people, and the bonds of patriotism and capacity for heroism binding Pole and Jew. The immediate inspiration for the poem was the brutal Russian suppression of a Polish patriotic demonstration in Castle Square in Warsaw on April 8, 1861, which resulted in a hundred fatalities.]

You—solemn Jewish Nation—
Are, in Europe, like a monument shattered in the East,
Borne everywhere by its fragments
On each of which an eternal hieroglyph is inscribed.

And the northern man,
Upon meeting you in a pine forest,
Divines the reflection of the
Sun of your homeland—

Which once upon a time did bathe
In the blue azure

Cyprian Kamil Norwid, "Żydowie polscy," in *Pisma Wybrane,* vol. 1, ed. Juliusz Gomulicki (Warsaw: Państwowy Instytut Wydawniczy, 1968), 487–88.

Artur Szyk (1894–1951), "The Young Jew Michael Landy Taking Up the Cross from the Hands of a Wounded Priest during the Demonstration of April 8, 1861, in Warsaw." Courtesy Żydowski Instytut Historyczny (Warsaw).

Like Moses in the waters of the Nile!
And he says: "He is great who once was so high,
And fell so low, and is as silent as you."

We sons of the North with flaxen hair,
The snowy clouds of eastern history—
Beyond the borders of occult mystery,
Right away, straight from the earth,
Beholding the high shrine of the heavens—
Like the sons of Hagar—through the essence of country;[1]
Like the sons of Sarah—through the toil of fathers;
We earlier than others—we entirely differently,

Looked unto you, though not despairing:
When coat of arms rent you and noble,
The cross stood in the breech—and did not lie![2]

Since history seemingly is *confusion,*
When, in fact, it is *strength and beauty*—
Since it is like a testament
Which a cherub on high looks after,

Then once again the Maccabee stood
Not in ambiguous anxiety with the Pole
On a Warsaw pavement.
—And when wealthier peoples on earth
Gave him not crosses, for which one dies,
But those from which it shines—
What then? He preferred instead
To stretch out defenseless arms, like David!

Great nation! Honor to you in those who
Did not bend before the Mongol-Circassian tempest—[3]
And, together with us, defended the God of Moses
With knightly gaze and bare chests.

---

1. Norwid alludes here to the diasporas of the Jews and the Poles, both of whom were driven from their homelands. Hagar was the Egyptian servant of Abraham who bore him a son, Ishmael. When Sarah, Abraham's wife, gave birth to Isaac, she had Abraham drive Hagar and Ishmael into the desert.

2. During the demonstration of April 8, 1861, a Jewish *gymnasium* student named Michał Landy raised up a cross from the hands of one of the fallen leaders of the demonstration and was himself almost immediately killed by a Cossack. This seems to be what the line in the poem refers to.

3. An allusion to the Russians, and the Cossacks, who put down the patriotic manifestation in Castle Square.

Like your elders in history,
Who, pointing to savages from above, cried out:
"I have endured!
I look unto the banner, not reckoning your men,
For once you were nothing, while I sucked milk —
Nature I know from an earlier time —
Hence I curse the bit —
And you shall remain on horse like a shepherd —
Without a *flock!*"

Part Two ■ From Positivism to Modernism

■ Józef Ignacy Kraszewski (1812–87)
The Jew: Contemporary Images (1866)

[Józef Ignacy Kraszewski was a phenomenally prolific writer (the author of some five hundred novels), many of whose works constitute a fictional history of Poland from prehistoric times through the period of the Saxon dynasty (1697–1763). Unlike Sienkiewicz, who later wrote historical romances in which fiction takes precedence over fact, Kraszewski was a disciplined student of history and an archivist who used primary source materials in order to recreate a given historical period as accurately as possible. Active also as a journalist, above all as editor of the Warsaw daily *Gazeta Polska* (*Polish Gazette*, 1859–62), Kraszewski was compelled to leave Warsaw because of political differences with the Polish civil authorities around the time of the outbreak of the January Insurrection of 1863. He settled in Dresden, where his long residence in the Saxon capital was used profitably for, among other things, research in the state archives for a series of novels set in the Saxon period of Polish history. Two of these novels, *Hrabina Cosel* (*Countess Cosel*, 1874) and *Brühl* (1875), are generally regarded as among the best of his historical fiction. Kraszewski's continued political activity in Dresden led to his arrest on a charge of treason and his sentencing in 1883 to three-and-a-half years imprisonment. But he was released after serving a little more than year because of his ill health. He then settled in San Remo, Italy, and died not long afterward in Geneva.

Liberal in outlook and imbued with the ideals of Polish positivism, Kraszewski turned to the status of peasants and Jews in several novels with contemporary settings. In *Latarnia czarnoksięska* (*The Magic Lantern*, 1843), a richly detailed picture of the life of the gentry in the Volhynian region of old Poland, Jews figure primarily as elements in a traditional landscape. The Jewish presence is much stronger in *Powieść bez tytułu* (*Novel without a Name*, 1855), about the ill-fated romance between a beautiful Jewish girl in Wilno and a young Polish poet who becomes her tutor. Realizing that love between them would be impossible because of the opposition of both Jews and Christians, she eventually drives him away by becoming a prominent actress and the mistress of a wealthy aristocrat. Kraszewski's most important novel about Jews remains *Żyd* (*The Jew*, 1866). He wrote it in Dresden and published it in Poznań under the pseudonym B. Bolesławita to avoid trouble with the Russian censors in Warsaw where he still had a house and family to which he hoped to return. Set in the period of the January Insurrection of 1863, the novel is built primarily around the figure of the Jewish idealist and Polish patriot, Jakub, who joins the insurgents, survives the insurrection, and finally settles in Italy with his wife. Of particular interest in the novel is the contrast Kraszewski draws between secularized, enlightened Jews for whom participation in Polish society and culture does not compromise fidelity to the Jewish faith and conservative Jews who regard acculturation as a profound threat to the traditional Jewish way of life in Poland. In the following excerpts, Jakub shares his life story and outlook with the Polish insurrectionary Iwas.]

Józef Ignacy Kraszewski, *Żyd: Obrazy współczesne* (Cracow: Wydawnictwo Literackie, 1960), 127–29, 133–36, 141–44.

"Listen," shouted Jakub, "admit it, you're a conspirator, aren't you?"

"So it is, and it can't be otherwise," replied Iwas. "All of Poland has been conspiring for over a hundred years. Oppression drives her to it; captivity raises generations of conspirators, in fear, darkness, silence, and danger. Where life cannot develop with all its energy conspiracies are inevitable, the natural fruit of despotism, the destitution that grows behind the dirty collar of its shirt . . ."

"I understand that," said Jakub, "but woe to the country that embarks on such a course; it has already lost confidence in itself and has recognized its own weakness. I understand only one conspiracy, ours, which has lasted a few thousand years and in which we have attained the epoch of the equality of rights and our regeneration. Our conspiracy has agglomerated our forces and united us into a strong and solid body. You and your conspiracies, with their feverish explosions, will attain nothing but a more morbid decline."

"Let's not discuss it," said Iwas, knitting his brows. "You don't have the same feeling as we do for Poland, nor have you experienced what we endure . . ."

"I beg your pardon," replied the Jew. "If this country is for anyone, it is for us, this country that gave us shelter, and where, despite occasional persecution, we grew by numbers and work. This country is our second chosen fatherland. If it still is not for all, it should be and will be. At the very least, I feel myself as much a Pole as an Israelite."

"Yes, but people like you — and with no flattery intended — cannot be anything but rare, and I say this knowing you for no more than several days. But in general your people can be reproached for not being very attached to this country in which you have been living for quite a long time in happiness and freedom and which has nourished you, raised you, enriched you . . . and recognized you as her own children."

"Easy now," replied Jakub, "look at history objectively. Religious fanaticism, ours as well as yours, and the arrogance of the nobility long stood in the way of the recognition of the Jews as citizens of the country. The Jews themselves are also to blame for never making the attempt to assimilate the language and customs of the country, for isolating themselves, for constituting a *status in statu,* a nation within a nation, for not working sincerely toward citizenship, which is acquired by self-dedication and blood.

"The fault is on both sides, and both sides should seek forgiveness and forget the past. This is another age, enlightenment is widespread, humane ideas are common to both of us, everything compels us to draw close to one another and become united. We extend our hand to you . . . don't reject us . . ."

"We, the younger generation, could we reject you?" cried out Iwas. "Can you imagine that? There still exist prejudices, repugnances, the vestiges of old, unextirpated ideas, the remains of past centuries . . . but the majority . . . sincerely extend their hand to you. Let us be brothers, but in spirit, not just in word, in deed, not just in appearance. Let us be brothers not only in time of success, but in work and pain as well . . ."

Saying nothing, Jakub extended his hand.

"That is enough for today," he finally said, "we understand each other and agree with each other easily, we, the younger generation. My contemporaries, the Israelite youth, think and feel the same as I, but just as among you, so we too have prejudices, old enmities, foul desires for vengeance nursed for centuries, and people who . . . Let us be forbearing, patient, and let us not allow ourselves to be carried away by passions breathing of hatred. . . . Love only reconciles, binds, and unites; let us aim for it and work at it."

[When the conversation resumes, Jakub expounds his religious beliefs.]

"As a Jew, I knew only my Bible until the time I entered school. The whole world was contained in it for me. But now I observed that as a human being I must come to grips with what humanity as a whole has done, achieved, and learned through the ages. My exclusive faith in the chosen people was at once somewhat shaken and they appeared to me in a rather different light. I became more humble and with a troubled soul, but a mind now more independent, I again returned to the Bible and in so doing became even more of a Jew, but of a different kind.

"Perhaps it's hard for you to comprehend me, as a Jew. I shall pause here in order to explain to you that our Israelite society, which has for so long been united by persecution, is divided into many different branches now that that persecution is coming to an end. The Jew today is no longer what he used to be when exclusion forced him to be only himself, to live, think, learn, and move in a narrow circle defined for him by the laws and customs of hostile Christians. . . . On occasion, a Maimonides or Spinoza emerged from this cramped little circle, but it was composed for the most part of a uniform mass of faithful and strict confessors of the Old Testament. We clustered around the Ark of the Covenant. . . . Today the Jews are freer, and, less restrained, walk different paths. . . . Many of them reject their traditional law and faith and seemingly accept another, while in reality they have none. . . . These are the ones I have to tell you about first.

"My protector, Tilda's father—to whom I owe everything—was precisely this type of Jew. Educated abroad, in a society that had become indifferent, he eventually lost respect for our faith and traditions, threw off the stern obligations of our rituals, and, without becoming a Christian, became the kind of person I described to you—one who reduces morality to mere calculation and makes reason his only guide.

"Nothing is sadder than people like him. Man is, after all, not only the most perfectly developed animal; above him exist other worlds, beings, and spheres of the spirit. Besides the body, man also has a soul, by which man is united with divinity, which inquires, has presentiments, soars above the earth and beyond the realm of the senses. Materialism and atheism satisfy neither society nor the individual; torn by them from the totality, they wither like flowers cut from their stems. Take away God, faith in the immortality of the soul, higher feelings and desires, and you will create—especially with our refined material civilization—something as hideous as our proper, cold, and dead present age. Our age conquers the elements, reveals the most hidden secrets of nature, yet is no longer able to differentiate good from bad, and designates honor and offense as intelligence or stupidity, awkwardness or practicality. Its measure is success, its divinity power, and *vae victis* (woe unto the vanquished) again resounds as a great echo above that desert intersected by rail lines and traversed by steam. . . .

"There is nothing sadder, I repeat, than those people who have broken with tradition, with all faith in the past, with all remembrance of it, and who make their way by reason along the path of material gain. . . . Such people are no rarity in our society or yours; in both they represent an equally sad phenomenon. The Christian who has rejected Christ, the Jew who has rejected Moses, give off the same stench of putrefaction. Such people are walking corpses whose horizon is limited by a short life devoted to some burning passion. . . . Outwardly happy, they are in their souls the poorest of people. Quickly satisfied, oversated with everything, bored, they end in apathy, ignorance, or madness. . . .

"The Christian world took so much from Mosaic law that it cannot deny its superiority without denying itself. Nevertheless, attributing them to the Talmud and rabbis, it has judged only superficially oddities that have accrued through the centuries; everything not understood in Judaism has been ridiculed, and trifles have been seized upon to mock it and make it abominable. All the literature on the subject pretends to illuminate our learning and elucidate our customs, yet proves in reality that neither has been understood. Laughter is easy and you can make a joke of whatever you want, even the flowers of the most wonderful poetry which in other literatures would be regarded as masterpieces . . ."

"I know nothing of your poetry," said Iwas.

"Did you ever read the ironic passages in the Talmud whose fancies, viewed dispassionately, would be regarded as nonsensical?"

"I've really read almost nothing."

"Would you be interested?" asked Jakub.

"Very."

"I know many passages and sayings by heart," said the Jew, "let's take, for example, the legend and description of Paradise."

[Jakub then discusses rabbinical concepts of Paradise and Hell.)

"The Hell of the Talmud is a necessary fulfillment of this image. The concepts of it share much in common with the Christian, since they developed at the same time. According to the book of Nischmas Chaïm, Hell is separated from Paradise by a very small space, according to some by a thin wall, just as virtue and vice are often separated by just a single moment. A river flows out of Hell just as from Paradise . . . but it is boiling whereas the river of Paradise is refreshing.

"Three routes lead to Hell, one from the sea, another from the wilderness, the third from the inhabited world. Hell has five kinds of fires that consume, devour, and destroy everything, but leave untouched the fire which consumes itself. . . . Hell is sixty times larger than earth. There are palaces there that govern the nether regions, and a triumvirate of leaders, the most important of whom is named Dumah. Countless scorpions and serpents attend them. Those who made a mockery of the holy books, scorned the religious leaders, behaved badly with people, and did not pray in the temple are locked in rooms and left to suffer. The shouts and screams of the torturers and tortured rise above the buildings. Two satans, Gimgums and Tassurina, gather the world over the empty talk that people carry throughout life and the shells of broken vessels that people smash in anger. Rabbi Simon mentions a third satan by the name of Sascharis, who tempts people to sin himself or through his attendants.

"The chief of the satans, Dumah, lives together with his subjects in a region of Hell known as Bor. He has many palaces here. In one of them, Shaches, a great fire burns, yet darkness and filth dominate. Three gates lead there: one of them is guarded by the satan Arshteria and millions of his attendants; the second is commanded by Tuskifa and Kos Hattarelah, the latter with a chalice containing a bitter drink, which is intended for those condemned to destruction; the third is presided over by Sanagdiel. Each category of sinners forms its own circle under the watch of a satan, just as in Dante's hell.

"The second region of Hell, which is also called Dumah, just like the chief, is even darker. Four gates lead to it, and different sinners enter through each. The Talmud calls the satan-guardians of each region by name and describes their duties. The last of them, Sachsicha, sows discord. This second region of Hell includes arrogant rabbis, false interpreters of the Bible, usurers, liars, those who laugh during prayer, and those who do not recite 'amen' when they are supposed to.

"Offenders of faith are incarcerated in the region of Tit hayovem, which corresponds to Dante's description at the end of canto 18 of the *Inferno*. This is where perjurers, the scorners of the poor and destitute, and unjust judges are tortured.

"There is only one entrance into the region of Sheol, and one guard, Ebah, who tempts people to wars and battles. His subjects are instigators of combat and murder. Imprisoned here are traitors and those who do not believe in resurrection." . . .

"I have expounded on this," said Jakub, "for the sake of proving to you that there is nothing funny in these apparitions of a feverish imagination, except perhaps for frivolous people. The teaching about Heaven, Hell, resurrection, purgatory, and atonement for sins is remarkably close to the Christian. There are many striking similarities; the character of the teaching, and even its peculiarities, are not unique to us despite the fact that they, too, bear the stamp of long servitude. This servitude can be felt everywhere—in our faith, legends, ceremonies, and in our entire life. That is why it is unfitting for us to throw out many absurdities, which have more to do with our servitude than with us; a martyrdom of thousands of years had to be reflected in everything touched by it." . . .

"First, by my Jewish education, and afterward by my European and human education, I became different, something new both to myself and to my compatriots — a Jew who respects his traditions without being superstitious. In the depths of my heart I preserved feeling and faith like the most precious treasure, but without rejecting the light of reason and the law of progress, and without excluding myself from the mainstream of humanity. This suits me and gives me complete peace of spirit.

"When I finished my studies, I was summoned to Warsaw by Tilda's father, my guardian. I still did not have the slightest idea of the situation of my coreligionists. In the countryside, I met only two types of Jews — old people faithful to the Law down to its smallest details and precepts incomprehensible or superstitious by today's standards, and those who were only brothers by blood and not by customs and spirit.

"I admit that I approached the capital of the Kingdom [of Poland] with curiosity, anxious about my future, knowing nothing about the world I was about to enter. Jews in the provinces lived, and still live, entirely apart from the Christians. Now I was to meet them here for the first time all mixed in with Christians if not by law, at least by custom. I confess that the early days after my arrival I was still unable to make head or tail of my surroundings. I met Jews who were no longer Jews, and others who were closed-mouthed about their origin, which nevertheless was visible on their brows . . . some among them drearily silent, incomprehensible. Most were still faithful to their faith but kept silent about it. It was evident at first glance that some sort of struggle was taking place here . . . the number, importance, wealth, and education of the Israelites already placed them in a position to demand the rights and recognition of citizenship. The old Polish nobility, the caretakers of a poorly understood national tradition, politely, but sneeringly, coldly, and cavalierly rejected those whom they had long considered newcomers. Dislike and distaste grew on both sides; the situation was unclear and false. Despite the fact that daily relations brought them together, necessity united them, and mutual interests on occasion reconciled them, memories, prejudices, and differences of faith still separated them.

■ Henryk Sienkiewicz (1846–1916)
Letters from America (1876–78)

[Henryk Sienkiewicz was Poland's first Nobel Prize winner for literature (in 1905). His international celebrity rests primarily on his novel of ancient Rome, *Quo Vadis?* (1896). In his own country he is known as the author of rousing, patriotic historical romances —*Ogniem i mieczem* (*With Fire and Sword*, 1884), *Potop* (*The Deluge*, 1886), and *Pan Wołodyjowski* (*Pan Michael*, 1887–88), set in seventeenth-century Poland, and *Krzyżacy* (*The Teutonic Knights*, 1900), about the fourteenth-century conflict between the German Order of the Teutonic Knights, on one side, and Poland and the Grand Duchy of Lithuania, on the other. Although often dismissed for his superficiality, particularly in the area of characterization, Sienkiewicz was a consummate stylist in Polish and remains eminently readable.

His *Letters to America,* which he originally submitted under the pseudonym Litwos, resulted from a two-year trip he took to the United States in 1876, when he was commissioned by a Polish newspaper to cover the Centennial Exposition in Philadelphia. There was also another reason for the trip. A group of artists and writers from Warsaw planned to emigrate to America with the purpose of establishing a commune in California; Sienkiewicz, who was to precede the group, assumed responsibility for finding an appropriate site. The commune, which was backed financially by Count Chłapowski, the husband of the distinguished actress Helena Modrzejewska, settled in Anaheim. The idealistic venture eventually foundered, but it provided Sienkiewicz the opportunity to travel extensively in the American West, his impressions of which are among the most interesting in *Letters from America.* Helena Modrzejewska went on to a successful career in the American theater under the name Helena Modjeska.

The following excerpts from Sienkiewicz's *Letters from America* are devoted to his observations on Polish Jews in America, and his positivist-shaped outlook on the need for greater collaboration between Polish and Polish-Jewish communities in the United States.]

San Francisco
9 September 1877

My dears!

I should have answered your last letter. I was a little angry with you for having my previous letter printed. Neither its form nor its style made it suitable for that, and your marginal explanations in some places altered or unduly generalized the meaning of my words. From the ending it's also possible to draw the conclusion that I have nothing but jeers for the Jews here, whereas I shall tell you sincerely that I have a lot of respect for them.

It was only here that I became convinced what an energetic and enterprising people they are. It is less surprising in Poland that the Jews have gained control of

Henryk Sienkiewicz, *Listy z podróży do Ameryki,* vol. 2 (Warsaw: Państwowy Instytut Wydawniczy, 1950), 227–28, 277–78, 300–302.

commerce and, in part, of industry; but here, where the population is industrious to excess, where competition is extremely keen and the struggle for existence is waged ruthlessly, the commercial abilities of the Jews realize their full potential. I shall tell you quite simply that in the field of trade, the Polish Jews hold their own against the Yankees, and if need be, could do so against all the devils put together. They come here in most instances without a grosz, without any knowledge of the language or conditions, in short, with only their two hands and a head on their shoulders. The day after their arrival each one of them opens a business. If anyone tries to cheat them, he is himself cheated. In bigger commercial undertakings, they are no less honest than other businessmen. I do not know a single Jew who, after a year's residence here, suffers from want. Each of them has money; each, as the Americans say, "is making a living"; and after a while each is worth such and such in cash. Some of them have made millions. Be that as it may. A still better attribute of theirs is that the Jews from the Kingdom of Poland never forget where they come from, where they lived before, and where the bones of their forefathers lie; on the other hand, Jews from Prussian and Austrian Poland prefer to identify with Germans. In a word, prejudice aside, the Jews are a hardy people. This element in our population should not be made light of, for the Jews possess exactly those traits which we Poles lack and which, added to our own, would create a quite impressive totality.

Such is my opinion, which I express openly, as do I also my belief that anyone of us who looks down on Jews from a position of some silly pretensions of birth, ancestry, and so on, is an idiot. I am not suggesting that we court them. When they deserve it, they should be given a good hiding (to use Prus's term) like anyone else. But by no means should we relegate them to the margins of our life. So much for that subject. . . .

The more a nationality can exert influence on the internal politics of the United States, the more importance it acquires. The more numerous, prosperous, and well organized the community, the more legislation it can achieve favorable to its own interests. The Irish and Germans have similar influence; the Poles, sad to say, none! Their numbers are too small, they are too poor, for the most part, and they count for too little. But the situation would definitely change if Jews were to become a part of any organized plan aimed at achieving internal unity among the Poles. I am not speaking now about German and Austrian Jews, who lean toward the Germans, but about Jews from the Kingdom of Poland who number at least 100,000 in the entire United States and who represent not only that number of votes but also possess capital. They are, for the most part, people of means. Shabby racial prejudices deserving only of contempt—which play such a great role in Europe—do not exist here. There would be nothing to hinder the attachment of Jews to various Polish organizations were it not for the fact that these organizations have a church-affiliated and religious character accommodating only Poles of the Catholic faith. The Jews themselves do not lack the desire. I heard that from the mouths of many of them. I do not have to add that that would bring incalculable advantages. All attempts at organization here fall apart over the lack of funds. But the Jews do possess funds. Other nationalities have their own schools and libraries, their own hospitals, institutions that guarantee assistance to new arrivals looking for work, and their own general treasury earmarked for support not only of single individuals, but of entire communities in case of fire, poor crops, floods, and locusts. The Poles could have everything if they were more numerous and wealthier, and they would be more numerous and wealthier if they united with Jews of Polish origin. But such a union has never taken place nor will it ever take place in view of the obstacles the clerics would put in its way. . . .

The Polish Jews I met in America were on the whole affluent. There are many of them in all the bigger cities and for the most part they have done well financially. Americans who have been here for a long time call all newcomers "greenhorns" and commonly exploit them at every opportunity. Our Polish Jew, however, thanks to his innate talent for business and aggressiveness, will arrive in New York on Sunday, for example, open a small business right away on Monday, and by Tuesday will run rings around the most cunning American who tries to cheat him. Here the scythe strikes a stone, hence the designation "Polish Jew" arouses justifiable apprehension among American profiteers. Because of their shrewdness, knowledge of the German language, and business initiative, our Polish Jews make out rather well in the United States and do not undergo the hardships, for example, of our peasants. At the recently discovered gold mines where adventurers quickly congregate, where the knife, the revolver, and the terrifying lynch law still prevail, where an American merchant reluctantly goes about his business out of fear of the danger to both his merchandise and his life, the first stores are generally established by our Jews. By their courtesy, kind words, and, above all, extension of credit, they win over the most dangerous adventurers and "regulators," as lynchers are called. Once they have the revolvers of such people on their side, the Jews then conduct their businesses safely under their protection. Profits are enormous in such localities because the miners pay for things with gold dust instead of with money. I saw stores of our Jews in precisely such conditions in Deadwood, Dakota; Darwin, California; and Virginia City, Nevada. Perhaps within a few years their proprietors will become millionaires.

When I consider the status of the Jewish population in the United States in general, I come to the conclusion that however much the peasant emigration is perilous both to our country and the peasant himself, the exodus of the Jews is beneficial to them. In Polish towns and villages there are hundreds of Jewish families who have nothing to live on and are engaged only in the harmful, unproductive business of middlemen. In the United States, however, where bare hands and a resourceful head can make one wealthy, where many branches of commerce have not yet been developed, broad opportunities for prosperity and profit would open up to them.

■ Eliza Orzeszkowa (1841–1910)
"Mighty Samson" (1877)

[Eliza Orzeszkowa was born into a landowning family in the Grodno district in eastern Poland. She is regarded as the first truly professional woman writer in the history of Polish literature. Her strong sense of social commitment, and her embrace of the feminist cause as reflected, for example, in her widely popular novel *Marta* (1873), owed much to her participation in the January Insurrection of 1863 and the subsequent dissolution of her loveless, arranged marriage. A prolific and uneven writer who rarely traveled from her native Grodno, Orszeszkowa addressed virtually every contemporary social issue dear to the positivists. Her novels are especially valuable for the remarkably vivid picture they afford of the Polish provincial life of her own time. Apart from *Marta,* the best of these— *Cham* (*The Boor,* 1888), *Bene nati* (*The Well-Born,* 1891), and *Nad Niemnem* (*On the Banks of the Niemen,* 1888)—deal with the peasantry and the impoverished gentry, and the relations between them.

Orzeszkowa also took up the cause of the Jewish community in her novels *Eli Makower* (1875) and *Meir Ezofowicz* (1878), which is the better of the two. Offended by obscurantism in any form, in the spirit of Polish positivism, Orzeszkowa, like Niemcewicz before her in *Levi and Sarah,* regarded Talmudism and Hasidism as the principal obstacles to the secularization of the Jews. Hardly unique in this respect, Orzeszkowa viewed such secularization as the precondition to the entry of the Polish Jews into the meanstream of Polish society and culture. There is no evidence, however, that she regarded Jewish assimilation as a stage in their transformation into Christians.

In order to write convincingly about Jewish life in Poland, Orzeszkowa read a great deal about Jewish culture and religion. Her knowledge, and compassion, come through clearly in her fiction and compensate for an undeniable didacticism and paternalism as well as for her simplistic treatment of the dynamics of intragroup conflict.

Among Orzeszkowa's shorter works of prose fiction dealing with Jewish life, the best by far is "Silny Samson" ("Mighty Samson," 1877). With her point of departure the premise that her fellow Poles look upon Jews as a kind of alien species, Orzeszkowa brings keen psychological insight into the transformative power of art in her story about a terribly poor, pious, and unworldly provincial Jew who takes the role of Samson in a Purim play.]

If you should ever desire, my reader, to find the equivalent of the term "Jew" in popular speech, take a historical dictionary, look under the letter *c,* and when you come across the name "Croesus" underline it and remember it, for you will then possess the information you sought. The synonym for "Jew" is "Croesus."

"Jew" and "Croesus" mean entirely the same. Everyone knows, of course, that the Rothschilds, above all, are to be found among the Jews. And there are also other bankers possessing I have no idea how many millions and palaces full of

---

Eliza Orzeszkowa, "Silny Samson," in *Nowele* (Warsaw: Czytelnik, 1957), 110–77.

gilding, sculptures, carpets, mirrors, and so on. Hence the simple deduction, just as two and two equals four, that the race from which issued the Rothschilds and other bankers is very wealthy and abounds in millions, palaces, gilding, sculptures, mirrors, and so on. And if some son of this tribe does not abound in all these things, then it is only because he himself does not want to as he can perhaps get along on what he has. If, however, he should so desire it, he would most certainly abound in everything.

Wealthy tribe! Fortunate tribe! I wholly acknowledge its good fortune and wonder only at the fact that Shymshel, the son of Gershun and husband of Tsipa, knows nothing, absolutely nothing about this wealth and the good fortune resulting from it. Seeing that total ignorance of Shymshel, I at once thought that he was merely pretending, that he was hiding in order to take better advantage of the goyim among whom he had most certainly chosen some *meropia,* or victim sentenced and delivered to the authority of the kahal for exploitation.[1] About such meropias, or victims, we have heard much of late. Upon closer examination, however, I convinced myself conclusively—to my still greater astonishment—that Shymshel, in fact, possessed no meropia and indeed knew absolutely nothing about wealth and all the beneficences of which it is the source. As concerns the gilding, statues, and mirrors, I even doubt that Shymshel ever saw them in his life except for the fact that a simple little mirror, a fourth of an arm in length, in a wooden frame without a trace of gilding or sculpture, hangs above a valise of Tsipa's. Six-year-old Esther, Shymshel's child, leans toward it a few times a day with the intention for sure of beholding in it her fiery ringlets and her sky-blue eyes laughing at the mirror, and the pale face of her father who smiles looking at the mirror and at her.

About other mirrors than the one in which a small part of a dirty wall is always reflected, or sometimes the playful little nose of Esther, Shymshel knows absolutely nothing, just as he knows nothing about a host of quite common phenomena and things though they exist on this earth. I must confess, however, with much embarrassment over this figure in my sketch, that the orbit of things and phenomena known to Shymshel is unusually small. Nevertheless, it must be said in all fairness that one must exclude from this ignorance of worldly things the tiny cottage which Shymshel knows perfectly and in all its details, first because he has been living in it for twelve years, and second because there is nothing in it to know apart from two beds heaped with beet-colored bedclothes, a huge stove with an opening as black as an abyss, raggedy clothing eternally drying in front of the stove, small windows in rotting frames, a table beneath one window, three small benches, one cat, and five children.

These last Shymshel knows very well, for he loves them very dearly. . . .

---

1. "Meropia"—a term of obvious Greek origin—occurs in cabalistic occultism and, like other elements in cabalistic magic, probably derives from Greek gnostic influence.

So much for Shymshel's children; but what about Shymshel himself?

The question as to who he is encompasses the question of his birth, that higher or lower position a person occupies on the ladder of the social hierarchy. As to his birth, I cannot tell you who his father was — a water-carrier perhaps, or a woodcutter. Some people say yes, others say no. All, however, agree with the assertion that he must have been very poor since his son began his formal education only in a *talmudor,* or free school.[2] That his place in the hierarchy must be high we can conclude from the words of Shymshel himself to his wife: "See where I've reached!" A person who pronounces such words with pride and satisfaction must have reached something important and high. Shymshel indeed possesses that position, which all of us are used to regarding as high, and esteem, and which arouses even a certain gratitude, since he is . . . I will truly surprise you, readers, when I say that Shymshel is — a scholar.

This information is not in the least contradicted by my previous assertion that the circle of things and phenomena known to Shymshel is extremely limited, if you should care to exclude at this moment from your memory and imagination all academies, universities, and institutions of higher learning that hand out diplomas to their students for erudition in branches of knowledge that you know at least by name. The scholarly institutions from which Shymshel derived his knowledge are called *talmudor, yeshivoth,* and *bet-ha-midrash.* They have grades the same as any elementary school, gymnasium, and academy. Not all Jews pass those grades. There are those who, because of a lack of talent, or will, remain in the first or second. Shymshel was not held back and graduated from them all. What is more, after reaching the first of these grades at the age of ten, the second at thirteen, and the third at eighteen, and then getting married in his eighteenth year, he still did not stop studying. He continued going to the bet-midrash and studying; entire evenings and nights he used to sit in his cottage at a table near the window and — study.

What, in fact, did he study? His religion, its history, its immensely numerous and subtle shades of meaning, the metaphysics contained in it and the fables, parables, axioms, and legends with which it is adorned. A large part of these — would you believe it? — can perhaps be compared to the pearls and flowers of human thought. Shymshel is then — how to say it? — a theologian, a metaphysician, and in part also a historian, that part, that is, which specifically and directly deals with the history of the Jewish people and its faith. Beyond this sphere of knowledge, in which he achieved a very high degree of fluency, he knows nothing, absolutely nothing, and apart from the action of continuously exercising his specialty he does nothing, absolutely nothing. The absolute immersion in a specialty quite far removed from the needs and demands of daily life would lead the daily life of Shymshel and his five children into inextricable difficulties had he not, at the age

---

2. A *talmudor* was a Jewish school devoted primarily to the study of the Talmud.

of eighteen, married the sixteen-year-old Tsipa. She was a clerk in a big grocery store and was familiar with business and its tricks. When she became the wife of a scholar (thanks to the matchmaking of the shopkeeper's wife), she felt so happy and honored by this marriage that to the person who bestowed this splendid fate on her she gave herself body and soul, with a tender and shy love, with deep respect and an indefatigable desire for boundless self-sacrifice. . . .

Shymshel and Tsipa thus married with a joint capital of thirty rubles. Besides that, Tsipa still had her trousseau consisting of three shirts, two feather beds, two dresses, and one quilted caftan.

They had nothing else besides these things at the time they married, yet they have been living together for twelve years. . . . In time they had nine children of whom four died and five lived. Certainly another five will be born of which three will die and two will be brought up, but nevertheless will live. It doubtless seems strange to you, and perhaps improbable, that such a family, blessed with such abundance — especially numerical — could live on a capital of thirty rubles. I myself was tremendously surprised until I got to know Tsipa better.

In appearance she is a small Jewess, utterly, as they say, simple. At the age of twenty-eight, she looks forty or more. Short, stooped, with shoulders on which her quilted caftan hunches up and shines less from the quality of the material than from old age, she threads her way through a crowd with a small, hurried, yet timid and somehow creeping step.

She seems eternally distracted by something, stunned, bewildered; only her dark eyes move very rapidly in her swarthy, withered face and frequently cast very lively glances. These glances betray a constant and rapid searching for something, and often a restless, alert, and passionate desire. It also sometimes happens that Tsipa's eyes assume a malicious look and then accord perfectly with her low brow, which is covered from her thick eyebrows to the very edge of a black wig by a countless number of small wrinkles.

Please refrain from making fun of this small, simple Jewess, who is neither aesthetic nor intelligent looking. She has accomplished a certain, quite important thing; she has resolved in practice a certain social question that the entire world has acknowledged to be exceptionally difficult to resolve, namely, the question of the equality of women with respect to earning a living. Tsipa has carried the resolution of the question to an ideal in view of the fact that for twelve years her earnings have supported herself, her husband, and five children, and that in all her endeavors to achieve that goal she has relied on capital amounting to thirty rubles.

With these thirty rubles, representing the foundation of her family life, Tsipa opened a grocery shop; additionally, she has been promised credit in an equal amount in the store in which she previously fulfilled the functions of a salesgirl. The most important task of any enterprise that wants to earn money is to find customers. From the very first day she opened her store, Tsipa began looking for customers and to this day keeps on looking for them, not because she was unable to find any, but because she loses them as soon as she finds them and then has to look for new ones. This loss occurs for different reasons, among which not the smallest role is played by certain secret activities to which Tsipa devotes herself evenings, after the store is closed, in a narrow corner of the store between a closet, the counter, and the wall. At such times an odd rustling emanates from the corner, as if something is being unstuck and then stuck back, emptied out and poured in.

Although these activities, to which the proprietess of the shop devotes herself at this hour, may appear mysterious in the dim light of the lamp that burns on the floor behind the counter, it would be an exaggeration to ascribe a tragic significance to them. Tsipa does not belong to any kind of Jewish plot to the detriment or for the destruction of the Christian population. She is not preparing in privacy and secret any injurious activity against her meropia, for I hasten to assure you that she does not possess any meropia of her own, and I even doubt that she ever in her whole life heard the sound of that word. She acts entirely on her own, without any solidarity with the rest of her people.

Her meropia is a collective entity bearing the name of—the buying public. The mighty authorities who compel her to those different emptyings and pourings by which she mixes good quality goods with poor ones, and even dreadful ones, are her learned husband, five children, and thirty rubles capital invested in the enterprise. Tsipa's meropia—the buying public—possesses, it seems, taste and a refined sense of smell, since its members, having barely made the acquaintance of her goods, cease to acquire them (alas, after many just complaints, shouts, and rebukes), so that searching out ever new clientele becomes for Tsipa a goal of unceasing effort and exertion. She puts herself out and curries favor in all sorts of ways: moanful petitions, kissing hands, giving everyone whatever they want, doing whatever services they require. In order to make herself useful to the public and earn an extra grosz from time to time, she has become a jack-of-all-trades: a public messenger, a letter-carrier, a procurer of servants, an intermediary between borrowers and lenders, sellers and buyers. She works in the store in fits and starts; her mother substitutes for her, or one of her sisters, or some neighbor. She herself spends entire days running from steps to steps; carrying heavy packages under her arm; hauling piles of old clothes on her shoulders; standing humbly on different threshholds with two baskets in her hands, one containing dried fruits, the other tea and bottles of wine; arguing with cooks and caretakers of houses who do not want to admit her to her benefactors; bribing her way around their rudeness with a pair of figs or a handful of nuts. Sometimes she becomes impatient with members of her own sex who create burdensome competition for her, and she conducts such arguments with them on the street that the guardians of the public order approach her and shake their fists at her to get her to quit the scene of battle. Once even, a good-sized piece of what used to be the velvet collar adorning her quilted caftan remained in the hands of these rough representatives of a great idea. . . .

There are those who have a somewhat better idea of Tsipa's domestic circumstances, and when they see her dark, wrinkled face, often damp from perspiration and exhaustion, and agitated by involuntary nervous tremors, they say to her: "What does that husband of yours do his whole life?"

At such moments the look of oppression disappears from Tsipa's face and is replaced by something akin to anger. "He has his own work," she replies gruffly, "he can't help me in the business."

"Then you are very unfortunate, Tsipa, to have such a useless husband."

When she heard this, Tsipa raised her head. "If I had ten daughters, I'd ask God to give them the happiness I have."

At these words her eyes sparkled and laughed; an almost tearful smile encircled her withered lips, and a flush of emotion or embarrassment overflowed her wrinkled brow to the very edge of her black wig.

Ha! Whoever could get Shymshel to help Tsipa would bring off a small miracle! In the early years of her marriage, before she knew the full extent of her husband's learning, Tsipa used to leave him in their little store to look after and sell the merchandise in her absence. Look after — indeed he did, and very conscientiously, for he sat like an unmovable rock behind the counter holding his head in both hands and pondering the question of how two contradictory assertions of Rabbi Gamaliel[3] and Rabbi Eliezer[4] in the Mishna could be reconciled, or what conclusions could be drawn from a certain statement by Rabbi Papa[5] from which a hundred and ten conclusions had already been drawn by various commentators. Shymshel, after all, was trying to draw the one hundred and eleventh conclusion from it, and while meditating on it looked after the little store entrusted to him without any unpleasantness or hindrance. But when it came to the second part of the work assigned him, that is to selling something, the matter became exceptionally difficult by virtue of the fact that conversation was to no avail since Shymshel had absolutely no grasp of the language in which buyers spoke to him.

[In conjunction with the coming Purim holiday, some of the Jews decide to stage a play about the events celebrated in the holiday, and to offer the part of Samson to Shymshel.]

Decided . . . what? Have we guessed? They have decided something! What could they have decided? Naturally something that is to undermine or painfully wound the Christian world, as the pamphlet would have us believe conclusively. I vow that it was written by a man of great wisdom but adapted to the Polish language by a man of still greater wisdom. It is called: *The Conquest of the World by the Jews.*[6] They (such a militant nation!) desire, and try, to conquer the world, and now they must have decided something leading to this goal.

3. The second-century Jerusalem patriarch who wrote commentary on the Mishna.

4. A teacher in a Jewish religious school in Jerusalem in the second century who also commented on the Mishna.

5. A Babylonian teacher of law in the fourth century and a commentator on the Mishna.

6. A reference to an actual anti-Semitic treatise, which appeared in Lwów in 1876 under the title *The Conquest of the World by the Jews. Demonstrated on the Basis of History and Contemporaneity by Major Osman Bey.*

So Yosel, the furrier, says that he and his companions have decided on the day of Purim . . . to give a play.

Is that all?

Just so. . . . To give a play for the benefit of the poor.

You don't mean it!

I do indeed.

Having thus decided to give a play for the benefit of the poor on Purim, they took it into their heads to ask Rebbe Shymshel if he would like to join their company.

Rebbe Shymshel has a very lovely singing voice; no one sings a lead role better than he does. . . .

What play do they intend to perform? They are going to do a play entitled "Mighty Samson," which Rebbe Shymshel surely knows (what does the wisdom of Rebbe Shymshel not know?) and which contains such pretty songs and pretty views! . . .

Of course, Shymshel will be Samson, just as Moishe will be Moses, Yosel Joshua, Itsek Isaac, and so on. You never imagined, dear reader, how names of splendid and universally esteemed memory are hidden behind names so modest that they are universally ridiculed! You often laughed at Moishe, Itsek, and Shymshel without knowing that you were dealing with Moses, Isaac, and Samson. . . . If you restrained from laughing a while, you would perhaps discover many other, similarly new, and quite engaging things. But laughter . . . If I were asked, like Aesop, what is the best thing on earth and at the same time the worst, I would answer — laughter.

Shymshel, or Samson, reflected a long time on the proposition made him. What was in fact expected of him was not meditation and not contemplation, but action, hence something with which Shymshel previously did not have the slightest relations.

Action terrified him. It was so difficult for him to walk, to move, to exert himself, in short — to act. Besides, would not such a frivolous thing as performing in a play undermine his seriousness and lower his dignity?

He thought about it a long time, then rose and said: "If the cantor says that I have such a nice singing voice, and if Rabbi Boruch asks me to do it, and if it is for the benefit of the poor, then I agree to take part in it."

The entire company was greatly pleased at the news that Shymshel himself was joining them.

Were Shymshel not a Jew, he would say, and he would have a right to do so, "I myself am poor"; but because he was a Jew he did not have the right to say that, and he did not. After all, his wife owned a business based on a capital of thirty rubles, every day she cooked barley soup with potatoes, and on Fridays and Saturdays she even bought a pound of meat or fish, which, I am sure you will agree, dear reader, was quite sufficient for a family consisting of seven people.

Possessing, therefore, all these conditions of life, Shymshel neither thought about the fact that he was poor or that performing in a play might somehow be to his advantage as well. . . .

One thing was certain: this day began a new era in the life of . . . Tsipa. In the weeks following Shymshel's joining the company, she experienced inexpressible pleasure and pride flowing in her bosom like a stream of honey!

Shymshel somewhat changed his sedentary ways, and frequently leaving his cottage for entire mornings, spent time at the cantor's where he practiced the art of singing, which, all joking aside, he possessed to a quite high degree even before. Evenings, therefore, the troupe of amateur actors gathered at his cottage in full force.

With that gracious pride peculiar to people occupying high position, Shymshel asked his temporary colleagues to do him this honor, and they acceded to his request with pleasure as well as a certain satisfaction of self-love. It is pleasant to be able to spend time daily with someone infinitely higher than ourselves. The tinsmith, the furrier, and the sign painter felt themselves honored by the possibility of a daily visit to the home of a learned man; but since they were occupied with low, coarse work, which of its nature consumed twelve, fourteen, or sixteen hours a day, the only time they could come was late in the evening.

When they arrived, the little cottage became as hot as a well-heated stove. They were suffocating, and when Shymshel noticed it he set a good example by removing his gaberdine and sitting on a table by the window in his waistcoat and white (not snow white) sleeves. When the guests saw that, they said "With your permission," also removed their gaberdines, and sat down wherever they found a place: on a trunk, on rickety chairs, and on the ground. This last position fell to the sixteen-year-old Meier, who was to play the part of Delilah, and to whom also, as the youngest member of the company, it was forbidden to remove the gray frock coat covering him (with the exception of his elbows, which it never covered).

The entire picture was composed in such a way that Shymshel, who sat on the table, prevailed over the whole group among whom the most prominent to stand out were the Philistine emperor, otherwise known as the sign painter, whose face and hands were stained red and blue, and the round face of Delilah, otherwise known as Meier, which was crimson from the heat and embarrassment like a peony and later shone as if sprinkled with dew. When all had seated themselves as best they could, they began the rehearsal, or singing in chorus and then solo, animated and directed by the furrier who stood to the rear and conducted with both hands, frequently prodding little Meier who doubtless out of shyness occasionally missed his cue. . . .

Purim! Purim! I do not know how many thousands of years ago the cruel Haman, the minister of King Ahasuerus, conceived a plan to crush the entire Israelite people. But they were saved by the wisdom of Mordechai and the beauty and goodness of Queen Esther. Haman was hanged, and the Israelites, saved from destruction, to this very day celebrate the anniversary of their rescue with such joy as if it were not the two thousandth or so, but the first or second, and in memory of the hanging of Haman bake cakes of special shape known as *hamantashen.*

Purim! Purim! All the Israelites of the town of Ongród were drawn into a whirlpool of extraordinary joy and happiness. From the elders to the children, from the well-to-do to the indigent, all rejoiced. (Only the Rothschilds and those other bankers doubtless no longer rejoice!) In every house, big and small, long, touching conversations take place on this day about the beautiful and good, oh how good, Queen Esther! Everywhere they bless her name and the name of the wise Mordechai. Fortunate people, this Mordechai and this Esther! In the bowels of the earth, their ashes have disappeared to the very last atom, yet their memory is still venerated today by millions of hearts, and what hearts at that—hearts that are unable to comprehend or feel anything tender, noble, or grand. These hearts—lowly, selfish, ungrateful—celebrate the holidays of their benefactors and saviors with joy, affection, and tender gratitude for the two thousandth something time. Oh, lowly, selfish, ungrateful hearts, let Esther and Mordechai attest that there is in you an inexhaustible supply of tenderness and gratitude!

Shymshel rejoiced with everyone else and for the entire day blessed Esther and Mordechai; but his joy was somewhat troubled by the feeling of abject fear he was experiencing not with respect to the public before which he was to appear, but because of the magnitude and importance of the task he had accepted. It was as if by presenting such a great man as Samson to people, he was in some way denigrating the memory of this man and thereby burdening his conscience with grave sin. No, he had to be handsome, great, powerful, the way Samson himself was! He even felt that waves of feelings never previously experienced were now gathering in his chest, that some powerful desires, akin to yearning, indeterminate sorrows and joys, were swelling his heart, which, as the evening approached, beat faster and faster, and kept growing and growing, as if constantly expanding. Throughout that entire day, he said nothing to Tsipa; he wanted to speak, but he could not. And Tsipa wept.

How could she help but weep since she could not be in the theater and see her husband appearing on the stage. She had been engaged for that entire evening by a certain lady who absolutely needed her services. Moreover, she had to mind the shop at a time when for sure no one would want to replace her. And so Tsipa wept as she ran as usual here and there through the streets of the town or sat behind the counter helpless and sad. . . . [Shortly thereafter, Shymshel goes to the theater where he will perform in the Purim play.]

At that moment Shymshel entered. Silence enveloped the dressing room, a sign of respect. Shymshel did not interrupt it with a single word. He approached the table upon which his theatrical costume was laid out, and he began to put it on with the kind of solemn look on his face and the same concentration of spirit with which he usually donned his *tallith* and *tefilah* before praying.

It was already time for the actors to finish their makeup. The hall was bubbling with the impatience of the spectators gathered in it.

What hall? Where was it? How did the company of actors acquire it for that evening's performance? That would take long to tell! There had been no small amount of trouble and torment connected with it. In the end, however, it existed. A large, cavern-like corridor led to it from the street. In the dark and misty depths of this corridor, a buffet, illuminated by a tallow candle, had been set up bearing an impressive abundance of sticky and mildly alluring sweets, *makagigi*,[7] slightly spoiled apples, and so on.

Crowds flowed along this cavern until they flowed into a very narrow and exceptionally long hall, with a floor covered, for the convenience of the spectators, with blocks of wood arranged in a sloping manner. As these blocks had rounded tops, it would be difficult to imagine standing on them comfortably. Were someone so inclined, he could also find something to complain about with respect to the illumination; it had been arranged in such a way that it lighted only one wall and several benches standing closest to the stage and reserved for the higher social spheres, while leaving the rest of the hall in darkness as gloomy as despair.

There was no orchestra (although the piece chosen for performance was an opera), but in the place usually occupied by an orchestra stood an armchair on which sat Yosel the furrier. He sat in it with his face turned not toward the stage, but toward the public. On this occasion, he had to direct not the actors, but the audience. The actors, who knew their roles perfectly, especially with the help and supervision of Moishe (the Philistine emperor), could take care of themselves splendidly. But the public was a tempestuous and insubordinate element.

In order, therefore, to control the frequently irregular movements of the audience, Yosel the director took a seat in the place customarily reserved for the orchestra.

And now the people standing on the rounded blocks of wood begin to stir and murmur with obvious impatience. . . . A minute more, and they would explode in a deafening roar. But then a curtain rose up behind the broad shoulders of Yosel. . . . The loud murmuring quieted down, and amid this grave-like silence the protracted, menacing roar of a lion, repeated several times, resounded.

The stage represented a desert.

Some palm trees appeared in the distance against a foggy background. An oasis, for sure, and from this oasis emerged a lion of powerful proportions, nut colored, and with flashing eyes. The king of the desert did not emit that frightful bellowing for nothing. He had a keen sense of smell and obviously sniffed a man approaching.

And here was that man. He entered, like the lion, from between the palm trees, only from the opposite side. We can imagine that it was Samson. But could it be

7. A confection made of nuts and honey.

Shymshel? What a metamorphosis! Tsipa herself, had she been there, would not have recognized her husband. He seemd taller, more manly; his costume, which he himself had designed, did not lack brilliance and authority. It consisted of a scarlet gown glittering with gold embroidery and a white, pleated cloak onto which cascaded a forest of hair black as night and extending in length to the waist. Samson's entire chest was covered with a diamond necklace and on his head he wore a gilded helmet with a huge plume adorned with diamonds.

I cannot conceal from you, dear reader, the fact that all the gold was false, and the diamonds merely spangles and beads. But there was nothing false in the countenance of Samson; the gravity and courage etched in it were as pure as could be. Clearly, the actor had so completely absorbed the role that he identified with the figure he had to represent.

Bold and sure of his strength, he approached the king of the desert; his flashing gaze was met with a calm, even mildly scornful look. Astonished at this audacity, the king of the desert arose and stood on his rear paws (Moishe, who was squatting behind the curtain, pulled a string wound around the rear paws of the king of the desert). He let out a protracted, terrible roar (what powerful lungs sign painters sometimes have) at which, when hearing it, the audience became terrified and did not dare breathe. But nothing frightened Samson. With a single leap he bounded across the stage, and before the great outcry of terror that the dread of the situation wrenched from the bosom of the audience had died down, he tore the king of the desert into two more or less equal halves.

"Bravo, bravo, bravo!" cried out the higher spheres seated on the benches, while from the darkness in which the ordinary spheres were sunk voices full of joy and triumph were heard, and they were so tumultuous that Yosel the furrier got up from his place and waving both arms toward the darkness, shouted: "*Shtill!*"[8]

The darkness fell silent, and Samson, standing on the edge of the stage, exhibited to the spectators a honeycomb found in the maw of the lion, of that unfortunate lion the two halves of which were lying at a distance from each other, its eyes, in death as in life, flashing frightfully.

As he showed the spectators the honeycomb, Samson's entire face wore an expression not merely of honey, but of a divine sweetness. Ripping the lion apart must truly have been an astonishing surprise for Shymshel who until then had no presentiment of such strength. It was obvious that his chest was filled with a great joy that expressed itself in a forceful breath and from which a song of pride and joy soon erupted. His voice was a beautiful, broad, and rather well-developed tenor.

Despite the not entirely perfect acoustics, the sounds of his voice filled the hall from one end to the other, and were so entrancing and pure, and flowed in so full and overflowing a stream, that even the higher spheres listened to them with

8. "Quiet," in Yiddish.

genuine pleasure; and as concerns the ordinary spheres, sunk in darkness, they erupted in such enthusiasm after the curtain descended that Yosel the director had to work long and arduously to impose some control over the movement of the public, which threatened all rules of order with utter destruction.

The second scene did not differ appreciably from the first in content, but its form was entirely different. We beheld a field grown over with wheat. At least fifty bales of straw were standing at a neat and orderly distance from each other. Samson was standing over the grain and singing. From his song we learned that these fields belonged to the Philistines, and that he intended to destroy them. Hardly did he finish singing his aria, which was swollen with fierce hatred toward the Philistines, when red foxes began running through the grain with the speed of lightning (this time not only Moishe, but his confidant, Itsek, and one of his men pulled certain strings known only to them).

Behind the foxes shone blue and purple will-o'-the-wisps that burned for a rather long time until they died out and filled the stage, as well as the entire hall, with thick smoke and the strong odor of sulfur.

The higher spheres, sitting closer to the fire and the sulfurous smoke emanating from it, withheld all applause on this occasion, as they were choking loudly and for a long time. But great joy reigned in the darkness, and this time Yosel the director did not subdue its manifestations, since he too was choking and coughing persistently into a red handkerchief.

The choking and coughing on one side and the fervent signs of satisfaction on the other lasted until the curtain went up again and the view of the stage inclined all to silence and attention. This time, despite certain insufficiencies in the scenic and decorative resources, the stage decor seemed engaging and picturesque even to the higher spheres occupying the benches and could have been so acknowledged even by spheres much higher than these.

At the feet of the palm trees, hence at the back of the stage, sat three Judean elders huddled close together. They were lamenting the misfortunes of their country brought on by the fierce vengeance wreaked by the ruler of the Philistines for the destruction of the Philistine fields by Samson's fire-bearing foxes. . . .

Their voices were trembling and exquisitely conveyed the patriotic anxiety and pain gripping their hearts. The words of their song informed us that the Philistine monarch demanded, as an indispensable condition of peace with the Israelite people, that "mighty Samson" be restrained and handed over to him. The Judean elders resolved to demand of Samson that he make this sacrifice and, as ransom for his endangered and severely distressed fatherland, voluntarily surrender himself to the hands of the enemy. They determined to go to him and implore him to do it, when he suddenly appeared. . . .

Shymshel, who from the time he became Samson, experienced the intoxication of pride and conquests, now felt himself gripped by fear and deep sorrow! But on the other hand, the sense of obligation and love for his native land strongly tugged at his heartstrings. Observe, dear reader, how his face changes! What deathly pallor covers his brow and cheeks! How his eyes belch forth fire of passion and despair and again are covered with the moisture of boundless pity!

Bravo! Bravo!

We were not beholding a simple actor, but a true artist who down to the smallest fiber of his being at that moment felt himself to be a man of powerful arms and a volcanic soul. He struggled for a long time . . . then suddenly extended both his hands to the Judean elders and emitted a great cry from his chest: "Bind me!"

This cry reverberated throughout the hall with the sound of immeasurable pain and lofty heroism. The Judean elders wept as they bound the arms and legs of the hero; the higher spheres here and there had tears in their eyes; from the depths of the distant darkness groaning and sobbing were audible, but Yosel the director no longer paid them any attention, since he too was weeping into a red kerchief held to his face. . . .

The curtain fell. A silence of deadly awe fell upon the auditorium, and only sobs could be heard in the darkness.

These compassionate souls were right to shed tears. Dressed in theatrical costume, Samson sat on the bench where the Philistines had placed him. He was deadly pale, breathing heavily, and with his eyes closed.

"Rebbe," Moishe spoke to him, "look at the palace which you are to topple on the stage. . . . Maybe it is too heavy for you. . . . We can make it smaller. . . ."

But only a hollow moan rattled in Shymshel's chest.

"My enemies have taken the light from my eyes," he whispered painfully. "I am blind and my eyes will never see the great works of the Eternal."

"*Hörste!*" the Philistines said to each other as they exchanged surprised glances.[9] "He thinks that we have really gouged out his eyes."

Suddenly Delilah moved through the dressing-room. Shymshel heard the rustle of her dress and raised his eyelids. His eyes hurled bolts of anger and despair; a dark flush spread over his pale face.

"What have you done to me? What have you done to me? You have destroyed me! I have lost my eyes through your great cunning; I have fallen into captivity and am destroyed!"

Shouting these words with increasing violence and force, he clenched his fists and rushed toward Delilah, who dropped her pink fan in fear and ran into the farthest corner of the dressing room where she hid behind a long flowered robe of one of the Judean Elders. Moishe also shielded her with his broad shoulders, and not daring to lift his hand to the learned man, stretched both his hands in front of him and called in a persuasive voice: "Rebbe! Ay, ay, Rebbe!" . . .

*   *   *

9. "You hear?" in Yiddish.

After the performance, the actors did not remove their theatrical costumes; on the contrary, they complemented them with various amusing additions. And since they were a bit tired, they drank a few bottles of honey wine in the dressing room and began singing in chorus a well-known, merry song. They continued their singing as they went out onto the streets of the town heading for the homes of the well-to-do merchants and the wealthy owners of town buildings. Lavish and hospitable receptions awaited them there; there they would dance, sing, and make merry through the entire night, and more than a single silver coin, even more than a single ruble note would fall into their hands and from their hands would pass the next day into the cash book of the poor, which the performance itself provided for abundantly and for a long time to come.

But among this merry and noisy troupe, which with outbursts of song and laughter now entered the quite wide steps leading to the dwelling of the merchant Rosendorf, Shymshel was absent. . . .

Having smashed the Philistines and himself beneath the overthrown palace walls, Shymshel arose from the dead, regained his sight, forgot all past humiliations and anguish. But not for a single second did he stop being "mighty Samson." No indeed; walking from one street to another, between the brick walls with windows now entirely dark or barely lit here and there, he ran in his mind through all the great deeds he had performed and he was filled with joy and pride.

Now and again the memory of the deceitful, unfaithful Delilah flashed in his memory. At such times a sort of melancholy, a sorrow, constricted his heart. But then he recalled his native Judea, which he had saved from blood, tears, and conflagration; he raised his head high, smiled, and sang more loudly and rapturously, and he strode across the uneven pavement of the dark street as if through laurels.

Shymshel thus crossed the boulevard and entered the alley. Mechanically, from habit, he made for his dwelling, and without thinking of what he was doing, singing all the while, he reached for the handle of the low door and stood on the threshhold of his cottage. He stopped, and for a few minutes stood as if rooted to the spot. Inside the cottage, on the table near the window, the lamp was burning; from its long neck a yellowish, smelly smoke drifted upward. Then the low, gray walls, the beds with their feather coverings, the old clothing strewn all around the ground and the trunk, torn and dirty, a few larger and smaller human figures, lying asleep here and there, created a chaos that was at first glance completely unintelligible both to his eyes and mind. But after a few minutes, he understood it, and awoke.

The marvelous, intoxicating dream took flight from him, and he comprehended that he was not Samson, that powerful athlete and poetic hero of the Bible, but Shymshel, the son of Gershon, a learned man of the present, who spent his past and would spend his entire future in this cramped, drab little cottage, over this book, which even now, as if surprised at the neglect in which it had been abandoned, lay open on the table with its long lines of verse writhing in the form of a serpent beneath the light of the lamp.

A strange thing! As he gazed at the book, an expression of distaste, almost of disgust, spread over Shymshel's pale face. He turned his eyes away from it, and slowly advancing a few steps, he sat down on the chair by the table. It was obvious that he was no longer able to look at the book, as he constantly averted his reluctant and sad gaze from it. A deep furrow arose between his eyebrows and cast over his entire face an expression of gloomy, almost angry, musing.

He had tasted a life of action, of sacrifice, of a tormenting yet at the same time exhilarating series of hardships and joys, defeats and triumphs. But it had all been just a dream, and now it was time for him to return to the yellowed, dead pages, to the eternally sitting, half-dead position, to infinite meditations, subtle distinctions, laborious studies.

"But what do I, what do people in general get out of all of this?"

He thought about people. . . . And what would he do now with that passionate, touching love for people that burned on the theatrical boards in the powerful bosom of Samson and remained behind in the weak chest of Shymshel. He felt strongly that it remained forever! How would he show it? How would he use it? With what deeds would he be able to pacify its burning desires? And what would become of the presentiment of that other love incited by the flaming eye and lithe waist of the Delilah-apparition; with the presentiment of that ardent and touching love that inhabited the great heart of Samson and now embraces the still-cramped heart of Shymshel, filling it with tears and sighs of unspeakable melancholy. . . .

Ideals! Shymshel did not know their name, but once they flew beneath his gaze, they bound his heart to them. Ideals of action, love, and glory flew beneath his gaze. . . . Oh! Where did the old, solitary ideal of his dry, subtle, and barren learning disappear; why did it become so small, like a grain of sand? Perhaps in the chest and head of this Jew, with his slender, nervous body, refined features, deep-set eyes, and thin lips, which trembled from every expression like a delicate leaf from a breath of wind? Or in the head and chest of this Jew, whose habit it was to cover the faces of his children with fervent kisses, and who, on dark nights, had angelic visions and perceived the existence of unknown, uncultivated layers of those feelings, imagination, and talents which, when they are known and cultivated, make a man capable of loving ideals and reaching for them with a strong, inspired arm?

. He lowered his head and examined his dress from top to bottom. A strange smile curled about his lips. Samson's white cloak fell about his knees and feet in soft folds; the scarlet robe radiated a golden luster; in the light of the lamp, the beads of his necklace covered his chest with the sparkle of rubies, emeralds, and silver; and on his forehead he felt the soft touch of the crest that hung from the knight's helmet. He smiled strangely, for a long while, until he lifted his arms and slowly removed the golden helmet with the crest from his head. He placed it on the table and gazed at it with flaming eyes from which after a while two large tears rolled down his pallid cheeks.

"Farewell, mighty Samson, great man, who taught me that there are heroic deeds in this world, a great love toward people, beautiful Delilahs, and . . . small, weak, unhappy Shymshels."

He learned that he had never been great, or wise, or happy . . . and he wrung his hands with such force that the bones cracked in their joints, and then he placed them on the back of his neck and began to unclasp his necklace of rubies, emeralds, and silver. He unfastened it, took it off, and held it before him in both hands. From beyond that net of shining strings gleamed his black eyes, brimming once more with large tears.

"Farewell, mighty Samson, great man!" . . .

■ Eliza Orzeszkowa
Meir Ezofowicz (1878)

[In *Meir Ezofowicz,* a minutely detailed picture of a Jewish shtetl, Eliza Orzeszkowa con-
trasts liberal and conservative traditions within the Jewish community and the attempt of
her titular hero to break free of the fetters of obscurantism and intolerance. Meir Ezofowicz, the young descendant of an ancient family proud of its enlightened, humanistic
traditions, is declared a heretic and expelled from the town of Szybów because of his
unwillingness to submit to the authority of the Cabalist rabbi Isaac Todros, himself the
descendant of an equally ancient family of Spanish Jews known for their asceticism and
fanaticism. Following his banishment, and the murder of his Karaite girlfriend, Golda, at
the hands of a band of Rabbi Todros's followers, Meir leaves Szybów to make his way alone
in an alien world. *Meir Ezofowicz* is Orzeszkowa's best-known novel outside Poland after
Marta. Its impressive knowledge of Jewish customs, beliefs, and learning—including the
prejudice against the Karaite sect—as well as its evident compassion, offsets its prolixity
and psychological shallowness.]

Far from the branch of the railway that cuts through the Belorussian regions, and
from the navigable river Dźwina that courses through them, in one of the re-
motest corners of Europe, in the midst of a vast, silent plain, at the conjunction
of two wide, sandy roads, which in the distance lose themselves in the depths of
a dark forest, lies a little town of several hundred houses. . . . The name of the
town is Szybów, and its population is mostly Israelite, with the exception of one
small street on the outskirts inhabited by very poor Gentile townspeople and
very quiet, old pensioners. It is the only street that is tranquil and where modest flowers bloom in summer. No flowers are to be found in any other part of the
town, and there is a constant hubbub. People are continually chattering and bustling about, either inside their houses, or in the narrow, dirty lanes that pass for
streets, or in the round, wide market square in the center of the town onto which
open the small, low doors of foul-smelling stalls. . . .

The importance attached to the town of Szybów by the Israelite population of
the Belorussian lands, and even beyond, in the broad expanses of Lithuania, may
be ascertained from a rather vexing occurrence that befell a certain nobleman,
who was more jovial than wise, in conversation with a certain humble Jewish
middleman, who was more jovial than humble. The Jew was standing at the door

Eliza Orzeszkowa, *Meir Ezofowicz* (Warsaw: Czytelnik, 1973), 9–25, 37–39, 57–65, 108–11, 114–15, 301–
9, 368–73, 407–8. There are two existing English translations of the novel, both weak, and with
unmarked textual abridgments: Eliza Orzeszko, *Meir Ezofovitch,* trans. Iza Young (New York: W. L.
Allison, 1898), and Eliza Orszeszkowa, *The Forsaken, or Meir Ezofowich,* trans. Edward Königsberger
(Bournemouth, U.K.: Delamare Publishing, 1980). Although the Königsberger translation is the better
of the two, it is also the most abridged.

of the nobleman's study, leaning somewhat in the direction of the latter's face; he was smiling, and was ready to be of service at a moment's notice or to utter a clever word in order to put the nobleman in a good mood.

The nobleman was in good humor and joked with the Jew: "Chaimek," he said, "have you ever been in Cracow?"

"No, m'lord, I haven't."

"Then you are quite ignorant, eh, Chaimek?"

Chaimek bowed.

"Chaimek, have you ever been in Rome?"

"No, m'lord, I haven't."

"Then you are quite ignorant, eh, Chaimek?"

The Jew bowed a second time, drawing a few steps closer to his master as he did so. About his lips played one of those shrewd, cunning smiles—typical of people of his race—about which one could never be certain if they expressed humility or secret triumph, flattery or mockery.

"I beg m'lord's pardon," he said softly, "but has m'lord ever been in Szybów?"

Szybów was some twenty miles distant from where the conversation took place.

"I've never been there," said the nobleman.

"So what now?" whispered Chaimek even softer.

The story remains silent as to what the jovial nobleman replied, but by using Szybów to repulse offensive statements, or rather to reciprocate in kind, it may be concluded that Chaimek regarded Szybów as of the same importance as Cracow and Rome to the nobleman, a center of civil and religious authority.

If Chaimek had been further questioned as to why he attached so much importance to the tiny little town in the middle of nowhere, he probably would have mentioned the names of two families that had lived for centuries in Szybów— Ezofowicz and Todros. The Ezofowiczes represented to a high degree a powerful element of secular glories, such as a large and well-connected family, wealth, skill at making profit and increasing their fortune. The Todroses, on the other hand, were the representatives of the spiritual element: piety, religious learning, and a purity of life so strict as to border on the ascetic. . . .

For centuries the Todros family had been regarded by the entire Israelite population of Belorussia and Lithuania as a perfect model and an inviolable ark of religious orthodoxy. Was this so in reality? Learned Talmudists here and there smiled somewhat strangely, and whispered sadly among themselves, at the mention of the talmudic orthodoxy of the Todroses. This famed orthodoxy gave the learned Talmudists a great deal to think about. But they represented a small number of doubters compared to the believing, worshiping masses, who descended on Szybów in droves, as if to some consecrated place, to render homage, to learn, and to seek counsel, comfort, and medicines.

Szybów had not always possessed such fame for its orthodoxy. Not at all.

Its founders were heretics, representatives in Israel of the spirit of opposition, Karaites. Once upon a time, very long ago, they had converted to their faith a powerful people inhabiting the land of Chersones,[1] which flowed with milk and honey, and they became its kings. Later, double outcasts from Palestine and the Crimea, they wandered the face of the earth with nothing but the memories of their past rule and with their one book of religion and law, the Bible. Invited by the Grand Duke Witold of Lithuania, a small number of them settled in his domain as far as Belorussia and there founded Szybów.

In those days a deadly quiet and darkness prevailed in the town on Friday and Saturday nights, since the Karaites, in opposition to the Talmudists, did not usher in the Sabbath with bright lights, loud merrymaking, and abundant feasts; instead, they greeted it in darkness, silence, sadness, and meditation on the fall of the Temple and national greatness. From the dark interiors of homesteads, from small, obscure windows, muffled, drawn out, melodious and plaintive sounds flowed forth. Fathers were telling their children about the prophets who smashed their harps above the rivers of Babylon and severed the fingers from their hands so as not to be forced to sing in captivity. . . .

A time came, however, when here and there on Friday evenings lights began to shine in the little windows of houses and the sound of spirited conversations and choral singing could be heard outside. The Rabbanites had arrived.[2] Worshipers of the Talmud, representatives of blind faith in the oral traditions, collected and transmitted by the *kohens, fanaits,* and *gaons,* they arrived in Szybów and drove out the heretics from their settlements. Under the influence of this invasion, the Karaite community slowly dissolved; the last blow was delivered by a man well known in the history of the Polish Israelites, Michał Ezofowicz, Senior.

This was the first Ezofowicz whose name emerged from the shadows of obscurity. His family, which had settled in Poland a very long time ago, was united with the local population by bonds of friendship thanks to the laws and customs of the Jagiellonian kings, which created in Poland an unusually high level of culture for those times. King Sigismund I gave him the title of Senior, or elder of all Jews living in Lithuania and Belorussia. . . . From the few references to him in history, the Senior must have been a man of strong will and energetic mind. He took the authority vested in him over his coreligionists into firm hands; those who refused to submit to him, such as the Karaites, he placed under a curse, thereby banning them from Israelite society and revoking their right to mutual assistance and friendship.

Under this blow, the sad and impoverished existence of the Karaites succumbed to its final dissolution. The descendants of the Khazar rulers, heretics,

---

1. The Greek name for the Crimea.
2. Followers of Maimonides (Moses ben Maimon, 1135–1204), the great Hebrew scholar, who is also known under the name Rambam, from the initials of the words Rabbi Moses ben Maimon.

Edward Gorazdowski (1843–1901). "Michael Ezofowicz Senior." Based on an illustration by Michał Elwiro Andriolli (1863–93) for Eliza Orzeszkowa's novel *Meir Ezofowicz*. Courtesy Muzeum Narodowe w Warszawie.

representing, as often happens, a minority in their society, to which they were objects of dislike and disdain, they left the town that had provided them temporary shelter, sustained only by their obstinate and exclusive attachment to the Bible and their poetic legends. They dispersed throughout the entire unfriendly world, leaving behind as the last traces of their two-hundred-year stay a drab collection of homesteads sprinkled over the Belorussian expanses and a few families who were fervently attached to the old graves and protected the bones of their fathers as well as the remains of the temple they had erected on a hillock that had been razed by the victorious Rabbanites.

The Rabbanites took complete possession of Szybów and, truth be told, with their drive, resourcefulness, and close cooperation with one another, transformed the shabby little town from a place of quiet, sadness, and poverty into one of bustling activity and wealth. For the most part, the Jews subject to the authority of the Senior made out well. Apart from material successes, the hope began arising among them that they would finally come out from under their intellectual darkness and social debasement. The Senior must have possessed a sharp, clear mind, for despite centuries of prejudice and superstition he could understand the spirit of the times and the needs of his people. It was certainly not out of religious fanaticism that he had expelled the Karaites from the womb of Israel, but to achieve purely administrative and broad social goals. Since he was, after all, a Rabbanite, he was obliged to honor and respect the religious authorities, but there were times when skepticism, this best and perhaps only road to wisdom, entered his mind. In one of his petitions to the king, in which he refuted charges brought against the fairness of his judicial decisions, he wrote sadly and somewhat ironically:

> Our books vary considerably in their commands, and we often do not know how to proceed when Gamaliel says one thing, and Eliezer another. There is one truth in Babylon, another in Jerusalem.[3] We heed the second Moses [Maimonides], whom some consider a heretic. I encourage the learned to write such wise things that the intelligent and simpleminded can both understand them.

During this same period a great controversy arose among the Jews of France and Spain as to whether worldly knowledge was prohibited or permitted to the believers in the Talmud and Bible. Opinions were for and against it, but could not long vacillate, since the partisans of the complete exclusion of Israel from intellectual works and the aspirations of human society constituted the overwhelming majority. Every society at one time or another experiences such a decline into darkness. . . . After several centuries of living in anxiety and wandering, in blood

---

3. A reference to the Babylonian and Jerusalem editions of the Talmud, which do not agree in all respects.

and fire, such a moment arrived for the Jews of the West in the sixteenth century. Long past were the days when famed doctors of worldly knowledge, beloved by the people, esteemed even by kings, had issued from their midst. Long past, and now forgotten and condemned, was also the great thought of Maimonides, who while granting the appropriate respect to the Israelite lawmakers also revered the Greek philosophers and endeavored to strengthen and consolidate biblical and talmudic scholarship on the basis of mathematical and astronomical truths. He openly confessed his desire to compress the two thousand five hundred pages of the Talmud into a single, clearly written volume. Rejecting unsound religious teachings without apology, he maintained that "the eyes of a man are placed at the front of the head, not the back, so that he can see ahead of him." And he preached that "the whole world will one day be filled with knowledge as the abysses of the seas are filled with water."

Four centuries passed from the time . . . the Israelite thinker disappeared from the surface of the earth. He was truly one of the greatest thinkers of the Middle Ages. A giant with the eye of an eagle and a burning heart had been succeeded by tired and embittered dwarfs, whose view of the world was blurred, narrow, and suspicious.

"Beware of Greek wisdom," exclaimed Joseph Ezobi to his son, "it is like the vineyards of Sodom that pour drunkenness and sin into the heads of men. When he heard of Jewish youth studying with gentile masters, Abba-Mazi exclaimed: "Alien people are entering the gates of Zion!" Then all the rabbis and elders issued a command henceforth prohibiting worldly knowledge to all under thirty years of age. "Only those who have enlightened their minds with the Bible and Talmud have the right to warm themselves at alien hearths." . . .

Similar controversies had also arisen in the same period among the Jews of Poland; but because they were less wearied by oppression than their brothers in the West, and because they lived in greater freedom and were more confident of their right to life and the future, they harbored less fervent loathing for "foreign tribes." On the contrary, a sizable faction among them clamored for secular learning and a brotherly relationship with the rest of mankind in intellectual efforts and aspirations. One of the people standing at the head of this faction was the Lithuanian Senior, Meir Ezofowicz. Mainly through his influence, the Jewish Synod issued the following proclamation to all Polish Jews:

> Jehovah has many Sefirot, and Adam various emanations of perfection. The Israelite must not rest satisfied with one kind of knowledge (the religious). The first should be holy learning, but that is no reason to neglect others. The apple of Paradise is the best of all fruit, but does that mean we must not eat the less tasty? . . . Jews were at the courts of kings, Mordechai was a sage, Esther, a wise woman, Nehemiah, a Persian councillor — and they brought their people out of bondage. Learn; be useful to the king and his lords, and

they will respect you. The Jews are as many as the stars in heaven and the sand in the sea; they do not shine like stars, yet everybody tramples them like the sand. . . . The wind carries the seed of different trees and no one asks whence comes the finest tree. Why should we not produce the cedar of Lebanon instead of blackthorns?

The man under whose influence this proclamation was written summoning the Polish Jews to turn their faces toward the light of the future, met face to face with another man whose eyes were fixed on the past and darkness. This was Nehemiah Todros, newly arrived from Spain, and a descendant of Todros Abulaffi Halevi who had been famous for his knowledge of the Talmud and his orthodoxy until he later let himself be carried away by the dark mysteries of the Cabala. Backing it with the dignity of his own person, he contributed significantly to the emergence among Jews of one of the worst errors to which the spirit of a nation can succumb. It is rumored that this same Nehemiah Todros, who bore the princely title of "nassi," introduced into Poland the book of Zohar, the quintessence of the pernicious doctrine, and that it was from that time on that studies of the Talmud and Cabala became mixed. This began to have an increasingly harmful effect on the minds and lives of the Polish Jews. History remains silent about the dissensions and conflicts brought on by this innovation among a people on the verge of emerging at last from the darkness that had so long enveloped them. But stories, piously passed from generation to generation, relate that in the struggle that was waged so long and fiercely between Michał Ezofowicz, a Jew of Polish descent, and Nehemiah Todros, the Spanish newcomer, the former was vanquished. Wracked by grief at the sight of his people being led astray, harried by intrigues hatched against him by his sullen opponent, he died in the prime of his life. His name was preserved in the Ezofowicz family from generation to generation. They were all proud of his memory, though with the passage of time they understood less and less its real importance. From that time on the great spiritual authority of the Todroses became unquestionable and the moral influence of the Ezofowiczes gradually diminished. The family, ousted from the field of broad social activity, now directed all their energies and talents to the accumulation of wealth. Their ships plied the navigable rivers, carrying huge supplies of all kinds of goods to faraway ports. Their house, which stood in the middle of the drab little town, more and more became a leading center of national finance and industry. . . . The Todroses, as poor as ever, continued to live in the wretched little hut near the temple; they despised everything that had the appearance of elegance, beauty, and even comfort, but they became renowned throughout the country and attracted to themselves the most pious sighs, the most burning dreams and longings of their people. And only once in the course of two centuries did one of the Ezofowiczes strive for moral as well as material leadership.

It was toward the end of the last century. In Warsaw, the great Four Years' Diet had assembled. Echoes of their deliberations reached as far as the obscure little town in Belorussia. The people living there pricked up their ears with interest, listened, and waited. News traveled from mouth to mouth that filled them with hope and anxiety: They were discussing the Jews!

"What are they saying about us? What are they writing about us?" These were the questions long-bearded Jews repeated to each other as they made their way along the narrow little streets of Szybów, dressed in their long gaberdines and their huge fur hats. The curiosity grew day by day to such an extent that it caused an unusual slowing of the usual financial and commercial traffic. Some even undertook the long and arduous journey to Warsaw, to be nearer the source of the news. Once there, they sent their brethren back in Belorussia long letters, crumpled and stained newspapers, and pages ripped from all kinds of pamphlets and books.

Among those who remained in town and listened for news most diligently and anxiously were two men: the Rabbi Nochim Todros, and Hersh Ezofowicz, the wealthy merchant. There was a silent, smouldering animosity between them. . . .

One day, a sheet of yellowed paper, crumpled from the long journey, arrived in Szybów from Warsaw. It contained the following words:

All differences of dress, language, and custom existing between Jews and the rest of the population are to be abolished. Everything concerning their religion to be respected. Even various sects to be tolerated provided they are not harmful to morals. No Jew to be admitted to baptism before he reaches the age of twenty. The right to acquire land to be permitted Jews; those desiring to take up agriculture to be freed from taxes for five years and provided with livestock. Marriage prohibited to men under twenty, and to women under eighteen years of age. . . .

The people of Szybów did not immediately express their opinion about what they read. One group, by far the smaller, looked with questioning eyes at Hersh Ezofowicz; the much larger one scrutinized the face of Rabbi Nochim Todros. Rabbi Nochim crossed the threshold of his hut, raised his thin arms high above his gray locks in a sign of danger and despair, and cried out several times: "A sybe! A sybe! Daige!"

"Misfortune! Misfortune! Sorrow!" repeated the crowd assembled in the courtyard of the synagogue that day. But at the same moment, Hersh Ezofowicz, who was standing at the very door of the house of worship, placed one white hand on the wide sash of his satin robe, ran the other across his dark-red beard, raised high his head covered with his costly beaver cap, and no less sonorously than the rabbi, but in an entirely different voice, exclaimed: "Ofenung! Ofenung! Frayd!"

"Hope! Hope! Joy!" repeated the small group of his friends in a more restrained voice, casting sidelong glances at the rabbi. But the old rabbi had keen hearing. He heard. His white beard trembled and his black eyes cast a fiery glance at Hersh.

"They will order us to shave our beards and shorten our garments," he called out sorrowfully and angrily.

"It will make our intelligence longer and our hearts wider," said the authoritative voice from the steps of the temple.

"They will harness us to plows and force us to till the land of our exile," shouted Reb Nochim.

"They will open the treasures of the earth before us and bid it be a homeland to us," said Hersh.

"They will not allow us to keep our kosher laws and will turn Israel into a nation of pork eaters."

"They will build schools for our children and will turn Israel into cedars of Lebanon from blackthorns."

"The faces of your sons will be covered with hair long before they will be allowed to take wives."

"When they get their wives their minds and arms will be stronger."

"We will be compelled to seek warmth from alien fires and to drink from the vineyards of Sodom."

"They will bring closer to us Jobel-ha-Gadol, the holiday of joy, when the lamb will lie down with the lion."

"Hersh Ezofowicz! Hersh Ezofowicz! Through your lips speaks the soul of your great-grandfather, who wanted to lead all the Jews into alien flames."

"Reb Nochim! Reb Nochim. Your eyes reflect the soul of your great-grandfather, who sank all the Jews in great darkness." . . .

Several thousand eyes darted from the face of one leader to the other; several thousand lips quivered, but — not a sound was uttered. Finally, the sharp, drawn-out shout of Reb Nochim pierced the air and reverberated through the temple courtyard:

"A sybe! A sybe! Daige!" the old man groaned, sobbing, his hands clasped above his head.

"Ofenung! Ofenung! Frayd!" exclaimed Hersh, raising a white hand and his voice full of joy.

The crowd remained silent and motionless for another moment, then their heads began moving closer together like waves rolling from side to side; their lips began murmuring like rippling water until suddenly several thousand hands were raised in a gesture of fear and pain and several thousand chests emitted a great cry in unison: "A sybe! A sybe! Daige!"

Reb Nochim Todros had won the day. . . .

Todros rejoiced and called upon all who believed in his wisdom and sanctity to rejoice with him. He had triumphed, but he wanted to triumph even more. Destroying the Ezofowiczes meant destroying a trend that aspired to the future and would fight with him who endeavored ceaselessly to transform the people into a petrification of the past. . . . Accusations, ill-will, and antagonism of every kind descended on Hersh Ezofowicz from all sides, as they had been brought centuries before against Michał Senior. It was loudly declared in the synagogue that he no longer observed the Sabbath; that he made friends with goyim; that he ate unclean meat with them at the same table; that in business disputes he avoided the Jewish courts and sought justice instead in those of the country; that he no longer submitted to the authority of the kahal and on more than one occasion even dared reproach them publicly; that he did not respect the zaddik or show Reb Nochim the proper esteem.

Hersh defended himself proudly, denying some of the accusations, admitting others, but justifying himself with arguments neither the people nor the elders were willing to accept. This lasted a long time, but finally stopped. The accusations died down and the intrigues faded away. So too did the person who was the object of all of them. . . . No one knew what he felt or thought about the last years of his life, for he confided in no one. He had a long talk just with Freyda before his death. His children were still too small for him to entrust them with the secret of his deceived hopes, vain efforts, and suppressed pain. He transmitted it to them through the lips of his wife. But did Freyda understand and remember the words of her dying husband? Did she want, and could she, repeat them to his descendants? No one knows. The only thing certain is that she knew the whereabouts of the hidden testament of the Senior, that eternal written heritage not only of the Ezofowiczes, but of the entire Israelite people, an unknown and disregarded heritage but one perhaps containing — who knows? — treasures a hundred times greater than those that filled the granaries and coffers of the wealthy merchant family.

The last wishes and thoughts of the Senior reposed thus in hiding, waiting anew the bold hand of a great-grandson thirsting for knowledge that would awaken them and bring them out into the open. Meanwhile, after Hersh's death . . . life in the little town grew dark from mystic fears and dreams, and oppressive and stifling from an implacable, petty, and soulless orthodoxy. . . .

[After breaking up an attack on the Karaite hut by a band of Orthodox boys, Meir Ezofowicz returns home late for the Sabbath.]

The young man did not join the family circle, but retired to the back of the room to recite the Sabbath prayers that he had missed that day. In doing so he did not make any movements of his body; he held his hands calmly crossed on his chest, his gaze fixed on the window beyond which hung the deep dark of evening. . . .

When the young man had finished his prayers, and approached the table to take his usual place, a hoarse voice . . . called out from amid the assembly: "Where have you been so long today, Meir? What were you doing in town so late, when the Sabbath had begun and nobody is permitted to do anything? Why didn't you

Edward Gorazdowski (1843–1901), "Sabbath" (1878). Based on an illustration by Michał El-wiro Andriolli (1863–93) for Eliza Orzeszkowa's novel *Meir Ezofowicz*. Courtesy Muzeum Narodowe w Warszawie.

celebrate Kiddush with the rest of your family? Why is your face pale and your eyes sad on a Sabbath, a happy day, when the whole heavenly family is rejoicing, and all pious people on earth are supposed to rejoice and keep their souls in great happiness?"

All this was uttered by a strange-looking man. He was a rather small, thin, dried-up creature, with a large head bristling with thick dark hair, a dark, round face endowed with a huge matted growth, and a great beard that betrayed a mortal aversion to combing and brushing. His round eyes moved from beneath protruding lids with incomparable speed, casting sharp glances all around. The thinness and dryness of the man's body were accentuated by his dress, which was even stranger looking than he himself. It was an outfit of uncommon simplicity, consisting of a long, sack-like shirt of rough gray linen, tied at the neck and waist with a coarse hempen rope; it fell to the ground, half covering his dark, completely bare feet.

Who was the man in the garb of an ascetic, with the eyes of a fanatic and the expression on his lips of deep, mystic, almost intoxicated fervor? It was Reb

Moshe, the *melamed* or teacher of Hebrew and religion, a supremely pious man. Whatever the weather, he was always barefoot and attired in the same linen sack; he lived like the birds on anything he could find, some grain perhaps tossed here or there. He was the right eye and the right hand of the great Szybów rabbi Isaac Todros, and after the rabbi the greatest object of respect and admiration in the community.

When he heard the torrent of questions directed at him by the melamed, Meir Ezofowicz, the grandson of Saul and great-grandson of Hersh, did not sit down, but stood erect, and with downcast eyes and evident timidity replied in subdued voice: "Rebbe! I have not been where people are enjoying themselves or doing good business. I have been where it is dark, and where very poor people sit in darkness and weep."

"Well now!" exclaimed the melamed. "Where can it be sad today? Today is the Sabbath; it's light and joyous everywhere. Where can it be dark today?" . . .

Meir did not answer. His face and downcast eyes expressed timidity and hesitation. Suddenly one of the girls who was sitting at the lower end of the table, the same one with the swarthy face and dark, playful eyes who a moment before had helped the great-grandmother into the family circle, clapped her hands merrily and cried out: "I know where it is dark today!"

All eyes turned in her direction and all mouths asked: "Where?"

Now the center of attraction, pretty Lia blushed and said more quietly and with a certain embarrassment: "In Abel the Karaite's hut, at the foot of the Karaite hill."

"Meir, have you been at the Karaite's?"

Although the question was asked by many voices, it was the melamed's shrill, sharp voice that towered over all the others. The young man's timidity began to give way to an expression of unpleasant and angry irritation.

"I wasn't with them, but I saved them from a terrible attack," he said more loudly than before.

"From an attack? What attack? Who attacked them?" the melamed asked in a mocking tone.

This time Meir raised his eyes and looked straight into the melamed's face.

"Reb Moshe!" he said. "You know who assaulted them. Your pupils did. They do it every Friday night. And why should they not do it, since they know . . ." He hesitated and again lowered his eyes. Fear and angry feelings were obviously warring inside him.

"Well, what do they know? Why didn't you finish, Meir? What do they know?" the melamed asked, laughing.

"They know that you, Reb Moshe, praise them for it."

Reb Moshe raised himself on his seat, his eyes flashed and opened wide. He stretched forth a dark thin hand and was about to speak but was not permitted to this time by the strong and sonorous voice of the young man:

"Reb Moshe," Meir said, bending his head slightly since it was obvious that humble bows did not come easy to him, "I respect you as my teacher, and I do not ask why you do not forbid your pupils to assault poor people at night; but I cannot bear to look at such assaults. . . . My heart aches when I see them, because I know that bad children will grow up to be bad men. If now they damage a poor man's hut and throw stones through his windows, they will burn down houses later on and kill people! They would have torn the hut down today and killed those poor people had I not come in time and saved them."

Saying this, Meir took the seat assigned him at the table. There was neither fear nor timidity in his face now. He felt deeply that justice was on his side and he looked around boldly. But at just that moment old Saul and his two sons raised their hands, and in one voice exclaimed: "The Sabbath!"

Their voices were solemn, and their eyes, which now turned to Meir, were stern, almost angry.

"The Sabbath! The Sabbath!" shouted the melamed, jumping up in his chair and throwing his arms wildly about him. "You, Meir, on the holy evening of the Sabbath, instead of saying the Kiddush, and filling your heart with joy; instead of offering your spirit into the hands of the angel Matatron who defends the generations of Jacob before the Lord so that He in turn would give it unto Sar-ha-Oloma, the angel above angels and prince of the world, and through him to the ten Sefirot, the great forces that created the world, to be brought at last by these ten Sefirot before the great throne of En-Sof, to be joined with him by a kiss of love; instead of all this you go and defend some people from some danger and watch over their house and lives. Meir! Meir! You have broken the Sabbath! You will have to go to the school and confess loudly before all the people that you are committing great sins and outrages." . . .

Meir answered, in a slightly trembling voice

"In our holy books, Rebbe Moshe, neither in the Torah nor the Mishna, there is nothing about Sefirots or En-Sof. But it is clearly stated that although Jehovah ordered the Sabbath consecrated, He allowed twenty people to break it in order to save one life."

The very act of answering the pious melamed, the right hand of Rabbi Todros, was an unheard-of and astonishing impudence. And if there was anything even faintly contradictory of his judgments! The bulging eyes of the teacher nearly burst from their sockets, so wide did they open and stare exasperatedly at Meir's face, which had turned pale from the skirmish.

"The Karaites," he yelled, tossing in his chair and pulling his hair and beard. "You saved the Karaites! Heretics, unbelievers, accursed! Why should you save them? Why do they not light their candles on the Sabbath? Why do they sit in darkness? Why do they cut the throats of birds and animals that serve for food from the back of the neck instead of from the front? Why do they not know the holy books of Mishnah, Gemara, and Zohar?"

He choked from his great excitement and then grew silent. In the interval, the pure, melodious voice of Meir resounded: "Rebbe! They are very poor!"

"En-sof is vengeful and implacable!"

"They suffer much from people's persecution."

"It is the Unfathomable who persecutes them," shouted the rebbe.

"The Everlasting does not command us to persecute. Rabbi Huna said: 'If the persecutor is just, and the persecuted an evil-doer, the Everlasting protects the persecuted.' "

Reb Moshe's face turned red. . . . Saul, from under his gray bushy eyebrows, cast a threatening look into his grandson's face and hissed: "Shhh!"

Meir bent his head before his grandfather, as a sign of humility and submission, and one of Saul's sons, in order to appease Reb Moshe as well as doubtless for his own edification, asked him what the differences were between the books of the Talmud, the Zohar, and the Cabala, and whether a properly pious man ought to study the first or the last.

Upon hearing the question, the melamed spread his elbows wide on the table, fixed his eyes upon the opposite wall, and with an expression of deep reflection, began to speak in a slow, solemn voice:

"Simon ben Jochai, the great rabbi who lived very long ago and knew everything that happened in heaven and on earth, says that the Talmud is nothing more than a wretched slave-girl, the Cabala a great queen. What does the Talmud contain? It is full of little, insignificant things. It teaches what is clean or unclean, what is allowed and what is not allowed, what is modest and what is immodest. What does the Zohar, the book of light, the book of the Cabala, teach us? It teaches us about God and his Sefirot. It knows and teaches all their names, what they do, and how they created the world. It is written there that the Lord's name is En-sof; his second name, Notarikon; his third, Gematria, and his fourth, Zirufi. The Sefirot, who are the great heavenly powers, are called: the source of man, the betrothed, the woman, the great face, the small face, the mirror, the heavenly level, the earthly level, the lily, and the apple garden. Israel is called Matrona, and God for Israel is called Father. God, En-Sof, did not create the world; He only created the heavenly powers, the Sefirot. The first Sefirot bore divine strength; the second, all the angels and the Torah (the Bible); from the third issued the Prophets. The fourth gave birth to divine love; the fifth, divine justice; the sixth, the power of destruction; the seventh, beauty; the eighth, splendor; the ninth, everlasting cause; the tenth, the eye that constantly watches over Israel and follows him wherever he goes and protects his legs lest they become injured, and his heads, lest great misfortune fall on them. All this teaches the Zohar, the book of the Cabala. And it also teaches where the Sefirot came from, and how they are divided, and how from the letters that make up their names, and from the letters that make up the names of God, all the secrets of the world can be divined. It is a great science, the greatest science for every Israelite. I know that many Israelites say that the Talmud is more important. But all of them who say that are stupid, and they do not know that until the earth trembles from great pains, and until God and Israel, the Father and Matrona, do not join in the kiss of love, the slave will not give way to the queen, the Talmud to the Cabala. And when will that time come? It will come when the Messiah arrives on earth. Then there will be Jobel-ha-Gadol, the great holiday of joy, for all pious and learned men! Then the Lord God will order Leviathan to be cooked, the great fish on which the entire world stands, and all will take their places at the great feast and will eat the fish, the pious and learned starting from the head, and the simple and uneducated from the tail!"

The melamed finished and sighed deeply after his long speech. Then lowering his gaze toward the table, he suddenly descended from his mystic heights to earthly realities. On a plate before him, exuding the fragrance of pepper and other spices, lay a portion of excellent fish. It did not come from Leviathan, in truth, but from some always tasty dweller of the waters. The melamed, who lived his whole life as an ascetic, liked the Saturday feasts and enjoyed them heartily. . . .

Rabbi Isaac Todros bore on his exterior person, and perhaps also in his spiritual organism, the unmistakable traces of the centuries-long habitation of his forebears in the burning climate of Spain. . . .

What was the real position he occupied in his community, and on what was it based? He was not a priest. Rabbis are not priests; and no nation is more distant from theocratic rule by its very nature than the Israelite. He was also not an administrator of the community, since civil affairs were dealt with by the officials of the kahal. The rabbi's function in the kahal was that of guardian over religious precepts and ceremonies. His was a higher position than the aforementioned. By birth he belonged to an ancient princely family among whose ancestors were many sages and pious and revered rabbis. He himself was a zaddik and chacham, an ascetic, some would say a miracle-worker, and exceptionally learned. . . . His learning embraced an incomparable knowledge of the holy books — the Torah, or Bible, least of all, the Talmud more, and the Cabala most of all. He was the leading Cabalist of his time, and that was the foundation of his greatness.

Someone who knows even a little about the faith of the Israelites might presume that the people of Szybów belonged to one of the numerous, dark sects of Hasidism who exalt the Cabala above all religious and secular learning. This was not so. They belonged to those Talmudists, who are especially numerous among the lowest social classes, who had simply joined the Cabala, which they regarded as a holy book and delighted in fervently, to the Talmud and Torah; in time these last two receded in importance. But Hasidism had also passed over the people of Szybów and left many traces behind. A considerable part of the population was actually Hasidic without knowing it, and it was said that Reb Nochim, the rabbi who clashed with Hersh Ezofowicz over their different ideas, had been a disciple of the Besht, the founder of this strange sect. Although he never completely joined

Jan Krajewski (dates unknown), "Rabbi Isaac Todros Making His Way through the Streets of Szybów" (1877). Based on an illustration by Michał Elwiro Andriolli (1863–93) for Eliza Orzeszkowa's novel *Meir Ezofowicz*. Courtesy Muzeum Narodowe w Warszawie.

them, he did introduce into the community of which he was spiritual leader a number of their basic ideas. The main doctrines were a boundless veneration for the Cabala, an almost idolatrous worship of the zaddikim, and deep, unshakable hatred toward the Edomites (foreign nations) and their learning. . . .

Rabbi Isaac's dark forehead was ploughed in deep furrows that appeared when he strained his thought in an effort to pierce the mysteries of earth and heaven through the proper combination of letters contained in the names of God and the angels. Gleams of rapture or gloom shone in his coal-black eyes, depending on whether he contemplated the incomparable bliss or boundless terror of the supernatural world. His back was bent from poring over the holy books, his hands trembled from the constant agitation of a mind contending with phantoms, his body dried up and his cheeks became deeply sunken from the torments of his spirit and the punishments of his body. . . .

He had been married off even before the slightest hair of maturity had appeared on his cheeks. But he soon divorced his wife when her bustling about hindered his concentration on pieties. His three children were being raised by his brother, and he himself, a hermit in his low, dark hut, lived a life stretched to the limit of fantasy, fervent prayer, and lofty mystic contemplations. He lived on the gifts sent him by his ardent worshipers. These gifts were small and insignificant; he would not take anything costly, nor did he even accept any payment for the advice, medicine, or predictions he bestowed on the faithful. . . .

His hut recalled the bare cells of hermits and anchorites. There was nothing in it but a low, hard bed, a white table near one of the windows, a pair of wooden stools, and some heavy boards, nailed to the wall, full of books. Among them were some twelve huge volumes in ancient print, bound in yellowed parchment. This was the Talmud. Above it lay: the Ozar-ha-kabod, written by one of Isaac's forebears, Halevi Todros, the first Talmudist who believed in the Cabala; Toldot Adam, an epic describing the first man and exile; Sefer Yetzira (the Book of Creation), an apocalyptic description of the creation of the universe; Kaarat Kezef, in which Ezobi admonishes the Israelites against the harmful influences of all secular learning; Shiur Koma, a visual description of God enlightening readers as to His physical being, the enormous dimensions of His head, feet, hands, and especially His beard, which according to the book, reaches the length of 10,500 parasangs.[4] But on the highest shelf, and the most worn from frequent use, was the Book of Light, the Zohar, the most extensive and most profound treatise on Chochma Nistar (Cabala), which in the name of Rabbi Simon ben Jochai, who lived several centuries before, was published by Moses of León in the thirteenth century. . . .

[The local Polish landowner, Kamioński, pays a visit to Rabbi Todros.]

"This way, please," said Yankel Kamionker, showing the squire the gates of the synagogue court.

---

4. An ancient Persian unit of measure, equal to about 3.5 miles.

"And where does your rabbi live?"

Kamionker pointed to the small dark hut close to the synagogue.

"What? In that little cottage?" . . .

The door of the hut was already closed, but several people still lingered at the open window, talking softly among themselves and from time to time glancing timidly inside. It was very silent within, and if someone knew in advance how diligently and indefatigably Isaac Todros worked for hours on end, he would doubtless suppose that he was now asleep or resting from all activity. Such a supposition, however, would be a grave error. With the exception of a few short hours at night, in which he dozed in a difficult, interrupted sleep typical of people of constantly strained intellect and frayed nerves, Isaac Todros never rested. . . .

Suddenly, the door opened, and on the threshold stood squire Kamioński. He stopped for a moment, and then said to Yankel who was following him:

"Remain here, Pan Yankel; I'll speak alone with the rabbi."

Saying this, he stooped in order to pass through the door of the hut, which was too low for his tall, stately figure. Once inside, he glanced curiously around. Opposite him, near a wall that was black from dust and dirt, sat a shabbily dressed man with pitch-black hair and beard, and a face almost orange in color, which he now raised up from the yellowed, ancient pages before him. . . . In a corner of the hut, low to the ground, appeared another human figure; but the young squire gave him only a passing glance. It did not even enter his mind that the man sitting on the bench, with holes in his sleeves and an astonished look on his face, could in fact be the Szybów rabbi, whose fame, spreading through the Jewish communities for many miles around, sent faint, fragmentary echoes even into the Christian world.

He approached the man and very politely asked if he might see the rabbi of Szybów.

There was no answer.

The man seated on the bench just craned his long yellow neck and opened his eyes and mouth still wider. Amazement, or perhaps some other sudden feeling, gave him the appearance of stupidity, almost idiocy. No wonder that Isaac Todros looked like he had been struck by lightning at the sight of the nobleman standing before him. He was the first Edomite who had ever crossed his threshold, the first he had ever seen up close, and the first who had spoken to him in a language whose sounds seemed to his ears utterly strange and unintelligible. If the angel Matatron, the heavenly patron and defender of Israel, or even Satan himself had appeared before him, he would have been less astonished and terrified; after all, he had close, if not direct, contact with supernatural beings. He studied them, knew their origin, their nature, their properties, and their functions. But this tall, stately man in his hideous clothing, which barely reached his knees, with the white, effeminate forehead and unintelligible language? Where was he from? Why did he come? What did he want? Was he a Philistine? A cruel Roman, who had defeated Bar Kochba, or perhaps a Spaniard, one of those who murdered the famous Abrabanel family and infamously drove his ancestor Todros out of Spain?

Kamioński waited a moment for an answer to his question, and not getting one repeated it.

"May I speak with the rabbi of Szybów?" At the sound of the somewhat raised voice the figure squatting in the corner moved and rose slowly. Reb Moshe, gaping in astonishment and looking dumbstruck into the face of the visitor, came into the light and hoarsely drawled the syllable "Hah?"

At the sight of the man dressed in such primitive simplicity, nowadays unseen anywhere else, the squire winced and barely suppressed a fleeting smile.

"My good man," he said, turning to Reb Moshe, "is that man deaf and dumb? I asked him twice about the rabbi of Szybów and got no answer." Saying this he pointed at Todros, who turned slowly toward the melamed and, craning his neck, asked:

"Wos sogd er? Wos will er?" ("What does he say? What does he want?") Reb Moshe, instead of answering, opened his mouth still wider, and at just that moment murmurs and whispers could be heard outside the open window. Kamioński glanced in that direction and saw the window filled with faces looking into the hut. The faces were inquisitive and a little frightened. He turned toward them and asked:

"Does the rabbi of Szybów live here?"

"He does," said some voices.

"Where is he then?"

A great many fingers pointed out the man seated on the bench.

"What?" exclaimed the nobleman. "That man is your wise and celebrated rabbi?"

The faces filling the open window radiated with a peculiar blissfulness and their eyes answered in the affirmative.

It was obvious that Kamioński was seized by a great desire to laugh, but he managed to restrain himself.

"And who is that?" he asked, indicating Reb Moshe.

"He is the melamed," said several voices, "a very wise and pious man."

Kamioński turned again toward Todros.

"Esteemed Rabbi," he said, "I would like to talk to you, alone, for a few minutes."

Todros remained silent as the grave, but his breath came faster and his eyes shone more brilliantly.

"Pan Melamed," said the nobleman to the barefooted man in the coarse shirt, "perhaps this is a day when your rabbi is not allowed to speak?"

"Hah?" Reb Moshe asked with his usual drawl.

Half amused, half angry, Kamioński turned toward the people standing outside the window.

"Why do they not answer?"

A long silence ensued. The faces looked at each other in evident perplexity.

"What do you expect?" replied one of the bolder ones. "They don't understand the language you're speaking!"

"For heaven's sake, what language do they understand?" exclaimed the squire.

"Well, they only understand the Jewish language!" answered the same person who spoke up before.

Kamioński opened his eyes wide. He could not believe his ears. He wanted to laugh, but at the same time an undefined anger gripped him.

"How can that be?" he asked. "You mean to tell me they don't understand the language of the country they're living in?"

Silence.

"So," someone finally said from the window, "they don't understand!"

There was an undercurrent of dislike in the voice that uttered that short sentence. At that moment Isaac Todros leaped from where he was sitting, stood erect, raised both hands above his head, and began hurriedly speaking:

"A day will arrive when the Messiah will awaken in a bird's nest suspended in heaven and will descend upon the earth. Then a great war will spread over the world; Israel will stand up against Edom and Ishmael, until Edom and Ishmael, vanquished, will fall at his feet like shattered cedars."

As he uttered the names Edom and Ishmael the speaker extended his index finger toward the Edomite standing in the middle of the room. His gestures were at once solemn and threatening, his eyes blazed passionately, and in an outburst of breath again repeated: "Edom and Ishmael will lie at the feet of Israel, like broken cedars, and the thunderbolt of the Lord's vengeance will fall upon them and crush them into powder."

It was now the Edomite's turn to look astonished. He indeed looked like a tall and mighty cedar, but certainly not like one that would soon suffer the catastrophe of being turned to powder. On the contrary. He was far closer to the catastrophe of Homeric laughter, which happily, though with no small effort, he managed to avoid.

"What does he say?" he asked the people crowding around the window. There was no answer. All eyes were riveted on the sage, while on the round, dark face of the melamed there was an expression of inexpressible rapture.

"My good people!" exclaimed Kamioński. "Tell me what he said!"

A voice from the window, heavy and coarse, but swollen as if with strange mockery and an equally strange desire for retaliation, answered with another question: "Did your gracious lord not understand?"

This naive and outlandish question put an end to the young man's strength of will. His sapphire eyes shone with untamed merriment and a long, loud peal of laughter burst from his chest. He turned to leave, still laughing.

"Savages!" he exclaimed at the door.

He kept on laughing as he crossed the courtyard of the synagogue, but the people who crowded round the rabbi's window turned their heads and followed him with looks of astonishment and deep humiliation. No wonder. The young man laughed, yet deep within himself he felt anger and resentment over the fact that Israelite sages, whom he saw a moment before, seemed to him like savage and terribly comic people, who did not even speak the language of the country whose air they breathed and that had nourished them for centuries. The people crowding into the rabbi's hut followed him with displeased looks almost tantamount to hatred because by his laughter he had blasphemed what they loved fiercely and revered above anything else. Poor sages of Israel and their worshipers who followed the Edomite with hateful looks! Poor Edomite, laughing at the Israelite sages and their worshipers! But poorest of all, the poor country whose sons, after journeying together for so many centuries, do not understand each other's heart and language. . . .

[Meir Ezofowicz is excommunicated and banished from the community for his love of a Karaite girl and his opposition to Rabbi Todros.]

"The shamos, the shamos, the shamos!"

The same man who a few minutes before had been keeping a vigil at the doors of the Bet-ha-Kahol, which was now as silent as a grave, made his way hurriedly from the gate of the synagogue courtyard across the square in the direction of the Ezofowicz house. He was on his way to announce the sentence of the tribunal to the accused and his family. . . . The door of the house was opened and shut again, and the shamos entered the drawing room. Glancing around anxiously, almost suspiciously, he bowed low before Saul.

"Sholom Aleichem" ("Peace unto you"), he said, in a low voice, as if he himself felt that the customary greeting this time harbored bitter irony.

"Rebbe Saul!" he began, in a somewhat more assured voice. "Do not be angry with your servant if he brings shame and misfortune into your house. I am fulfilling the command of our great rabbi, and all our elders and judges, who today sat in judgment upon your grandson, Meir, and whose sentence I am ordered to read out to him and to all of you!"

A deep silence greeted his words. At last Saul, who stood leaning on the shoulder of his son Rafael, said in a low voice: "Read."

The messenger unrolled the paper he was holding in his hand, and in a loud voice began to read, or rather sing out: "Isaac Todros, the son of Baruch, rabbi of Szybów. together with the judges and elders of the kahal, who constitute the tribunal of the community of Szybów, have heard the charges, confirmed by many witnesses . . . that the strong-willed, impertinent, and disobedient Meir Ezofowicz, son of Benjamin, committed the following grave transgressions and crimes unheard of ever in Israel:

"(1) Meir Ezofowicz, son of Benjamin, failed to observe the Sabbath according to the rules and decrees of the Law of Israel. Instead of giving himself up on this

Teofil Konarzewski (dates unknown), "Town Elders Angered by Meir's Defiance" (1877).
Based on an illustration by Michał Elwiro Andriolli (1863–93) for Eliza Orzeszkowa's novel
Meir Ezofowicz. Courtesy Muzeum Narodowe w Warszawie.

day to the reading of holy books and the memorization of the countless prescriptions of the Talmud and the impenetrable secrets of the Cabala, he dared defend the dwelling of the Karaite heretic and he raised his hand in anger against Israelite children. . . .

"(2) Meir Ezofowicz was seen reading the accursed book, *More Nebuchim* (*Guide for the Perplexed*), of Moses Maimonides, the false sage, excommunicated by many saintly rabbis and learned men. He also persuaded his companions and friends to read this book, thus acquainting them with the heresies and abominations contained in it. . . .

"(5) Having hair grown on his face and beard he refused to get married and insolently broke his engagement to the Israelite girl Mera, daughter of Eli, thereby showing his resolution to avoid the righteous bonds of marriage.

"(6) He maintained an impure friendship with Golda, the granddaughter of a heretic, whom Rabbi Isaac and the elders of the kahal through their great charity allowed to live in the home of his fathers, although the Karaites, who voluntarily fell away from the bosom of Israel and refused to acknowledge the holiness of the Talmud and Cabala, are unworthy of being borne on the surface of the earth. . . .

"(7) He did not pay due respect to the learned Israelites, opened his mouth to impudent quarrels with Reb Moshe . . . and dared raise a criminal hand against him, knocking him to the floor of the cheder, turning a table over on him, thereby causing great commotion and bringing fear and pain to Reb Moshe, and grief and scandal to all Israel. . . .

"(9) His audacity and impiety knowing no bounds, he extracted the writing of his ancestor, Michał Senior, from its hiding place, where it should have rotted away and turned to dust, and with criminal boldness went to the bet-midrash in order to read it before a large crowd of people, thereby gravely shaking their faith in the old laws and traditions of Israel. We have been told that the document is full of the most malicious counsels and the gravest blasphemies the ear of Israel ever heard. We consider the reading of said document as the greatest of all his great crimes. On the basis of the laws contained in our holy books, and the power given us, in accordance with these laws, over each and every son of the house of Israel, we decree:

"Tomorrow after sunset a great and terrible curse will be pronounced against the impertinent and disobedient Meir Ezofowicz, son of Benjamin, through the mouth of Rabbi Isaac, son of Baruch, for the hearing of which all the Israelites of Szybów and its environs will be summoned by the shamoses, and Meir Ezofowicz will be cast out from the bosom of Israel and ignominiously expelled from the house of Israel. All of you who remain faithful to your God and His Law, live in peace and happiness with all your brethren in Israel." . . .

[Following his expulsion, Meir seeks out his Karaite sweetheart, Golda, and attempts to persuade her to leave Szybów with him. She refuses, despite her love for him, because of her devotion to her elderly grandfather, who has nobody else to look after him. Before he leaves, Meir entrusts her with the "testament" of Michał Ezofowicz, Senior. Golda and her grandfather are killed by fanatical followers of Rabbi Todros who come seeking the document. Meir, however, recovers the papers from a child to whom Golda had given them for safekeeping and takes them with him on his journey into the world.]

It seemed as if the sight of the papers roused Meir from sleep, reminded him of something important, summoned him to something holy and necessary for him. He passed both hands over his forehead and then took the Senior's legacy from the child's hands. When he felt it in his hand, he raised his head and his eyes again shone with courage and strength of will.

He looked at the town waking up from sleep and said something in a low voice, more in thought than words. He said something about Israel, its past greatness and its great sins, and that he would never desert it and not return curse for curse, that he would carry the covenant of peace to other nations, drink at the source of wisdom and come back sometime. . . .

Then he began slowly ascending the hill. . . .

Has the humiliated, excommunicated youth, torn from everything, achieved the goal he so ardently desired? Has he found in the wide, unfamiliar world people ready to open their hearts and doors to him and show him the way to the source of wisdom? Has he returned, or will he return to his place of birth and bring with him forgiveness and that light by the power of which the "cedar of Lebanon" will arise in place of the "lowly blackthorn?" I do not know. The story is too recent to have an end, because this story, and many, many other stories like it, are far from any ending. Reader, of whatever tribe blood flows in your veins and whatever place on earth you pay homage to God, if you meet Meir Ezofowicz on your way hesitate not to extend him your sincere, brotherly hand in help and friendship.

■ Aleksander Świętochowski (1849–1938)
"Chava Ruby" (1879)

[Aleksander Świętochowski was a prolific writer and journalist, and a leading representative of Polish positivism. He addressed a variety of contemporary issues in his works,
among them the situation of the Jews, and has been held in high esteem for his cham-
pionship of a democratic reorganization of Polish society. His plays and prose fiction tend
generally to be overshadowed by his journalistic writings, which are devoted mainly to the
advocacy of the philosophical and scientific views of positivism. "Chava Rubin" ("Chava
Ruby," 1879) is one of his best stories.]

I call my honorable readers' attention to the fact that the persons and events I
mean to deal with in this story belong to a social stratum that does not remuner-
ate their spokesmen, and that I have, therefore, undertaken to describe them quite
disinterestedly. I consider this reservation necessary lest the tribunal of public
opinion, in judging my motives, find grounds to accuse me of intentionally pan-
dering to the coreligionists of my heroes. I must, therefore, begin by explaining
that the surname Ruby implied only what Chava and her husband Simcha would
have liked to be, and not what they really were. For they were so poor that it
would not have been in the least derogatory to their financial status had they
chosen the humble name of Sandstone. Simcha's great-grandfather, wishing to
possess at least the name of a precious stone, and to transmit it to his family as a
magic word, called himself "Ruby." But it had helped neither him nor his descendants. Simcha was a Ruby in a setting of perfect misery. He lacked, indeed, nothing that is necessary to suffocate a poor wretch. Being a Hasid he would sit in the
temple uninterruptedly; convinced he came "of very good stock," he considered
himself an outstanding personality whom the world was duty bound to support
and whom it would not let perish; and finally, his weak chest had, for some years
past, rendered him unfit for any manual work. The death of his father ruined
him definitively, for he inherited one-fourth of a house in Kazimierz-on-Vistula,
or rather, one-fourth of a tumbledown hovel whose window-sills had sunk below
the muddy street level, and which the town assessor himself deemed exempt from
taxation, as it was doomed to be demolished. Nevertheless, Simcha was proud of
his heirloom, which entitled him to call himself a landlord. He took two tenants
into the one room that was all he owned, and ever since he either quarreled with
them, or kept promising them repairs "next spring," or else he sat on the bench
in front of the house, basking in the sun or feeding boiled potato peel to his three

Aleksander Świętochowski, "Chava Rubin," trans. Ilona Ralf Sues, *Polish Short Stories*, ed. Jadwiga
Lewicka (Warsaw: Polonia Publishing House, 1960), 57–85. Translation slightly amended.

chickens. He even neglected the synagogue. Illness, hunger, conceit about his descent, and the dignity of being a realtor — all contributed to paralyze the poor Jew completely. Whenever he found idleness boring, he would go down to the market and tell passersby about the many prospective buyers of his property (which no one wanted). As the tenants never paid their rent, the reader may wonder how Simcha managed to live with his four children.

And it is to solve this mystery that we need Chava Ruby.

An artist familiar with restoring damaged paintings would call thirty-year-old Chava a beautiful woman. In fact, anyone might still notice her regular features, finely drawn nose, sparkling dark eyes, exquisite tiny ears, and attractive smile; yet all this was disfigured by marks of such utter misery that I'd rather talk about Chava's diligence than about her beauty. And diligent she was, as diligent as any Jewess must be to keep a husband and four children alive on a working capital of three rubles. Had Chava been born a Catholic, she would be earning several złotys every day and living in comfort. As a Jewess, however, with so many jobs being *treife* (impure) all she could do was act as an intermediary procuring the most necessary commodities, and that yielded her an average profit of some twenty or twenty-five groszy a day. Provided, of course, she made a big effort. It meant running at daybreak to a settlement, three versts from the town, picking up a supply of milk and delivering it to many homes; it meant making the rounds in several villages to find a few pots of butter or cheese for the wives of some officials; it meant carrying petroleum from the town to a neighboring estate. In a small town where everybody has everything he needs right at home, or easily available, there's very little a middleman can do unless his own requirements are very modest. Therefore, Chava had to chase after those twenty-five groszy from sunrise till late at night. It was a vicious circle, for the inadequate working capital rendered any bigger business transactions impossible. Of course, had she had fifty rubles at her disposal, she would, within three years, be wearing satin dresses on the Sabbath, and the Kazimierz aristocracy would bow to her politely. But all she had in circulation was those three rubles. There was only one way to increase her capital: a series of audacious and lucky transactions. She did possess the two essential assets needed to achieve that end — ambition and courage. She kept dreaming about prosperity and about taking chances. Once she almost took ten gallons of honey on account, but she refrained for fear she might lose all her fortune. Then, when she learned that someone she knew had bought the honey and made four rubles profit on it she burst into tears and made up her mind to take a decisive step on the very first occasion.

One day she was trotting down to the Vistula River to buy some eels, when she saw a group of fishermen who seemed very excited. They had just caught three sturgeons. Chava thought at once: "What about buying them?" With a faltering voice she asked for the price.

"Five groszy a pound wholesale," said one of the fishermen. "There'll be about 150 pounds."

Chava started to bargain passionately.

"Take it easy," said the fisherman. "We haven't caught a sturgeon in a month. You'll sell 'em at a złoty a pound."

Chava was so thrilled at the mere thought of such a profit that she agreed to the price and gave them three rubles on account "for the moment." She expected to pay the rest after making a quick sale. On her way to town with the fishermen, she was seized by the fever of expectation, her cheeks were flushed, in her mind she was making the rounds of the households where she might offer the fish: the assistant judge, the clerk, the clerk's assistant, the notary, the mayor, the assessor, the tanner. . . . Fifteen groszy a pound, or maybe even a złoty! Chava's eyes sparkled again with that brightness they had lost long ago, and a happy smile parted her lips. She adjusted her bonnet and began to walk so briskly that the fishermen with their load of sturgeon could barely keep pace with her. — But then again, what if no one cared to buy the fish?

One hundred and fifty pounds of sturgeon, for Kazimierz, where not more than thirty persons could afford such a luxury on a weekday! She stopped in a panic, breathless, but a moment later her courage came back, she pushed her kerchief off her head and hurried ahead.

"Go and wait in my house," she told the fishermen and got hold of one sturgeon. "I'll be back right away; I'll just change some money."

Without waiting for their reply, she went down a narrow lane toward the other end of the town. Chava was too experienced in her trade not to realize that if she wanted to sell so many pounds of fish she had to make her round of the small town aristocracy strictly by importance of their rank. She therefore hurried first to the assistant judge's, though other clients of hers lived along the road.

Her calculations proved correct. The judge's wife bought the whole sturgeon for three rubles after relatively little bargaining; that meant more than eleven groszy a pound!

On her way home, Chava was delighted at the prospect of a big profit, and yet anxious about her future sales; she felt sorry one moment and happy the next.

"Well, never mind," she told herself, hurrying on, "one time you sell cheaper, one time you get more. She's bought a whole fish and she's paid cash. I could give the two other fish away for free, and I'd still have my three rubles."

"My three rubles!" she cried loudly, squeezing the bill in her pocket. "I owe them five złotys, I'll pay them; ain't two sturgeons worth five złotys?"

Chava spotted her husband in front of the house: he was talking with the fishermen and poking at the sturgeon with a stick. The children stood around eyeing the fish fearfully.

"Call this a fish? Some fish that!" he was saying with disgust. "Who will eat that? Some starveling. Who will pay money for that? An idiot! Ayayah, a delicacy! She didn't give you a deposit, did she?"

"She did," replied one of the poor fellows, "but she don't show up with the balance."

"Gevalt, she don't show up! So I don't have a house? So I am not a proprietor? My property not worth five złotys?"

At the sight of his wife, Simcha suddenly raised his voice with pride.

"There ain't a penny on my mortgage, so there's plenty room for two sturgeons. Me, I don't handle such stuff. I've said it: I got a house — Simcha the proprietor."

Chava silenced her husband with a blunt remark and turned to the fishermen: "I gotta pay you another three złotys."

"Five," they retorted.

"What' d'you mean? A ruble and a złoty a piece."

They began to argue. With Chava it was a habit, and then too, she hoped to make up for having sold the first sturgeon too cheaply. But her effort proved vain.

When the fishermen had left, she sat down on the bench in front of the house and wiped the sweat off her face with her apron, taking no notice of her whining children pulling her in different directions. Finally she took two pears out of her pocket, bit each in two and stuffed the pieces into the four open mouths.

"Simcha," she called her husband who stood with his hands folded on his back and gazed at the moss-covered shingles of his house, "taken them fishes inside."

"They won' catch cold there. Let them lie," he replied phlegmatically and slouched away coughing, headed for the town.

Chava shook with anger, her eyes filled with tears. She hated her husband for his laziness and sickness, as much as one can hate under the yoke of hard work. If Simcha were healthy, she would still have felt some attachment to him; if he were lazy for religious reasons, she would have patiently borne the whole burden of maintaining the family. But Simcha shunned every bit of work because of his Hasidic habits and because his illness had made him sluggish. A sick parasite still breeding — can there be anything worse for a poor wife who has to feed the whole family?

Chava kept silent, busy with her sturgeons, which had to be gotten rid of fast, lest they spoil in the July heat. Deaf to the renewed cries of her children, she hurried to a house nearby to call on one of her customers, the assessor's wife; she found her in the garden.

"Ahya, my dear lady, I got something extra for you! Haven't said a word about it yet to anyone! A fresh, delicious, extra fine sturgeon!"

"A sturgeon," said the cashier's wife, "is no fish. It is no fish. Last year I marinated twenty pounds, and then I had to throw half of it away; even the kids wouldn't eat it."

"You don't mean it, Madam! The late notary preferred it to any other fish. The assistant judge's wife keeps reminding me 'Pani Simcha, Pani Simcha, when will you bring me a sturgeon?' "

"Well, I might, after all — if it's cheap . . ."

"For you, it will be a złoty a pound."

"Run along, then. At that price I can get salmon."

"I myself had to give twenty-five groszy; I must make something on it."

"At fifteen groszy, I'd take thirty pounds."

"And what'll I do with the rest? Aye, my dear lady, such a tasty fish — it's almost a pity to eat it. Well, I'll run over to the mayor's wife, maybe she'll share with you.

But when the mayor's wife heard that Chava (who had, for a moment, over-looked the hierarchy) had gone first to the assessor's wife, she chased the Jewess.

"The rotter," she screamed, slamming the door shut. "Offering me the leav-ings of some assessor's wife! I won't forget that in a hurry!"

Chava had not time to worry over that reception; she rushed on. But the god of commerce had evidently decided to punish her for her audacious venture, for she couldn't get anyone to buy either a whole or even half a sturgeon. Some people were out, others had no cash. After running all over town in vain, Chava returned home quite depressed.

What now? That question is as horrible a nightmare to a merchant whose frieghter loaded to capacity develops a leak in mid-ocean as it is to a poor ped-dler whose sturgeons no one wants to buy. In time of danger, the first thought is to save one's capital. Having paid the fishermen, Chava was five złotys short. She therefore cut one sturgeon in half with an axe and took it over to the assessor's wife. If she got the whole sum, she would have a net profit of two rubles, even if the rest of the fish rotted. Oh, sweet hope, oh, rare and lucky day! Two rubles profit for a few hours of running around! Richer people than Chava would be willing to peddle fish were they sure of success.

But that day the very ground under Chava's feet seemed to turn to water.

First, the assessor's wife declared that she wouldn't give fifteen but only ten groszy a pound, and that she would pay the bill the following day. So Chava didn't have the three rubles in her pocket, and hadn't earned any ready cash during the greater part of the day. Dismayed at that thought, a strange determination in her face, she walked home pensively.

It was one o'clock in the afternoon. Simcha was plucking beet leaves and throwing them to the chickens, but they wouldn't be fooled. The children were huddled by the wall, chewing pods of unripe peas, a handful of which their father had brought home from the town. When they saw their mother, they began to scream. Chava picked up the youngest, kissed it and went into the house.

"Buy them a pound of bread," she told the woman tenant, putting down four groszy, "I gotta go out again."

She paid no attention to the howling child, rushed out, grabbed the sturgeon lying under the window, threw it across her shoulder and went in the direction of a suburb.

"Where are you off to, Pani Simcha," asked an old woman sitting on a porch with a stocking in her hand.

"To Puławy, dear lady," replied Chava drawing near and kissing the old woman's hand.

"Carrying a sturgeon? For whom?"

"No idea. Impossible to sell it here. I got yet another half sturgeon at home."

"I'll take that. My grandson is here on his vacation from school—he's a big eater. But will you manage to carry such a load to Puławy?"

"Oh, my dear lady, I can barely stand on my feet. I haven't eaten anything today; I don't even know if I'll be able to cook a meal for the kids. But what else can I do? Fish won't keep long. I've bought three sturgeons: the assistant judge's wife took one, paid eleven groszy a pound; the assessor's wife took half a fish, at ten groszy. I still have the rest and am on my way to Puławy. I haven't earned anything so far. I haven't even got back all of my three rubles. And if I lost that money of yours, I'd have to eat dirt with my children."

The old woman to whom Chava was confessing so openly was the widow of the late gardener on the princes Czartoryski's estate in Puławy. After the loss of her beloved masters, and later of her husband, she couldn't bear staying at a place that held so many sad memories. She moved to Kazimierz, where she managed to live with her crippled daughter on her modest savings and some support from her many relatives. It was she who had, two years earlier, lent Chava those three rubles which enabled her to carry on all her business and which she kept intact with particular care.

Nothing, not even the promise of an immediate big profit, would allay her anxiety whenever all or part of those magic three rubles were out of her hands. If that did occur she was deadly afraid and imagined herself at the edge of a precipice where she and her whole family were bound to perish. It was that fear which prompted her to try and sell the sturgeon without delay. Five złotys were missing of the three rubles!

The characteristic feature of her relationship with granny Włostowicka was Chava's sincerity. She would lie to everyone of her small-town lady customers; to the old woman she never told anything but the truth.

"How much did you pay for the sturgeons?" grandma asked.

"Five groszy a pound," replied Chava.

"Then you have made a profit."

"At the assistant judge's, yes, but the assessor's wife didn't give me the cash."

"Well then, go ahead, my dear. I don't know who is living in Puławy nowadays, but it seems some well-off families are gathered there."

Chava kissed the old woman's hand and left. It was no joke walking the ten versts from Kazimierz to Puławy with fifty pounds of fish on one's back. The stur-

geon thrown over her shoulder seemed to wag its head skeptically at her courageous undertaking. But, tired and hungry though she was, she plodded along at
a good pace. After the third verst, she rested. A gentleman driving past spotted
the fish at her feet and ordered his driver to stop.

"What have you got there?" he asked.

"A sturgeon," she replied, her heart thumping.

"Oh, just a sturgeon," he muttered derisively and drove on.

What if the people in Puławy wagged their heads the way he did? Chava
jumped up and walked on. After another two versts, she sat down again and
meditated over her troubles. A two-wheeled cart passed by, headed for Puławy; a
Jew, probably picked up on the road, was sitting beside the driver. The driver was
a familiar figure in Kazimierz; he delivered the mail, a dismissed soldier, excommunicated by the church, and occasionally beaten up by the police for drunkenness. He was on his way with some mail and had taken on a passenger for his own
account.

"Franek, hi, Franek," she called, "wait a moment!"

"What's up?" he asked, without stopping his horse.

"Give me a lift to Puławy!"

"You'd have to hitch up your fish alongside my mare, or else she can't make it."

"It ain't far! A rabbit could get there in three leaps!"

"Go on and leap."

"Oh, come on."

"Where you'd sit? On Moshek's lap."

"I'm sure there's a little room for me." Without waiting for his reply, she tried
to scramble up.

"Cough up a złoty first," cried Franek.

"Don't be silly, I won't hold out on you." Off they went.

"How come it's you driving the mail cart today?" she inquired.

"Andrzej's child died," replied Franek, "so the boss sent me instead. Hell of
a job."

"You'd rather walk all over town and to the villages to deliver letters?"

"Who says I walk? I'd be a damn fool to wear out my boots. If there's a letter
to be delivered to a farm, I look around for a cart. If I find one, okay, if I don't, I
wait. Paper ain't a flower, it don't fade."

"But if it's urgent?"

"It ain't urgent to me, unless my pocket's empty."

"D'you get many letters for the countryside?"

"The devil knows. I don't deliver them all, just the ones where it says they
gotta be delivered by messenger and those that the gentlemen of the post office
ask me to deliver against a receipt: 'registered' and 'insured' letters."

"Do they pay well?"

"Nonsense. Sometimes they give me some kopecks, and sometimes a bit of grain. I told that guy in Uściąż last Sunday that I ain't no sparrow and want no grain thrown to me. The gentleman from Połanowka is a decent sort — yesterday he gave me a ruble for a letter."

"A ruble!" Chava cried excitedly. "Why it ain't even a mile to Połanowka."

"Six versts. Well, then I got myself a few drinks, and had some words with the postmaster, he hit me over the head, and I gave him a piece of my mind. He said he would fire me, the son of a bitch. Now, there, we've almost reached the post office. Get off, Jews."

Chava jumped down.

"God'll reward you," she said.

"What's that, you louse? Want me to collect the fare from your god? Cough up that złoty!"

"You're crazy, Franek, a złoty for that bit of a ride?"

If you don't give me ten kopecks, I'll cut a piece off your fish."

He produced his knife, ready to make good his threat.

"Stop it, you scoundrel," screamed the Jewess in despair, "here you are, you bandit."

Franek threw the fish down on the ground, collected the fare from Moshek, and drove on whistling a tune. Chava continued along the road with her load over her shoulder, and turned into an avenue leading to St. Mary's Institute. That was where she was surest of selling it. But she was disappointed right away, for the housekeeper told her that foodstuffs were bought only in big lot, and that while she would be ready to take a score of sturgeons, one fish alone was of no use to her.

Chava wept leaving the Institute. "What if everybody refuses to buy?" she thought. A fish can't wait long. She trudged along the street, hoping that a passerby might stop her and ask for the fish. There were quite a number of people gaping at her, but no buyer. At last an elderly gentleman stopped and asked:

"For whom is that?"

"It's for sale," Chava replied.

"Fresh?"

"Just caught."

"He looked the fish over.

"How much do you want for the whole fish?"

"Five rubles."

"Will you take four?"

Chava's heart filled with joy.

"Oh, my dear sir, it's too little. That's as much as it cost me."

"Will you take four?" .

"Where d'you want me to deliver it?"

"To the house over there, to Doctor Pryski. They'll pay you." He scribbled a note, handed it to the Jewess, and walked off.

Had Chava been Lot's wife, and had a rain of fire poured down on Puławy, she couldn't have clinched the deal faster and run away in a greater hurry. There are creatures to whom a few rubles profit lends wings! On her way home Chava kept laughing, clapping her hands, talking to herself of pleasant things — in short, behaving as if the mere joy of having earned a few rubles had driven her crazy. But a human body demands its rights, although it may forget about its needs in a moment of excitement. The Jewess had not eaten a thing except some boiled potatoes left over from the day before; and it was almost night. Exhausted from hunger, tired after chasing around the whole day, she felt her legs going limp as soon as the first feeling of joy had worn off. She dragged herself to the first village and entered the inn. Franek was sitting at a table with a young stranger; they were going over a batch of mail together and drinking vodka. The Jewish innkeeper stood a little way off, watching their gay feast with curiosity. Franek was tipsy.

"Some fellows in the service have such dainty fingertips," he was saying to the stranger, "they can tell right away if there's money in a letter."

"There sure is some in this one here," said his companion, "it's fat and bulky. How 'bout opening it?"

"Fine, let's!"

Busy with her own thoughts, Chava did not pay much attention to that scene; she bought two buns, went in front of the inn, sat down on a tree stump and started to eat. Through the open window she heard their loud laughter, and once she even heard Franek's voice distinctly, threatening: "I'd let her have it, all right!" But it meant nothing to her.

A moment later, Franek came out of the inn, quite drunk, staggered to his cart and clambered up awkwardly.

"Hi, Jewess, comin' along?"

"No," replied Chava.

Franek burst out laughing, lashed out and struck her across the back with his whip, then he whipped his horse and drove off, shouting:

"You old bag, you think I'm tryin' to court you?"

Chava screamed with pain, cursed him, and wept. Her appetite was gone; she put the rest of the bun in her pocket and headed for home. What didn't she think of on her way! She thought of the half sturgeon she had left at home, of the two fish she had sold, of the cart fare she had paid, of her hungry kids, and the delicious supper she was going to serve them, of delivering mail, of Franek and his whip. Her husband was perhaps the only thing that didn't come to her mind. Chava's face mirrored the flow of thoughts, and her lips kept uttering abrupt words — figures of her groszy's accounts. To us who know the inside story of her sturgeon deal, this won't seem strange. After all, she had made a profit of over three rubles that day (not counting the amount the assessor's wife owed her). Three rubles net profit! One has to be a she-wolf to understand all the joy of getting a leg of beef for one's young ones!

Twilight was falling when Chava reached the village opposite Kazimierz. Walking along the ditch, she heard someone snoring loudly, and a little way off, she saw a mare placidly pulling an overturned wheel cart across the meadow. That, Chava guessed, was probably drunken Franek's way of speeding up the exchange of ideas by mail, and, recalling the effectiveness of his whip, ran away as fast as she could.

You would be mistaken, dear reader, if you thought that the encounter made Chava ponder the whims of fate our correspondence is subjected to. Not at all. On the contrary; she considered Franek lucky to be able to deliver the mail and to have gotten a ruble for a letter in Połanowka.

At the sight of the little light in her window she quivered with delight. It was a long time since she had come home with so big a profit, a long time since she had served them as rich a dinner as she would tonight! Above all, she was happy that ten-month-old Itsek, who was kept quiet all day long by feeding him potatoes, would, at least, get something tasty that was appropriate to his age. To save time, she stopped at the market first, bought a quart of flour, three groszy worth of butter, half a pint of milk, and one fig. She was still a long way off when she heard the desperate cries of the children in the house. A mother belonging to another social class would probably have been scared out of her wits thinking that something had happened to her family. But Chava knew well that it was only the chorus of four little empty stomachs.

"Hush, hush, baby," she called entering the room where two boys were sobbing in a corner and the little girl was trying to pacify Itzek who was howling loudest.

Chava kissed him and stuck the fig into his mouth. She divided the rest of her bun between the three others and thus silenced all her brood.

"Where's father?" she asked her eldest daughter.

"He went to perform a marriage; he'll stay on at the wedding."

"He's cooked nothing?"

"He didn't eat."

Within an hour, efficient Chava sat down with her children to a rare meal of dumplings and potatoes with melted butter poured over them, and milk added for Itzek. The dumplings were the highlight of the feast, for the daily housekeeping budget of fifteen groszy did not allow such luxury. Potatoes, dwarf pears, gruel were the Rubys' usual fare.

I would be hard put to describe the wonderful dreams Chava dreamt that night. They were like those of a fellow who had drawn a winning lottery ticket, or of a beggar who had found a sack of gold, or, as I said before, of a she-wolf who had buried a leg of beef near her lair.

"Where've you been traipsing around?" Simcha nagged her the following day. "You got no husband, no? So you can go promenading around. How much did you make?"

Chava kept silent, reluctant to disclose the amount she possessed for fear that her husband (who, for the past three years, had been thinking of buying himself a housecoat to boost his dignity as a landlord, and of repairing the house) might want to grab her money.

"Quite a lady, aren't you?" he continued. "Buying sturgeon for yourself. What's going to happen with that half sturgeon? Who's going to take it?"

"I'll sell it," she replied curtly and walked out, taking the fish along. But where? She had been to almost every household. Suddenly, recalling yesterday's incident with Franek, she thought of the post office. True enough, Pan Chrząstkiewicz gave his wife only a token household allowance and refused to pay any debts, but whenever he did have any money (which happened usually when a peasant woman mailed some money to her husband in the army), the postmaster was generous with housekeeping expenses and settled all debts in cash. At first Chava was afraid of a possible encounter with Franek, but then she told herself that with Pan Chrząstkiewicz present, Franek wouldn't dare act the way he did on the road to Puławy. So she went.

The Kazimierz post office stood on a high hill, probably to permit Pan Chrząst-kiewicz's team of horses, harnessed to the express mail coach, to start off in a gallop and give the passengers the fleeting illusion that they were not quite as phlegmatic as they looked. Chava was still at the foot of the hill when she heard the postmaster cursing. It was not very safe to arrive at such a moment with her sturgeon; yet, wouldn't it be a pity not to find out what the hollering was all about? After a moment's hesitation, Chava slipped into the bushes for cover and picked her way cautiously uphill. The reason for the row became clearer to her with every step.

"I'll have you put in chains," yelled Chrząstkiewicz. "What did you do with these two letters, you scoundrel? Why is this one ripped open? Where have you been loafing till this morning? You son of a bitch! Do you think I'll take the re-sponsibility? You'll rot in jail! You won't ever see the light of day again—you'll croak there, you dirty dog!"

Blows followed these words, then a horrible howl, a wild scramble, and finally someone jumped crashing through the bushes right above Chava. It was Franek running away from the postmaster. The Jewess screamed and ran instinctively toward his pursuer.

"That thief," Chrząstkiewicz was yelling and panting. He stopped at the sight of her. "I'll fix him all right!"

"What did he steal?" asked Chava cautiously.

"The mail. He cut open the letters, he lost them or destroyed them. No, I won't let him get away with it, not ever!" Chrząstkiewicz vociferated pounding the ground with his stick. "Jędrzej, go downtown and fetch me a quire of paper. I'll write that report right away."

While Jędrzej went for the paper and his master shut himself up in his office to think about his report, Chava stepped into the kitchen. The postmaster's wife was so worried over the incident, she could talk of nothing else at first, but eventually she let herself be induced to consider the question of the sturgeon.

"I would buy it," she said, "if Ferdy gave me the money, but I doubt it. That rascal robbed the mail. There may have been something for us in it, too; it's a big loss. . . ."

"It's him that's robbed the mail, so it's him that'll get the clink," Chava comforted her. "Sure, it's trouble, but it isn't your fault."

"How much does this piece weigh?"

"Maybe twenty-five pounds, maybe a little more. I'll sell it cheap."

Suddenly the door opened and Chrząstkiewicz burst into the kitchen.

"Have you got time, Pani Simcha?" he asked.

"For what?"

"Pan Kopf from Uściąż sent word yesterday asking me to forward a certain letter to him as soon as received. That scoundrel didn't get back with the mail until today. He's fired, he is. Now can you take that letter over to Pan Kopf? He'll make it worth your while."

"If you wish, I'll go there right away." Chava left her sturgeon in the kitchen and rushed out.

Obviously providence had turned a new leaf in the book of her destiny. Only yesterday Chava had dreamed of Franek's good luck, and today she was headed for Uściąż with a letter! Sure, Uściąż was the place Franek scorned because people there paid for errands only with grain, but first, kasha was nothing Chava would disdain, and second, one never could tell, the postmaster might send her tomorrow to Połanówka, where they paid a ruble for a letter. Now that Franek was fired, all she had to do was to get on the right side of the postmaster.

At that point Chava laughed, thrilled with joy over a new, great, dazzling idea. What the idea was, we shall see later. Meanwhile, we must say, in fairness to Pan Kopf, that he rewarded the Jewess generously for delivering the letter. He ordered that she be given half a gallon of peas, a quart of flour, and some carrots, and, being a connoisseur of beauty, he even stroked her chin and said:

"I'll ask Pan Chrząstkiewicz to let you deliver all my mail."

Chava bowed obediently and left. And that day she and her children ate an opulent meal.

She returned to the post office with the receipt, but Chrząstkiewicz had not finished his reports. The one to the authorities, stating that two registered letters had been lost on the way by the postman, had caused him no difficulty, but the other one, to the mayor—his mortal enemy—in which he demanded Franek's arrest, kept him busy for an hour. He changed phrases, crossed them out, rewriting whole passages, and succeeded at last, after a lot of trouble, in elaborating a document that seemed to do justice to his dignity and to the importance of the case.

"I have dismissed Franek," he told Chava proudly, shaking the ink off his pen onto the table. "If you do a good job, I'll appoint you postwoman."

The Jewess bowed and thanked him moving her lips silently. A maid entered just then.

"Does master wish to eat the sturgeon cold?"

"Oh, that's right," Chrząstkiewicz remembered. "How much do I owe you for the sturgeon?"

"Don't mention it," she replied.

"Well, call for the letters."

He went out. Thus, on 13 July 18—— Chava Ruby was formally confirmed as a postwoman appointed to deliver ordinary and registered mail in the town and in the countryside, the fees being left to the discretion of the addressee. The news spread rapidly throughout Kazimierz and reached the city hall simultaneously with the report.

"Have you heard that!" shrieked the mayor's wife, bursting into her husband's office. "Chrząstkiewicz has fired Franek and appointed that herring peddler, that Ruby woman, in his place!"

"He's just sent me a report about Franek's having committed a theft, asking that I put him in jail."

"If you ever agree to that, I'll say you're an utter idiot! Don't you remember how Chrząstkiewicz insulted you at the notary's? Will you believe him that Franek has robbed the mail? And then again, that awful Jewess who dared bring me a piece of sturgeon yesterday—leftovers the assessor's wife didn't want! Well, do as you like. Anyway, I've already hired Franek to be our watchman."

"But if he actually is a thief?" the mayor wondered.

"He won't be when he's with us. And after all, we've got to run things our own way."

The mayor had his own way indeed. He refused to arrest Franek and hired him to serve at the town hall.

Franek wasn't the kind to give way easily before another, and he was even less willing to do so now that he had the formidable support of the mayor, or rather of the mayor's wife. Besides, as he also knew of a series of secret dealings being carried on in the post office, he was sure that Chrząstkiewicz wouldn't go too far pressing the matter of his guilt for fear of retaliation. Thus he decided not only to face the storm but also to take revenge on the Jewess who had taken his place and whom he suspected of having denounced his tampering with the mail at the inn.

To be fair, we must admit that the motives Franek gave for his anger were those of any "righteous citizen" and sounded as if they were taken straight from one of those learned treatises published with the aim of destroying the Jews. The rays of true light sometimes penetrate down to the lowest strata of society. Franek was a case in point; though he had never read any treatise against Jews, nevertheless he felt within him the inspiration necessary to bring forth such a work.

"The hell with the job," he told his friend, another townhall watchman, "I wasn't born yesterday, I can always find work, and I did find another job. But to have a mean Jewess snatch the bread right out of your mouth is a shame on mankind and an insult to God."

"You think he's going to keep her?"

"Sure he will. He'd jump into the fire after any skirt, and into the water after any Jew. And besides, do you think he won't get his share in the racket? I never stuck my hand into anybody else's pocket, and what I made, belonged to me, but she'll have to split her soul with him. He's hollering I robbed the mail so he can get rid of me just because I was decent and looking after my own job."

"Sure, everybody knows that."

"Oh, those Jews, those Jews. Sons of bitches, they crop up everywhere. You get your teeth into something, and they'll tear it out of your mouth. The vermin! They ought to be herded together and drowned in the Vistula."

"Right you are."

"Our bread turns into stone. With them, sand turns into bread."

"Whatever we touch goes wrong; they get away with everything. Tripping us up at every step."

"You said it!"

"I won't let that rag peddler get away with it; I'll fix her all right."

Notwithstanding these threats, Chava delivered the mail unhampered without having to stop her own trade, and both occupations were profitable yielding sometimes as much as half a ruble a day. Although she had not yet delivered any letter to Połanowka, where, according to Franek, they paid a ruble for it, she was getting plenty of kasha, peas, potatoes, flour, old clothes, and money, as there was a lot of correspondence going on just then, people were generous and the new postwoman knew how to please them. The most telling proof of prosperity were the pudgy faces of her children who were getting two warm meals a day, and the tiny bag which Chava kept on her chest under her bodice. In that tiny bag were the ten rubles she had saved, a first installment for new Sunday outfits for the six Rubys. Six, I repeat, for Chava had decided to buy even her husband a new housecoat, which was a sure sign of her prosperity.

While she was ever more successful, Franek's good luck was letting him down. One day two silver spoons were missing from the sideboard. The mayor's wife might have suspected someone else, but the mayor felt a policeman's aversion to the new watchman and fired him on the spot. Franek swore that he was innocent, but it didn't help him—the severe master would not change his mind.

"It's all because of that damn Jewess," he told the other watchman on leaving the town hall. "So long as she kept out of it, everybody considered me a decent fellow."

With this well-founded claim, he went straight to the inn, where, by a curious concatenation of circumstances, his credit had considerably improved simultaneously with the disappearance of the spoons. After washing down some of his sorrow with a series of double vodkas, he wept bitterly and complained to Srul's wife of his misfortunes and of the woman who had caused them.

"What's she got to do with it?" the innkeeper's wife defended Chava. "Has she double-crossed you?"

"Why did she get into the cart, with her sturgeon, I ask you? Eh?" Franek muttered. "I crossed myself, she climbed up. And, right away, it was no longer the mare that pulled the cart but a he-goat! I'll strangle her, I will! And if I don't strangle her, she'll starve to death anyway."

"Nothing will happen to her," said Pani Srul sternly. "Now she is able to eat roast goose. She's just been here; today she's got a letter for Połanowka."

"For Połanowka," screamed Franek, his eyes popping out of his head. "That's my ruble. I'm going to deliver that letter to my gentleman. To Połanowka!"

He ran out of the inn like a lunatic, stumbling, and headed for the country.

Chava had indeed to deliver a registered letter in Połanowka that day. Out of respect for the manor where they rewarded messengers so generously, she decided to dress with special care. Just about the time Franek was leaving the inn, she returned home to change. Having washed with particular care, wearing her new skirt and shoes, a white bonnet, and wrapped in a blue kerchief, she looked so pretty that one could, for once, forget her diligence and remember her beauty. Satisfied with her appearance and sure of earning a good bit of money, she kissed her children and left on the errand.

The road to Połanowka was bordered on one side by hills covered with undergrowth, and on the other by the Vistula. Halfway to the village the road turns uphill and passes through a narrow gorge. When Chava reached the gorge, she saw a man lying on the roadside. The old uniform coat, the worn leather cap, the mud-stained clothes reminded her of Franek. "Maybe it's him," she thought. He surely won't attack her in broad daylight. Drawing nearer, she no longer doubted that it was her predecessor. Embarrassed by this encounter, she wanted to go round the sleeper, but he had evidently spotted her, for he got up and went toward her. Chava was gripped by fear, but she decided not to run away.

"Where you headed?" Franek asked hoarsely.

"To Połanowka," the Jewess replied trembling.

"What for?"

"To deliver a letter."

"Hand it over, and be quick!"

"Why?" cried the Jewess. "It's not addressed to you."

"Hand it over," Franek roared and grabbed her by the throat.

Chava tried to free herself, he tightened his hold and hit her several times so furiously with his fist on the head that she crumpled and collapsed at his feet. Then he tore open her clothes and found the letter and the little sack on her chest.

It seems beyond any doubt that Franek was not out to murder Chava and rob her of her money. He had not planned that originally; he became a murderer and a thief because he hit her too hard in his fury and took her little bag. He did it only to take his revenge. Grabbing the letter, he ran off in the direction of Połanówka. It was not until he reached the outskirts of the village that he sobered up and realized that his errand was not safe this time. He turned back, got off the road where he had left his victim, and disappeared into the bushes.

Meanwhile, Chava, half dead and unconscious, had to wait a long time for help. It was an hour later that a butcher from Kazimierz drove by and saw that she was still alive. He put her in his wagon and drove to her home. No messengers were sent out, no doctors came running to save the injured woman, no one but the desperately crying four children and her coughing husband tried to bring her to. Finally, the news of the incident reached grandmother Włostowicka who came immediately to the rescue and called a medical practitioner. Leeches were applied to the poor bruised head and that seemed to give her some relief, but the high fever persisted and the patient continued to push somebody away, to reach for her chest, to call for the little bag, which, alas, wasn't there. Without any money, treatment was impossible. They did fetch the money the assessor's wife owed for the half sturgeon, but that was just enough to buy some potatoes for the children and to prolong the mother's coma.

Chava died after two days of suffering, without even telling them that Franek had robbed her of ten rubles, and without returning the three rubles to grandmother Włostowicka.

Poor Chava. I do forgive you for having wanted to work in my country and to have your children eat its bread.

■ Wiktor Gomulicki (1848–1919)
"El mole rachmim . . ." (1879)

[Wiktor Gomulicki was a respected and prolific poet of the positivist camp known especially for his poems devoted to everyday Warsaw life. It was Gomulicki more than any other Polish poet of his time who legitimized the urban landscape in Polish poetry. In this respect, he paralleled the literary orientation of the majority of Polish positivist prose writers, above all Prus and Sienkiewicz, for whom modern urban society and culture displaced the previous preference for the countryside and the life of the provincial gentry. "El mole rachmim," about what at first appears to be a quite ordinary Jewish wedding, is one of the best Polish poems on a Jewish subject and became one of Gomulicki's most popular poetic works.]

It was in the courtyard of a Jewish house
On a summer's eve. I made my way there in secret.
Faith, instead of uniting, divides and distances.
A wave of black heads stirred among the walls.
Itsek the quilt-maker was marrying the daughter of the junk peddler.
And guests and the curious filled the courtyard.
The place was shabby, and the people ordinary.
A few aroused geese gaggled in the vicinity of a nearby barn;
Bedding was being aired out on the railing of a balcony.
From a kitchen the unpleasant smell of fried fish wafted past.
And in a corner two acacias were dying of dryness.
The sky shone of stars like — a golden Sabbath candleholder;
Even the fleecy wool of the clouds was unsoiled by gray.
And the night was full of royal splendor.
Itsek stood beneath an old scarlet canopy,
In ceremonial robes, bathed in light and smoke.
He was a swarthy stripling, half man, half child.
Among Jews, love seizes a person deceptively;
It leads him over the abyss with closed eyes
And throws him into the embraces of a woman unexpectedly.
Everyday figures of the street composed the throng,
People whom one sees at market during the day:
Peddlers, middlemen, vendors, porters.
A fever inflamed their bearded faces

Wiktor Gomulicki, *Wiersze wybrane,* ed. Paweł Hertz (Warsaw: Państwowy Instytut Wydawniczy, 1960), 28–31. The title of the poem derives from the opening words of the Jewish prayer for the dead.

And they were gilded by the light of the wax *avduli*
(Of candles, that is, in which the flames nestle close to each other
As in the lightning-plaited sword of the archangel).
At times, foreheads bent forward like ears of corn.
They jabbered, but to no one did the ceremony seem
"The solemn drollery of Beaumarchais."
Itsek covered his face with a kerchief, while one of the congregation,
Not a chaplain, but an ordinary man — only paler
And sadder than others — sang
While his gaze encompassed everything.
The song, though matrimonial, was not happy.
Two curly headed boys accompanied it by shouts,
And the whole crowd with a half-plaintive, half-wild murmuring.

I looked on this scene interestedly, a bit coldly.
Itsek, though covered by a luminous and smoky cloud
And solemn amid the rubbish and litter of the courtyard, as though before
    an altar,
Was for me only Itsek, a poor quilt-maker;
Nor did I see anything poetic in any of the others:
To me they seemed ordinary people, who guard
With equal diligence their beards as well as their faith and possessions.
Vainly did their swarthy faces acquire a mysterious aspect
From the radiance of the new moon and the flames of the candles:
None of them captivated with an inspired or melancholic countenance.
Suddenly the singing stilled. You'd say that it scattered in the distance.
The windows of the wedding chamber were opened with a bang.
The bride could be seen sitting weeping in the midst of a crowd of women.
The *chazen,* with sparkling eyes and patriarchal beard,
Raised his arms above her
And recalled her father who died young,
And who today was absent from the family celebration. . . .
His words brought forth a great cry, and during the lamentation,
During the sobbing of the women and the wringing of hands,
He led a song which rings with a funereal note,
El mole rachmim . . . Although brimming with tears
The song flowed on calmly, bearing to the feet of the Lord
A heartfelt grief, and thoughts restrained by force;
Thus weeps a grown son over the grave of his father.
Then, laced through with a sadness that ushers forth from graves,
It lost in a flicker faith and hope,
Grew in power and, torn by the perturbation of pain,

It drowned in the burning tears and lamentation of the women.
No, not of one grave, but of a million graves
It became a loud weeper, and, maddened with pain,
Raced to wail over old cemeteries,
Over the bones of Israel, which
Are scattered over the entire earth like grains of a barren sand.
And over this sowing, which may perhaps be poor,
And over the silent weeds that grow on the graves,
And over the fact that the weak spirits of their sons have become stunted,
And because this night of bondage is so long, so long . . .
Nothing restrained the song . . . It surged on like a stream
When it turns into a foamy river after a storm;
The singer had sparks in his eyes and his breast was trembling;
His forehead, which he uncovered, pushing his cap back on his head,
Ran with sweat. The song moved even an old grannie,
Whom paralysis had made a corpse and a rock;
The glass of her half-dead pupils grew misty.
Everyone in the room was crying, seized with a profound grief,
And when the *chazen* recalled holy Jerusalem,
The mother, who though her white face shines from afar,
Died centuries ago for her first children;
When he recalled the merciless cruelty of fate,
The wretchedness, persecution, wandering, martyrdom,
And happiness lost forever, forever —
The pain became more real, the wounds of the heart bloodier.
Throughout the room the madness of despair blew with a wild beat
And burst forth in a huge, hopeless roar . . .
I listened to the song with a breast swollen with feeling;
And these people complaining loudly before God,
Proud of their great past, emboldened by their great pains,
Strangely grew in size in my eyes — and became noble.
I no longer saw the shabby stains on the canopy,
The garb of Itsek, or even Itsek's name no longer upset me.
The ordinariness of these bearded faces disappeared for me,
And I became like a man who . . . daydreams.
The courtyard . . . no, it was now a flowering valley
Somewhere at the base of Mt. Lebanon, which climbs to the sky
And roars with a forest of dark cedars, as though singing.
The moon poured forth silver springs on this valley,
The heaven covered it over with a crystal bell,
The desert breathed with a hot breath,

And palm trees cooled like fans of leaves.
Between heaven and earth there was no envy —
The countenance of Jehovah looked from above, smilingly
Blessing the valley, its people and the lambs in it;
The crowd of the faithful whispered prayers and bowed to the Lord,
The aroma of nard and saffron floated in the air;
Like a serpent, the stream unwound its silver-scaled plexus —
And stars shone like a golden Sabbath candleholder.

■ Klemens Junosza (Szaniawski) (1849–98)
"The Tailor" (1884)

[A popular novelist and short story writer, Klemens Junosza (whose real name was Klemens Szaniawski) became known for his almost anthropologically detailed pictures of the economic hardships of the provincial Polish landowning gentry. He applied the same literary method to his extensive writings about rural and urban Jewish life. Although compassionate in his depiction especially of impoverished Jews, as in the stories translated here, "Łaciarz" ("The Tailor") and "Froim," Junosza did not flinch from portraying members of the Jewish community who devoted their energies to the exploitation of others. This is the subject of his well-regarded novel *Żywot i sprawy I. M. P. Symchy Borucha Kaltkugla ksiąg pięcioro* (*The Life and Affairs of the Honorable Symcha Boruch, Juggler of Five Account Books*, 1895). In 1889 Junosza also published a sociological treatise on the Jews under the title *Nasi żydzi w miasteczkach i na wsiach* (*Our Jews in Towns and Villages*); excerpts from this work follow the translation of "Froim." Although doubtless sincere in his desire to deal even-handedly with Jewish life in Poland as he understood it, Junosza's less flattering portraits of Jews earned him a reputation for anti-Semitism that he never succeeded in throwing off.]

A sad spring night rocked the Podlasian gentry village to sleep.

The little houses and barns sank in darkness as if in some huge vessel full of a rare, diluted ink. From time to time, fleetingly, from behind heavy lead-colored clouds blown from above by a stronger wind, a small star appeared and immediately disappeared from view, like a person stealthily crossing a frontier.

The silence was funereal, solemn; lights were turned out, people slumbered. Only the strong wind, gamboling about the fields, dug in and contended with the old forked willow and tore the last yellow leaves from its broken and twisted branches.

The heavy trunk of this sick consumptive, its upper body rent by lightning, was hollowed on the inside; its heart had already fallen out from the side branches, and in this way a kind of strange flute was fashioned of the willow tree from which breaths of wind extracted whimsical tones.

From the distant forest the protracted, sad wailing of hungry wolves sometimes wafted, and they became a single voice reverberating amid the darkness and stillness.

People slumbered in a hard, stonelike sleep, that sleep bereft of dreams and apparitions which is the lot of those who work hard with their hands.

To a person who handles a plow the whole day long or wields a flail well, even

---

The story "Laciarz" first appeared in the newspaper *Kurier Warszawski* in 1884. It was subsequently included in Junosza's collection *Z mazurskiej ziemi* (*From the Mazurian Land*), which was also published in 1884. My translation follows the text in Klemens Junosza (Szaniawski), *Obywatel z Tamki i inne opowiadania* (Warsaw: Czytelnik, 1960), 151–74.

a hard bench suffices as a comfortable bed. Many an otherwise fortunate individual would envy such a sleep.

For several hours now, the cocks having announced midnight long before, Morpheus ruled absolutely over this gentry hamlet; all its inhabitants were snoring for all they were worth, as befitting true poor country squires.

On this gray spring night, in one of the small cottages, situated on the edge of the hamlet, a white, uncertain little light twinkled and the panes of glass reflected the shadow of a man bent over, bowed, continually executing monotonous, measured, mechanical gestures with his hand.

Who is awake in the village at so late an hour? To whom did the bizarre thought occur to burn a light on a night granted for the purpose of sleeping? Let us have a look inside the hut.

It is big enough, with two small windows. In the chimney, hissing and cracking, glow two damp birch slivers along the white bark of which a white glimmer of flame flits from time to time. It stops for a while and again retreats to its parents, two coarse burning firebrands, draws fresh strength from them, and stronger than before, now rich in bloody reflection, throws itself on a sliver with new ardor and with a yet hotter kiss tears the white skin from it.

In another corner of the hut stands a large bed supporting a huge feather comforter covered with a striped kilim. From under one corner of it can be seen a woman's nightcap and part of the brick-red face of a lively gentlewoman.

Beneath the chimney, in a handful of fresh straw, snores the right hand of the mistress, the squat Brygida, evidently enjoying pastoral-idyllic dreams since she frequently makes a gesture as if energetically turning away from harm somebody's stray livestock.

Stretched out on a bench beneath the wall is a boy about twelve, the youngest member of the family. His head propped up against a sheepskin coat folded in four, his hands beneath his head, he lies as quiet and peaceful as when in summertime, herding oxen before daybreak, he gazed in quiet contemplation at stars wandering about the sky and at those milky ways along which, according to folk legends, saints and angels walk.

Pan Onufry himself, the owner of the cottage and land, is asleep on the opposite side, in the great room, where a pine tree coated a yellow color pretends to be an ash tree and homemade linen covering the table imitates a tablecloth.

Pan Onufry sleeps like a corpse, like the rest of his household sleeps, like his wife who raged and bellowed hundreds of times the whole day long and chattered away even twice as much!

In the room that serves as both servants' quarters and kitchen, where a fire is burning in the fireplace, only one being is awake, but he is completely alien to this home.

It is a shabby little Jew, pale, frail, thin, distinguished by a particular pointedness of forms.

A sharply pointed Crimean cap, pushed somewhat to the rear, covers the top of his head; from beneath it protrude short curly side-locks, like two drills screwed into his temples. The cap is no doubt contraband, but this poor little Jew has tasted so little of the sweet fruits in his life that perhaps this forbidden yet essentially innocent one is his only comfort and personal pleasure.

Spectacles in a brass frame perch on his nose, and through the glass of these antique pince-nez, possibly the property at one time of some old, very old monk, penetrating dark eyes, and a sharp gaze, are visible, the latter to some extent concealed by a teary mist which like a tulle curtain falls on vision tired from work and lack of sleep.

The elongated face ends in a thin, pointed little beard in which, like white stitching against the background of a black garment, silver threads of premature grayness shine.

His concave chest, sunken and spare, attests through its heavy, interrupted breathing how much work his poor lungs have to assume in order to maintain their owner's life.

Pointed elbows, gaunt, sharply ended fingers, and legs as thin as twigs make up the whole, which resembles a skeleton enclosed in a double case: human skin and a few lengths of black, well-worn camlet.

This frail being so passionately devoted to work is Yudka Silberknopf, the first Warsaw tailor in all of Łosice and its environs, as he himself asserts.

Before him on a table lie scissors, a handful of buttons, a few balls of thread, a piece of wax stuck on a small board, and a snuffbox made of birch bark and a little leather strap and filled with green Ukrainian tobacco.

From time to time, when the teary fog covers his eyes more and his lids acquire the weight of lead and begin to fall helplessly, Yudka's thin fingers draw out of the snuffbox a portion of green powder and his freshness temporarily returns.

Bigger tears flow into his eyes, wash away the fog, and once again his gaze more swiftly follows the stitches of the needle, which must sew a fine Warsaw coat with such a large collar the likes of which the count himself never wore.

Besides the tobacco, the table also contains a small bottle of vodka, a piece of bread, two onions, and a pinch of salt in a piece of paper. But Yudka, a practical man, does not drink the vodka now nor eat the onions because he knows full well that in a few hours, when he is sewing the sleeves, and there to the east, between earth and heaven, a pale band has become clearly outlined and roused the cocks to their third crowing, he will not feel well somewhere in the vicinity of his heart.

At that moment he will feel such a contraction in the pit of his stomach and such a terrible faintness that he will almost fall from his stool. He will become weak, he will see spots flashing before his eyes, very pretty red, green, blue, gold, and gold-spotted black spots and then all black ones that will quickly begin to unite and form a single black whole.

Then a light tremor will run along his spine, huge drops of perspiration will appear on his brow . . . his sunken chest will begin working hard . . . and for a moment it will seem to him that Jehovah became impoverished and barely has enough air and that, naturally, only for wealthier Jews.

Yudka knows such moments well—this is not the first time he has experienced them. Afterward, he begs forgiveness of his Creator for having such a sinful suspicion; but it did seem to him that there was no more air for the poor.

That is also why, since he knows such matters, that he does not immediately drink the vodka. The time will come for that, no need to look at the clock . . . Green and gold spots flash before his eyes . . .

When the time for that comes, Yudka will get up, straighten himself, moisten his temples with water, wash his hands, turn his eyes to where a gilded band already separates earth from heaven, and utter a short prayer.

This prayer will consist wholly of expressions of gratitude. Yudka will declare: "Thank you, God, for not making me a woman; thank you for not making me a slave, or a dog!"

Or: "Thank you for the fact that I am an able man; that I am a free man and can work eighteen hours a day; and that I am the first Warsaw tailor in the whole town of Łosice and all its environs and not some ugly and stupid animal."

Afterward, with clean conscience, Yudka will pour a tiny bit of his drink on the ground and sip the rest of it slowly, delighting in each drop, which at once brings an animating warmth to his chilled, tremor-shaken organism.

After downing the vodka, he will consume a small quantity of bread with a huge quantity of salt and will eat an onion—but just one—since such onions are not encountered daily. They are large, smooth, pale red, with a particular silver sheen, and can serve as the real adornment of the Sabbath feast. It is for that reason that one of them must be kept in reserve, in the deepest pocket of a threadbare gaberdine.

Having addressed the matter of nourishment, his eyes red, but with an artificially induced sprightliness, Yudka blows on the fire and places in the fireplace two flat-irons with handles bound in rags, two irons as black as his lot in life and as hard as that relentless necessity which bends his neck to the ground and powders his beard with premature gray.

Before the loudly snoring squire and his household awake from their sound sleep, and before Yudka finishes his elegant Warsaw coat that resembles a huge bag, let us retreat in thought and in a few hurried strokes attempt to trace the biography of this tailor.

It will not contain pretty and aesthetic images; dirt, hunger, ignorance, and superhuman work are the four pillars supporting the life of this person.

The power of memory did not fix in his mind any pretty or poetic images. However far back into the past his thought might reach, it would find only drabness, gloom, and filth.

If he dreamt of anything in his youth, then it would only have been about silver rubles or perhaps about great success in talmudic learning. But neither wealth nor scholarship were inscribed in the book of his destinies.

He inherited from his father a trade that he had to keep up.

In this very same town his great grandfather sewed the gentry ample *czamary*[1] and accessories as well as sturdy rain-cloaks.

Those were lovely times!

They live to this day in the family tradition of Yudka; they pass in the living word from generation to generation, for there is something to tell about after all!

The nobleman was loath to part with a grosz, but spared nothing when it came to provisions. His cheapness, however, was legendary!

It was nothing unusual for Yudka to have an entire pike for the Sabbath, and sometimes even on a weekday meat made an appearance at his table.

There was plenty of work on the estates, his profit was frequent, and his wealth so considerable that when great grandfather gave granny Royza in marriage, her dowry included four ducats edged in pure gold, and in addition he also gave a silver thaler for luck.

Those were the days, and how!

Yudka's grandfather, who inherited from his father part of the house and the workshop, no longer had such a fate. Nevertheless, he praised his own times for he created a masterpiece of the tailor's art, a masterpiece about which he liked to tell his grandchildren . . .

He made a dress coat!

A dress coat for none other than the mayor, for his wedding. It was splendid — dark blue with gilded buttons, a waistcoat with white flowers to go with it, and trousers of canary-yellow nankeen.

Everything fit like a glove. The dress coat was elegant, long, with narrowish sleeves; a real gem. The entire outfit created a magnificent effect that beggars description.

Ha! In those days people had taste, dressed up like dolls, and were lords! They paid five złotys to have an outfit made up, and without any bargaining.

His grandfather had two sons, so that Yudka's father got only one eighth of the house. The times also worsened a bit. The business began to decline and lowered itself to sewing peasant's overcoats and antediluvian, though always fashionable, surtouts for the poorer gentry who worked their own land.

It was in this period that our hero saw the light of day.

As reliable as memory may be, I recall three or four emaciated little Jews, bent over a narrow table sewing away for all they were worth.

At another table, the father, as thin and dry as a lath, a master tailor whose hair had already turned gray, was cutting a large piece of cloth with dull scissors. The scissors gave off an unpleasant grating sound, while Yudka, who was crawling

---

1. A type of coat with strings instead of buttons worn by the old Polish gentry.

around beneath the table, eagerly grabbed the cuttings, which meant to him what mechanical dolls, pretty big rocking horses, or bicycles mean to wealthy children.

The father was very kind-hearted and did not deny his son the little pieces of cut cloth. But even a father's generosity has its limits. So when the boy tore a piece that could be used for a patch, his parent confiscated the booty and punished him by striking him several times on the shoulders with his yarmulka.

With a piercing scream, Yudka snuggled up beneath protective wings, which is to say beneath his mother's apron. It was only here that he experienced a certain consolation in his misery, since his mother shoved a piece of potato in his mouth, hit him on the neck with her fist, and tossed him out the door shouting: "Gay weg! Dy paskidnik!"

Which means: "Go on, little angel, be off with you, go run around a little in the open air."

The potato calmed Yudka's agitated nerves, his joy returned, the more so since he came across a group of entrepreneurs of equal age and outlook who were building an attractive two-story house out of shavings collected around the yard, making in the process a racket as great as what accompanied the building of Jericho.

Yudka's youth followed an unvarying pattern. In winter he warmed himself beneath the stove, in summer in the sun. He fed himself, or rather was fed, on potatoes and radishes. When he was disobedient or bad in other ways, his father struck him with his yarmulka and his mother with whatever she happened to have in her hand at the time.

When he turned six his father began thinking about his education.

This education descended upon him like lightning, sudden and unexpected. He was taken to school just the way someone might have been taken off to the army in the old days.

On a certain lovely morning (for usually in the dark moments of life mornings always appear very lovely), two older, twelve- or thirteen-year-old Jewish lads arrived, took the little culprit by the hands, and dragged him off with them. He has to be given credit for the fact that he defended himself valiantly. Holding fast to the pavement with his feet, he shouted, struggled, but finally had to yield to overpowering force.

Led down several narrow streets, he was finally thrust into a dark, stuffy room full of children who stared at the new arrival with curious, widely opened eyes.

At a separate little table in the room sat a man of learning and great wisdom . . . and a strangely stern face. In front of him lay a thick book bearing the traces of the fingers of many generations each of which in all likelihood used more tobacco than soap since the corners of the pages were completely blackened.

The master had a stern look, and when he gazed at the auditorium with his big black eyes fear gripped the lot of them. Reddish hairs stuck out from under his faded plush cap, and a long brownish beard fell to his chest.

The master held in his mouth a long-stemmed deep porcelain pipe. Little pieces of black tobacco, identified by the label on the packet as "Select Swicent, Fine-Cut," glowed in this vessel, which a certain very wealthy merchant had brought him many years ago as a present from Gdańsk.

The bluish smoke of the select, finely cut narcotic united with the heavy, stifling atmosphere of the school and created a scent utterly unlike the fragrance of roses, violets, or lilies of the valley.

Seized by anxiety, Yudka looked in dread at the master, at his brownish beard, and at the pipe stem about which the tales of the younger generation of future merchants and citizens of the town asserted that in a strange way it clung smoothly to one's back and greatly facilitated the comprehension of the intricate letters of the Hebrew alphabet.

In the course of his longer stay in the sanctuary of learning, Yudka became personally convinced that such tales were not the fruit of invention and fantasy, but the absolute truth. Besides his great scholarship and highly refined mind, the master possessed a strong right hand and did not in the least spare the expensive stem in the noble purpose of inculcating learning.

The system of education was quite simple and unsophisticated. The master bypassed the mind and aimed straight for the memory—across the back. It was not his fault that this route became the one he followed most frequently.

In order to save time he passed over all explanations and observed that exalted and very simple pedagogical principle which is the basis of the game known as "Father Virgil":

Father Virgil taught his children—
Few there were, just twenty-two—
Come on, children, come on, children!
Come on do just what I do!

The learned *melamed* of Łosice, the esteemed rebbe Yoyna Gewaltlehrer, played "Father Virgil" with his pupils by first reading, slowly, loudly, with a melodious declamation and constant swaying back and forth, after which all the children together repeated the words he read imitating the intonation of his voice and executing precisely the same movements of the master.

This is a splendid system and, apart from many others, has the one great virtue, which is unknown to modern pedagogues, of saving the school the expense of a sign.

The great tumult, which is a lot cheaper than a plaque with the appropriate inscription, informs passersby and the nearest inhabitants as to the existence of the sanctuary of learning. At the same time it affords the director of the school the most eloquent testimony that the young people are not idling but instead passionately and diligently applying themselves to scholarly work and exercising their minds.

Tadeusz Popiel (1862–1913), "Holiday of the Torah" (1889). Courtesy Żydowski Instytut Historyczny (Warsaw).

Rebbe Yoyna thus fairly enjoyed considerable recognition as a wise and energetic pedagogue insofar as he succeeded in teaching young people the loveliest things from books which he certainly could read but of which he understood nothing.

Yudka spent five years in this sanctuary of learning, and after acquiring the closest familiarity with the pipe stem of the esteemed master, made such progress that he read the holy books with the loveliest lachrymose intonation, and swayed over them so adroitly, so rhythmically, it seemed as if he had a spring set in his back.

Although he grew manly in spirit, Yudka did not become manly in body. He was thin and pale, and curiously like a young asparagus artificially dislodged from an old root.

No blush ever appeared on his pale-dull face. Only his large, wide-open eyes, although stamped with the sign of weariness, had the appearance of life.

For a future tailor, the education drawn from the inexhaustible well of the esteemed rebbe Yoyna more than sufficed, and as a result Yudka was ordered to leave the cheder and take up a place at a tailor's workshop, in fact at the famous workshop where his grandfather had sewn that dress coat unique in the history of the local tailoring establishment and which still lived in the memory of the town's oldest inhabitants.

Yudka thus left the cheder without sadness and without tender memories and entered his new occupation also without great joy.

He threaded needles, sewed on buttons, affixed patches, and learned from his father the proper way to pat down garments on clients' backs so as to prove to them that a tight fit was comfortable and a wide one went beautifully with their figure, and that all worthy people in the entire district would have to praise the cut and that the count of Wywłoka himself did not possess a better garment in his Varsovian and foreign wardrobe.

While engaged in this work the heretofore straight spine of Yudka slowly and unobtrusively began getting crooked, and his left shoulder, no longer able to stay on the same level with his right one, drooped somewhat.

In the future these minor defects made Yudka a purely civilian tailor, whereas otherwise he might have become a hero and gathered laurel wreaths on the field of battle, for which he did not, however, have an inborn affection. From childhood he preferred the needle to the bayonet and the sight of marching soldiers filled him with dread.

During his professional practice, Yudka used to go on outings into the neighboring environs at his father's side. On such occasions, besides the necessary tools, they took with them two bags in which they brought back something for the provisioning of Mama Ruchla's larder.

After six years of practice, Yudka was already a young man and an accomplished tailor. He possessed a festive camlet capote, which he had sewn himself, a black woolen belt, and boots. He wore a cap pushed to the back of his head and prepared himself for a journey to very distant places, almost to the end of the world.

In a white cloth stall, with his father and several other members of his family, he set out on a trip to Sokołów, where he had a certain small matter to attend to.

He had to get married there.

The truth of the matter was that he had never seen the pretty panna Bayla

Goldwasser, the daughter of the local "chabou," who was to become the chosen one of his heart and his lifelong companion. But so what if he had never seen her?

Even if he had seen her, would her dowry have increased by even a single cent? Would the pretty Bayla be able to cook potatoes any better? Or buy an emaciated chicken in the marketplace any cheaper?

Not in the slightest. So why bother about any additional waste of time or expense?

The wedding procession was already awaiting the bridegroom, with an orchestra composed of a fiddle, flute, and tambourine. The money that was spent on the wedding!

The bride and groom were conducted beneath an old faded canopy, married, feted at a wedding party, and thus Yudka began a new life.

Once she removed the veil from her face, the pretty Bayla revealed herself to the eyes of her husband. Her face was red and somewhat freckled, her figure on the dumpy and thickset side. To tell the truth, there wasn't much to get excited about; but it must be assumed that even if Bayla possessed the charms of the biblical Judith or Shakespeare's Jessica, that would have been a very secondary matter for our hero and of little effect on him.

This lad, already a husband now, if he ever dreamed about anything, it would have been the least about women. He was still so young and had seen so little beauty in his short life, and had heard so little about the emotions in general, that he didn't have and indeed couldn't have had the slightest qualifications to be the hero of a novel.

His marriage was nothing more or less than a business transaction arranged mutually between his father and Shmul Goldwasser, the leading tailor in all Sokołów.

The fathers each contributed thirty rubles toward a capital account for the young pair, while Yudka was obliged to live at his father-in-law's for the first three years of his marriage, to eat at his table, and to train further in his profession. When the three years were over, he and his wife were to return to their home town and to spend the next three years under his father's roof, after which he would take possession of the capital with interest and would begin living independently from his own labor.

The program was carried out in full.

I don't know if in those first three years the young married couple looked deeply into each other's eyes, held hands, or whispered sweet nothings in each other's ears, but it seems to me that they did not. He spent all his time in the workshop, whereas she divided her time between the kitchen, the cradle, and the market at which she permitted herself some small speculative trades. It must be admitted, however, that they were true to each other and that neither one of them experienced the desire to cast a glance in another direction. Why should they? They barely even looked at each other.

When they returned to their home town, Yudka threw himself into a frenzy of work. He wore a capote that was two inches shorter, had his boots cleaned several times a year, and hung a sign with the inscription "Yudka, Warsaw Tailor" above the door of his house. Why Warsaw I shall explain at once.

Yudka was not lying. A part of his expertise, to be sure not direct nor straight but over several stages, flowed to him from Warsaw. In order to explain this more easily to the reader, I have to compose something on the order of a miniature Book of Genesis of this wisdom.

Yudka's last level of training took place in the studio of his father-in-law, master Shmul Goldwasser.

Shmul studied with Hershek Fajn in Biała; Hershko studied with Yankel the Handsome in Siedlce; Yankel studied with Abram Gelbfisz, the great tailor of Lublin; Abram Gelbfisz completed his studies with Boruch Włodawer in the Praga district of Warsaw; and finally Boruch Włodawer had apprenticed with Chaim Tabaksblum, who not only owned his own workshop in Warsaw but was even the twenty-sixth part owner of the cheap goods store in Krasiński Square.

Hence nobody can deny that part of the knowledge of Chaim, through a series of intermediate stages, came down to Yudka, and that this master had a certain right to be titled a Warsaw tailor.

He was entitled to this right all the more by virtue of the fact that he even possessed a colored picture from a journal from 1846, which it was possible to admire from the street through a window only to the extent allowed by the dusty panes and mass of flies.

Despite his dowry, however, and his numerous clientele, good fortune did not accompany Yudka. His father died; he himself had been seriously ill on several occasions; he had eight children; his expenses were heavy; and medical care consumed his funds. Yudka began to grow gray, and was coughing all the harder.

He had just one happy, though short, moment in life.

One summer he began renting a fruit garden. What a paradise that was!

He used to sew in a straw hut in the fresh air and every Sunday came back with a load of pears. What an abundant life he had!

Bayla prepared a wonderful soup from worm-eaten apples that had been prematurely knocked down from trees by the wind, and there were plenty of green chives, young potatoes, and radishes.

How delicious to live rather than die!

During this period of his life Yudka even sang. He did this every Saturday, after the Sabbath had ended and myriads of stars began glowing in the dark-blue summer sky. He sang some *mayufes* in a trembling voice, his gaze fixed on the pale fog that arose above the nearby lake like a spirit, and listening raptly to the croaking of frogs and the screeching of corncrakes.

This happiness lasted a short time!

The financial aspect of his business was anything but splendid. Storms ruined much of his fruit, prices were unexceptional, and thieves accounted for some of his losses. He had to renounce this type of enterprise in the future, the more so since the small capital he had left went for the dowries of his two eldest daughters, who together with their husbands settled in with their father.

On top of all that, another tailor set up shop in town. He was called a "Petersburg Tailor," since he had been a musician in the army and had served for a time in a regiment as far as Brest whence he imported such fresh styles that in the face of them Yudka's old journal lost its authority.

This competition was lethal. The best clientele transferred to the fashionable Abramek, while Yudka, a bag on his shoulders, wandered from village to village looking for work on the estates of the gentry, both big and small.

For the past several days, as a matter of fact, he has been working for Pan Onufry. He has been working diligently, since in this period of time he sewed a lovely mantle for Pani Onufry, made over an old overcoat into a jacket for Panna Brygida, patched up and restored some ten different articles of clothing, and by the end of this night was to complete his masterpiece—the greatcoat for Pan Onufry himself.

For all of this, besides a load of wood and provisions, provisions which Pan Onufry swore solemnly to deliver in his own cart the following week, Yudka was supposed to receive in cash four silver rubles.

The masterpiece absolutely had to be finished on time.

"Listen, Jew," Pan Onufry announced, "I'll pay you, you scoundrel, as a gentleman, but remember the coat's got to be ready for Friday morning since I won't go to the church fair in anything but my best outfit."

"But I beg your lordship," Yudka explained, "I haven't slept the whole week."

"Then why didn't you bring an apprentice along to help you?"

"What can an apprentice earn here, sir, when I myself earn so little?"

"I told you, do as you wish, but just so it's ready."

"Well then, I'll do it, but would your lordship add just a half a bushel of potatoes for the kids . . . please don't spare it, sir, times are so hard now."

"Oh, devil with . . . ! All right, I'll give you as much as you can lift so long as you get the thing done. I'll also procure you work at my neighbor's."

This promise was a spur to Yudka; he would stay up working a fourth night in a row, but besides the wages agreed upon, he would receive a half a bushel of potatoes, and the prospect of new work also meant something.

And so he betook himself zealously to his work, and when the golden band began to appear in the east, and he had already sewn on the sleeves to his masterpiece, only then did weakness overcome him. Colored rings flickered before his eyes with extraordinary speed and immediately began turning black. At such moments, as was his custom, Yudka came to his own aid by means of a glass of vodka and a pungent onion with bread.

When his strength recovered and he was all set to press the coat, Brygida jumped out of bed and started a fire in the fireplace sufficient to roast an entire calf.

Pani Onufry also arose.

"How greedy the little Jew must be for profit if he's been sitting up all this time," she said.

"Begging your pardon, ma'am," answered Yudka, "every poor thing is very greedy, but greedy or not, when his lordship goes to the church fair he's going to look just like the count of Wywłoka. A piece of clothing like this is a rare thing!"

Pani Onufry carefully examined the coat, found fault a bit with the sewing, criticized the pockets, but on the whole was content that her esteemed husband had achieved such elegance at a cheap price. But when she cast a glance at Yudka's face, all drained of color and exhausted, and at his eyes as red as a rabbit's, she felt sorry for the Jew and declared: "Would you like something to eat? You look just awful, Yudka."

"Thank you kindly, ma'am, but what can I eat here? I'm not allowed to eat what you people eat."

The woman admitted that he was right.

"What's true is true," she said, "everyone has to respect his own law . . ." after which she opened a cupboard, poured out a glass of vodka, and set it on the table.

"Go on," she said, "at least this you can have!"

The second glass of vodka in a row and the heat from the fire in the fireplace had their effect. Yudka came to, his face turned bright red, and even his mood brightened. He made jokes as he tried the baggy coat on Pan Onufry and smoothed it over his broad shoulders.

"Well, Małgosia?" asked the freshly decked-out squire. "Have you seen the likes of it?"

"There's nothing to say, the Jew knows his business. He sewed you a nice garment all right."

"Let your lordship himself judge how it lies," said Yudka as he smoothed out the wrinkles with the palm of a hand. "Let someone else try to make such a fine coat! That's a real piece of work; it's a work of art! Oy vey, your lordship looks he was all set to go off to some great wedding. I've earned my half bushel of potatoes."

"Well, I gave my word . . . I'll keep it. I'll see that you get what I promised."

"That won't be until Tuesday; maybe your lordship can at least give me a quarter today for my children; I'll take them home with me. I'm sure they don't have anything to eat at home. For such fine work let them have those few potatoes to eat!"

The squire led the Jew to the pile of potatoes, helped him fill his sack with a good quarter bushel, then paid him the money he owed him, and they parted.

Pan Onufry and his wife headed for the fair. In his new coat, a red shawl about the neck, and freshly shaved, he had an unusually festive air. His wife, on the other hand, attired in a huge mantle of antediluvian cut, looked like a little haystack.

Yudka left on foot.

He bore the heavy sack, which contained two tailor's irons besides the potatoes, on his stooped shoulders.

The road was full of mud. A heavy, gray fog hung in the air; the contours of trees and wayside bushes appeared indistinctly from behind it.

It was nearly two miles to town, and Yudka had to reach it before sundown since it was Friday and the Sabbath was about to begin.

He counted on his light weight, on the wooden tailor's measure with which he supported himself, and finally on the possibility of some peasant catching up to him and giving him a lift the rest of the way in his wagon. After all, everyone knew him in these parts.

In order to make it easier to walk, he gathered up the ends of his gaberdine and attached them to his belt from the back. This gave his capote the appearance of a kind of dress coat the tail of which kept dragging along in the mud the deeper it got.

It's no easy matter walking on foot along a bumpy road full of quaggy mud, especially when carrying a fairly heavy load. Oh, it's anything but easy! But Yudka was being propelled home by his great joy.

He had such a splendid week; he earned so much! He was going to have a wagon full of wood and some provisions; he had four whole rubles in his pocket and on his shoulders he was carrying a quarter bushel of potatoes!

It was worth hurrying home with such copious earnings!

So he walked along the road and thought.

In the beginning, his thoughts concentrated on the sum he had earned. He kept reckoning and figuring what he could buy for those four rubles and how much a wagon of wood and the provisions he was going to receive additionally were worth. These things on his mind, he walked very fast, so fast that he felt himself getting warm. His face began to burn, and his heart was working strenuously.

He had to slow his pace and finally came to a halt, set his load on the ground, lit up a smoke, and started looking around to see if perhaps some peasant wagon was approaching.

He then ascertained that he had not yet come two versts. As far as his eye could reach, the road was completely empty; but several wagons were traveling from the opposite side. A lame beggar, having taken his crutches under an arm, was also hurrying in the direction of the fair. He was actually running at a brisk pace and was singing a song of not very pious character. Everyone was heading in the other direction!

He was reminded of his conversation with Pani Onufry and he began thinking about her. He himself said that poverty was greedy and grasping, and because of the fact that poverty is greedy on account of it's being forever hungry, the well-to-do have clothes made to order.

That's true, he thought, being poor is a nasty business, and hunger is strangely like a whip; it beats, beats hard. A water-carrier's horse receives plenty of blows; it pulls a lot of water and gets a little hay in return. For these hard times, the horse isn't doing badly, but a tailor makes out worse. Why worse? Because a horse needs only hay and has neither a wife nor eight kids, doesn't have to arrange the Sabbath feast or give his daughters in marriage.

Yudka began to envy the horse, but the thought disturbed him. Phew! What am I thinking! A horse is an animal whereas he is the leading Warsaw tailor in all Łosice. He thanks God each and every morning for making him a human being. A horse is stupid whereas he drank for five years from the well of wisdom at the learned rebbe Yoyna's. After they die horses are consumed by dogs whereas he is going to be lying comfortably in the ground beneath a stone with a candleholder engraved on it. His soul will go to his illustrious forebears.

No! The tailor does not envy a horse's fate. Besides, he had such handsome earnings this week!

He had already rested and then resumed his travel. But a strange drowsiness took hold of him as he walked. He stared blankly at the gray fog, took one step at a time automatically, but his steps became increasingly slower.

His legs grew heavy as if someone had attached a piece of lead to each one. They did not want to follow a straight path but kept on swaying uncertainly and describing circles like a drunk.

But Yudka is not drunk; he just feels somewhat weak.

It's a trifle, certain to pass. It's not the first time he's experienced it. Oh, it's happened many times!

It's just drowsiness, drowsiness that causes the head to ache a little and the body to shiver. Sometimes a person can get sick from it, and sometimes it passes. It often passes. Yudka knows that it's possible to get used to it, and anyway a little wagon may yet come along . . .

But alas, there is none in sight.

He has already come halfway, but what is this? The town is not drawing any nearer; on the contrary, it seems to have grown even more distant. And his sack has become frightfully heavy. Did the squire dump peas in it instead of a quarter bushel of potatoes?

No, they really are potatoes. They oppress the back . . . oppress it something awful; but why are they so terribly heavy? When he first took them on his back, they didn't seem so, and he didn't want to sleep then any more than he does now.

His eyelids fall helplessly and his legs refuse obedience. He absolutely has to have some sleep. It's impossible to go any farther.

Fortunately, there is a hillock by the side of the road, a rather dry one. Parched, yellowed grass protrudes from it. An oak tree must have stood here once; a wide black trunk gives evidence of it.

A splendid place for a rest.

Yudka put his sack on the trunk and then sat down on the hillock.

He still has time. The fog let up a little and a pale, sleepy sun that slipped out from behind the clouds from time to time attests to the fact that it is not yet afternoon. He can still reach the town before sunset.

Yudka sits and thinks, why did the Lord give a poor man stupid legs that faint? For sure because He endowed him with a delicate mind. And that is the truth.

But that doesn't apply to all people. What splendid legs, for example, every commission agent has, the way he chases after business like a rabbit! But then again he can't sew a fine Warsaw coat, or go without sleep for several nights in a row.

That's destiny for you. Either talent or health. Yudka has talent.

He counts in his head all the capotes he's sewn in recent times; they were lovely capotes! He then tries to guess what Bayla has prepared for the Sabbath. For sure many very good things. A splendid thing, Sabbath. On this day he always eats and sleeps and praises God. Whoever invented Sabbath must surely have been very wise. Oh yes!

Yudka's thoughts go back to the past; ever new images form as in a kaleidoscope. The whole story of his life stands before his eyes. He feels himself growing weak. Why again?

Fatigue and sleep are demanding their rights.

His head falls on his chest; his entire body at last inclines in an involuntary gesture. The tailor places his hands beneath his head, stretches out his legs, and falls asleep. Two crows, cawing, circle overhead. They finally come to rest in a field and from afar, their heads bent, observe the sleeper. Afterward they fly up to the sky again and from on high watch him attentively, cawing loudly. They are no doubt wondering why this Jew is sleeping alongside the road. They are aware that he hasn't yet died. Ha! Crows know about such things.

The sun is already beginning to set. A rack wagon, harnessed to three spirited horses, is traveling quickly along the road despite the mud. In the wagon, in a seat made of straw, sits Pan Jacenty, a local estate steward; Grzela the carter is driving. They are evidently going after some piece of farm equipment since the wagon was well lined with straw and was carrying enough fodder for a few days.

"Hold on, Grzela, hold on!" calls Jacenty. "Have a look, who's lying over there?"

Grzela restrained the horses.

"Looks like some Jew, sir."

"Is he drunk, or sick?"

"Eh, sir, maybe he's dead. If that's so, we better get out of here or they'll take us in as witnesses."

"No doubt, but we've got to have a look. If he's alive, let's take him into the wagon; but if he's dead, we're away from here fast!"

Grzela jumped down from the wagon.

"Sir! It's that Jew from Łosice, Yudka, but he's got to be alive since he's still breathing."

"Jew, Yudka!" Pan Jacenty shouted. "If you're not home by Sabbath, you'll catch it, you rascal!"

At this exclamation, Yudka started suddenly, looked around with the unconscious eyes of someone apparently insane, and for a moment couldn't figure out where he was and what was happening to him.

"Come on, take a seat, scoundrel!" Grzela shouted. "We'll take you to Łosice."

Thanking them, bowing to the ground, the tailor clambered onto the wagon with his heavy load and told the steward where he was going.

"But to just fall like that along the road, as if you weren't a person," the steward said as if speaking to himself, "well, I never!"

"I beg your lordship's pardon," replied Yudka, "but there's a saying we have: a chicken isn't a bird, a goat isn't cattle, and tailors aren't people."

"What do you mean, not people? Then what are you?"

"Well, y'know, maybe they're people, but not like people, just tailors."

"Tell me another one! Who ordered you, my good man, not to sleep for four days?"

"Nobody ordered me, but you see, m'lord, every person has to live. A tailor also has to live a little, but if he wants to live then he can't sleep, and if he wanted to sleep, then he couldn't live; it's really a simple matter."

"There's a shrewd Jew for you," Grzela interjected, "he's got an answer for everything!"

A few hours later, at a separate, spread table, Yudka sat attired in a new capote and a pointed fur cap.

Some of the children were still awake; others were yawning in corners. Pani Bayla, dressed in sort of a strange hairpiece decorated with flowers and yellow ribbons, placed on the plate of her husband and master a piece of fish heavily seasoned with spices. And this husband and master, and the head of his family, was thinking about how beautiful the world is, how tasty the *kugel,* how delightful life, and how blessed the Sabbath!

He did not come down with typhus, for such sleeplessness, headaches, and shivers sometimes pass . . . especially when one is used to all the pleasures of life.

■ Klemens Junosza (Szaniawski)
"Froim (A Sketch from Nature)" (1899)

Amid the sands and marshes of Podlasie, in an out-of-the-way, wooded region, there was a poor and wretched little town. Perhaps there were a hundred homes in it, and perhaps not, who can remember, especially since several years ago or so, all of a sudden, a fire broke out and turned the entire town into a pile of charcoal and rubble. Were it not for the excavated fireplaces, nobody would have known that once upon a time there had been a human settlement in this place.

Usually after a fire, the Jews raised a great cry and lamentation, tore their garments, pulled the hair from their heads and beards, wept as they once had after the destruction of the Temple, gathered what aid they could and took up collections in neighboring districts. But after a few months the tears of the victims dried, their groans grew silent, and immediately thereafter the grating of saws and the knocking of axes could be heard. Like a mushroom after rain, the town grew up again, seemingly new yet as poor as before and maybe even dirtier.

Huts that looked as if they had just been thrown together stood in four rows around a marketplace. In the open doors of small shops stood merchants inviting in the very rare customers. Children were rolling in the sand and pensive goats were pondering what they could find to eat.

It seems that the same subject was a constant concern to the whole, largely Jewish, population of the town.

Fairs took place here six times a year, and the entire town eagerly looked forward to them.

Six times a year a much desired market opened for shabby caps, peasant boots, patched sheepskin coats, and other items appropriate to a similarly inelegant wardrobe. Life and activity seethed before every fair. Jewesses threw themselves into a frenzy of baking cracknels, gingerbread, poppy-seed cakes, and similar tidbits. The male Jews, on the other hand, brought in shoddy goods and manufactured beer, vodka, and all kinds of other drinks just so long as they were tasty and scalded peasant mouths the way they were supposed to, like fire.

How it was all done is not my affair. Suffice it to say that on the eve of the fair everything was ready. Happiness shone on every face, and even the shrill squeaks of the unclean creatures that had been driven to market seemed to be filled with the joy in the heart of this famished mercantile throng eternally thirsty for a grosz.

When night had fallen, the carts had driven off, and the last drunk had been

"Froim (Szkic z natury)," originally published in the fifth volume of the posthumous edition of *Tanie Wydawnictwo Dzieł Klemensa Junoszy* (Warsaw, 1899). My translation follows the text as given in Klemens Junosza (Szaniawski), *Obywatel z Tamki i inne opowiadania* (Warsaw: Czytelnik, 1960), 175–86.

hauled out of the tavern, the town again descended into its usual lethargic sleep.

The shopkeepers dozed in their cages, the Jewesses, seating themselves on the thresholds of their habitats, were knitting stockings . . . and learned people were bending over their holy books from morning until nightfall. But if someone unknown happened to be riding through the town, everyone awoke from their apathy, and the entire population went in a body to take a look at the carriage or coach and to ask the traveler or coachman who he was, where he was going, for what reason, and what his business was.

Chickens and goats arrived to collect the remains of the fodder, and one scholar after another, having abandoned his books, willingly turned himself into a commission agent for the sake of earning a few groszy.

In the very middle of the marketplace stood an old, dilapidated, red building that towered above the small wooden huts. It was a large hostelry with a shop, a taproom, dirty "quarters" for their traveling lordships, and a big stable where at the very least a platoon of cavalry could be comfortably quartered.

This hostelry endured all the fires and avoided destruction in the fiery sea of flames, avoided it despite the fact that fire was raging on all sides of the marketplace, despite the fact that the roofs of houses collapsed with a roar scattering millions of sparks, and despite the fact that the wind was hurling burning firebrands about.

Ignorant people declared that the hostelry was untouched by fire because it stood apart, was built of stone, and was covered with a Dutch roof. But whoever had the slightest bit of education, whoever knew the taste to be found in wise tomes, knew that the reason lay elsewhere. The hostelry didn't burn down because it couldn't, and even if someone wrapped it from top to bottom in matches, drenched it in pitch, and strewed feathers all over it, fire still wouldn't touch it. That is because of the conviction people had that a long time ago a word was pronounced of far greater strength than sulphur, pitch, and all the powers of black devils. Of even better proof (about which old Jews relate even today, and which for the eternal memory of the matter is inscribed in the books of the kahal) is the fact that when, fifty years ago, or maybe more, there was a lot of tumult, violence, and confusion in the world, when half the population fled the town and the other half hid in cellars, when there was as much roaring as during a storm and fiery balls flew through the air, the whole town went up in smoke, but the hostelry remained, and what's more, those who were shooting, entered it in order to drink vodka. History asserts that they didn't pay for the vodka because they didn't have to, but they didn't destroy the hostelry either, since they couldn't, since according to belief it would remain standing for centuries.

Whoever wants to laugh, let him, but there's hardly a lad in town who doesn't know that a hundred years ago, and maybe even earlier, a great man, who was pious, just, learned, and who had great power from God, in a word, a rabbi, stopped off in the inn once on his travels. But he wasn't just any ordinary rabbi;

he was a great one, a very great rabbi who was known the world over—the kind of rabbi Jews came in droves to from different towns, fifteen, twenty, or maybe even twenty-five miles distant! To the town's great fortune, because his wagon broke down and his horses were exhausted, the rabbi was overtaken by the Sabbath in this of all places. Thus it was here that he took the baths, recited his prayers, and spent an entire day in the hostelry. He ate pike with saffron, *kugel, tsimes* made from carrots, and drank splendid kosher wine, the best the town had to offer. The way he was received, it suffices to say that out of gratitude he pronounced a mighty word that henceforth the hostelry would forever be spared from fire.

People naturally regretted the fact that that holy word did not extend to the entire town, but they later became convinced that the wise rabbi knew well what he was doing. After all, a fire isn't the kind of thing on which, essentially, a lot is lost, whereas rebuilding a town is indeed the kind of thing from which it's possible to make something in hard times. A simple and ignorant person often complains about what is because the simple person is blind and can't see what will be. The learned person, on the other hand, a great and just person, knows what was, what is, and what will be, and therefore every word of his is wise.

Jews from other towns offered a lot of money to purchase the hostelry, for possessing such a building is the same as having great happiness. But neither the owner at the time nor his successors wanted even to hear about such a proposition. They spat in disgust whenever anyone brought up the issue and they regarded every such amateur as a stupid and impious person. And they were right, for who could imagine getting rid of such an esteemed and valuable keepsake, and of such a great honor deriving from its possession, for a song.

And so the hostelry remains in the possession of one and the same family from that memorable Sabbath in the history of the town down to this very day.

Its present owner (for he is still living, in honor and peace) is old Froim.

We made his acquaintance accidentally, in passing. . . . Our horses were exhausted pulling a heavy carriage through the yellow Podlasian sands, and they justifiably deserved a rest.

We rode into the wide gates of the hostelry. Our party consisted of several young people inclined to gaiety and games.

"Hey! Hey!" one of them shouted. "Master innkeeper, show yourself!"

The innkeeper didn't jump out at this summons, but instead a girl with disheveled black hair, full of feathers, ran out and announced that here you could get everything you could in Warsaw, and even more than in Warsaw; but it so happened that the fair had taken place a week ago and the peasants consumed everything they could lay their hands on so that at the present moment there was absolutely nothing left.

The truth is, this announcement didn't bother us very much since we were coming from a vacation in the country and our hospitable hostess had loaded up the carriage with so many provisions that we could have traveled on them

God knows how far. We ordered the horses given oats, the disheveled little Jewess brought Maciek a glass of booze, while we took a basket of food along with us and made ourselves comfortable in the guest room.

In the adjacent room sat an old Jew with a long beard as white as snow, with a velvet cap on his head, and taking no notice whatsoever of our arrival, was reading something from a huge book spread out on a table in front of him.

"Pan Abraham! Innkeeper!" one of our party called out. "Come on over, tell us, what you've got? What can we get here?"

The Jew got up, straightened himself, and entered the room stroking his beard.

"I am not Abraham," he said bowing. "My name is Froim. I see that you gentlemen are not from here, since you don't know old Froim."

"Froim, Froim," repeated one of my companions. "My late grandfather, who lived in these parts years ago, often mentioned that name."

"Pardon me, what was your grandfather's name?"

"He had the same name as me," replied the visitor, "Brzozowski . . . he once had an estate in these parts known as Black Ford."

A particular radiance shone in the Jew's eyes.

"Pan Brzozowski," he exclaimed, "Pan Brzozowski, the grandson of Pan Walenty . . . his own grandson! Please, let me have a look at you! Yes, yes, you resemble your grandfather. Only he didn't like laughing the way you do."

My companion was slightly embarrassed.

"Well, no matter, no matter," said Froim, "young gentlemen sometimes like to laugh at an old Jew. That's what young gentlemen are for . . . that's what an old Jew is for, to be laughed at."

"But please . . ."

"Your late grandfather understood things differently, and so did I. But it's true, the world was different then. Today things aren't any good, no good at all . . . but maybe it's better; God knows what He's doing."

"What do you mean? What are you saying? That it's better that things aren't good in the world?"

"I'll explain it to you. They laugh at me because I read books, and sometimes I read all day long and all night long. When gentlemen come here they say that Froim spends his whole life thinking about trifles, about stupidities. You know what, sirs? You say that once you drive a nail into a wall and then take it out, there is a hole in the wall. Well, it's as if Froim thinks his whole life where did the wood go from the place where the hole was made?"

They burst out laughing.

"But that's not true. Froim is thinking about something else. He's thinking about what is written that the world will get worse and worse . . . people's heads will begin to get confused, their hearts will become harder than stone, and the Lord will punish people . . . and after the punishment, they will mend their ways and things will be good again in the world. The wolf will eat grass again with the she-goat and will do her no harm. I believe that God will deliver His punishment soon, because things are getting worse and worse and are going to get even worse. Wrongdoing, falsehood, and deception will grow worse than now. When someone sees another person with bread, he'll want to take it away from him. If one person is stronger, he'll seize someone else's property, his happiness . . . he'll take away his life. And why does he take it away? Because it belongs to him? Because he has some right to it? No, only because he happens to be stronger. A time will come, such as has never been, and such pressure on people, such as has never been, and such a wailing of the unfortunate, such as has never been, and such woe, such wrongdoing, and such injustice, such as have never been. It's already beginning, it's already beginning. . . . I'm an old man; I won't live to see what will happen. But you gentlemen are young; you have a long life ahead of you. You'll discover that everything is turning worse."

"Phew! Forget it, Pan Froim," Brzozowski exclaimed. "Did we come here just for you to frighten us with such images? Come on now, better be a gracious host and fetch us some wine, if you have any wine, by the way, in your cellar."

Froim smiled bitterly.

"Why shouldn't I have any wine?" he asked.

"No doubt some swill the likes of which the world hasn't yet beheld?"

"What harm will it do you to try a little of this swill? If you don't like it, I won't force you. The trial is free."

He summoned the servant who before long brought wine and glasses.

As soon as the bottle was opened, a gorgeous aroma filled the entire room. Although we were anything but connoisseurs, we understood that we had before us no mean demonstration of cellar archaeology.

"That's some kind of old wine," said Brzozowski.

"Not very old," answered Froim. "My father imported it when the French were stationed in our town. There were a lot of them, of these Frenchmen, I remember it all perfectly; it was more than just a few years ago," he added with a smile. "Pan Brzozowski, have a drink. . . . Your grandfather was very fond of wine. Drink your health; I won't charge you any more than I did your grandfather, and your grandfather I charged the same as my father did the French . . . a ducat a bottle, no more."

He got up, looked to see if there was anyone in the next room, and after shutting the door sat down beside us and spoke softly: "How happy I am to see you, Pan Brzozowski; how happy I am that I've seen you. You immediately reminded me of your grandfather, Pan Brzozowski of Black Ford, my best friend. It was no shame for your grandfather that he was my friend, that he had a friendship with a Jew, for the Lord God created all people on earth and even ordered the first human being to call himself the 'son of earth.' Every faith and every religion comes from God, just as from God comes the commandment that man live honorably in the faith God gave him. It is from one God that we have life and death, happiness and unhappiness, wealth and hunger . . . we have everything from one, for there are not two gods, or many gods; there is just one God for all faiths and all people. . . . Your grandfather used to say the same thing and never despised a Jew. He despised only cheating, swindling, thieves, robbers, and when he had reason to despise, he never asked if it's a Jew or not a Jew, he just despised the individual, the scoundrel. Your grandfather had a great mind and a great heart. He even looked death as calmly in the eyes as I look at this bottle.

"How can you know that?" I asked.

"I saw it, I saw it with my own eyes," he answered calmly. "But please, drink up, gentlemen, such wine is worth drinking, there isn't much of it left in the world any more. The late Pan Brzozowski and I had an acquaintance as old as this wine. We were together through thick and thin. He defended me once when I was in great trouble, and I have only him to thank for the fact that I am still alive on this earth and that I can praise the Lord. It was a long time ago, gentlemen, a long time ago, but I remember it. I was about to to die, but for what? I myself don't know, but I was staring death in the face. Your grandfather ran up, saved me. . . . I passed out. . . . No wonder, I wasn't a soldier . . . that's not a Jewish business and not the Jewish nature. . . . My father, my grandfather, they weren't soldiers either. But your grandfather, Pan Brzozowski, your grandfather was a courageous man. I waited a long time to repay the kindness and the day came. It was when your grandfather was again threatened with misfortune. The Lord God, who some-times gives strength to the weak, allowed me to save him. I was very much afraid at the time, I can't deny it, I was awfully afraid, but I did what I had to."

"Pan Froim," said Brzozowski, "then you're the Jew my grandfather had so many good things to say about?"

"I surely am that Jew, just as surely as I respected your grandfather, and he me. I dealt with him honorably; I made money from him, but I never skinned him, never wronged him the way people do in the world. He lived, and I lived; he earned his, and I earned mine, even earned quite nicely, praise God. But when misfortune struck, he lost, and I lost. We didn't shed any tears. . . . God gave, God took . . . that is His will. Sometimes God even wants to test a person: if he is pious and just in good fortune, will he be the same in misfortune? And do you know, Pan Brzozowski, why your grandfather lost his estate? Through misfortune. And there are different kinds of misfortune. One is like a stone that can injure a per-son's head when it falls from above; another can be like an entire mountain of rocks, which when it falls down can destroy everyone. It was such a mountain descended on us!"

We didn't interrupt as the old Jew sighed deeply and continued as follows:

"Oy, oy . . . it was a long, long time ago. You young gentlemen weren't even alive at the time. But I was alive, and Pan Brzozowski's grandfather was alive. An entire mountain descended on our shoulders, for that was God's will. We didn't cry, we didn't renounce God, for you know that sometimes God sends misfortune so that something good can be made of it. So we suffered and praised God, Pan Brzozowski in his way and I in mine, and we asked God to let us bear misfortune and to turn that misfortune into happiness. But the good Lord didn't hear us, He had other plans for us and did not turn misfortune into happiness, but instead wanted to test people and so gave them yet worse misfortune. That was the way He wanted it, so you have to accept it. Dew falls to earth so that grain can grow better; the same with the tears that fall from people's eyes—that's also not in vain. God keeps thousands of angels to note down, weigh, measure, and keep an account of that crying which God may sometime have need for. I don't know if you have understood me well, gentlemen, but I know that what I am saying is right, the truth, the way one ought to speak. The world isn't decent now, because people have forgotten God, expelled goodness from their hearts, and replaced it with malice, rancor, envy, and greed. One person acts as if he'd like to tear everything right from another's throat, worse than a dog; another, as if he'd like to ruin and destroy everyone and everything. . . . It's bad, very bad. And I expect even worse."

"Why are you such a pessimist, Pan Froim?" I asked.

"I don't understand what that word means," he replied, "and I don't even want to understand. I'm neither what you called me nor what someone might think. I am an old Jew . . . of the old-time Jews."

"Old?"

"Old, sir, an old Jew, not today's kind. There is a difference. And the wine you're drinking, it's different than today's . . . and everything nowadays is different than before . . . only God's strength is always the same; only His word never changes."

After saying that he became sadly pensive.

Night had already fallen, everything grew quiet in the room, the disheveled little Jewess brought in a thin Sabbath candle and set it in front of us. A red glimmer from the candle threw fantastic shadows against the wall and floor. A brass Sabbath candlestick suspended from the ceiling looked like some hideous chandelier, like that mountain of misfortune that descends, as Froim said, on fathers, on children, and on their children's children. And Froim himself, a serious, gray-bearded old man, in that indistinct, flickering light, seemed to be a prophet crying out: 'Woe unto you, woe! For your hearts have become hard as rocks!' "

The horses were already fed and rested. Maciek also harnessed them and rode up to the inn with a clatter. We said goodbye to Froim, who accompanied us to the door and said on the threshold: "Gentlemen, Pan Brzozowski, don't avoid our little town and old Froim. You'll still find a little of the wine that remembers the French. But come again soon, for time flies, oy, oy, how it flies! It flies like a bird on wings, it flies like the wind blowing in the fields . . . blowing a little, carrying things along with it a little. . . . So hurry, gentlemen, for soon you'll be saying that there aren't any people like the late Pan Brzozowski, nor such wine that remembers the French . . . that there isn't . . . that there isn't old Froim either."

"Live a hundred years," I said as I mounted the carriage.

"Thank you for the kind word," he said, "but what would I do here?"

"How's that?"

"With whom would I live? When I say to you that nothing remains of the old days, there aren't even . . . and I am ashamed and sad to say this . . . there aren't even Jews, as they used to be."

*   *   *

We rode off.

Refreshed, the horses snorted merrily as they pulled the carriage briskly along the sandy highway. My colleagues, drowsy from the old wine, were dozing, while I looked around as much as the shadows of a summer night permitted. Stars shone above this sad, wooded district of Podlasie. The fog assumed fantastic shapes as it rose upward from marshes and meadows.

It seemed to me that in this indistinct, whitish mist I saw the dignified figure of Froim. I saw his gray beard, spreading wide, and his gaunt hand raised up; the old man's dry voice seemed to reach me on a breath of wind . . .

■ Klemens Junosza (Szaniawski)
Our Jews in Towns and Villages (1889)

Our anti-Semites say: this Jew is bad, that Jew is no good, the other is still worse, and they try to support their assertions with proofs. May I be permitted to ask, what then are we to do with the Jews? We have no right to, nor any possibility of annihilating this mass of people by force, or of expelling them. As they have existed among us, so shall the Jews continue to exist among us, on the same soil, and we will not find a means of hedging ourselves off from them or distancing ourselves from them. We must continue to remain with them in commercial and economic relations, since we have no way not to.

The law in force has introduced a line of demarcation beyond which the Jews are not free to settle.[1] And since there are no prospects for overruling this law, the Jews, therefore, will continue to exist, live, and multiply in the Kingdom of Poland and neighboring provinces as they have down to the present.

The emigration of Jews to America, an emigration about which so much has been written and discussed in recent times, does not contribute much to a lessening of the importance of the Jewish question, or even to any sizable diminution of Jews in the provinces where they are permitted to reside. That is because many more Jews are born than emigrate, and the ones who emigrate are predominantly only those who are no heavy burden for society either because they possess some capital or because they know a trade.

Thus we do not have the slightest possibility of parting with the Jews. The tempests of history drove them here, and the lack of foresight of our legislators created of them a nation in a nation and safeguarded their separateness until the present day. We must reckon, therefore, with accomplished facts. And since we cannot part from them, we must live alongside them and exert every effort to make that life as bearable as possible for both parties.

It is indeed true, when we look about and see what is happening, when we read and hear what is written and said, that we cannot say that we are on the right road.

On one side, there is dangerous bitterness, and on the other, melancholic sorrow, and on both mutual recriminations and reproaches. Take the current literature on the question: the Jew is a demon, the Jew is a martyr—again the vicious circle from which there is no way out.

The anti-Semites paint the Jews in the darkest colors; the philo-Semites as-

Klemens Junosza, *Nasi Żydzi w miasteczkach i na wsiach* (Warsaw: Nakładem Redakcyi "Niwy," 1889), 126–32.

1. A reference to the Russian Pale of Settlement, which limited areas of Jewish settlement in Russia proper.

cribe to them extraordinary virtues. From one side and the other we hear only outbursts and declamations.

Why not put the question on a practical foundation? Why not treat it calmly? Why not say, fate has joined us, we cannot separate, we must live alongside one another, so let us find a "modus vivendi" as convenient as possible to both parties?

What has happened has passed; history does not move backward. We have to deal with what is, and help ourselves as best we can.

Let us not be frightened by the imaginary apparitions of those Jews who have already broken away from Jewry; let us not be intimidated by their seemingly exceptional, supernatural enterprise; let us not be anxious about the phantom of some secret league striving to rule the world. Let us rather turn our attention to things that exist, to the fact that we have next to us a million ignorant, fanatic, and hungry people. Neither the notorious "Alliance Israélite,"[2] nor the millions of Baron Hirsch,[3] nor any machinations of the Rothschilds should preoccupy our minds, but rather that mass of people populating our cities and towns, those half-savage Hasids, those beggars who resort to anything for the sake of ekeing out a living.

Here is the core of the so-called Jewish question, here is its main source!

It is true that much has been written among us, and for a long time, about the reform of backward Jews. But all desiderata expressed on this issue have again become enclosed in a vicious circle.

If we look at the literature on the subject, past and present, we encounter the same motifs. "Vodka is a harmful tool in the hands of a Jew, so let us forbid him to traffic in vodka"; "The Jew cannot work productively, so let us direct him to the trades and agriculture"; "The Jew differs from the rest of the population in dress, so let us cut off his side-curls and shorten his gaberdine." The results of this have always been the same. Despite restrictions and edicts, Jews have trafficked in and still traffic in vodka secretly, and even openly; despite efforts to direct them to the trades and agriculture, they do not take themselves very eagerly to the first, and not at all to agriculture; they continue to distinguish themselves by their dress and speech, and despite everything, they remain just as they have been for centuries.

2. The Alliance Israélite Universelle, which was founded in Paris in 1860, was the first modern international Jewish organization. Imbued with the ideals of the French Revolution, it has sought above all to defend the civil rights and religious freedoms of the Jews, and to serve the cause of Jewish regeneration.

3. Baron Maurice de Hirsch (1831–96), who was born in Munich to a family of very wealthy industrialists but lived mostly in Belgium and France, was an outstanding Jewish philanthropist. Concerned about the plight of the Jews in Russia, in 1888 he proposed to establish a network of craft and agricultural schools for them. When the Russian government adamantly opposed the plan, Hirsch launched his most ambitious project, the Jewish Colonization Association, which sought the resettlement of Russian Jews primarily in Argentina. Hirsch provided millions of dollars for the Association and also became one of the biggest financial backers of the Alliance Israélite Universelle. His benefactions have been estimated at over $100,000,000.

Why? Do the Slavic tribes possess so few assimilationist talents? Is the Jewish race so vital and strong that it can never be assimilated? Neither one nor the other. Frenchmen, Germans, Englishmen, and others come to us, and after a number of years living among us — in the second and third generations — entirely forget about their origins, and become citizens warmly attached to the country in which they found hospitality. We have many such families and their names would fill whole pages. Concerning the second assumption, it is also contradicted by the fact that there are countries in which the Jews differ from other citizens only in religion; they speak the national language, do not know Yiddish or Hebrew (knowledge of the latter being reserved to clerics and scholars), and are not distinguished by dress. In a word, they are completely assimilated.

Why, then, is it different with us?

First of all, because all reforms applicable to Jews were superficial; not one of them touched the very core of Jewishness, never entering the sphere of the education of children, nor in any way encroaching upon independent Jewish institutions. The Jews were allowed to manage their own affairs any way they wanted; to educate children the way they pleased; to develop spiritually wholly independently. Hence they developed unnaturally, sickly, monstrously.

The Polish Jews developed into a species, unlike any other, which Moses surely never had in mind. In the time of Moses, eleven tribes occupied themselves with material, temporal matters; the twelfth lived from tithes and devoted its time to learning and the service of God. In Poland, all generations of Jews have occupied themselves with erudition, while a small number of them spend their time collecting tithes . . . from us. That is the way it is, unfortunately.

Coming to us mainly from Germany, the Jews brought with them from there their speech, which with various distortions and changes has remained to this day their national and domestic language. No one ever compelled them to study our national language, Polish; no one interfered with their internal affairs. They settled in cities, gathered trade into their hands, since neither the peasant nor the noble had any enthusiasm for it, and created their own, exclusive world, which exists to the present day. Living entirely apart, they began to immerse themselves in religious studies, and erudition (along with wealth, and sometimes even more than wealth) became the height of Jewish dreams and ambitions.

Neither in Jerusalem, nor in Babylon, nor even during the greatest development of rabbinical studies in Spain, nowhere has the Talmud had so many researchers and commentators as in the dirty one-horse towns scattered about the fields and forests of our fatherland. One can say that a new Palestine arose here.

■ Adam Szymański (1852–1916)
"Srul of Lubartów" (1885)

[Adam Szymański's literary career was shaped by the Siberian exile to which he was sentenced in 1878 because of his political activities during the Russo-Turkish War. It was while in Yakutsk that he wrote his first stories, collectively published under the title *Szkice* (*Sketches*, 1887). *Szkice* attracted much favorable attention because of the stories' poignant picture of the hardships and sufferings endured by Polish exiles in the bleak wastes of Siberia. Szymański's grasp of the mentality of the exiles, by and large ordinary men, was paralleled by his obvious fascination with the harsh Siberian landscape. The story "Srul of Lubartów" has long been regarded as one of the best in the collection.]

I

It happened in the year . . . , but no matter what year. Suffice it to say that it happened, and that it happened in Yakutsk at the beginning of November, a few months after my arrival in that capital of frosts. The thermometer was down to 35 degrees Réamur.[1] I was therefore thinking anxiously of the coming fate of my nose and ears, which, fresh from the West, had been making silent but perceptible protests against their compulsory acclimatization, and today were to be submitted to yet further trials. These latest trials were due to the fact that one of the men in our colony, Piotr Bałdyga, had died in the local hospital two days before, and early that morning we were going to do him a last service, by laying his wasted remains in the frozen ground.

I was only waiting for an acquaintance, who was to tell me the hour of the funeral, and I had not long to wait. Having wrapped up my nose and ears with the utmost care, I set out with the others to the hospital.

The hospital was outside the town. In the courtyard, and at some distance from the other buildings, stood a small shed—the mortuary.

In this mortuary lay Bałdyga's body.

When the doors were opened, we entered, and the scene within made a painful impression on the few of us present. We were about ten people, possibly a few

My translation is a revised version of the one included in *Tales by Polish Authors: Henryk Sienkiewicz, Stefan Żeromski, Adam Szymański, Wacław Sieroszewski*, trans. Else C. M. Benecke (Oxford: B. H. Blackwell, 1915), 119–36. The original appears in Adam Szymański, *Szkice*, 2d ed. (Petersburg: Nakładem autora, 1890), vol. 1, pp. 5–18.

1. The Réaumur temperature scale was established in 1730 by René-Antoine Ferchault de Réaumur. Its zero was set at the freezing point of water and its 80 degree mark at the boiling point of water at normal atmospheric pressure. Once widely used, the Réaumur scale all but disappeared in the twentieth century.

more, and we all involuntarily looked at one another; we were standing before a cold and bare reality, not veiled by any vestige of pretense. . . .

In the shed, which possessed neither table nor stool, nothing but walls with hoarfrost and a floor covered with snow, lay a large, bearded corpse, equally white, and tied up in some kind of sheet or shirt. This was Bałdyga.

The body, which was completely frozen, had been brought near the light to the door, where the coffin was standing ready.

Never shall I forget Bałdyga's face as I saw it then in the full light of day, and washed by the snow. The rough countenance was marked by a strange, indescribable pain; the large pupils and projecting eyeballs seemed to look far away into the distance toward the stern frosty sky.

"That fellow—he was a good sort," one of those present said to me, noticing the impression that the sight of Bałdyga made on me. "He was always steady and industrious; people in worse straits used to go to him and he'd help them. But he was as stubborn as can be; he believed to the last that he would go back to the Narew [River]. Yet before the end came it was plain that he knew he would never make it."

Meanwhile, the petrified body had been laid in the coffin and placed upon the small, one-horse Yakut sledge.

Then the tailor's wife—a person versed in religious practices—undertook on this occasion the office of priest and began to sing "Ave Maria," while we joined in with voices broken with emotion. After this we proceeded to the cemetery.

We walked quickly; the frost was invigorating and hastened our steps. At last we reached the cemetery. We each threw a handful of frozen earth onto the coffin. . . . A few deft strokes of the spade . . . and in a moment only a small freshly turned mound of earth remained to bear witness to Bałdyga's yet recent existence in this world. This witness would not last long, however—scarcely a few months. The spring would come, and, thawed by the sun, the mound on the grave would sink and become even with the rest of the ground, and grass and weeds would grow on it. After a year or two the witnesses of the funeral would die, or be dispersed throughout the wide world, and if even the mother who bore him were to search for him, she would no longer find a trace on the earth. But, indeed, none would seek the dead man, not even a dog would ask for him.

Bałdyga had known this; we knew it too, and we dispersed to our houses in silence.

The day following the funeral the frost was yet more severe. There was not a single building to be seen on the opposite side of the fairly narrow street in which I lived, for a thick mist of snow crystals overspread the earth, like a cloud. The sun could not penetrate this mist, and although there was not a single living soul in the street, the air was so highly condensed through the extreme cold that I continually heard the metallic sound of creaking snow, the sharp reports of the walls and ground cracking in the frost, or the moaning sound of a Yakut. Evidently those Yakut frosts were beginning that reduce the most terrible Arctic cold to insignificance. They fill human beings with unspeakable dread. Every living thing feels its utter helplessness, and although it cowers down and shrinks into itself for protection, it knows quite well—like the emaciated cur surrounded by a pack of fierce mastiffs—that all is in vain, for sooner or later the implacable foe is bound to be victorious.

And Bałdyga was continually in my mind, as if he were alive. I had been sitting for an hour at my half-finished task. Somehow I could not stick to work; the pen fell from my hand, and my unruly thoughts ranged far away beyond the snowy frontier and frosty ground. In vain I appealed to my reason, in vain I repeated the doctor's advice to myself for the tenth time. Hitherto I had offered some resistance to the sickness that had consumed me for several weeks; today I felt completely overcome and helpless. Homesickness was devouring me, eating me alive.

 I had been unable to resist dreaming so many times already; was it likely I should withstand the temptation today? The temptation was stronger, and I was weaker than usual.

So begone frost and snow, begone Yakutsk! I threw down my pen, and surrounding myself with clouds of tobacco smoke, plunged into the waters of feverish imagination.

And how it carried me away! My thoughts fled rapidly to the far West, across taigas and steppes, mountains and rivers, across countless lands and cities, and spread a scene of enchantment before me. There on the Vistula lay my native plains, free from misery and human passions, beautiful and harmonious. My lips cannot utter, nor my pen describe, their charm!

I saw the golden fields, the emerald meadows; the dense forests murmured their old legends to me.

I heard the rustle of the waving corn; the chirping of the feathered poets; the sound of the giant oaks as they haughtily bid defiance to the gale.

And the air seemed permeated by the scent of those aromatic forests, and those blossoming fields, adorned in virgin freshness by the blue cornflowers and that beauty of spring—the innocent violet. . . . Every single nerve felt the caress of my native air. . . . I was touched by the life-giving power of the sun's rays; and although the frost outside creaked more fiercely, and showed its teeth at me on the window panes more menacingly, yet the blood circulated in my veins more rapidly, my head burned, and I sat as if spellbound, deaf, no longer seeing or hearing anything round me . . .

II

I did not notice that the door opened and someone entered my room; neither did I see the circles of vapor, which form in such numbers every time a door is

opened that they obscure the person entering. I did not feel the cold: it pene-
trates human dwellings here with a sort of shameless, premeditated violence. In
fact, I had seen or heard nothing until suddenly I felt a man close to me, and even
before catching sight of him, found myself involuntarily putting to him the usual
Yakut question: "*Toch nado?*" ("What do you want?")

"If you please, sir, I am a hawker," was the answer.

I looked up. Although he was dressed in ox and stag's hide, I had no doubt
that a typical Polish Jew from a small town stood before me. Anyone who had
seen him at Łosice or Sarnaki would have recognized him as easily in Yakut as
in Patagonian costume. I knew him at once. And since, as I have said, I was as
yet only semiconscious, and had asked the question almost mechanically, the Jew
now standing before me did not interrupt my train of thought too harshly; the
contrast was, therefore, not too disagreeable. Quite the reverse. I gazed into the
well-known features with a certain degree of pleasure; the Jew's appearance at
that moment seemed quite natural, since it carried me in thought and feeling to
my native land, and the few Polish words sounded dear to my ear.

The Jew stood still for a moment, then turned, and retreating to the door,
began to pull off his multifarious coverings.

Then I came to myself, and realized that I had not yet answered him, and that
my sagacious countryman, quite misinterpreting my silence, was anxious to dispose of his wares to me. I hastened to disabuse him of the idea.

"In heaven's name, man, what are you doing?" I cried quickly, "I don't want to
buy anything; I don't need anything. Don't unload yourself for nothing, and go
away with God's blessing!"

The Jew stopped undoing his things, and after a moment's consideration, came
toward me with his long fur coat half trailing behind him, and began to mumble
quickly in broken sentences: "It's all right; I know you won't buy anything, sir.
I saw you, for I have been here a long time, a very long time. . . . I didn't know
before that you had come. . . . You come from Warsaw, don't you, sir? They only
told me yesterday evening that you had been here four months already; what a
pity it was such a time before I heard of it! I would have come at once. I have
been looking for you today for an hour, sir. I went to the very end of the town,
and there's such a frost here, confound it! . . . If you will allow me, sir—I won't
interrupt for long? Just a few words . . ."

"What do you want of me?"

"I'd just like to have a little chat with you, sir."

This answer did not greatly surprise me. I had already come across not a few
people, Jews among them, who had called solely for the purpose of "having a
little chat" with a man recently arrived from their country. Those who came were
interested in the most varied topics imaginable; there were the inquisitive and the
gabbers; there were the people who only inquired after their relations; and there
were the politicians, including those whose heads had been completely turned.

Among those who came, however, politics always played a specially important part. So it did not surprise me, I repeat, to hear the wish expressed by a fresh stranger, and although I should have been glad to rid my cottage as quickly as possible of the unpleasant odor of the ox-hide coat—badly tanned, as usual—I begged him in a friendly way to take it off and sit down.

The Jew was evidently pleased. He took a seat beside me at once and I could now observe him closely.

All the most common features of the Jewish race were united in the face beside me: the large, slightly crooked nose and penetrating hawk's eyes, the pointed beard the color of a well-ripened pumpkin, the low forehead surrounded by thick hair; all these my guest possessed. And yet, strange to say, the haggard face expressed a certain frank sincerity and did not make a disagreeable impression on me.

"Tell me where you come from, what your name is, what you are doing here, and why you wish to see me?"

"Please, sir, I am Srul, from Lubartów. Perhaps you know it, just a stone's throw from Lublin? Well, at home everyone thinks it a long way from there, and I used to think so too. But now," he added with emphasis, "we know that Lubartów is quite close to Lublin, a mere stone's throw."

"And have you been here long?"

"Very long; three good years."

"That's not so very long; there are people who have lived here for over twenty years, and I met an old man from Wilno on the road who had been here close to fifty years. It's people like that who have really been here a long time."

But the Jew snubbed me. "As to them, I can't say. I only know that I have been here a long time."

"You must certainly live alone, if the time seems so long to you?"

"With my wife and child—my daughter. I had four children when I set out, but, may the Lord preserve us, it was such a long way, we were traveling a whole year. Do you know what such a journey means, sir? . . . Three children died in one week, died almost immediately. Three children! . . . An easy thing to say! . . . There was nowhere even to bury them, for there was no cemetery of ours there . . . I am a Hasid," he added more quietly. "You know what that means, sir? . . . I keep the Law strictly . . . and yet God punishes me like this . . ." He grew silent with emotion.

"My friend," I tried to say to console him a little, "under such circumstances it's hard to think about it; but God's earth is everywhere."

But the Jew jumped as if he had been scalded.

"God's? What do you mean 'God's'? In what way is it God's? What are you saying, sir? It's fit for a dog! It's damned! . . . God's earth? . . . You mustn't talk like that, sir, you ought to be ashamed! Is it God's earth that never thaws? This earth is cursed! God doesn't wish human beings to live here; it wouldn't have been like this, if He had wished it. Cursed! Bad! Damned! Damned!"

And he began to spit about him, and stamp his feet, threatening the innocent Yakut earth with tightened lips and his shriveled hands, and muttering Jewish maledictions. At last, exhausted by the effort, he fell rather than sat down at the table beside me.

All exiles, without regard to religion or race, dislike Siberia. Evidently a fanatic Hasid couldn't hate it half-heartedly. I paused until he had calmed himself. Educated in a severe school, the Jew quickly regained his composure and mastered his emotion, and when I gazed questioningly into his eyes the next moment, he immediately answered me: "You must pardon me; I do not speak of this to anyone, for to whom should I speak here?"

"Then there are very few Jews here?"

"You call them Jews, sir? They're the kind that don't observe the Law, not a one of them."

Fearing another outburst, I would not, however, allow him to finish, and decided to change the conversation by asking him straight out what he wanted to talk to me about now.

"I should like to know what's happening there, sir. I have been here so many years, I still haven't heard what's going on there."

"The way you ask me, I can't tell you everything all at once; I don't know what interests you, politics perhaps?"

The Jew was silent.

I concluded that my present guest, like many of the others, was interested in politics; but as I myself lacked a grasp of the subject, I began to give the stereotyped account I had already composed with a view to frequent repetition of the situation of European politics, our own, and so forth. But the Jew fidgeted impatiently.

"Then this does not interest you?" I asked.

"I've never thought about it," he answered candidly.

"Ah, now I know why you have come! I am sure you want to know how the Jews are doing, how trade is going."

"They are doing better than I am."

"Quite right. In that case, you would doubtless like to know if living is expensive for us now, what prices at the market are like, how much for butter, meat, and so on."

"What do I care how cheap it may be there, if I can't get anything here?"

"Quite right again; but what the devil did you actually come here for?"

"Since I don't know myself, I ask you, sir, how am I to tell you? You see, sir, I often get to thinking . . . I think so much that Ryfka—that's my wife—asks: 'Srul, what's the matter with you?' And what can I tell her, for I don't know myself what it is. Perhaps some people would laugh at me?" he added, as if fearing that I might be among them.

But I did not laugh; I was interested. Something, the cause of which he himself could not explain or express in words, was evidently weighing on him, and his unusually poor command of language added to this difficulty. In order to help him, I reassured him by telling him that I was in no hurry, as my work was not urgent, and that I wasn't going to lose anything if we chatted for an hour, and so on. The Jew thanked me with a glance, and after a moment's thought opened the conversation thus:

"When did you leave Warsaw, sir?"

"According to the Russian calendar, at the end of April."

"Was it cold there then or warm?"

"Quite warm. I traveled in a summer suit at first."

"Well, just fancy, sir! Here it was freezing!"

"So you've forgotten have you that our fields are sown in April, and all the trees are green?"

"Green?" Joy shone in Srul's eyes. "Why, yes, yes—green. And here it was freezing!"

Now at last I knew why he had come to me. Wishing to make certain, however, I was silent: the Jew was evidently getting animated.

"Well, sir, you might tell me if we now have any . . . but you see, I don't know what it's called; I have already forgotten Polish," he apologized shyly, as if he had ever known it—"it's white like a pea blossom, yet it's not a pea, and in summer it grows in gardens round houses, on those tall stalks?"

"Kidney beans?"

"That's it! Kidney beans! Kidney beans!" he repeated to himself several times, as if wishing to impress those words on his memory for ever.

"Of course there are plenty of those. But are there none here?"

"Here? I have never seen a single pod these past three years. The peas here are what at home, forgive me, only, only . . ."

"Pigs eat," I prompted.

"Well, yes! Here they sell them by the pound, and it's not always possible to get them."

"Are you so fond of kidney beans?"

"It's not that I'm so fond of them, but I often get to thinking—it's pleasant, after all, begging your pardon—how a grove may be growing round my house. Here there's nothing!"

"And now, sir," he began again, "will you tell me if those small gray birds are still there in the winter; you know the ones, they're like this," and he showed me on his finger. "I have forgotten their names too. There used to be a great many of them! When I prayed by the window, how they used to swarm all around! But who ever took any notice of them there? Do you know, sir, I could never have believed that I'd ever think about them! But here, where it's so cold even the crows fly away for the winter, little things like that couldn't last. But they are sure to be at home, aren't they? They are there, aren't they sir?"

But I did not answer him now. I no longer doubted that this old Jew, this fanatic Hasid, was pining for his country just as much as I was, and that we were both sick with the same sickness. This unexpected discovery moved me deeply, and I seized him by the hand, and asked in my turn: "Then that was what you wished to talk to me about? Then you are not thinking about people, about your heavy lot, about the poverty pinching you; but you are longing for the sun, for the air of your native country! . . . You are thinking of the fields and meadows and woods; of the divine creatures inhabiting them, whom you never even had the time to get to know in your poor life. But now that these beautiful pictures are fading from your recollection, you fear the solitude surrounding you, the vast emptiness that meets you and effaces the memories you value? You want me to re-call them to you, to revive them; you wish me to tell you what our country is like?"

"Oh yes, sir, yes, sir! That was why I came here," and he clasped my hands, and laughed joyfully, like a child.

"Listen brother! . . ."

And Srul listened, all transformed by listening, his lips parted, his gaze riv-eted on mine. He kindled me, he inspired me by that look; he wrested the words from me, drank them in thirstily, and laid them in the very depth of his burning heart. . . . I do not doubt that he laid them there, for when I had finished my tale he began to moan bitterly, "*O weh mir, o weh mir!*" His red beard trembled, and huge tears, pure tears, streamed down his emaciated face . . . And the old Hasid sobbed for a long time, and I cried with him.

Much water has flowed down the cold Lena since that day, and not a few human tears have rolled down suffering cheeks. All this happened long ago. Yet in the silence of the night, at times of sleeplessness, the statuesque face of Bałdyga, bearing the stigma of great sorrow, often rises before me, and invariably beside it Srul's yellow, drawn face, wet with tears. And when I gaze longer at these appari-tions, many a time I seem to see the Jew's trembling, pale lips move, and I hear his low voice whisper: "Oh Jehovah, why are You so unmerciful to one of Your most faithful sons?"

■ Bolesław Prus (Głowacki) (1847–1912)
The Doll (1890)

[Bolesław Prus, whose real name was Aleksander Głowacki, was one of the leading writers of prose fiction in the second half of the nineteenth century. A prolific, and popular, short story writer and novelist, Prus was imbued with the ideals of positivism and addressed a broad range of social issues in his writing. His major novel was *Lalka* (*The Doll*), a huge work set in contemporary Warsaw and dealing primarily with the issue of the pernicious effects of lingering romanticism. This is embodied in the figure of Stanisław ("Stach") Wokulski, a man of gentry origins who must earn his living as a shopkeeper in the aftermath of the insurrection of 1863. His vestigial romanticism manifests itself above all in his love for Izabela Łęcka, a vacuous young woman of an aristocratic family that has known better days financially. Prus uses the relationship between Wokulski and Izabela to explore attitudes toward class and commerce that had become wholly anachronistic in light of the new economic and social realities of postinsurrection Poland. But in its broad canvas of everyday contemporary Warsaw, *The Doll* is much more than the story of the ill-fated romance between Wokulski and Izabela. Sympathetic toward the Jews, and aware of their growing importance in Polish trade and industry, Prus depicts in *The Doll* the growing hostility toward the Jews rooted in a sharpening economic competition. The focus of the interest in the "Jewish Question" in the novel is Wokulski's plan to sell his business to Jews and the reverberations this produces among his fellow Poles. Many of the events in the novel are viewed through the eyes of Ignacy Rzecki, a clerk in Wokulski's store, whose own brand of romanticism takes the form principally of an unadulterated Napoleon worship. Rzecki's observations are presented in the novel in the form of first-person narrative identified as "The Memoirs of an Old Clerk." It is also from Rzecki's perspective that the novel's major Jewish characters, Szlangbaum and Szuman, are viewed. Of a traditional, Orthodox background, it is Szlangbaum who eventually takes over Wokulski's business. Through the contrasting figure of Szuman, Prus examines the outlook of a secularized Jew who is both proud of his heritage yet contemptuous of conservative, traditional Jews like Szlangbaum. In the following excerpts, Rzecki's comments appear in the first person.]

This Szlangbaum (I have known him for some time) is of the Hebraic persuasion, but an upright person. Small, dark, stooped, unshaven—in a word, you would not give two cents for him when he sits at the cash desk. But just let a customer come in (Szlangbaum works in the department of Russian textiles), and my God,

Bolesław Prus, *Lalka*, 2 vols., ed. Józef Bachórz (Wrocław: Zakład Narodowy im. Ossolińskich—Wydawnictwo, 1991), vol. 1, pp. 259–60, 274, 480–84; vol. 2, pp. 340–41, 342, 348–49, 387–88, 389, 465–67, 491–92, 493–95, 496–98, 507–9, 565–66. For a complete translation of the novel into English, see Bolesław Prus, *The Doll*, trans. David Welsh (New York: Twayne Publishers, 1972).

he twirls like a top! Now he is at the highest shelf on the right, now at the lowest drawer on the left, and at the same moment again beneath the ceiling somewhere on the left. When he begins tossing bolts of cloth around, he resembles a steam engine rather than a man; when he begins unfolding and measuring, I think he must have three pairs of hands. Moreover, he is a born salesman, and when he starts recommending goods, all in an exceedingly grave tone, then word of honor, he puts even Mraczewski to shame! Too bad, though, that he is so small and ugly; we have to get him a stupid but handsome man to assist with the ladies . . .

Thus Szlangbaum is a decent citizen in the full sense, yet everyone dislikes him, since he has the misfortune to be a Hebrew . . .

In general, I have noticed for about a year that animosity toward the Hebrews is increasing; even people who, a few years ago, called them Poles of the Mosaic persuasion, now call them Jews. And those who recently admired their industriousness, their persistence, and their talents, today see only exploitation and deceit.

When I hear such things, I sometimes think that a spiritual twilight is falling on mankind, like night. . . .

*   *   *

Dr. Szuman is also a Hebrew, but an unusual man. He was even supposed to be christened once when he fell in love with a Christian girl; but as she died he dropped the matter. People say he even poisoned himself from grief, but was saved. Today he has entirely abandoned his medical practice. He has a large fortune, and occupies himself investigating people and their hair. Small and yellow, he has a piercing gaze before which nothing can be hidden. . . .
[Rzecki has come to the court where the auction of the house belonging to Izabela Łęcka's family is to be held. The principal bidders will be Wokulski, who plans to offer an excessively high sum in order to help the family financially, and the Baroness Krzeszowska, a distant relative of the Łęckis, who comes prepared to offer considerably less. But oppressed by a crowd of Jews in court for another case and the lamentations of the Baroness Krzeszowska over being temporarily abandoned by her lawyer, Rzecki flees the building.]

Ignacy fled from the vestibule to the other side of the street; on the corner of Kapitulna and Miodowa Streets he dashed into a café and hid himself in such a dark corner that even Baroness Krzeszowska would not have noticed him. He ordered a cup of foaming chocolate, hid behind a torn newspaper, and saw that in this small room was another, still darker corner, in which sat a certain magnificently plump individual and some hunchbacked Jew. Ignacy assumed that the grand personage was at least a count and owner of great estates in the Ukraine, and that the Jew was his agent; however, he overheard the conversation going on between them.

"Sir," said the hunchbacked Jew, "were it not for the fact that no one in Warsaw knows your excellency, I wouldn't even give you ten rubles for the business. But as it is, you'll make twenty-five . . ."

"And stand an hour in a stuffy courtroom," the personage muttered.

"True," the Jew went on, "at our age it's hard to stand, but such money doesn't go on foot either. . . . And what a reputation you'll have when people find you wanted to buy a house for eighty-thousand rubles!"

"So be it. But I want the twenty-five rubles in cash right now . . ."

"Heaven forbid," the Jew responded, "you'll get five rubles now and twenty will go to pay off your debt to that unfortunate Selig Kupferman, who hasn't seen a cent of yours in two years, even though he got a court order."

The grand personage banged the marble-top table and started to leave. The hunchbacked Jew caught him by the coattails, sat him down in his chair again, and offered six rubles in cash. After bargaining several minutes, both sides agreed on eight rubles, of which seven would be paid after the auction and one right away. The Jew resisted, but the majestic gentleman dispelled his hesitation with a single argument: "After all, damn it, I have to pay for our tea and cakes!"

The Jew sighed, pulled a badly torn little piece of paper from his greasy wallet, straightened the paper out, and placed it on the marble-top table. Then he rose and lazily left the dark little room, whereupon Ignacy recognized old Szlangbaum through a hole in his newspaper. . . .

Since he had not found what he was looking for, either in the café or in the church, Ignacy began strolling about in the vicinity of the court building. He was quite confused: it seemed to him that every passerby looked him mockingly in the eye, as if to say: "Wouldn't you be better off, you old rascal, minding the shop?" or that one of the "gentlemen" was about to leap out of every passing drozhki to tell him the shop had burned down or collapsed. So again he thought that maybe it would be better to give up the auction as a lost cause, and go back to his account books and office—when he suddenly heard a desperate shriek.

It was some Jew or other, leaning out of a window of the court and shouting something to a crowd of his coreligionists, who in response rushed to the door, pushing, thrusting tranquil passersby aside and stamping their feet impatiently, like a frightened flock of sheep in a crowded shed.

"Aha, the auction has already started!" said Ignacy to himself, following them up the stairs.

At this moment he felt someone take hold of his arm from behind, and, turning around, saw that same majestic gentleman who had obtained a ruble on account from Szlangbaum in the café. The grand gentleman was obviously in a hurry, for he was making way for himself with both fists among the packed mass of Hebrews' bodies, shouting: "Out of my way, kikes! I am going to the auction!"

Contrary to their customs, the Jews made way and looked at him with admiration: "What money he must have!" one muttered to his neighbor.

Ignacy, infinitely less aggressive than the grand personage, delivered himself up to the favor and disfavor of Fate, rather than push his way through. The stream of Hebrews surrounded him on all sides. In front he saw a greasy collar, dirty neckerchief, and still dirtier neck: behind, he could smell the odor of fresh onion; on the right, a grizzled beard pressed against his collarbone, and on the left a powerful elbow was squeezing his arm almost to the point of numbness.

They thronged about him, pushed him, and clutched at his coat. Someone grabbed his legs, another reached into his pocket, someone struck him between the shoulder blades. It reached the point where Ignacy thought they would crush his chest. He raised his eyes to Heaven, and saw he was already within the door. Now! Now! . . . They were stifling him . . . Suddenly he felt an empty space before him, struck his head against someone's charms not very carefully veiled in a frockcoat, and was inside the courtroom. . . .

[Some time after Wokulski's return from Paris, where he thinks of settling, Rzecki again encounters Councillor Węgrowicz and Pan Szprott, the commercial traveler, whom he once challenged to a duel over Wokulski's romance with Izabela. The conversation in the tavern again turns on the rumored sale of Wokulski's store to Jews.]

The respectable councillor already had six bottles in him, so he began laughing and said: "Pshaw! I'm in the habit of crossing myself, but they won't let you do even that once you switch from Christian bread to Jewish challah. People are saying, aren't they, that the Jews have bought your shop?"

I thought I was going to have an apoplectic stroke. "Councillor," I said, "you're too serious a man not to tell me where you heard this news!"

"The whole town's talking," replied the councillor, "and besides, let Pan Szprott here explain."

"Pan Szprott," I said, bowing, "I wouldn't want to offend you, the more so since I asked you for satisfaction, and you refused me like a scoundrel . . . Like a scoundrel, Pan Szprott . . . However, I must tell you that you're either repeating gossip, or making it up yourself."

"What's that?" blustered Szprott, banging the table with his fist as he had done the previous time. "I refused because I'm not in the habit of giving satisfaction to you or anyone else. Yet I'll repeat that the Jews are buying that shop of yours . . ."

"What Jews?"

"Devil knows — the Szlangbaums, Hundbaums — how should I know?"

I was so overcome with anger that I ordered beer, and Councillor Węgrowicz said: "Sometime there's liable to be a nasty row with these Jews. They're strangling us, driving us out of our jobs, buying us up — it's hard to cope with them.

No point in trying to outcheat them; but when it comes to bare fists, then we'll see who'll come out on top . . ."

"Right you are!" added Szprott. Once the Jews grab everything you've got, in the end you'll have to take it all back by force, to keep a balance. Just have a look, gentlemen, what's happening just with this bunch!"

"Well," I said, "if the Jews buy our store, I'll join the rest of you. My fist still carries some weight . . . But in the meantime, for heaven's sake, don't spread rumors about Wokulski, and don't stir up people against the Jews, because there's enough bitterness without that!" . . .

[Shortly after the encounter with Węgrowicz and Szprott, Rzecki also discusses the possible sale of Wokulski's store with Dr. Szuman. Rzecki is the first speaker.]

"Never mind what's the matter with me, but I've heard that Stach is selling the store to the Jews . . . Well, rest assured, I have no intention of working for them."

"What's this, anti-Semitism got you, too?"

"No; but it's one thing not to be anti-Semite, and another to work for the Jews."

"So who will work for them, then? For even though I'm a Jew, I won't wear the livery of these Yids. In any case," he added, "how did such thoughts get into your head? If the store is sold, you'll have an excellent position in the company trading with Russia."

"That company is uncertain," I interposed.

"Very uncertain," Szuman answered, "because there are too few Jews in it, and too many magnates. . . ."

"I've almost sold it," replied Wokulski.

"To the Jews?"

He jumped up from his chair, and thrusting his hands in his pocket, began walking about the room.

"To whom else would I sell it?" he asked. "To those who don't buy the store when they have money, or to those who'd buy it just because they have none? The store is worth some hundred and twenty thousand rubles. What am I supposed to do, throw it in the mud?"

"The Jews are dislodging us something awful."

"From what? From positions we don't hold, or ones we ourselves force them to take, thrust them into, beg them to take? None of our fine gentlemen will buy my store, but every one of them will give a Jew money to buy it . . . and have him pay a good percentage on the capital invested."

"Is that so?"

"Of course it is. I know who's lending Szlangbaum the money . . ."

"So Szlangbaum is buying it?"

"Who else? Klein, Lisiecki, or Zięba? They'd never get the credit, and even if they did, they'd probably squander it."

"There's going to be trouble sometime with the Jews," I muttered.

"There already has been, and it's gone on for eighteen centuries, and what's the outcome? The most noble individuals perished in anti-Jewish persecutions, and the only ones who survived were those who were able to protect themselves from extermination. And so what kind of Jews do we have today? Persistent, patient, deceitful, united, cunning, commanding in a masterful way the only weapon left them — money. By wiping out everything that was better, we made an artificial selection and protected the very worst. . . ."

For a moment they were silent, and did not look at one another. Szuman was moody, and Rzecki almost ashamed.

"I would like to talk to you about Stach," Rzecki finally remarked.

The doctor impatiently put the papers aside.

"What can I do to help him?" he muttered, "He's an incurable dreamer who will never regain his senses. He is moving disastrously toward material and spiritual ruin, like all of you, and your entire system along with you."

"What system?"

"Yours, your Polish system . . ."

"And what would the doctor replace it with?"

"Ours, the Jewish one . . ."

Rzecki almost jumped out of his chair. "Only a month ago, weren't you calling the Jews 'kikes'?"

"Because they are. But theirs is a great system; it will triumph, when yours goes bankrupt."

"And this new system, where is it to be found?"

"In the minds that have emerged from the Jewish masses and ascended to the peaks of civilization. Take Heine, Börne, Lassalle, Marx, Rothschild, Bleichröder, and you'll discover the new paths of the world. It's the Jews who paved the way for them: despised, persecuted, but patient and full of genius." . . .

"Take the Łęcki family; what have they done? They squandered fortunes, all of them: the grandfather, the father, and the son, who was left with thirty thousand saved by Wokulski — and a beautiful daughter, as collateral.

"But what have the Szlangbaums been doing in the meantime? Making money. The grandfather made money, so did the father, so is the son today, who until recently was but a modest clerk; but within a year he'll give our commerce a real shake-up. . . .

[When it becomes obvious that Szlangbaum is to be the new owner of Wokulski's store, Rzecki muses further about him in his memoirs.]

This Szlangbaum is an odd fellow. I'd never have thought, when I knew him as a poor wretch, that he'd turn up his nose so. Already, I see, he's made the acquaintance — through Maruszewicz — of barons, through the barons, of counts, though he hasn't yet been able to reach the count who is very polite to the Jews, but keeps them at a distance.

And when Szlangbaum turns up his nose, there's an outcry in town against the Jews. Whenever I drop in for a beer, someone always grabs me and scolds me because Stach sold the store to Jews. The councillor laments that the Jews are depriving him of a third of his pension; Szprott complains that the Jews have ruined his business; Lisiecki weeps, because Szlangbaum has given him notice as of midsummer; but Klein keeps silent.

They're already beginning to write against the Jews in the newspapers, but still stranger is the fact that even Dr. Szuman, although himself a Hebrew, once had the following conversation with me:

"You'll see, sir, that in a few years there's going to be trouble with the Jews."

"Pardon me," I said, "but didn't you yourself praise them recently?"

"I did indeed praise them, because they're a race of genius, but with vile characters. Imagine, sir, that the Szlangbaums, old and young, wanted to cheat me, me . . ."

"Aha!" I though to myself. "You're beginning to get converted again, now that they've tickled your pockets . . ."

And, to tell the truth, I completely lost my liking for Szuman.

But what they're saying about Wokulski! A dreamer, an idealist, a romantic . . . Perhaps because he never did anything nasty.

When I repeated to Klein my conversation with Szuman, my wasted-looking colleague replied: "He says there will be trouble with the Jews in a few years? Put him at ease, sir, it will come sooner . . ."

"For God's sake," I said, "why?"

"Because we know them well, even though they're flirting with us," Klein replied. "They're sly! But they've miscalculated . . . We know what they're capable of, if they had the strength."

I regarded Klein as a very progressive man, perhaps even too progressive, but now I think he's a great reactionary. Besides, what does that "we" and "us" mean?

And this is supposed to be the age that followed the eighteenth century, which inscribed on its banners: freedom, equality, fraternity! What the devil did I fight against the Austrians for? What did my comrades die for?

Jokes! Premonitions! The Emperor Napoleon IV will remake everything. Then Szlangbaum will stop being arrogant, Szuman will stop boasting about his Jewishness, and Klein won't threaten them. . . .

[Near the end of the novel, Dr. Szuman also tries to dissuade Wokulski from selling his store to Szlangbaum and in doing so reveals his own ambivalent attitudes toward his fellow Jews.]

"By all means . . . A fine idea . . . ," said Szuman ironically. "And so that they might hold you in higher esteem, let them take on Szlangbaum as director. He'll fix things for them! The way he did for me . . . These Jews are a race of genius, but what scoundrels they are!"

"Come now . . ."

"Please don't defend them in my presence," cried Szuman angrily, "because I not only know them, I can sense them . . . I'd give my word that at this very moment Szlangbaum is digging a trap for you in that company, and I'm certain he will worm his way in there, for how could the Polish nobility get along without a Jew?"

"I see you don't like Szlangbaum?"

"On the contrary; I even admire him, and I would like to imitate him, but I can't! And just now the instincts of my forebears are beginning to awaken in me — an inclination toward business . . . Oh, nature! How I wish I had a million rubles, in order to make a second million, and a third. . . . And become Rothschild's younger brother. Meanwhile, even Szlangbaum is deceiving me. I've moved for so long in your world that in the end I've lost the most valuable attributes of my race . . . But they're a great people; they will conquer the world, and not even by intellect, but by cheating and insolence."

"So break with them, become a Christian."

"I wouldn't think of it. In the first place, I wouldn't break with them even if I became a Christian, and then again, I myself am such a phenomenal Jew-boy that I don't like hoodwinking people. In the second place, if I didn't break with them when they were weak, I won't break with them today, when they are powerful."

"It seems to me that now they are weaker, if anything," Wokulski interposed.

"Is that why people are beginning to hate them?"

"Come now, hate is too strong a word."

"For goodness sake, I'm not blind or stupid . . . I know what they're saying about the Jews in the workshops, taverns, stores, even in the newspapers . . . And I am certain that any year now new persecutions will break out, from which my brothers in Israel will emerge still cleverer, still stronger, and still more united. And how they will repay you at some future time! They are scoundrels, I grant you, but I have to acknowledge their genius and cannot get rid of a certain liking for them . . . For me, a dirty Jew-boy is dearer than any well-scrubbed young master; and when I looked into a synagogue for the first time in twenty years and heard the singing, there were tears in my eyes, I swear . . . But what's there to talk about . . . Israel in triumph is beautiful, and it's pleasant to think that this triumph of the oppressed is partly my doing." . . .

*   *   *

Szuman pondered. "Do as you like," he said, taking his hat, "but the fact remains that if you leave your company, it will fall into the hands of Szlangbaum and a whole pack of disgusting Jews. But if you stay, you might bring in honest and respectable people who don't have too many faults, and all the Jewish contacts."

"In either case, the Jews will dominate the firm."

"But without your help, ultraconservative Jews will do it, whereas with your help, university-educated ones will."

"Isn't it all the same?" Wokulski replied with a shrug.

"Not at all. We're linked with them by race and a common position, but our views divide us. We have education, they — the Talmud; we, reason — and they, cunning; we are rather cosmopolitan, they are particularists, who don't see beyond their synagogue and council. As far as common enemies are concerned, they are splendid allies, but when it's a matter of the progress of Judaism . . . then they are an intolerable burden to us. That is why it is in the interests of civilization that the guidance of affairs be in our hands. The Jews can only dirty the world with their gaberdines and onion, but not move it ahead. . . . Think about it, Stach!"

He pressed Wokulski's hand and left, whistling the air: "O Rachel, when the Lord in His mysterious goodness . . ."

"So," thought Wokulski, "a conflict is stirring between progressive and backward Jews over us, and I am to take part in it as an ally of one side or the other . . . A fine role! Oh, how it bores and wearies me! . . ."

"People are saying in town," Rzecki went on, "that you're leaving the company."

"Yes."

"And that you are relinquishing it to the Jews."

"Well, after all, my partners are hardly an old wardrobe that I am discarding," Wokulski exploded. "They have money, they have heads on their shoulders. . . . Let them find other people and work things out."

"Who can they find, and even if they could, whom will they trust, if not the Jews? And the Jews are seriously thinking of this business. Not a day passes but Szuman or Szlangbaum visits me, and each tries to persuade me to manage the company after you."

"In fact, you are already managing it."

Rzecki made a gesture. "With your ideas and your money!" he replied. "But never mind. . . . From this, I see that Szuman belongs to one party and Szlangbaum to another, and they both need a strawman. In my presence, they tear each other to pieces, but yesterday I heard that both parties have already come to an understanding."

"Clever!" Wokulski murmured.

"But I've lost my feeling for them," Rzecki replied. "After all, I'm an old clerk, and I tell you that with them, everything depends on humbug, cheating, and trash."

"Don't insult them too much," Wokulski interposed, "after all, we're the ones who reared them."

"Not we!" Rzecki cried angrily. "They're the same everywhere . . . Wherever

I ran across them — in Budapest, Constantinople, Paris, London — I always observed the same principle: give as little as possible, and take as much as possible,
both materially and morally. They may be all right on the surface, but underneath
they're treacherous!"

Wokulski began walking about the room.

"Szuman was right," he said, "that dislike of them is mounting, if even you . . ."

"I don't dislike them . . . I'm stepping out of the picture . . . But just look at
what's happening here! Where don't they crawl in, where don't they open stores,
what don't they reach out their hands for? And each one, as soon as he occupies
some position, brings in after him a whole legion of his own people, by no means
better than we are, even worse. You'll see what they'll do with our store; what sort
of clerks there'll be, what merchandise . . . And hardly have they seized the store,
than they're worming their way into the aristocracy, and already have their sights
on your trading company . . ."

"It's our own fault . . . our own fault," Wokulski repeated. "We can't refuse
people the right to acquire positions, but we can defend our own." . . .

A few days before the final date, Wokulski summoned his attorney and asked
him to inform his partners that in accordance with the agreement he had with
them, he was withdrawing his capital and leaving the company. Others could do
the same.

"And the money?" asked the attorney.

"It's already in the bank for them; I have accounts with Suzin."

The attorney left, upset. That same day the prince called on Wokulski. "I've
been hearing extraordinary things!" the prince began, shaking him by the hand.
Your attorney is behaving as though you really intended to desert us."

"Do you think I am joking, prince?"

"Well, no . . . I just think you noticed some disadvantages in our agreement
and decided . . ."

"To bargain, so as to force you to sign another agreement that will lessen your
interest and increase my income?" Wokulski snapped at the bait. "No, prince, I
am completely serious about leaving."

"You will disappoint your partners . . ."

"How? You gentlemen formed the company with me only for a year, and you
yourselves wanted business conducted in such a way that a month after the dissolution of the agreement each partner could withdraw his investment. That was
your express desire. I have contravened it only to the extent that I shall return the
money not within a month, but within an hour after the company is dissolved."

The prince sank into an armchair.

"The company will continue," he said quietly, "but your place will be taken
by . . . Hebrews."

"That is by your own choice."

"Jews in our company!" sighed the prince. "They will want to speak Yiddish at committee meetings. . . . Our unhappy country! Our unhappy language!"

"Don't let that frighten you," Wokulski interrupted. "The majority of our partners are in the habit of speaking French at committee meetings, and so far nothing has happened to Polish, so in all likelihood it won't be damaged by a few phrases in Yiddish."

The prince blushed. "But Hebrews, sir . . . A foreign race . . . Now, too, a certain animosity toward them has begun . . ."

"The dislike of the crowd proves nothing. But who really is preventing you gentlemen from collecting sufficient capital, as the Jews have done, and entrusting it, not to Szlangbaum, but to one of the Christian merchants?"

"We don't know one we can trust."

"But you know Szlangbaum?"

"In any case, we don't have sufficiently talented men of our own," the prince interrupted. "They are clerks, not financiers . . ."

"And what was I? I was a clerk, too, even a bus boy in a restaurant; besides, the company brought in the promised profits."

"You're an exception."

"How do you know you wouldn't find more exceptions in winecellars or behind counters? Go look for them."

"The Hebrews come to us on their own."

"There you have it!" Wokulski exclaimed. "The Jews come to you, or you go to them, but a Christian parvenu can't even come to you because of the obstacles he encounters on the way . . . I know something of this. Your doors are so tightly closed to merchants and industrialists that they must either bombard them with hundreds of thousands of rubles in order for them to open, or they have to squeeze through like a bug. Open your doors a little, and maybe you'll be able to get along without the Jews." . . .

At the end of July, Henryk Szlangbaum celebrated his birthday as owner of the store and director of our company. Although he didn't do half as well as Stach did last year, all of Wokulski's friends and enemies gathered, and drank Szlangbaum's health . . . until the windows rattled.

Oh, people, people! For a full plate and a bottle you'd crawl into the sewer, and for a ruble God knows where else. . . .

[In the final excerpt from his memoirs, Rzecki notes the worsening resentment toward Jews and the contradictions in Dr. Szuman's character.]

But bad feeling against the Jews grows constantly. There is no lack even of rumors that the Jews trap Christian children and kill them to make matzoh out of them.

When I hear such stories, heavens, I rub my eyes and ask myself whether I'm raving in a fever, or whether my entire youth was a dream. But what angers me most is Dr. Szuman's pleasure at the ferment.

"Serves the kikes right!" he says. "Let them make a row, let them learn some common sense. They're a race of genius, but such scoundrels you won't break them in without a whip and spurs . . .' "

"But, doctor," I replied, for I had already lost patience, "if the Jews are such rascals as you say, even spurs won't help."

"Maybe they won't improve them, but they'll drive an extra measure of sense into them, and teach them to hold hands tighter," he replied. "If the Jews were more united, well . . ."

■ Bolesław Prus (Głowacki)
Chronicles (1875, 1876)

[Prus began his literary career in 1872 on more than a single front. Besides writing for a few positivist journals, he also contributed to humor magazines and around the same time started penning short pieces on a broad range of social issues, expressing essentially a positivist outlook. These articles appeared in a variety of newspapers and periodicals on a weekly basis; Prus referred to them as *kroniki* (chronicles). So enamored did he become of his "chronicles" that he continued to write them throughout his long career. The many volumes that they comprise represent an extraordinary panorama of contemporary Warsaw society, which Prus observed with remarkable keenness. But Prus was no less a social commentator than an observer of social phenomena, as the following two chronicles dealing with Jewish issues make clear. Prus's *Chronicles* have long been admired by Polish readers for their clarity of style and sharpness of wit as much as for their social observations.]

A few weeks ago, the annual meeting of the Mutual Aid Society of Salesclerks of the Mosaic Confession took place. Last year the organization possessed a capital fund of 1,946 silver rubles, and a circulating capital of 3,479 silver rubles. For the year 1875 the following persons were elected to the board of directors: Pan Adolf Peretz, chairman; Pan Davison, secretary; Pan Hirschsohn, treasurer; Pan Breslauer, accountant, Pan Silberbaum, librarian, and Pan Poznański, manager.

The Society has existed since 1856, and in recent times has attracted favorable attention for its activity and honorable intentions. For several years it has organized for its members popular lectures, and at the last session, by a vote of 87 to 57, changed its previous name — *Salesclerks of the Mosaic Confession* — to a more general one, which permits subjects of other persuasions to enroll in it.

It is an important fact, rooted in very noble motives. It must be understood that salesclerks of Christian persuasions still do not possess a similar organization and have tried in vain to establish one. These efforts have today been renewed; what fruit they will bear remains to be seen.

The change of title and the offer of hospitality to colleagues of other religions who lack their own center have attracted the attention of our intelligentsia and have occasioned debates, naturally only in private circles. The noble intentions have been acknowledged, but as for taking advantage of them, opinions have been divided. As a result, it has been agreed that it would be inappropriate to enter an organization established a long time ago and with capital acquired by labor other

Bolesław Prus, *Kroniki* (Warsaw: Państwowy Instytut Wydawniczy, 1956), vol. 1, part 2, pp. 220–23. The first excerpt from Prus's *Chronicles* originally appeared in the journal *Niwa* on June 1, 1875. The second excerpt is from Bolesław Prus, *Kroniki* (Warsaw: Państwowy Instytut Wydawniczy, 1953), vol. 2, pp. 561–72. It originally appeared in the journal *Ateneum* in November 1876.

than our own. On the other hand, should a license be obtained for an association of Christian salesclerks, it would be appropriate to strip it of any exclusive features and so pave the way for the sought-after merging of both organizations.

This plan is very attractive since it allows salesclerks of Christian confessions to manifest those same good feelings that animated the salesmen of the Mosaic faith. Nevertheless, it has one quite weak aspect, namely, it does not indicate how salesclerks of Christian confessions are to behave in the event that they do not obtain a license for a separate association.

We would propose another, incomparably simpler plan, namely, that the salesclerks of Christian confessions honorably and sincerely accept the offer of their colleagues and enter their association, governing themselves henceforth by common laws and jointly assuming management. The ceremony of union may indeed be statelier, whereas ordinary entry would be . . . just that, ordinary. The effect would be the same, however, and that would be the creation of yet one more point for the rapprochement and fraternization of strata, which should accomplish this as soon and as perfectly as possible.

"Oho," you'll say, "a new Judeophile has arrived on the scene," and you won't be wrong—I am a Judeophile, and I have gone so far in granting Jews equality of rights in my noble and Christian heart that I do not distinguish them from the rest of my beloved fellow inhabitants of this country. I do not hesitate for a moment to acknowledge their virtues, and I make fun of their deficiencies and absurdities whenever the occasion permits.

According to my no doubt limited outlook, the so-called Jewish question presents itself the following way. We have two races that are different in language, customs, and religion, and that keep their distance from each other and look at each other askance. Now why are they distant from each other and why do they regard each other with distaste? Can it be because for more than five centuries they have been sitting opposite each other?

If these several hundreds of thousands of Jews were to be suddenly expelled from the country, the greater part of them would most certainly perish while those remaining would live in dire poverty. The country would gain as much as a person who for relief had the arteries ripped from his body. This circumstance demonstrates that the races under discussion, despite all their sulking and dislike, already constitute an organic whole.

Why do you sulk? Because the Jews have come to dominate trade. But then why did you let it out of your hands, and then again, why don't you try to regain it? . . . True enough, the Jews practice usury. But are there no usurers, and indeed infamous ones, to be found among arch-Catholics, and moreover among highly educated people? . . . That may be true, but why do the Jews speak a jargon? . . . But don't your aristocracy and pseudo-aristocracy also speak a jargon, which in fact they learn from childhood? . . . You say that the Jews are slovenly; but remember that you equal them in slovenliness. You accuse them of cheating you; but why do you allow yourselves to be cheated? . . . Those are all evasions, schoolboy evasions; better to beat one's chest and declare straight out that these two races are inimicable to each other only for the reason that they are equally ignorant, equally prejudiced, arrogant, and intolerant.

At the bottom of every human heart lies a worm that troubles the peace of the world and breeds violence and eternal hatred. It is called — lack of respect for the person who is different from us. We scream bloody murder if someone gets in our way, yet we're surprised that others shout when we do the same thing to them. We take offense when this one or that one flees our friendship, like a dog from flies, but we forget the fact that a sign of fraternity is kindliness and tolerance, and not grabbing someone by the hair. Oh, these are dangerous principles, and they can often be turned against us to our great harm.

With regard to mutual relations, we suffer from a strange confusion. Here's a woman, for example, who doesn't want to work as a teacher among Jews, although her father used to light their ovens when he was alive. Another doesn't want to be a wet nurse to them, doubtless from fear that young Moshek will suck out her stupidity along with her milk. Then there's the fellow who loudly declares that he would never marry a Jewess, but doesn't ask if she would be given to him. Or the one who today assures us that he would never extend his hand to a Jew, although yesterday he looked for a job from Jews with a humble expression on his face, and tomorrow will kiss their beards for a loan. Heavens, who needs this nonsense, this bandying about of words whose purpose seems to be to prove one's good intentions and feelings of self-worth but in reality demonstrate an emptiness in head and heart and a lack of understanding of one's obligations toward society as a whole.

The Jews undoubtedly can learn many things from us, but there is a lot we can learn from them as well. They are frugal, honorable, at least among themselves, and above all united. I believe that if we had an exchange, we could offer them our coats of arms in return for such attributes; the question is, would they accept them!

The Jews also have certain unsympathetic traits, however superficial, which alienate us from them. A fractured Polish, great arrogance, boastfulness, and a disdain for those poorer. These are not pleasant attributes in society. But the solution is simple. Let us draw closer to them and live with them, and above all let us show them, by our own behavior, the superiority of modesty over a turning up of one's nose, and perhaps things will change for the better.

Oh, I beg your pardon! It seemed to me that I was in a club of Christian salesclerks and unwillingly struck out on these evangelistic paths. I completely forgot that I am, after all, addressing progressive and liberal readers who have been abiding by these principles from time immemorial, and who therefore have no need of my counsels!

*   *   *

In the last few years a question has again arisen in our journalism that has troubled us for eight centuries. An ineffectual effort to resolve it was made at the end of the last century, and from that time down to the present many books, pamphlets, and articles have been devoted to it, however, not with the best results. We are speaking of the Jewish question.

In the literary, practical treatment of this matter certain intervals have always occurred. Whenever the public wished to examine it more closely, for the sake of reaching a decisive conclusion, important events turned public attention in another direction. In the meantime, the question has resolved itself from the political and legal point of view, without our participation. The Jews have been made the equal of the Christians in all respects. They are free to own real estate, to fulfill the functions of doctors and officials; they are free to pursue agriculture, trade, and commerce without limitations, and to enter a variety of educational establishments. In short, they have acquired among us today what Western Europe granted them at the end of the last century, and which they are fairly entitled to, namely, rights of citizenship.

In this way then the Jewish question has already been resolved, but only by a third. The legal emancipation of the Jews is by no means the whole story. They still remain to be accepted by society, by the families and individuals that make up society. Moreover, in order to facilitate that acceptance, they must reform themselves, and while holding to their religion, they must rid themselves of those distinct traits thanks to which — without benefit to themselves, or rather to their own harm and to general offence — they represent in society not the healthiest element. The blacks in America also lived to see legal equality with whites, but despite that they are treated in social relations like a foreign race, inferior and hostile.

After what we have said, it is easy to understand that the present journalistic discussion on the Jewish question no longer addresses such questions as: should the Jews be granted equality of rights, and to what extent. It takes place instead in the sphere of economic and social relations between Christians and those confessing the Old Testament. . . .

But it is one thing to acknowledge someone as equal to oneself, and another to call that person a friend and brother. Enthusiasm passes quickly, the old bad blood among neighbors remains, and only time and further consideration of the issues can improve the situation.

Now that we understand the basis of the Jewish question today, we ask in turn how does literature deal with it?

If we surveyed only the novels of recent years, we would have to say favorably in answer to the question. In truth, in our greatest belletristic works, Jews, with few exceptions, are treated most sympathetically.

Journalism, however, is another matter. Yet even here objective and favorable opinions can be read; even here voices are raised in defense of the Jews. Nevertheless, the majority of papers are ill-disposed toward them. Humorists poke fun at their poor Polish; non-humorists dispute their social and economic position in an emotional manner, which, in fact, resolves nothing. . . .

The Jews are strangers. The Jews are unproductive and harmful, and so . . . one must fight against them, treat them like enemies. That is their view.

The Jews must be rendered harmless and productive; both we and they must be raised up and ennobled. That is our view.

Out of fairness, it behooves us to point out that each of these formulas is only a formula. The whole difference between them rests on the fact that the first is a cry of despair that offers no remedies but rather sows discord and irritates a dangerous wound; the other, however, is an appeal to the harmony and mutual labor of Christians and those Jews who have raised themselves above the dark masses of their coreligionists, have sunk roots in Christian society, but at the same time have not drawn away from their own kind.

Before proceeding further, let us recall the history of the Jews, if only in the most general way. Their history is sad beyond expression. Persecuted terribly while in Egypt, they left their prison in order, after a certain number of centuries had passed, to enter Babylonian captivity. Returning anew to their own country, they fell under Persian domination, later under the rule of the Macedonians, and finally under that of the Romans.

Eighteen centuries have elapsed from the time the Jews, because of their desire to cast off the yoke of emperors, lost their homeland forever. During this war, their capital was destroyed, more than a million of them died in the field, and the rest were scattered throughout the world. From then on there is hardly a corner in certain parts of Asia and Africa as well as in all of Europe that they did not visit in the course of their wanderings and where they were not persecuted. Fate played terribly with this tribe. Hardly were they given land, property, the possibility of educating themselves, and access to the highest offices, when not long afterward they were deprived of everything and forced to differentiate themselves by their dress, live in special quarters, and so on. And as if that were not enough, they were converted en masse, burned, imprisoned, and finally expelled.

Spain, France, England, Italy, Germany, each in turn gave ample evidence of their moral fortitude. It seemed that the Jews were sentenced to inescapable annihilation. Fortunately or not, they found a country that saved them, and that country was ours.

For a long time Poland was called the bulwark of Europe because it rescued it from the Mohammedan tidal wave. Poland was something else as well: it was a sanctuary in which the most unfortunate members of the human race found shelter. That the Jews were not exterminated is our virtue or fault. They are ten times more numerous among us than in Prussia, 34 times more numerous than in Turkey, 100 times more numerous than in England, and 340 times more numerous than in Belgium. No wonder that the forebears of today's Jews, who so willingly make use of a German dialect, called Poland *Paradisus Judeorum* (the Jewish paradise), and Cracow the *New Jerusalem*. . . .

The first groups of them arrived in Poland as early as the tenth century. Things went well for them until the fifteenth century; they had broad privileges, and they enjoyed the protection of kings. Later on, as a result of intrigues on the part of the clergy, but mostly for their separatism, the declining bourgeoisie grew to hate them, and schoolchildren and soldiers harassed them.

In the eighteenth century, when the poverty of the country reached its zenith, the Jews were held responsible for the economic decline and were forbidden to deal in spirits, to conduct business, or to pursue trades. They themselves again showed no inclination toward agriculture, both because they had become disaccustomed to it in the course of many generations and because they saw the wretched lot of the peasants of the time, to which they themselves had often contributed.

Although the oppression in our country never reached the grotesque proportions it did elsewhere, nevertheless, the eighteenth century was the worst period for the Jews among us. Their only consolation might have been the fact that there existed a still more unfortunate class [the peasants], which they exploited and troubled. Even very serious people of that period declared outright: "The Jewish nation is accustomed to trickery, deception, indolence, thievery, and robbery," and Staszyc referred to them as "a winter and summer locust plague."

But in this time of moral and material decline, both of the country and of the Jews, voices favorable to them were raised. "A strange claim," declared Mateusz Topora Butrymowycz, "to want the Jew to be useful to a country that was not his homeland; to want him to be industrious, when the fruit of his industry was not assured him; to want him to be friendly and faithful to someone who constantly oppressed him; to want him to respectfully wear fetters and to kiss the hand that put them on his neck." Another author prescribed "a constant and eternal *concordatum* between two nations fighting in one country"; and Jacek Jezierski, the castellan of Łuków, at a session of the Sejm, declared: "I hold the Jews to be Polish citizens and useful ones, for I know no other merchants in Poland. The good regulation of the Jews will increase treasury revenues and will facilitate the circulation of money by several millions."

But perhaps even then people used to say that "whoever speaks for the Jews, has already taken, and whoever is against the Jews wants to take." A good system for relieving the mind of the burden of such questions; just a shame that it leads nowhere.

If the constant pressure, pursuits, and persecutions, which were interrupted by brief periods of relief as if to provide the Jews rest, comprise the content of Jewish history, then the question arises; what traits could a nation of such experience develop? Can one suppose that the ordinary human being would not repay annoyance and contempt with hatred; or that for the sake of shielding himself from the consequences of violence, he would not take recourse to hypocrisy and deception, or that he would not fall back on usury when all other roads of earning a living were obstructed? Is it surprising that, hounded on all sides, they united among themselves like conspirators, that pressed because of their religion, they fell into religious fanaticism?

All present defects of the Jews are their own doing as well as that of all Europe. History also shows that this nation possesses noble attributes. When they were allowed to take advantage of the treasures of the new civilization, they brought forth outstanding people, and when a society embraced them, they did not hesitate to shed their blood for a common cause. When they were given a field to work, they quickly enriched themselves and the country along with them.

A few weeks ago, Pan Chmielowski summarized in *Niwa* a book about the Talmud by August Rohling.[1] What strange things we meet there! "The whole world belongs to the Jews . . . ," "Skinning a *goy* is permitted . . ." To deceive him, kill him, insult his wife is also permitted, as is taking vows falsely; cursing nonbelievers and their religion is even a necessity! . . . And so on.

We are not surprised by the fact that Pan Chmielowski repeats with horror such awful maxims, but rather that he expects explanations from "enlightened Israelites." Among the young workers of our literature, Pan Chmielowski is undoubtedly considered erudite; he knows history and modern philosophy, which teaches that everything must have a reason. For that reason, Pan Chmielowski is waiting for explanations from the Israelites, as if he himself did not know that the perverse tenets of the Talmud are a summary of the principles by which the "nonbelievers" were governed in their relations with Jews, and that alongside the objectionable tenets there are also some such as "Do unto others as you would have them do unto you."

I cannot claim any knowledge of the Talmud, except for what I know from the essay of Pan Kramsztyk; *a priori,* however, I offer two hypotheses:

1. That in the Talmud, besides the tenets dictated by despair and vengeance, there must also be those dictated by justice, love, and gratitude. In their studies, readers are most influenced by those principles corresponding most to their environment. A Romanian Jew may derive poison from them; a French Jew, nourishment.

2. In the opinion of those fluent in this learning of our Jewish citizens, the Talmud is not at all a dogmatic book, but rather a collection of interpretations. Even

---

1. Chmielowski's article, "Zasady Talmuda" ("The Principles of the Talmud"), appeared in *Niwa* 10 (1876):669–82. It was based on the second edition of August Rohling's book published in Lwów in 1875 under the title *Zgubne zasady talmudyzmu do serdecznej rozwagi Żydom i chrześcijanom wszelkiego stanu podał* . . . (The harmful tenets of Talmudism presented for their sincere consideration to Jews and Christians of all classes).

without that, however, one must assume that it does not exert too decisive an influence on the character of the Jews. If books truly had such an effect on people, then how honorable Christians would have had to be!

From thoughts about the general question of the Jews, I digressed to the Talmud for the purpose of making the observation that, regardless of the esteem this book has among unenlightened Jews, one should not attach too much importance to it. The Jews have been, are, and will be what their surroundings make them. That, it seems, is an appropriate point of departure. For the same reason I would advise putting less emphasis on opinions even of the most famous rabbis of the past and more on the present-day situation and customs of the Jews.

Much attention has been devoted to the dress, side-locks, jargon, and prohibition against certain foods of the Jews. As far as I am concerned, I leave all that to them, and I advise others to do the same and to think instead of the most important reform of all: *the reform of marriage.* Jews marry too early, multiply too energetically, and this way fall into a poverty that compels them to seek illegal and criminal gains, and that in turn harms society.

Despite all the kind feelings I have for the Jews, I cannot conceal the fact that I am frightened by the rapid growth of their proletariat. I also strongly suspect that their immoderate haste to enter into marriage is one of the factors contributing to the destruction of a certain part of the strength of the country. . . .

They comprise 13% of the population. Let us assume that the Jews represent half of the artisans, or 6%, which certainly is not small; that 4%, or all tradespeople, are Jews, which is too many; and that finally 1%, or 60,000 people, belong to the agricultural stratum, are lawyers, doctors, financiers, and so on. Hence 6% + 4% + 1% = 11%; since Jews make up 13½% of our population, or 150,000 people of different sex and age, that means that 42,000 of this number are men of productive age who are occupied with something other than agriculture, industry, or trade . . .

They indeed work, but at what? Since these producers, such as they are, satisfy the needs of the population, there remains to them only to gratify caprices, encourage indolence, and exploit weaknesses. Let us have a look at the owners of portable stalls making calls at inns, where they are always intruders and barely of any use, or at peddlers of cheap candies and cakes. Let us have a look at commision agents, who just as willingly minister to laziness, and to passion, and finally at spirits dealers and tobacco salesmen, who facilitate intoxication and nervousness among the masses. The profits of such merchants is unusually small, and their poverty great. Many of them turn to other fields after going bankrupt in one. When trade strengthens, the number of these wretches decreases, but it grows exceptionally fast in times of stagnation. Their adversity is not at least isolated; it takes its toll, in the name of solidarity, above all on their coreligionists, and further — on the whole of society.

The malady we characterized above is not the exclusive privilege of "Jewry";

under the name "proletariat" it troubles all societies. Do you imagine that even among our Christian populace there are no proletarians? Indeed there are; they beg, they steal, they cheat, they become parasites, or they die as a result of an exhaustion of their strength, since Christian solidarity does not always support them.

In all likelihood the proportion of our proletariat of both religions to the general population is no lower than what we find in the West. The reasons, however, are different. In the West the malady stems from overpopulation and the excessive predominance of capital over labor; with us, on the other hand, it has historic conditions. I believe that if the peasants had been enfranchised, for example, a hundred and fifty years ago, our country would be a lot better off in many ways.

Speaking parenthetically, of both our proletariats, the Christian and the Jewish, the latter is the more numerous, at least in proportion to the mass of respective coreligionists. By virtue of the fact that it is more active and more enterprising, that it multiplies faster than the Christian, it is more harmful; it is, in fact, even *very harmful.*

But has our journalism, confronting such a malady, understood it properly? Has it offered remedies? I assert decidedly that it has not! Condemning the Jews to the masses as leeches, faulting them for their unproductivity, appealing to the Christians that they *defend themselves,* does not heal but only worsens the malady. Addressing this issue until now under the term "society," they have understood only Christians. By their outcries they have supported separatism, as a result of which we must regard their good intentions as the most harmful in their results.

As an axiom in inquiries of this type, one must accept the fact that Jews and Christians represent a single whole; they are elements of a single organism, despite the differences in faith, language, customs, and even traditions. They cannot get along without us, nor we without them. Were we able to get rid of the Jews, a great number of them would perish, and the rest would fall into misery. If they went away from us, the country would meet with misfortune. The strengths of the local Christian populace are not abundant enough for a part of them to be returned to fields now worked by Jews. We would experience a sudden lack of merchants, a lack of wagon drivers, artisans, capitalists, and commission agents; the country would suffer an increase in the cost of living, and there would arise a poverty resembling that of the Middle Ages. Soon, instead of 815,000 Jews already becoming assimilated, 600,000 Germans would enter. That would be the most dreadful blow that our society could ever encounter. The country would certainly recover, but after a few generations we would have to send for our exiled brethren of Jewish origin.

Summarizing what we have said about the present situation of the Jews among us, it appears that regardless of their differences and the small percentage of harmful proletariat, the overwhelming majority of them are beneficial, and beneficial to such an extent that thanks to them the sum of attributes of the Jewish population considerably surpasses the bad they cause the country as well as themselves.

It seems that our perspective on the Jewish question is public-spirited, worthy of both tribes, and doubtless the same as that held by Kings Kazimierz, Mieczysław, and Sobieski, by such nobles as Butrymowicz, Jezierski, Czacki, and by such writers and intellectuals as Mickiewicz and Lelewel. Those who treat the matter from the separatist and even persecutorial position undoubtedly also find predecessors among whom the students at medieval educational institutions occupy a considerable place.

From our position, the way to deal with the Jews is immediately adumbrated; it can be characterized by a single term — brotherhood. One must traffic with them in societies, be concerned about their hospitals, schools, temples, and shelters, give them work and accept work from them, learn their ways, cease ridiculing their defects, and support their poor on an equal level with the Christian. I know that this program will upset a certain percentage of my readers, but for their consolation I add the following:

Look how much has changed among them over several years, how many among them have become good citizens, how nicely the educated speak, and especially women, how their children study, even the poorer. Show me a single charitable institution, or some other serving the country, to which they would not contribute time and money.

And finally, I ask you to direct your attention to the fact that even in many small towns and villages, in the very heart of them, two parties contend with one another: a progressive one and a backward one, and that the first — if it does not triumph — it at least holds its own. From what they were formerly, a nation within a nation, the Jews are slowly becoming transformed into a party; from a Jewish class there will arise a bourgeois class.

In what I have said I do not address Christians exclusively, but honorable, enlightened citizens of both persuasions. Let us struggle! But let us struggle not with people, but with darkness, misery, prejudice, and frivolousness, regardless of whether they reside in a peasant hut, a nobleman's court, the salon of a financier, the basement of a Christian proletarian, or the shop of a follower of the Old Testament. Only on this road can individuals and societies be raised up.

We direct these thoughts above all to the attention of journalists. Let us not stir up old strife, which is sufficiently strong as it is. It would also be worthwhile to abandon certain antiquated separatist formulas, which we constantly use in a way that is sometimes unpleasant to the Jews and explain nothing. I count among these worn-out formulas such terms as "starozakonny" [of the Old Testament] or "wyznania mojżeszowego" [of the Mosaic confession]. If these formulas have no sarcastic meaning, by the same token they have no logical one and look as if someone had written "Pan X, blond, wearing a green necktie, went abroad . . ."

The sole tangible result of the tactics of our journalism so far has been the provocation of the *Israelite,* a newspaper devoted to the affairs of the Jews.[2] Not long ago distinguished by a conciliatory spirit, this paper has today become a polemical organ. Let us not be surprised that the *Israelite* has become contentious in defense of principles represented by it; nevertheless, we regret it. For our common cause, it would be better if the *Israelite* left the provocations of journalists–economic inquisitors to the rebuke of their opponents of the same religion. . . . However, one must confess that even in our own journalism healthier trends are manifesting themselves. The proof of this is the moderate and tactful discussion of "hajzówki" between Jacek Soplica and the *Israelite,*[3] and finally the above-mentioned summary of the black stains of the Talmud by Pan Chmielowski, to which, as far as we know, Pan Grosglik, an authority on the Talmud, is supposed to answer in the same *Niwa.*

2. A secular, Polish-language newspaper devoted to Jewish issues. It was founded in 1866 (the first number appeared on April 6, 1866) and ran for forty-seven years.

3. A reference to the erroneous belief at one time that in the town of Zamość, besides their legal owners, properties, Jewish as well as Christian, also had secret owners (*hajzówki*) whom only the Jews knew and whose names were entered in a register held by a rabbi or the elders of the Jewish community.

■ Maria Konopnicka (1842–1910)
"Mendel of Gdańsk (A Sketch)" (1897)

[A very popular, if not very gifted, poet, Maria Konopnicka is most admired for her social activism and her literary embrace of the poor and downtrodden. Her poetry is full of moving images of the wretchedness of poverty in big cities and small peasant villages. Her literary career began after she left her much older husband, a landowner, and settled in Warsaw together with their six children. Although she wrote movingly of the degrading conditions in which workers lived and worked, she has long been thought of primarily as a poet of peasant life. In this respect, her most impressive achievement is the long epic poem *Pan Balcer w Brazylji* (*Mister Balcer in Brazil*, 1910), which deals with the migration of large numbers of Polish peasants to Brazil where they were employed mainly in the clearing of virgin forests. Konopnicka spent twenty years writing her epic poem. Although it contains a number of vivid passages, the work is read today for its historical and sociological interest.

Konopnicka's commitment to the impoverished and socially marginalized extended as well to the Jews of whom she wrote mostly in her prose fiction. Her best effort in this respect is the story "Mendel gdański" ("Mendel of Gdańsk," 1897).

Apart from her poetry and prose fiction, Konopnicka published children's literature, critical essays, and translations from the works of German, French, Italian, and Czech writers.]

Since yesterday, some disturbance has taken hold of the street. Old Mendel is surprised and more often than usual fills his short pipe as he looks out the window. He has never seen these people here before. Where are they going? Why are they joining the workers hurrying to the excavation of the foundation beneath the new home of the riveter Greulich? Where did these ragged teenagers come from? Why are they looking around entrance halls that way? How come they have money all of a sudden to go to a tavern?

Old Mendel shakes his head sucking on the small, bent, cherry-wood stem of his pipe. He knows this quiet little street so well. Its physiognomy, its movement, its voices, its pulse. . . .

And how could Mendel of Gdańsk not know all this, since for the past twenty-seven years he has had his bookbinding shop in the same room beneath the same window and so for more than a quarter of a century has stood alongside it in his leather apron? And while his dry, sinewy, and now somewhat trembling hand tightens the wooden screw of the press, his eyes, from beneath thick, gray, overhanging brows, look at the little street, which is like a separate world enclosed within itself in the midst of a great city.

Maria Konopnicka, "Mendel Gdański. Obrazek," in *Nowele,* ed. Tadeusz Budrewicz (Warsaw: Ludowa Spółdzielnia Wydawnicza, 1988), vol. 2, pp. 69–87.

Mendel knows the little secrets of this world by heart. He knows when the cough of the old archivist who brings him thick, dust-laden folios of musty papers for binding is worse or better; he knows the smell of the pomade of the little ward for whom he sews together the records of his benefactor; he knows when Joasia comes from the wife of the counselor with the request that he "set nicely behind glass" a congratulatory scroll on which a gilden angel uncovers himself and reveals a young man with a bouquet of roses in his hand; he knows when the student living in the attic goes without supper; and he knows from which side will run up the breathless schoolgirl asking him to bind "in blue and with gold strings" some romantic poetry transcribed on letter paper.

He knows everything. Everything that one can see to the left and right with a gray, swift eye, and that one can hear to the right and left with an ear, and that one can think about for hours at a time hammering like a woodpecker with a bookbinder's hammer, leveling and cutting off huge sheets of paper, boiling glue, and mixing colors.

And everyone knows him as well. A stranger rarely drops in; everyone else is like a member of his household.

The old, bald watchmaker shouts "good day" to him in summer through an open window opposite him and asks about Bismarck; the consumptive rope-maker attaches to his door handle his long, hemp strings, which he twists, panting, in the narrow, semi-dark lobby of the tenement house; the gaunt student from the attic, with legs like compass shears, sticks his head on a long, thin neck in his doorway in the evening and borrows a candle from him, which "he'll give back right away, but he's still got about an hour's writing left." Sometimes the stall-keeper hands him a black radish through a window in exchange for colored scraps of paper from which her boys make kites renowned the length and breadth of the street; the landlord's son spends time with him waiting for a free moment when Mendel will give him cardboard for pasting on soldiers cut out of paper, all the while marveling at the big handles of the shears, weighing a hammer in his hand, and thrusting his nose into a glue pot, nearly trying it. All of this taken together creates a warm, informal atmosphere, an atmosphere of mutual friendliness. Old Mendel must feel good in it. His seventy-seven years notwithstanding, he is still spry. Composure and dignity are inscribed on his face withered from labor.

His hair is very gray, and his long beard is completely white. His sunken chest puffs and pants beneath a quilted jacket, and his humped back somehow never seems to want to straighten out; but this is nothing to fret about so long as his legs and eyes hold out and so long as he still has strength in his hands. When he has difficulty breathing, and the small of his bent back aches with pain, old Mendel fills his little pipe with tobacco from a blackened pouch tied round with a string, and smoking it, relaxes a while. The tobacco he uses isn't very choice, but it gives a lovely, blue smoke that Mendel likes. This blue smoke has something else special about it, the fact that various distant things can be seen in it and things that happened a long long time ago.

He can see in it his wife, Resia, with whom he enjoyed living for thirty years, and his sons, who like leaves driven by wind went their separate ways in order to make a living, and the children of his sons, and all kinds of sorrows, and comforts, and cares. And most distant of all he can see in it his youngest daughter, Leah, who was given in marriage so early and who passed away so early and who left him only a single grandchild. When old Mendel lights his pipe, a kind of quiet murmur escapes from his mouth. As he smokes and the blue smoke brings him distant images and those that never return, this murmur grows, becomes stronger, and nearly becomes a groan. This human soul, the soul of an old Jew, also has its sadnesses and anxieties, which he drowns in work.

In the meantime, his neighbor brings in in one hand a small pot of soup filled with pieces of a softened roll and in the other a covered plate containing meat and vegetables. Old Mendel takes this modest meal from her, but he doesn't eat it right away; after setting it down on a small iron stove, he just waits. The waiting doesn't last long. At two sharp the door of his room opens noisily, with a bang, and in comes a small gymnasium student. He is dressed in a long overcoat into which he has plenty of room to grow and in a huge cap thrust toward the back of his head; a knapsack is slung over his back. He is a boy about ten who inherited his glittering hazel eyes, long dark lashes, and small mouth from his mother, old Mendel's youngest daughter, and his aquiline nose and high narrow forehead from his grandfather. Small and thin, the boy seems even smaller and thinner when he sheds his coat and remains just in his school blouse girdled with a wide belt. Old Mendel worries about him constantly. The boy's transparent complexion, his frequent cough, his frail chest and bent shoulders, arouse in the old man an incessant anxiety. He therefore chooses the best pieces of meat for him, pours out the soup, and sets it before him on a plate. When the boy has eaten his fill, he pats him on the shoulder and then encourages him to go out and play with the other children in the courtyard.

The boy rarely allows himself to be persuaded. He is exhausted from his lessons, his heavy coat, sitting in school, the long walk, and from the burden of his knapsack. He also has a lot of homework for tomorrow. He has a tendency to shuffle his feet as he walks, and even when he smiles his hazel eyes have a certain melancholy about them.

A few moments after his meal, the boy sits down at the simple pine table and proceeds to remove his books and notebooks from his knapsack. Old Mendel returns to his workbench. Although the boy goes quietly about his business, repeating his lessons in an undertone, every now and then he lightly knocks the stool on which he is rocking, his thin elbows leaning on the table, and sure enough disturbs the old bookbinder at work. The latter turns his head around in order to look at the boy, and though he can reach for his glue with a hand, he gets up to get it from the other side of his bench so that he can pinch his grandson on his pale, transparent cheek, or stroke him along his short, soft hair as dark as a mole's fur. The boy is evidently accustomed to these caresses, for he interrupts neither his eager murmuring nor his rocking on the stool. The old bookbinder is completely satisfied with this; muffling the flopping of his slippers, he returns on tiptoes to his workbench.

On Friday just before evening the scene changes. The boy studies alongside the window, rocking strenuously on the stool, which no longer has the same momentum. The pine table is now covered with a tablecloth and on it the neighbor sets out fish, macaroni, and a fat, beautifully ruddy duck just brought in from the baker's. A tin candleholder with knobs with strangely twisted arms illuminates the room in festive, solemn way.

Old Mendel has on a rather worn but still attractive black robe with a wide belt around it into which he is fond of placing his exhausted hands. A yarmulka covers his gray hair, while the creaking of his new knee boots with their long tops fills the room with a kind of merry rustle. When the table has already been set, the boy washes, combs the mole's fur atop his small, elongated head, buttons his fresh collar and clean cuffs, and, his hands folded behind his back, stands straight and serious while his grandfather reaches for his tallith and prayer book on a shelf.

A moment later the old Jew's labial, humming song of prayer reverberates throughout the room. His voice passes through all ranges, from a brassy low to the high where his singing moves from a groan and a kind of fervent lament into passionate, imploring, and sobbing accents. Under the spell of his singing, a nervous tremor takes hold of the small gymnasium student; his pale little face becomes even paler, his big eyes grow immeasurably wider, flicker, and fill with tears. He looks at his grandfather as if bewitched; his mouth opens in spasmodic yawning. Fortunately, the grandfather soon closes the prayer book and with a blessing begins the Sabbath feast.

It happened once, in summer, that the sons of the locksmith Kołodziejski and the shoemaker Pocieszka gathered beneath the window of the old bookbinder and peering through it into the room all lit up with Sabbath light, began making fun of and mocking the prayers.

Just at that moment the old parish priest happened to be passing by. Glancing into the window and seeing the praying Jew calling out to God in his own way with such a groan, he tipped his hat. The scene was mute, but eloquent beyond words. The boys scampered away as if blown by a wind, and since then the tranquillity of that poor room has not been disturbed.

Until the day before yesterday . . .

And in fact even the day before yesterday nothing really happened. Except that the boy returned from school without his cap and breathing as hard as a hunted rabbit. At first he didn't want to say anything; only after he was interrogated at length did he confess that some ragamuffin shouted at him "Jew! Jew!" So he ran away and lost his cap and was afraid to go back for it.

A wave of anger struck old Mendel in the face. He straightened himself up, as if he suddenly grew, spat, and then seizing the boy hard by the shoulder, thrust him to the table and ate dinner in silence.

After dinner, he neither returned to his workshop nor filled his pipe. Breathing heavily, he paced the room. The boy also didn't start doing his lessons, but stared at his grandfather with a frightened look. He had never seen him so angry.

"Listen, you!" Mendel finally blurted out, standing before the boy. "When I took you in a little orphan and looked after you, and was a nursemaid to you, and a mother as well, I didn't look after you and nurse you just for you to be stupid! And when I began your education, sent you to school, and bought books for you, it wasn't just for you to be stupid! Yet despite all that you're growing up stupid and you don't have any brains at all! If you had any brains, you wouldn't be ashamed, you wouldn't cry, and you wouldn't run away just because someone yells 'Jew' at you. When you cry on account of that, and run away, and on top of that lose a pretty, new cap that costs nearly five złotys cash, well, despite everything you're stupid, and all the schools, the books, the learning, they're worth nothing!"

He took a deep breath and began speaking again, but now in a gentler tone of voice:

"Well, what do you mean 'Jew'? Eh, what kind of a Jew are you? You were born in this city, after all, so you're no stranger; you belong here, you've got a right to love this city as long as you live honorably. You shouldn't be ashamed that you're a Jew. If you're ashamed of being a Jew, if you regard yourself as good-for-nothing just because you're a Jew, what good can you ever do the city were you were born, how can you ever love it? Well?"

He cleared his throat for a moment and then stood again before the boy. This time, however, he looked at his frightened little face with a certain tenderness. He put a hand on his head and said with gravity:

"It is a beautiful thing to be an honest Jew! Remember that! Now go study so as not to be stupid and I'll buy you another cap. You don't have any reason to cry, the whole thing is silly!"

The boy kissed his grandfather's hand and took himself to his books. The old bookbinder, however, was more disturbed by the matter than he wanted to show the child. He walked around the room for a long time without finishing urgent work that had already been begun and spitting in corners as if he had eaten something bitter. He was unable to digest the bitterness even during the night since he rose the next morning even more stooped and old-looking than usual. When the boy left for school after fastening the straps of his knapsack, the old man went to the window and looked after him anxiously for a long time.

This anxiety did not leave him even at work. Upset by something, he filled his pipe more often than usual and kept going up to the window and looking suspiciously at the little street he knew so well and for so long. Doubtless because of the same upset, the movement in the street, its voices, its pulse seemed to him different than usual.

However, when the boy returned from school happy because he got a good grade and delighted by the new cap, which leaped to his eyes the moment he stepped in, the old man forgot about his premonitions and whistled while he worked—either for himself or for the sake of the boy—just the way he used to in the old days.

After lunch the ward, smelling of musk, came by for his master's records.

"How's everything?" he asked.

"Everything's fine, thank God!" answered Mendel.

"They're going to beat up on Jews, huh?" the odoriferous ward interjected, smiling idiotically.

"Well, if they beat, so they beat!" replied Mendel of Gdańsk, concealing the expression the words evoked in him. "And who, pray tell, is supposed to do the beating, the government?"

"What's the government to do with it?" the little ward shot back with a laugh.

"Well, if it's not the government, then thanks be to God!" said Mendel.

They both laughed, the little ward mindlessly, the Jew with evident strain.

He was angry that this conversation had taken place in the presence of the child. He looked at the boy from beneath knitted brows. The boy fixed his big eyes on the ward and only when the latter was beyond the threshhold did he lower them, darkened and burning, to the pages of his book. As if taking no notice of this, old Mendel began whistling again. But his whistling had something in it of the wheezing of a chest burdened by a great weight. The note softened, grew faint, and dropped off to sleep with a rasp or a groan.

It had already become dark in the room when the stout watchmaker, in the gray havelock he constantly wore in those days, squeezed past the narrow door.

"Did you hear the news?" he asked sitting on the edge of the table at which the boy was studying.

"So what do I care about news?" retorted Mendel. "If it's good, then it'll still be good when it's not news; and if it's bad, well, why should I have to listen to it?"

"They say they're going to beat up on the Jews," said the fat watchmaker, shaking a foot in a low-cut shoe with a shiny metal buckle.

Old Mendel blinked a few times nervously; a sudden trembling passed over his lips. But he recovered quickly and said in a tone of jovial kindheartedness:

"Jews? What Jews? If it's the ones who are thieves, who hurt people, who are highway robbers, who skin a poor person, then why not? I'll go beat them myself!"

"Oh no," laughed the watchmaker, "all Jews."

A sudden light flared in Mendel's gray pupils; but it was extinguished by a half-lowered eyelid, and he answered seemingly indifferently:

"Now why should they want to beat all Jews?"

"Why?" the watchmaker unhesitatingly shot back, "Because they're Jews!"

"Well," said Mendel, his gray eyes blinking, "why don't they go to the forest and beat birch trees because they're birch trees, and fir trees, because they're fir trees?"

"Ha, ha!" the watchmaker burst out laughing. "Every Jew knows how to twist things! But the birch tree and the fir tree are our own, in our forests, grown up out of our soil!"

Mendel all but choked as an answer rushed suddenly to his lips. He bent a bit toward the watchmaker and stared deeply into his eyes.

"So what did I grow out of? What soil did I grow out of? Haven't you known me for a long time? You've known me for twenty-seven years! Did I come here as if to a tavern? Ate, drank, and didn't pay? No, I didn't come here to any tavern! I grew up in this city like the birch tree in the forest! I ate a piece of bread here, that's true. I also drank some water, that's true too. But I paid for that bread and water. With what did I pay? You want to know what I paid with?"

He held out both his toil-worn, emaciated, and veiny hands.

"Well," he called out with a certain vehemence in his voice, "I paid with these ten fingers! Do you see these hands?"

He again leaned forward and shook his thin hands in front of the watchmaker's shiny face.

"These are hands that didn't bring that bread and water to the mouth for nothing! These are hands that have become all twisted from knives, pincers, screws, and hammers. I paid with them for every piece of bread and for every glass of water I ever ate and drank here. I even added these eyes that can't see very well any more, and this back that refuses to be straight, and these legs that are tired of carrying me!"

The watchmaker listened indifferently, toying with his watch chain. The Jew became impassioned with his own words.

"Well, and where's my remuneration? My remuneration is in school with the children, the young men, and the young women who are studying books, who keep accounts, that's where. It's in the church, too, when people go there with books . . . It's with the parish priest because I repair books for him, may he be well!"

He raised his yarmulka and then added:

"My remuneration is in these good hands!"

"That's what they say," replied the watchmaker diplomatically, "but a Jew is always a Jew!"

New sparks flashed in the eyes of the old bookmaker.

"So what else should he be? Should he be a German? A Frenchman? Maybe he should be a horse? Since he became a dog a long time ago, he's already one!"

"That's not the issue!" the watchmaker pompously replied. "The issue is that the Jew shouldn't be a stranger!"

"Is that what it's about?" answered Mendel leaning back and withdrawing his elbows. "Just tell me right away! There's a wise word for you! I like hearing words of wisdom! Words of wisdom are like a father and a mother to a person. I'd walk a mile for a wise word. Whenever I hear a wise word it's as good as bread to me. If I were a wealthy man, a big banker, I'd give a ducat for every wise word I heard. You say the Jew shouldn't be a stranger? So, I say the same thing. Why not? Let him not be a stranger. Why should he be a stranger, why should he make himself a stranger, when he's himself? Or do you think that when rain falls it doesn't get the Jew wet too; that when wind blows it doesn't strew the Jew's eyes with sand as well, just because the Jew's a stranger? Or maybe you think that the brick that falls from a roof misses the Jew because he's a stranger? Well, I'll tell you, my dear sir, that it doesn't miss him. And the wind doesn't miss him, and the rain doesn't miss him! Have a look at my hair, my beard . . . They're gray, and white . . . What does that mean? That means that they've seen many things and remember many things. I'll tell you, sir, they've seen great fires and a great conflagration, and great lightning strike this city, but one thing they didn't see is Jews being spared these fires and conflagration and lightning! And just as night falls on the city, it falls on the Jews as well, and the sun doesn't shine on the Jews any longer either!"

He drew a deep, heavy breath . . .

"You know my name, don't you? Well, my name is Mendel of Gdańsk. The reason I'm called Mendel is because there were fourteen children in the family and when I was born I was the fifteenth, here in the Old Town, in this narrow little street, right behind these yellow buildings, where the apothecary's is. You know where? So, when I was born, there were fifteen of us, a whole *mendel*.[1] That's how I got the name Mendel. What was my late father supposed to do with the lot of us, drown us? He couldn't drown us! First, because he feared God, and second, because he loved his fifteen children, so much so that when mother brought us herring he cut off just the head for himself and gave the whole herring to the children so that they'd have something to eat and not be hungry. That's how he loved them."

He cleared his throat. He turned red, his eyes lit up with sudden recollection. But he restrained himself and spoke further with a jovial smile on his face that barely concealed a bitter irony.

"But I, Mendel, saw that any fifteen of anything has a hard time in life, so I had only half a dozen children, and my daughter, Leah, well, she just had one son and she died in great pain. But if she had lived, and had six sons, and seen what I've seen, she'd have died six times from the pain!"

He spoke faster and faster, his voice strained with emotion, as he bent toward the watchmaker and penetrated him with a burning gaze. A moment later, he straightened up, drew a deep, heavy breath into his old chest, and smiling dolefully, declared:

"So we didn't call him Mendel; we called him Jakub instead."

1. *Mendel* in Polish means fifteen of anything.

"Kubuś, come here!"[2] he called, as if remembering the boy's presence for the first time. And when the boy rose from the table, scuffing his shoes in front of the watchmaker, and approached his grandfather, the old man stroked him on the head and said:

"Kubuś, that's a name that even the gentleman here can be proud to give a worthy son. . . . He shook his gray beard and clasped the boy still closer to his side.

"You know, I'm not only called Mendel, but also Mendel 'of Gdańsk.' So what does it mean to be 'of Gdańsk'? It means a person or a thing that comes from Gdańsk. You know that, do you? There is Gdańsk vodka, and a Gdańsk trunk, and a Gdańsk chest of drawers . . . If they can be of Gdańsk, so can I. I'm not 'of Paris,' I'm not 'of Vienna,' and I'm not 'of Berlin'; I'm 'of Gdańsk.' You tell me I'm a stranger. How can that be? If I'm 'of Gdańsk,' that makes me a stranger? Is that what you're saying? Has the Vistula River gone dry? Don't the rafts still go down it from our city? Don't those money-grubbing boatsmen of ours still exist? Is all that foreign? . . ."

The watchmaker smiled and put his hands on his sides.

"So let's say I don't know you! Is there anything you've thought up here that some Polack couldn't have handled better? You're called 'of Gdańsk,' so right away the place is yours! Ha, ha, ha!"

The old Jew shook his head and smiled too. The playfulness of a sophist shone in his eyes, but his smile was bitter, prickly.

"Mendel of Gdańsk and Jakub of Gdańsk," he said seriously after a moment's pause, turning to his grandson and as if passing on to him the dignity of his name and tradition.

"Well, what is this Mendel of Gdańsk? He's a Jew, born in this city, lives in this city, from his own work, has the graves of his father and mother, his wife, and his daughter in this city. He'll lay down his own bones in this city.

"Well, and what is this Kubuś of Gdańsk?" He thrust the boy an arm's length from himself back into the middle of the room but still held on to him.

"Well, he's a student. He sits in school, on a bench, sits alongside his fellow students, looks at a book, writes, learns. And what does he learn for? He learns in order to have intelligence. And where's he going to go with that intelligence once he has it? He's never going to go with it to any foreign place. He's not going to drown it in water or burn it in fire, or bury it in the ground. He's going to be smart for this country, he's going to use his intelligence for this city. There's intelligence enough in this country without him, and it'll still be there when Kubuś has it. Do you think that'll be an excess? Too much? You can't think such nonsense. When he has intelligence he'll know things I don't know and you don't know. Maybe he'll even know that all people are the children of one God and that all people are supposed to love each other like brothers."

He again tugged the boy close to himself and embracing him around the neck

2. "Kubuś" is a nickname for Jakub in Polish.

leaned over and whispered to the watchmaker: "He's a sensitive child . . . an orphan . . . with a very soft heart . . ."

He patted the boy on the face and said: "Go on, darling, go to sleep; tomorrow you've got school."

The boy again scraped his shoes in front of the watchmaker, pressed his grandfather's hand to his lips, and disappeared behind the beaded curtain that separated the room from a small alcove.

The old Jew blinked a couple of times, cleared his throat, and asked as he stroked his beard: "Now, begging your pardon, sir, who was it was saying they're going to beat Jews? I didn't want to ask in the child's presence so as not to frighten him for anything in the world, since he's very sensitive. But now I can ask you about it without any bad feelings."

He smiled in a complimentary way, ingratiatingly, his gray eyes looking coaxingly.

The watchmaker, somewhat taken aback by the Jew's previous arguments, immediately sensed his superiority.

"That's what they say . . . ," he muttered casually, puffing out his lips.

"But who's saying it?" the Jew asked, his eyes turning from mellow to sharp, calculating.

"People are saying it," the watchmaker muttered in the same tone of voice.

The old Jew sprang back two paces with a nimbleness nobody would have imagined of him. Gaze burning, lips snorting, he thrust his head forward like a goat.

"People? People are saying it?" he asked with a hissing sound, his voice getting increasingly louder. "People?"

With each word spoken, he leaned forward more, almost sitting down. The watchmaker looked on indifferently, playing with his watch chain and swaying a foot back and forth. He observed, however, that alongside his the figure of the Jew was inconsequential and ludicrous.

"Why does that surprise you so?" he asked coldly.

But the old bookbinder had already calmed down. He straightened out, put his arms akimbo, tossed his beard upward, and squinted.

"You're wrong, sir," he said, "people aren't saying it, vodka's saying it, the tavern's saying it, anger and stupidity are saying it, a bad wind that's blowing is saying it."

He raised a hand and gestured contemptuously.

"You sleep soundly, sir. And I'll sleep soundly too, and the child there will sleep soundly! There's a lot of sadness in our city and a lot of ignorance, and a lot of misfortune, but our city hasn't reached the point yet where the people in it are biting like mad dogs. Oh, you can put your mind at ease!"

He tightened his lips and with a serious mien reached for the heavy tin candlestick as if wanting immediately to light the guest's way to the entrance hall. The watchmaker pushed himself down from the table, tightened his havelock, secured on his head the hat that had slipped down somewhere on his neck, tossed out a "goodnight," and left.

The Jew then returned from the door, put the candlestick back on the table, tiptoed to the alcove, opened the curtain, and listened attentively. From inside the alcove the feverish, uneven, hoarse breathing of a child could be heard. A small lamp in the shape of a green glass globe was burning on a table. He slipped off his old slippers, went up to the bed, and gazed anxiously, inquisitively, at the flushed face of the boy. He stood for a moment that way holding his breath, then sighed, withdrew from the alcove, and sat down firmly on his stool, resting his hands on his knees and shaking his gray head. He was stooped now and looked as though he had aged by at least ten years. His lips moved soundlessly, his chest breathed deeply, and his eyes remained glued to the floor. The thin candle in the tin candlestick expired with a hissing noise.

*   *   *

On the following morning the small street awoke as quiet as usual and as peaceful as usual. From the crack of dawn Mendel of Gdańsk was at his workshop in his leather apron. His huge scissors were gnashing impetuously but firmly through paper; the screw of his press squeaked, tightened to the last turn; the worn blade of the long narrow knife shone in the morning sun; snippets of paper fell with a rustle to the right and left. The old bookbinder worked feverishly, zealously; the sleepless night was visible on his haggard, deeply furrowed face. But after he downed the wretched coffee brought him by his neighbor in a large faience teapot, his spirits picked up, he filled his short little pipe and went to wake his grandson.

The boy had somehow overslept. For a long time during the night he tossed about like a fish, but now he was fast asleep. A thin beam of sunlight falling into the alcove through an opening in the beaded curtain fell on his eyes, his mouth, and his frail bare chest; alighting on his soft, dark hair and on his long, lowered eyelids it kindled golden-brown, twinkling glimmers.

The old man looked tenderly at the child. The wrinkles left his brow, his mouth widened, his eyes squinted and took in the light. He finally broke out into a happy, quiet smile, and drawing a huge puff of smoke from his pipe, leaned over and let it out directly beneath the boy's nose. The boy choked, came to with a start, opened wide his golden eyes and began rubbing them with his hands clenched into two thin little fists. He then began bustling about concerned that one of his lessons was unfinished. Books and notebooks that hadn't been put away were still lying on the table. He had no time to drink up his morning coffee and he didn't want to take for play period the roll filled with two slices of hard-boiled egg. Instead, he just threw his books into his knapsack, uncertain whether or not he was going to be late. But no sooner did he head for the door with his overcoat over his shoulders when the door was flung open and the thin student from the attic pushed him back into the room.

"Run, they're beating up Jews!"

He was clearly very agitated. His long, pockmarked face seemed even longer and more ravaged. The step he took from the hallway to the room separated his thin legs a huge distance from one another; his little dark-gray eyes shot out sparks of anger. The terrified boy rolled like a ball of yarn toward the table, dropping his coat and knapsack on the way.

The old man stood paralyzed. But he came to soon and, his face ablaze, lunged at the student like a wildcat.

"What do you mean 'run'? Where's he supposed to run to? Why should he run? Did he steal something from someone, that he should run away? Is he some place here where he doesn't belong? In someone else's home? He's in his own place here! In his own home! He didn't steal anything from anyone! He's going to school! He's not going to run away!"

He jumped up to the student standing in the doorway, shriveled by rage, tensed, fuming, and tugging at his beard.

"Do as you want!" the student retorted roughly. "I told you . . ."

He was about to withdraw his exceptionally long legs from the room when the old bookbinder grabbed him by the tail of his threadbare overcoat.

"As I want? What kind of talk is that, what I want! What I want is to have some peace. I want to eat in peace the bread I work for! And I want to bring up this orphan, this boy here so that he'll become a man, so nobody'll spit at him when he's not guilty of anything! I don't want to suffer any harm or anyone else to either. I want justice, for everyone to fear God! That's what I want. I don't want any running away! I was born in this city, had children in this house, I didn't do anyone any harm, I have my workshop here . . ."

He didn't finish; a dullish roar, as from a distant gathering storm, turned a bend in the street. A sudden cramp passed over the student's face, a barely audible curse fell from his compressed lips. The old bookbinder remained silent, straightened himself, and extending his thin neck listened attentively for a moment. The roar drew closer quickly. A protracted hooting, laughter, calling, outbreaks of shouting, and crying could be heard. The little street was in turmoil. Gates were locked, shops were boarded up, some people ran right toward the roar, others ran away from it.

Suddenly, the boy began sobbing loudly. The student banged the door shut and disappeared into the empty hallway. The old Jew kept listening, seemingly unaware either of the boy's sobbing or the student's exit. He looked as if he had withdrawn into himself; his lower lip hung loosely, his ears were pricked. The trembling of his old knees was visible through his leather apron; his face turned from red to brown, from brown to yellow, and from yellow to chalk white. He resembled a person who had been struck by a bullet. A moment more and the old, frail body would shatter and collapse.

All the closer, all the clearer, the roar at last descended on the deserted street with a huge outburst of shouting, whistling, laughing, and cursing. Hoarse, drunken voices merged with the satanic squealing of adolescents. The very air seemed drunk on the yelling of the mob. An animal-like frolicsomeness took hold of the street; it squeezed it and coursed through it wildly and deafeningly. The crash of broken shutters, the din of rolling barrels, the tinkle of shattered glass, the rumble of stones, the grating of iron rods—all seemed live participants in this horrid scene. Like flakes of thickly falling snow, feathers from ripped pillows and bedding flew out and dropped down. Now only a few weathered market stalls separated Mendel's room from the unbridled throng. The boy stopped sobbing and trembling all over as if in fever pressed close to his grandfather. His large dark eyes grew even darker and shone gloomily from his pale face. How strange! The child's embrace and the near and unavoidable danger strengthened the old Jew. He placed a hand on his grandson's head, took a deep breath, and though his face was still as white as a sheet, he summoned fire, and life, to the pupils of his eyes.

"Sh," he whispered comfortingly.

Only now did he still the cry, which itself had died down, stifled by great fear. Only now did the child's previous sobbing reach his consciousness. Just at that moment a few women—the rope-maker's wife with a child in her arms, the portress, and the marketstall-keeper—rushed into the long, narrow hallway.

"Get away, Mendel!" shouted the portress from the threshhold. "Don't let them see you! I'll put a holy picture or a cross in the window as fast as I can. They're already up in the other rooms . . . They won't go there!"

She grasped the boy by a hand.

"Hurry, Kubuś! Into the alcove . . ."

They formed a circle around them, shielded them, and pushed them toward the beaded curtain. They knew the Jew from way back; he was an obliging, good person. Other residents of the small tenement house began crowding in behind the women. The room filled with people.

Old Mendel leaned one hand heavily on the boy's shoulder while with the other he pushed the women away. He came to his senses completely in the course of that one moment.

"For heaven's sake, Janowa!" he said in a hard voice as resonant as a bell. "For heaven's sake! I thank you for wanting to give me your holy things, for wanting to save me, but I don't want to put a cross in my window! I don't want to be ashamed of being a Jew. I don't want to be afraid! If they don't have any pity, if they want to do harm to others, then they're not Christians, so that cross or image won't do any good. They're not people. They're just wild beasts. If they were people, Christians, then the gray head of an old man and an innocent child like this would also be like something holy to them. Go on, Kubuś . . ."

And dragging the child after him, despite the noisy protests of the others gathered in the room, he went to the window, threw open both shutters with a thrust of the hand, and stood there in his open jacket, his leather apron, his white beard trembling, his head raised high, hugging to his side the little schoolboy in his school blouse, whose large eyes opened ever wider and were fixed on the howling mob.

The sight was so touching. The women began sobbing.

The gang in the street caught sight of the Jew in the window and, passing the abandoned market stalls, threw themselves toward him.

The heroic boldness of the old man, the mute summons to human feelings, was taken as an insult, as mockery. Here they didn't have to look for some barrel full of vinegar to roll away, a case of goods to be broken, a feather bed to be torn open, a basket of eggs to be smashed. Here there erupted that savage lust for hurting, that instinct for cruelty, that lurks within a person, like a conflagration taking hold of a crowd, a mob . . .

They hadn't reached the window yet when a stone, hurled from the midst of the crowd, struck the boy on the head. The lad shouted, the women rushed to him. The Jew let go of the boy's arm, didn't even look around, but raising both hands, directing his gaze high above the howling mob, whispered with lips turned white:

"Adonai! Adonai!" And huge tears ran down his furrowed face.

At that moment he was a true *gaon,* which means tall, noble.

When the front rank of the throng reached the window, they found an unexpected obstacle in the form of the frail student from the attic. With disheveled hair, his uniform undone, he stood beneath the Jew's window, tightened his fists and crossed his arms, and set his legs apart like an open compass. He was so tall he covered almost half the window. Anger, shame, contempt, and pity shook his bared chest and like flames coursed across his dark, pock-marked face.

"Hands off the Jew here!" he snarled like a mastiff at the first who ran up. "If not, come on, have a go at me, you hoodlums, bastards, good-for-nothings!"

He was trembling from head to toe and couldn't even summon his full voice, so overcome with anger was he. Sparks seemed to stream from his small dark-gray eyes.

He was beautiful as Apollo at that moment.

Some of the more sober of the gang began withdrawing. The figure of the young man and his words struck them with their strength. The tall student took advantage of it; jumping through the low window into the room, he pushed the Jew aside and took his place at the window himself. The throng dragged past the window with a mute din. Taunts, threats, yells, and curses accompanied the procession. The tumult then receded, quieted down until it became an indistinct, distant rumble . . .

*   *   *

That evening nobody studied at the pine table and nobody worked at the workbench. From behind the beaded curtain, from the alcove, the quiet groaning of the child could be heard every so often. Otherwise, complete calm reigned. If not for a broken pane in the window, if not for the overcoat and student knapsack thrown on the floor, there would not have been a trace of the storm that had passed by here in the morning.

In the alcove, behind the curtain, lay Mendel's grandson with bandaged head. The green lamp burned alongside him, and the thin student sat on the edge of the bed holding his hand.

The face of the student was the same as usual, a pockmarked, ugly face; only in his eyes shone unextinguishable fires, stirred from the bottom of his soul. He sat without saying anything, frowning, angry; from time to time he threw an impatient glance at the dark corner of the alcove. Old Mendel of Gdańsk was sitting in the corner, motionless, speechless. Crouching, his elbows resting on his knees, his face hidden in his hands, he had been sitting like that since noon, from the moment he learned that the child was out of danger.

This immobility, and the old bookbinder's silence, disturbed the student.

"Pan Mendel," he finally grunted, "crawl out of that corner once and for all! What are you doing, sitting *shivah*?[3] It's just a little fever and nothing more. In a week the boy'll go back to school, as soon as his skin's grown back a bit. And you, you're sitting as if on a sack of ashes. After all, nobody died."

The old Jew remained silent.

After a while he finally raised his head and replied in a voice trembling with passion: "You're asking if I'm sitting shivah? Yes, I am! I've scattered ashes on my head and I've got a heavy sack on it, and I'm sitting in the ashes, and my feet are bare, and I'm doing a heavy penance, and I have great pain, and great bitterness . . ."

He grew silent and again buried his face in his hands. The small green lamp lent his gray head a peculiar, spectral-like illumination. The boy groaned once or twice and again everything fell silent. But then, amid the silence, Mendel of Gdańsk once again raised his head and spoke:

"You say that nothing of mine died? You're wrong. Something did die—what I was born with, what I lived with for sixty-seven years, what I hoped to die with . . . What died is my love for this city!"

---

3. The Jewish period of mourning following a death and burial.

■ Gabriela Zapolska (1857–1921)
"The Anti-Semite" (1897–98)

[After an unsuccessful attempt to establish herself as an actress, above all at Antoine's Théâtre Libre in Paris, Gabriela Zapolska devoted herself to a literary career. A prolific, if hasty, writer of novels, short stories, and plays, she combined elements of both positivism and naturalism in her work. Known for her jaundiced outlook on life and her venomous pen, she gained a certain notoriety for her sensationalist writing and her delight in exposing the hypocrisy of the bourgeoisie. She was a better playwright than novelist; her best work for the theater was the antibourgeois satire, *Moralność pani Dulskiej* (*The Morality of Mrs. Dulska,* 1907). The strong contemporary Polish interest in the "Jewish question" is reflected in several of Zapolska's works, among them her two plays with ghetto settings, *Małka Szwarcenkopf* (1897) and *Jojne Firułkes* (1898), and her long story "Antysemitnik" ("The Anti-Semite," 1897–98). "The Anti-Semite" manifests Zapolska's desire to enter the struggle against anti-Semitism, in the spirit of the positivists. This element is lacking in her "Jewish" plays, which take place wholly within a Jewish milieu; however, like the positivists, Zapolska emphasizes the need for dynamic change within the Jewish community by contrasting progressive and obscurantist attitudes, particularly with respect to the position of women. On the basis of such plays as *Małka Szwarcenkopf* and *Jojne Firułkes* and several of her novels and short stories, Zapolska merits recognition as perhaps the leading feminist of Polish modernism.]

Of the 186 gulden won in the dark den that resembled a coffeehouse, only 47 remained.

According to the promise he made his comrades, he had to let the rest go as well.

It went on cheap, watered-down champagne, snacks, liqueurs, caviar, and other poisons, the remains of which stained the linen on the restaurant table.

Szatkiewicz drank a mixture of Rhine wine, port, Kümmel, beer, mustard, salt, and curaçao. It was of indeterminate color and dreadful taste, but Szatkiewicz did not want to yield to the pale Witwicki, who had a reputation for drinking similar potions. They felt the effects usually at daybreak when the adulterated drinks they had consumed began stimulating them. They then prepared exquisite brews with the delight of a pharmacist just beginning his career.

Afterward—they drank slowly—they observed one another from beneath swollen eyelids. They didn't even wince, but instead assumed the expressions of martyrs suffering voluntary torments for some ideal. Only the small, bluish eyes

Gabriela Zapolska, "Antysemitnik," in *Szkice powieściowe* (Cracow: Wydawnictwo Literackie, 1958), 85–171. This is volume 10 of Zapolska's collected works (*Dzieła Wybrane*). The novella first appeared in the journal *Życie,* in installments, from November 27, 1897, to June 18, 1898. The first book edition was published in 1899 as a bonus for new subscribers to *Życie*.

of Witwicki were clouded over, although his mouth wore a bitter, ironic smile. Szatkiewicz's round, babyish face, on the other hand, was flushed. Spasmodically tightening his grip on the stem of a glass, he kept drinking, and drinking, and drinking. . . .

Szatkiewicz now leaned against the arms of a chair and stared blankly at the large, black, unattractive mirror, which, like a mythical bird, sad and motionless, hung on the wall above a small console table on which lay a pile of hats. Behind him someone was playing on an untuned piano, something from Schumann—*Warum* perhaps, impatient and desperate[1]—wailing with longing in this saloon atmosphere so saturated with smoke and the murmur of gossip whose sole purpose was the physical and moral undressing of women both known and unknown. . . .

He stretched out his hand and unconsciously drew a devil's wings on the tablecloth with a broken toothpick. At the same time, a single thought kept running through his mind:

"Where am I going to get forty-five guldens by tomorrow?"

But Witwicki, who had expressed his opinion about the lack of "culture" of the average Cracovian, drew toward himself the basket with the remaining rolls and began drilling small holes in each one. He then extracted the middle and filled the cavity with pepper, cigar ashes, toothpicks, mustard, capers, and anything that came to hand. He worked diligently, all the while sticking out his pointed tongue shaped like a stinger. The young people seated around him were extremely interested in this cultural labor and kept on giving him suggestions, which he accepted with a smile full of disdain and superiority. He sealed up the apertures of these "stuffed" rolls in this manner and put them back in the basket, pleased with himself and the world.

Szatkiewicz felt out of sorts for a while. He wanted in some way to defeat Witwicki's sense of superiority. Mechanically thrusting a hand into his pocket, he encountered a woman's horn-rim hairpin. He took it out and tossed it on the table. The poor, frail little hairpin, a bad imitation of tortoise-shell, suddenly looked black among the emptied bottles of liqueur and the salt scattered all around. Witwicki reached for it greedily and shoved it into a roll as fast as he could. The figure of the thin, dark chorus girl, whom in moments of good humor he called "bat," flashed before Szatkiewicz's eyes. She lost the hairpin the day before when she left him at the entrance to the theater. He noticed it in the light of the street lamp, bent down, and picked it up. The girl disappeared into the shadows; he intended to return the hairpin to her today when he escorted her to the theater, but he didn't go to her. Instead, he drank the whole night, and afterward worry over the forty-five guldens troubled him like a nightmare. He paid no attention

---

1. The title of one of the piano miniatures in the *Phantasiestücke* cycle by Robert Schumann (1810–56).

to what was being said around him. He saw before him the black apparition of
the landlady of his hotel to whom he owed rent and who either fell in on him
herself or sent waiters up to him every day. . . .

Without saying anything, Szatkiewicz began observing his host. He was a
bearded, angular "romantic" with a big, black beard and dreamy eyes. He worked
at the same newspaper as Szatkiewicz but held a superior position. He had a desk
that wasn't cracked, a small carpet beneath his feet, and a certain standing with
the editor-in-chief.

His name was Binder and he had been at the paper a long time, for several
years, and he was what's called a "pillar," that is the editor's right-hand man. He
was a crypto-decadent and confessed to it only in bars and only after consuming
a quantity of beer. It still isn't profitable to be a decadent in Cracow, and Binder
liked wearing a fashionable coat and new gloves. But pale faces, convoluted pictures, and moody poetry still attracted him. He lumped all "isms" together and
called them "decadence," and himself a secret "ist," not in deed or in life, to be
sure, but in his desires. He worked for a so-called sober and healthy newspaper,
so he kept his "isms" in his pocket and covered them with an honorable kerchief
of small-town, run-of-the-mill, journalistic philistinism. During the day he was
"untouchable," but at night he played cards ferociously with colleagues from rival
papers or declaimed Tetmajer's poems[2], a mug of beer in hand, at Hawełka's.[3]

At times like that Szatkiewicz looked at him with a strange hatred. Yet he drank
the whole night at his expense. They came there straight from a coffeehouse where
they had gone after a theatrical premiere with the intention of finishing the review
they had in fact written before the performance. Cards consumed all their attention, and it was late at night that they remembered the text that still hadn't been
sent. But the matter was easily resolved. On the marble tabletop of the so-called
anti-Semitic forge, the management of the theater, the author of the play, and the
actors taking part in the production were abused with a damaged and leaky pen
point. There had existed, after all, since the beginning of the season an irrevers-
ible order for a similar method of "harassment" of the theater, and the staff of
the *Kurier Narodowy* (*National Courier*)[4] grasped the order with the tenacity of
people drowning whom fate allowed to find a straw in the waves of the river.

After "disposing" of the premiere in this manner, they fondly surrendered
themselves to their impassioned cards, and the result of this arduous labor last-

2. A reference to the popular turn-of-the-century poet Kazimierz Przerwa-Tetmajer (1865–1940).

3. A well-known restaurant on the Main Square in Cracow. It was named after its founder, Antoni
Hawełka.

4. Published in Kraków from 1889 to 1893, the *Kurier Narodowy* was the anti-Semitic organ of the
Christian Democrats. It was edited by Józef Orłowski. After the paper's closing, an additional forty-
one numbers (October 15–November 24, 1893) appeared under the name *Nowy Kurier Narodowy* (*New
National Courier*). The *Głos Narodu* (*Voice of the People*), a successor paper, continued the extreme
anti-Semitic line of the other two. It is possible that the paper referred to in the novella is a composite
of all three.

ing several hours was *souper* in a *chambre separée,* with champagne, piano music, fragrant partridges, hissing gas, and the wailing from time to time of songs heard in the luxurious rooms of the Odeon or Friedmann's. . . .

At dinner, Binder had mentioned something about establishing a conservative newspaper; this meant, of course, anti-Semitic, for otherwise there was "no business" in Cracow. And from that moment on everyone began bowing low to him and laughing whenever he said something that was supposed to be witty.

Only he, Szatkiewicz, and Witwicki behaved coldly and indifferently. There was thus a knot of sympathy between him and this pale decadent.

There was no doubt in his mind that Witwicki would lend him the money.

If he just had . . . but his doubt began to wane . . . The pale journalist tossed two silver guldens at the fellow who was supposed to be watching the coats and hats but was dozing over an old newspaper.

Szatkiewicz's mood improved.

He himself got dressed and even though his ears were buzzing he made his way down the carpeted staircase. . . .

But by now the whole group had slowly begun moving toward Market Square. Dragging past Szpitalna Street, which was empty and dark, they entered Market Square and unconsciously, as if directed by force of habit, they went in the direction of Hawełka's shop. . . .

Szatkiewicz tried to stay behind the others alone with Witwicki. He succeeded, since the pale young man, who felt an instinctive dislike for Binder, involuntarily separated himself from the whole group. He even leaned on Szatkiewicz's shoulder, and melancholically rapping his cane against closed shop doors, dragged along his boredom and twenty years of age. Szatkiewicz sought in his mind the point at which he might begin a conversation with his request for a loan. Along the length of Szpitalna Street, he pondered how best to cloak the coarseness of his words. He did after all possess a considerable inbred delicacy of feelings, which even work on the *Kurier* was unable to uproot.

But when they came out onto Market Square, Witwicki removed his hand from Szatkiewicz's shoulder: "I'm rather tired," he said, "I'd best go sleep!"

Szatkiewicz was seized with despair.

"Walk with me at least to that other street lamp!" he asked, thinking that at the first street lamp he'd at last be able to cough up his request. But Witwicki stopped and repeated with the obstinacy of a peevish child: "I'm going to sleep!"

And then suddenly he burst out shouting like a hoot owl, and his voice fell into the wind and the foggy night and broke against the panes of closed, dark windows.

Szatkiewicz seized him by the hand.

"What are you howling about?" he asked.

Witwicki smiled bitterly.

"I'm bursting with culture!" he declared, beating his chest.

He then fell silent and began staring into Szatkiewicz's face, blinking his eyes and shifting his weight from one foot to the other. Szatkiewicz made the same movements and had the same expression on his face. And both began simultaneously:

"Perhaps you could lend . . ."

They both broke off, momentarily confused, after which Witwicki was the first to break out laughing:

"Just great! I'm going to sleep!" he exclaimed and turning on a heel disappeared in the darkness of Floriańska Street.

Szatkiewicz remained alone. He stood for some time in the middle of the sidewalk and, consumed by sudden anger, buttoned his coat up all the way. He looked with hatred at the handful of his comrades fading into the distance, Binder in the lead. Nobody noticed that he was no longer among them; nobody gave a thought either to his person or to what was going on in his soul. Why, then, did he spend so many hours with them and give them a part of his existence? He felt lonely, very poor, very small, and very deserted. He reminded himself that in all likelihood he'd soon have to buy a new pair of shoes, and the thought moved him to tears.

In the twenty-second year of his life, he himself had to think of himself and buy his own clothing. Alcohol made him all the drowsier. He felt a need to get things off his chest, to unburden himself. Even when he was in school the other kids used to annoy him without understanding that the only thing he wanted to do in class was sleep. . . . Then afterward he went on to the university, but it just bored him. Nothing ever worked out for him in life and probably never would. . . .

II

The following morning Szatkiewicz woke up with a hangover and a foul taste in his mouth. He looked around with a sleepy gaze. It was cold in his hotel flat, into which day shone skimpily through a small window looking out on a smelly courtyard. The furniture was crooked and ugly; the only thing that stood out strangely against the shabby walls, indeed in the whole place, was a clean mahogany bed, empire style, with bronzes. It was a splendid piece of furniture, huge, majestic, taking up fully half the room. The bronze decorations, though somewhat tarnished, looked impressive against the dark background of the wood. On the inside, the bed contained linen that was no longer fresh, an amaranth quilt edged with rumpled sheeting, and beneath it all the small, thin body of Szatkiewicz.

The head of the young journalist was sunk in crumpled pillows. His eyes seemed dark only from afar; they were nice eyes, large, dreamy, sleepy. He reached mechanically for cigarettes and matches, but remained motionless for a long moment, an unlit cigarette in his mouth. He felt that he ought to get up, get dressed, and go to the newspaper, but at the same time he felt that he lacked both the strength and desire. The state in which he found himself at the time was known as "sickness of the will." A physician referred to it as the consequence of neglected neurasthenia. Szatkiewicz himself, however, assigned no name to his sickly indolence, even in his own mind. He simply said, his arms stretched out: "I want nothing!"

He stared at the window from which hung freshly washed cheap bluish curtains. This detail irritated him. Why did the curtains have to be washed? He was already used to their dirty, grayish color. In his absence, who had the desire to remove the curtains from their hooks, wash them, and put them up again? For what purpose? Why?

His lack of money again began irritating him. He knew that he had to provide the *Kurier Narodowy* with a sensational piece about some Jewish villainy, something about usury and its terrible effects — in short, something completely "new" and "piquant" on that subject known and used by all those organs that supported themselves by rousing the passions and fanning racial hatred.

But Szatkiewicz's anti-Semitism was no more than a means to an end, and the young journalist had a large debt to pay off. But his heart wasn't really in it; his zeal lacked wings. They were cut off by his account at the office, a disastrous one which in his recklessness he had not foreseen. Another advance was absolutely out of the question. His monthly salary was almost twice spoken for. Those fifty guldens, for which he was obligated each month to pour out a certain dose of hatred against Jews, socialists, and anybody else who had the misfortune to be disliked by the newspaper, had long ago been consumed by life, coffee shops, clothing, rent, the Odeon, Friedmann's, and other similar needs and pleasures of this wretched existence. Szatkiewicz didn't have many debts for the simple reason that nobody would lend him money or extend him credit because of the uncertainty of repayment. His position became lamentable, the more so since he had to conceal it both at the office and among his friends so as not to lose a certain kind of charm that always surrounds a person "of means." This meant a lot to Szatkiewicz; he felt instinctively that it placed a person in an advantageous light and lent him substance in the eyes of his employers.

Nevertheless, lying in bed any later than noon was impossible lest that jeopardize his job at the paper. So Szatkiewicz procrastinated. He began dressing in deadly silence. Something loomed through the curtains and began stirring on the windowpanes. It was as if a huge pigeon were shaking out its feathers. And then Szatkiewicz noticed that strange white transparent light was filling his room.

He rapidly approached the window and raised the curtain.

The roof of the apartment house across the street, of which Szatkiewicz had a view, was covered with a thick clean layer of snow.

Szatkiewicz shut his eyes and remained that way for a moment, suspenders hanging from his hands. Snow acted on his sick and oversensitive nature the way it does on every neurotic. At that moment he felt pulled somewhere far off, he didn't know where — to the mountains or the steppes; just to where there was a lot of snow, strewn with diamonds of sparks, and where unseen sleighs gliding across the surface could be heard in the distance.

A knock on the door interrupted this snowy daydreaming.

A waiter poked his head in through the half-opened doorway. Szatkiewicz trembled. Every morning this lightbrown head with a smooth meaningless mask of a face put in an appearance and Szatkiewicz heard the words: "Your bill, sir?"

But today was different. The waiter said nothing about the bill and just delivered the following announcement: "There's a young lady at the gate who wants to see you!"

Szatkiewicz shook his head: "Tell her to come up at once!"

"Yes sir!"

The waiter disappeared. Szatkiewicz began dressing again, but without haste. He knew very well who was waiting for him at the gate. He would have to lie about why he hadn't come for her at the theater. This woman couldn't understand that he wanted nothing, even her, her pretty eyes, her alluring smile . . . Nevertheless, barely washed and with his hair scarcely combed, he descended the dirty carpeted stairway. . . .

Although she saw him from afar, she did not go up to him but waited as if a little confused and frightened. When Szatkiewicz drew close to her she raised her large, hazel, tired eyes to him and asked: "You're not angry at me?"

"Why should I be?"

"For sending up for you."

"No, but you could have just come up yourself. You could have warmed yourself, had some tea . . . I would have ordered cakes sent up . . . Maybe you'll come after all, eh?"

He knew in advance that she would refuse him and wouldn't for anything come to his apartment; but without waiting for her answer, he began walking hurriedly in the direction of Market Square, in this way compelling her as well to distance herself from the hotel. She walked alongside him, or rather behind him, trying not to muddy her shoes in the melting snow on the sidewalks. Little of her face could be seen between the brim of her dark-blue hat, pulled down far over her eyes, and the edge of the high collar of her black jacket of fake Persian lamb. But her features seemed quite regular, her nose a bit too upturned, her complexion dull, chalk white, her mouth small and somewhat semicircular and heavily daubed with carmine lipstick. She was tall, on the thin side, but with quite broad hips, which swayed as she walked with a certain indolent charm.

Szatkiewicz was shorter than she was, and on the whole seemed to fade and diminish in stature despite the fact that when he strode out onto the street he reminded himself that he worked for the *Kurier* and had to maintain a "sturdy" expression on his face. Hence he thrust out his chest, raised his shoulders, and walked with the look of a tamer of wild animals.

Silently, they entered Market Square, which was then all white with snow. Frozen pigeons were huddling along the walls of the Church of Mary.

"Poor birds!" the young woman said, pointing in the direction of the church.

Szatkiewicz shrugged: "How many times I've asked you not to point to things when you're walking with me."

The woman blushed deeply.

"Maybe that's all right on the stage, but not on the street!" Szatkiewicz went on.

A moment of silence. They continued walking, passing shops on their way. Finally, she replied timidly: "Are you in a bad mood today?"

"Yes!"

"Something didn't go well?"

"No!"

"Why didn't you come to the theater yesterday? I was waiting for you!"

Szatkiewicz wanted to shout at the top of his lungs, in a shrill voice, that he simply didn't want to, that he preferred to go off to a bar, to drink and get high in the company of Binder and Witwicki; but almost involuntarily he answered:

"We worked late at night at the paper, we were busy writing . . . we have a very important and urgent job to do now."

They entered the arcades of the Cloth Hall.[5] A dark passageway filled with market stalls on both sides loomed before them inside the building. The cold, dampness, and the wretchedness of everyday haggling seemed to lurk in the darkness. Audible from afar were the entreaties of Jews encouraging peasant woman to buy things. At the very edge of the passageway the bright reeds of the baskets placed in the first stall took one by surprise with their immaculate freshness amid the dark grayness of the colorless surroundings as a whole.

It had stopped snowing, and behind the windows of the shops looking out on the Square beneath the arcades the goods were elegant and colorful. Flowers by the bunches were growing out of greenery. Here and there behind a pane of glass one could see the amethyst violet of a velvet hat or an entire cascade of pale-green crêpe.

Szatkiewicz slowed his pace for two reasons. In the first place, he wanted to delay his arrival at the paper; in the second, when this woman was at his side he always felt calmer and more cheerful. He rested in her presence and he wanted to prolong the moments of such rest.

She walked as though lost in thought and at that moment far from him and everything surrounding her. Suddenly she asked him, her gaze fixed on the stone pavement: "I . . . I'd like to ask you something."

"Ask!"

---

5. *Sukiennice*, in Polish. The Renaissance Cloth Hall in the middle of Market Square in the heart of Cracow.

"You probably know this better than anyone else . . . Is it true that tomorrow they're going to attack Jews?"

Szatkiewicz shrugged his shoulders.

"I don't know. Where'd you get the idea?"

"People were talking . . ."

"Well, maybe . . . But what do you care about the Jews?"

"Nothing . . . Just wondering."

They emerged from the arcades and turned in the direction of Cobblers' Street.

"Besides," Szatkiewicz began again, "where did you get the idea that I ought to know something about when Jews are going to be beaten up?"

The woman said nothing for a short time, but finally retorted deeply lowering her head on her chest:

"Because you write for a paper that's always picking on Jews."

"So what about it?"

"Nothing . . . I just thought . . ."

Snow began falling again. She opened the damaged part-silk umbrella, but it was obvious that her wishes to the contrary she couldn't bring herself to get closer to Szatkiewicz to protect him with it. . . .

Since Irma didn't want to talk about her family it was easier to discuss the theater. He then asked her: "How much do you make?"

Her eyes suddenly flashed. She began speaking willingly and fast. She even became animated; she raised the hand with the needle in it and remained that way while her lips moved rapidly.

She made barely forty guldens and from that salary had to buy her own stage and street clothes, pay for her apartment, electricity, laundry, and . . . oh, she had so many other expenses! She sighed saying those words and the fire in her eyes began dying out. Her dark pupils wandered about the walls as she again repeated: "So many expenses!" And then she fell silent.

Astonished, he looked all around. A tidy little room, clean, warm, brightly lit. So very different from the hovel in which he spent his sad existence. And this woman was able to afford all this on forty guldens a month. She had respectable shoes, she was always decently dressed, and on the street even gave the impression of a certain inexpensive chic. He, however, was always in his tailor's and laundress's debt; the same for restaurants. Yet he went around almost shabbily attired and often hungry. This, too, was evidently a secret which she knew and understood.

"How can you get by on such money?" he finally brought himself to ask her.

"It's hard," the woman answered, "often very hard, but what can I do? We have supernumeraries who get paid only by performance, and that's worse. But we're all happy now because we're going to be doing a Jewish play that calls for a lot of women and is going to have a good run. So we'll make a little money . . ."

"And nobody helps you?" Szatkiewicz asked.

She looked in his direction with gloomy eyes:

"What do you mean by that?" she asked.

"I just thought maybe family, or perhaps you're divorced or separated from your husband and collect some alimony."

"Nobody's paying me any alimony, and my family doesn't help me out at all. But sometimes I do some business with them."

"What do you mean 'business' "?

"Well, you know, in the theater you often need this or that . . . and you get it here or there . . ."

Szatkiewicz was delighted; at last he found a key to the mystery.

"Oh . . . your family owns shops, do they?"

"They do!"

She said this unwillingly, almost under her breath, and then tightened her lips. But he pressed her no further. He felt dreamy and sleepy. . . .

A creaking of the door awakened him. He opened his eyes without moving. Irma was standing in the half-opened doorway and was talking to someone on the other side.

"I'm coming right away!" reached Szatkiewicz's ear.

An indistinct whisper, then Irma's answer again:

"Go on, mama; I'll wake him up now!"

With all his energy, Szatkiewicz bestirred himself and made an effort to get up from the couch. Hearing his rustling, Irma banged the door closed and came up to him. She was somewhat pale, tired, and her eyes were slightly reddish. Nevertheless she managed a cheerful and forgiving smile when she saw how difficult it was for Szatkiewicz to awaken completely.

He got up, straightened his hair, rubbed his eyes, and stammered excitedly:

"I dozed off . . . odd . . . I've been sleeping the whole day . . . it must be late . . . I've got to get back . . ."

But she tried to be hospitable:

"Why don't you stay a little longer."

Szatkiewicz, however, declined, despite the fact that a desperate feeling of sadness constricted his heart at the recollection of his unheated and unpaid for hovel in the hotel annex.

"No, no; I've got to go . . . What time is it?"

"Eleven-thirty."

"Heavens! I slept so long. And what did you do the whole time, my dear Irma?"

This was the first time he had shown any concern as to what she was doing, and this weak proof of caring made a definite impression on Irma.

"I was just sewing and looking at you," she replied with great simplicity and an almost childlike charm.

He took her hand and squeezed it firmly so pretty and appealing did she seem to him at that moment. Then he leaned over to her and thrust his still sleepy eyes close to her lips:

"Kiss me!" he said in a childish, coddling voice.

With a strange, passionate, and long embrace she began kissing his large attractive eyes and soft lashes, which she brushed slowly with her tender, fresh mouth.

A murmur could again be heard near the entrance door, as if a mouse was scratching it.

Irma pushed back lightly from Szatkiewicz whose senses had become aroused under the influence of the warmth emanating from her entire body.

"It's already late!" she said, as if with regret.

Her eyes were covered by a kind of mist, her mouth half open, parched.

Szatkiewicz looked around him once again.

"I'd like to stay longer!" he said finally, a note of entreaty in his voice.

But pushing him gently toward the door, she again said: "It's already late!"

She opened the door. In the entrance hall, a small oil lamp, set on wooden crate, was burning. The moment Irma opened the door, someone on the other side made a dash for the half-open door of the neighboring apartment. Szatkiewicz heard only the characteristic shuffling of feet, like the snapping of big slippers, and caught sight of the small, stooped figure of a woman. He went into the hallway, but near the crate bumped into something small and soft that gave way beneath his feet like a trampled puppy. He bent down. In the faint light of the lamp he beheld a small boy, maybe about three years old, in a pink pinafore.

Szatkiewicz was at once struck by the red color of the boy's hair. The hair was cropped close, almost down to the scalp, which showed through the nearly scarlet stubble with a luminous whiteness. Looking at the boy from above, all that one could see was the reddish-gold ball of his small head and large ears that stuck out terribly. Little legs bent into the shape of a spider, deformed by rickets, protruded from beneath his shift. The child was dirty and greasy although his clothing was whole and warm. Covered with a long, gray, woolen kerchief, he stood glued to the crate, tiny, poor, quiet, contorted, and sleepy.

Szatkiewicz looked at the child with a curiosity he could not explain to himself. The child seemed very dirty and frightfully Jewish. Szatkiewicz pointed to it with the tip of the umbrella the way one points to a mangy kitten sitting on the edge of sewer grating and asked: "Whose brat is that?"

Something like indecision passed over Irma's face. "I don't know," she said, "probably a neighbor's."

Szatkiewicz began descending the stairs. "So there are Jews living opposite you?" he asked. And without waiting for an answer, he added: "You've got to get out of here; it's unpleasant having neighbors like that."

She didn't answer, but leaning on the balustrade she shined the lamp at him which she had taken with her from the table. He looked at her. Illuminated from the side, in her blouse bright as dawn falling freely about her body like a soft silk nightshirt, she was exceptionally pretty. The triangle of her face assumed an even greater ascetic thinness and transparency. Appearing almost dreamlike in the dark stairway, she seemed like one of Odilon Redon's apparitions. . . .

Szatkiewicz went down the stairs with this impression and even when the drowsy watchman opened the gate for him, sighing and breathing heavily, he clung to this vision which hung above him so charmingly at the last moment.

Meanwhile, as soon as she heard the clatter of the gate closing, Irma turned quickly to the child nestled in the little corner:

"Well?" she asked, hurriedly bringing the lamp into the room and returning to the hallway. "Well? Is Bernard going to go to sleep?"

The sound of her voice was lovely, soft, caressing. She leaned over to the child, drew him close to her, and took him in her arms. The red-haired child brightened his contorted and wretched face. His greenish eyes, full of tears, beamed with happiness.

"Mama!" he stammered, half asleep, pressing his little red head into the woman's bosom.

Wrapping him in the kerchief, she took the small oil lamp into her hand and went with him to the neighboring door.

"Auntie!" she called, lightly kicking the door with her foot. "Take the lamp, auntie, and go to sleep!"

The door opened. An old woman, covered in a long quilted caftan, appeared in it. On her head she wore a kerchief pulled down so far over her eyes that beneath it the only thing visible was a sparrow-hawk nose and a long, creased chin.

"*Git!*"[6] she said taking the lamp.

Irma then headed for her own room. The child had already fallen asleep in her arms, his little face buried in her neck. She entered the room, locked the door behind her, and went up to bed. She then sat down on it and began to undress the child. Sleepy, he fussed.

"Hush!" said the young woman. "Wait, dear, mama will put Bernard to sleep!"

And the red child repeated, without opening his eyes: "Mama will put me to sleep!"

IV

The next day, good fortune greeted Szatkiewicz. An old acquaintance, who had left Cracow for a certain period of time, met him on the A-B line. This old acquaintance owed Szatkiewicz ten guldens. What's more, this old acquaintance (miracle of miracles!) gave Szatkiewicz back his ten guldens without hating or

6. Yiddish for "good."

resenting him as usually happens in such cases. The two of them even went to Hawełka's and downed beer and wine — an uncommon fact, since justice compels one to admit that it was hard to find an acquaintance like this in Cracow and even unlikely. Along with the ten guldens, fancy, insolence, and cheerfulness entered Szatkiewicz's heart. He decided not to ask his editor for an advance, but instead to "keep himself" just as he had before so that nobody on the paper might suspect the material hardship in which he found himself. He was still a novice in the world of journalism, and had come to the *Kurier Narodowy* by a fortunate turn of events (the patronage of a certain count). Not having money seemed to him a terrible thing, hideous. He concealed it like a wound. Now, ten guldens facilitated his existence for several days. He decided to live frugally and stretch out the money as long as possible. . . .

Szatkiewicz henceforth began to treat Binder and other colleagues lightly. They seemed to him mercenary hacks, bent over work assigned them by a superior. He, however, rich in the prospect of writing a new play, something in the style of . . . [Gerhart Hauptmann's] *The Weavers*, felt superior to them and to everyday details.

The newspapers forwarded from Vienna reported on the *succès d'estime* of a new play by Hauptmann. Reading these reviews, Szatkiewicz made a wry face.

"That's the way it usually is with artificially pumped up fame. But when I write something along the lines of *The Weavers* . . ."

It didn't even enter his head that *The Weavers* was a work by Hauptmann.

With no less irony he glanced at the specially fabricated (with dictionary in hand) "original" telegrams and letters from Paris.

Anti-Semitic outbreaks in Algeria now provided the *Kurier Narodowy* with ample fodder. There was hardly a page without "Jew this" or "Jew that." If this lucrative and profitable red flag so redolent of the Christian love of one's fellow man wasn't waved every fourth line, Binder himself added some "Jew" or other, often apropos of nothing at all.

That day at the paper there was an arid spell with respect to Jewish crimes and villainies. Reporters brought in nothing special. For the time being the imagination dried up. But there absolutely had to be some Jewish criminal or other to be fed to the readers. The Dreyfusards piled up falsified telegrams and articles breathing of noble tolerance even toward Christians: "Judge ye not lest ye be judged yourselves!" But that was all "from there," from "rotten" France, from the "new Babylon." But here, from the pavements of Cracow, something had to be stirred up, instigated, transmitted in the form of slander. And from under the pen of Binder and one of the honorable reporters a splendid plant blossomed, which in the silliness of its form lost even its poison and dishonorable goal.

On a certain street someone ordered a Jew (!) to install panes of glass in windows shattered by the wind! News of this dreadful concession to the benefit of Jews, of this insolent support of non-Christian trade and industry, was displayed

in a prominent place and began with the words: "We inform in astonishment that
Pan . . . summoned a Jewish glazier to install panes in his building, and so forth
and so on." There then followed the usual litany of hateful words composed according to a well-worn formula and intended, like a pigeon from Noah's ark, to
bear the olive branch of peace and unity even to a very tempestuous and dis-
united Galician society. . . .

With a salary paid in advance, Szatkiewicz did not feel himself solidly bound
to this newspaper where Jews were so splendidly and constantly drawn and quartered.

"This isn't a newspaper, it's 'Jew-bashing,' " crossed his mind like a flash of
lightning. But at just that moment Binder came up to him and took him by the
arm in a confidential manner.

"I've got to entrust you with a certain mission," he declared in a subdued voice.

"What do you have in mind?"

"You see," Binder began, "I can't be involved in it myself, because . . . well, I
simply can't and that's all there is to it. But you can handle it easily. You've got a
connection with the theater, haven't you, with a member of the chorus . . ."

Szatkiewicz felt depressed. "With a member of the chorus!" That didn't sound
very nice. So he denied it emphatically.

"What's going on? Someone spreading rumors?"

"Take it easy!" Binder laughed. "You want to save her honor, is that it? Don't
bother. You were seen several times entering Turliński's Restaurant.[7] She was
walking behind you!"

Szatkiewicz squinted, pretending that he was trying to remember.

"Oh, yes! Irma . . . That's her name, as I recall. Yes! But *sans conséquence* [noth-
ing to it] . . ."

He studied his nails and waved his hand. "*Sans conséquence,*" he repeated.

He was glad that he could embarrass Binder this way since he didn't understand French despite the fact that he often quoted Lemaitre, Sarcey, and other
masters of the Parisian feuilleton who were known even to most coffeehouse
waiters.

"In the present campaign against the management every piece of backstage
news has considerable importance," Binder went on. "We've got to take advantage of any misunderstanding between the artists and the management, arguments among the actors themselves . . . you know the rest—different kinds of
domestic news, rumors, scandals . . . who's living with whom, who's broken off
with whom . . . Especially if there was some scene smacking a bit of scandal; that
would be very, very useful to us. It's been quiet there for too long. . . ."

7. The restaurant operated by Ferdynand Turliński in the Hotel "Pod Różą" ("Under the Sign of
the Rose") in Cracow. In 1895 Turliński opened the Café-Réstaurant du Théâtre opposite the Teatr
Miejski (Town Theater) in Cracow. It became a popular meeting place for artists and writers.

He stopped and started laughing to himself as if pleased by a sudden and agreeable thought.

"If we managed to set them all at odds with each other, if anarchy reigned there for good, that would be very handy indeed for us, eh?"

Szatkiewicz winced a bit.

"That's a dangerous mission," he said. "You know, actors are a nervous breed; they can try to take revenge later on."

Binder burst out laughing.

"Then one writes about the dignity and unassailability of the press, about the fact that the position of critic is holy, that the attacks of comic players wounded in their self-love have no significance for us and leave us . . . cold! That's it!"

He remained silent a moment, then added: "But what the public reads and thinks about them is already a win for us. Besides, that's what the editor wants and he instructed me to ask you about it . . ."

After which he also added, nonchalantly: "The editor said that you are the only one capable of handling this smartly."

But Szatkiewicz wanted to turn the situation to his advantage.

"I'll do it," he declared, "but under one condition!"

"And that is?"

"That I be placed in charge of the whole section of theater reviews and not just short notices as I have been!"

Binder knitted his brow.

"That I can't promise you," he declared after a long moment of silence, "you're a little too young, and new, and you don't have the professional training . . ."

"Oh!" exclaimed Szatkiewicz. "Professional training! It strikes me that that's superfluous at the *Kurier*. Besides, you yourself don't have any!"

They looked each other in the eyes with barely concealed hatred: the "older man" with ironic contempt and at the same time a certain apprehension regarding the "young one," who knew how to mine phony phrases stolen from Warsaw critics and lacked any professional training; the "young one" with the hidden malice of a little mutt whose teeth are full grown and who sees a bone macerated and gnawed by the already dulled teeth of an older mastiff.

They remained silent for a moment after which Binder drawled through clenched teeth: "I'll talk to the editor about it!"

"Please!" replied Szatkiewicz, strutting and puffing himself up. "In any case, I'll let my colleague take over my reports!"

This was the first time he used the term "colleague" with reference to Binder. He wanted to let him know by this that he regarded himself as of equal standing at the paper.

When Binder returned to his office, where he again occupied himself with the manufacture of patriotism, the Christian spirit, and the pogrom against the Jews, Szatkiewicz sprawled out in an armchair and began reading the German papers.

He had to put together a "special correspondence" about the art of Hauptmann on the basis of them, and this undertaking strangely appealed to him. He was delighted that he could give a "thrashing" to some notable.

Hauptmann's *Sunken Bell,* which he had absolutely no idea of, got on his nerves "from afar." He had already referred to the play once in his article as a "sick delirium." Now he was happy that he could quote himself. It gave him importance and strength in his own eyes. . . .

*   *   *

But one particular feeling took possession of him at the same time. He wanted to have some gentle female form next to him, to feel a small, friendly, and calm hand on his shoulder. He wanted to be "a pair," but he was alone. This came to him as a moral desire, not just a sensual one. And unconsciously he directed his steps toward the theater. There at least was one woman who was attracted to him, with whom he could be informal, and who he had a certain right to think that for the time being anyway was "his property."

Shadows lurked beneath the theater building, some strange, imperceptible silhouettes. Several stagehands in high kneeboots, with the looks of healthy, sturdy roisterers, were standing on the steps talking politics. Shafts of light fell from the actors' dressing rooms. . . .

Szatkiewicz approached one of the stagehands and asked him to go to Panna Pasmantieri's dressing room and tell her that someone was waiting for her. But the stagehands tossed Szatkiewicz a contemptuous look, since from their point of view anyone who worked for the *Kurier Narodowy* was a "nobody." All the stagehands, like working people and not speculators in human passions, led by their instincts, represented a party hostile to the *Kurier Narodowy.*

"You can go yourself to her dressing room!" replied one tall, strong, heavyset fellow and returning to his comrades continued the interrupted political conversation.

Szatkiewicz knew that he was not permitted behind the curtains. The *Kurier's* attacks on the management and the entire theater had closed that path to him forever. He used to go there often and had had a fine time in the company of the witty and merry artists. But now he had to remain on the other side of the door. He felt inexpressibly bad. Why? After all, he had no personal brief against either the management or the performers. For a little money he had to be an exile and endure the contempt of stagehands.

He then turned to some boys crouching near the wall.

"One of you go to Panna Pasmantieri and tell her that I'm waiting for her."

He pulled a crown from a pocket and tossed it into the small hand of one of the boys with considerable meanness, wanting in this way to embarrass the stagehands. But they paid him no attention. One of them extracted a paper from a pocket and began reading it beneath a lantern. Others, forming a closed circle, listened to him attentively.

As Szatkiewicz looked at this group of men, the chaotic plan of the play he intended writing again came to mind. These people in the clothing of simple workers, grouped together in the beam of light falling on them from above and engrossed in the contents of the printed word, assumed the aspect of one of the scenes preparing the spectator for an outburst, a catastrophe, something powerful . . . He forgot that just a moment before they had looked at him angrily and couldn't stand him. Now they consumed all his interest. They penetrated his brain with their rapt figures. Slowly they became his property.

Suddenly the door opened slowly and Irma came through it, wrapped in her jacket with the high collar. The stagehands didn't stir in the slightest, their attention fixed wholly on the one who was reading. Irma descended the steps and approached Szatkiewicz.

"Here I am!" she said. "I guessed it was you who sent for me. I'm glad."

She took him under the arm and led him to the street.

"Come on. You must have frozen standing outside like that!"

He walked with her as if rudely awakened from his scenic vision about which other foggy and unclear visions had begun to take shape in utter chaos. But with the gentle movement of a caring woman she began buttoning his coat around the neck, and taking one of his hands into her own she walked across the square surrounding the theater conversing merrily and with an animation unusual for her.

She had gotten a small but good role, that of a nun. She was going to have a costume with a huge white hat, the kind that looks like outstretched wings. The director told her that she'd look very nice in the costume because she has, well, a figure, and that if she applied herself she wouldn't do badly at all.

"You'll teach me!" she said imploringly. "You know all about such things and you'll tell me how to say my lines and in what tone, because I'll be quite scared!"

He nodded his assent.

"I'll teach you, of course I'll teach you . . ."

They reached the corner of the street. Suddenly she slowed her step.

"Are you showing me home?"

He grasped her hand nervously.

"No," he said almost softly and beseechingly. "Come to me today. I'm not in the mood to be alone!"

There had to be in his request the voice of a craving heart for Irma answered a moment later with touching simplicity: "Fine, I'll go!"

And so the two of them went together to that hovel called a room located somewhere beneath the roof of a smelly hotel. It was dark on the balcony. Waiters were dozing in corners. When they entered the room they did not light any candles but instead, like thirsty travelers, plunged at the spring of each other's mouths and drank long soothing kisses amid the murmur of words whispered tremblingly in the darkness.

Finally, when he turned on the light, Irma's eyes were struck by the wretchedness of the surroundings in the midst of which her soul was swooning from an excess of sensual pleasure. Poverty crawled from every corner, poverty and neglect.

The young woman sat down on a broken chair and looked around in astonishment. Szatkiewicz, in the meantime, looked for candle ends in drawers. He did not want to call and awaken the waiter. Besides, because of his unpaid rent he was sure to meet with refusal. That was one affront he wanted to avoid at all costs.

Speaking slowly, Irma said at last: "You . . . you're so poor!"

He jerked impatiently.

"I'm not poor . . . I get a good salary at the paper. Why do you say that I'm poor?"

She remained silent, feeling that she had committed an indiscretion, that by that involuntary word she had shaken his self-esteem.

"I am not poor!" Szatkiewicz repeated. "It's just that I'm never home so there's no one to keep order."

He was afraid that his poverty weakened his gravity and importance in her eyes. He also feared that it might alienate her for good. Just a moment before she had been so wonderfully passionate and now seemed so gentle seated on the edge of the chair with her hair unwound about her flushed face. . . .

"If you like, I'll order dinner," he said reaching for the bell handle.

But she replied quickly:

"No, thank you, I've already had dinner."

Szatkiewicz felt deep gratitude toward that tactful girl. He wanted to express it somehow. He approached her and pressed his head into her untwined hair.

"Why do you address me so formally? Call me by my first name," he whispered.

Surprised yet happy, she asked: "If you don't mind. What is it?"

"Zygmunt."

"What a nice name." . . .

He had no idea when or how he fell to his knees and nestled his head against her, his eyes shut, tired and drowsy. It felt blissful to him.

From time to time just the sound of the electric bell summoning waiters could be heard.

She turned bright red as if that submissive gesture of a man surprised and even frightened her, but she quickly composed herself despite the fact that her lips whispered: "Please get up!"

She put her hand on Zygmunt's head with a dominating gesture peculiar only to women who feel themselves spiritually superior to their lovers. She said nothing for a long time, and her eyes, riveted on the window panes behind which a lowered roller blind showed gray, seemed to sink into worlds and shadows that were incomprehensible to her.

Finally she said slowly and distinctly: "Why do you hate Jews so?"

But at that moment he hated no one. He felt quiet, calm, and good. His cheek resting on Irma's knee, his hands lowered to the ground, he sat like a small, poor child, tired and drowsy. And in an almost unintelligible whisper, he finally replied: "I don't hate them at all . . . Where did you get the idea?"

"Oh . . . well, because of the things you write about them."

He shook his head sadly: "I write . . . because I have to!" he blurted out, almost humbly. "You see, that's what they pay me for."

"Oh!"

The woman reflected for a moment.

"And who pays them to order Jews to be picked on like that?"

"Them? Who?"

"You know, the editor . . . the publishers . . ."

"Them? No one."

Irma raised her eyebrows in surprise.

"They do it on their own then? Na, I don't believe it! From that they make a *geszeft?*"[8]

She pronounced the last word gutturally, with a Jewish accent, but suddenly catching herself, added hastily: "I mean to say 'profit!'"

Szatkiewicz either did not want to or couldn't oppose her. For what reason? For whom was he going to cross swords? And in the final analysis what concern was it of his?

"There must be some profit in it for them!" Irma repeated. "Otherwise, I ask you . . . They're constantly writing that they're Christians and forever taking pride in it. But the Christian faith is based on love of one's fellow man, or at least that's what the priests say. So why is the *Kurier Narodowy* constantly stirring things up against their fellow man? If they're Christians, then they ought to be kind to others; after all, the Jew's a human being too, isn't he? What do you say?"

He listened to what she was saying in surprise and felt an obligation in some way to refute her simple but effective arguments.

"Yes, but the Jews hate Christians, don't they?"

She smiled and replied simply:

"So what if they do? Just because Jews behave badly does that mean that Christians should behave worse? If they're supposed to be better then they should set a good example."

She was silent for a moment and then added: "You know, I'm sure, that it's easier to reach an understanding with someone, even a Jew, through kindness rather than through meanness! Besides, didn't God assign each human being a piece of earth and say—this is for a Catholic, and this for a German, and this for a Ukrainian, and this for . . . whomever? God after all has such a right, doesn't He? And since God created Jews, then it must have been so that they too would live on earth . . ."

Szatkiewicz shrugged his shoulders.

---

8. Yiddish for "business" (in Polish spelling); *Geschäft* in German.

"My dear . . . you don't know about such things. They're economic questions, racial ones, so it's better not to talk about them!"

She saddened and a fog covered her eyes.

"Maybe," she said. "I know I'm stupid, but it seems to me that Christ never threw stones at anyone; he just forgave people and spoke kindly to them."

They both fell silent. . . .

Finally, Irma said softly and affably: "I'll be coming here more often, all right?"

He nestled still closer to her knee.

"Come, by all means!"

"Because everything here is very . . . (she hesitated) disorderly. You'll see how I'll tidy up the place; right away it's going to look different."

He shook his head affirmatively.

"As you like . . . but what's unnecessary order to me; I'm hardly ever here."

"But at night, you sleep here, don't you?"

"At night it's dark, you can't see anything."

"No matter, it all becomes visible in the morning. Besides, it's unpleasant to wake up in such a mess."

After a moment's reflection, she added: "Everything would look different with curtains and a little rug on the floor . . . like in my place . . ."

Szatkiewicz gestured indifferently: "Who needs them?"

"It's always more elegant that way. And you don't have to pay right away either. I'll give you a . . . I know someone who'll let you have everything on installment, and even . . . money, if you like."

Szatkiewicz raised his head. "Money?" he thought. "Maybe there is a way out, maybe I can lay my hands on those forty guldens I badly need."

But Irma was quick to add: "Only, I don't know if you want to have dealings with that person."

"Why not?"

"Because it's . . . a Jewish woman."

Szatkiewicz was surprised.

"So what?"

"Well, I just thought . . ."

Irma stammered, broke off, then finally finished what she was about to say: "Since you're always writing against Jews!"

"What has one thing to do with another?"

He got up from the floor, suddenly pleased with the prospect of extricating himself from the trap he had been in for such a long time.

"Who is she, this Jewess," he asked, "do you know her?"

Irma burst out laughing happily.

"Oh! I know her very well! Besides, all the girls from the theater know her since she's been doing business with them for twenty years! She's a . . . kind of . . . theater Jew. I'll send her to you, all right?" . . .

Struck by her charm, Szatkiewicz grasped the hands extended him.

"Fine, send her to me in the morning."

"Yes, yes! And I'll have a rug, curtains, everything necessary, brought to you."

She shook the mass of her hair down onto her shoulders and began looking for the double pins.

"A second, I'm coming!"

But they didn't leave for quite a long time and the candle had gone out long before when Irma had to grope her way in the dark to find her hat, veil, and gloves. She smiled happily and, poorly dressed, with her hair barely fastened over the nape of her neck, she at last stood on the threshold of the room. "Let's go!" . . .

Szatkiewicz walked silently, looking straight ahead. He felt that he was surrounded by cold and terrible misery. The more he moved forward the more it seemed to him that he was sinking ever deeper into a morass from which he could not escape and in which he was going to perish. Then suddenly he heard Irma's voice: "If it's so Christian, why doesn't the *Kurier Narodowy* devote itself to seeing there was less want instead of making trouble for Jews and other people?"

Szatkiewicz said nothing in reply, but just quickened his pace.

"Forgive me, I don't know," Irma went on, "but it seems to me that if I were a man who made his living writing, I'd sooner write about such poor people . . . and I'd just have to make people come to their senses so they wouldn't let others die of hunger."

She stopped for a moment, and then resumed:

"I know myself that when I read something in a paper I don't forget it, and I try, if they offer good advice, to behave that way. And if they write about poverty in some paper, I first feel better because I see that there are others who are poorer than I am and that what I have seems a lot to me, and afterward I'd like to do something good for others. Don't you feel the same?"

Szatkiewicz mumbled something indistinct instead of answering.

Irma began laughing quietly.

"How stupid I am," she declared, "after all, you do write for papers so it doesn't make that kind of an impression on you. You know what?"

"What?"

"It must be hard to be a writer . . . and dangerous."

"Why?"

"Because they beat you up!"

"Nobody's struck me yet."

"I'd be afraid."

Szatkiewicz puffed himself out like a turkey.

"You are stupid. It's best not to talk about things you don't understand."

Irma grew suddenly humble.

"Fine, I'm sorry."

They were just passing the building in which the *Kurier* was located. It was dark. Evidently the serpent, having emitted the last drops of its venom, had fallen asleep. Nevertheless, an unusual, elusive atmosphere surrounded that forge of libel and paid hatred. Even the cloak of night, which smothers, if only temporarily, all pain and suffering, was unable to drive beneath the stars this enormous and inexplicable human hatred. This atmosphere gripped Szatkiewicz from the moment he entered it. He remembered the paper, Binder, the post of critic offered him, and he experienced a waning of ambition, of vanity, of accession to power, of reaching the top, and especially of the desire to oppress others.

He reminded himself that he was supposed to bring a bunch of behind-the-scenes tales as the basis for his future theater criticism. He turned to Irma. He felt that she had been somewhat hurt by his previous rudeness. He took her arm, put it around his shoulder, and embraced her firmly, the way students in love do.

"Are you angry?"

"I? No!"

The pressure of his hand made her as happy as the most tender caress.

He explained further.

"You know, I'm fed up with these newspapers, editorial boards, and the whole *Kurier.* I'm too worn out all day long by printed nonsense to be occupied with it even when I'm with you. Better tell me something about yourself, or . . ." He hesitated a moment: "Or about the theater . . ."

She lit up at once.

"About the theater? But there's nothing to say. . . . The same old thing, except for when the extras got into an argument once in our alleyway, maybe because one of them was from the summer theater in Cracow Park and the others said something to her . . ."

"I didn't mean the extras. What's new with the actresses?"

"Oh! You mean the women who get dressed in separate dressing rooms?"

"Yes!"

"Well, I don't know a lot because they're always mum at rehearsals and when they're performing they're all taken up with their roles and costumes. I'm rather timid around them."

Szatkiewicz grew impatient.

"But really now, you must have heard something. Why aren't they playing *Countess Sarah* tomorrow?"[9]

"I'm really not sure. But it seems to me that the two women who were supposed to play ingénues weren't happy with each other, and the woman who plays Sarah, she got angry about something because she went upstairs, to the secretary, and came back down again very mad . . ."

"Aha . . . Did she say anything?"

"No . . . I just know she was mad. 'Cause when she's in a good mood, she

9. A play by the then popular French writer Georges Ohnet (1848–1918). It was written in 1883.

always asks for a chocolate drink and cake and has them on the stage, but when she gets mad about something, then she doesn't send for the chocolate."

"Aha . . . So she didn't drink chocolate?"

"No!"

"So you don't know anything else?"

"No!"

They had reached Irma's house.

Szatkiewicz stopped in the middle of the sidewalk.

"My dear!" he began sweetly. "Please, find out what happened between the two ingénues and why the other actress was angry."

Irma began to laugh.

"You like such woman's gossip?"

"With a passion."

The chorus girl was truly happy.

"Then good, I'll tell you things once in a while. Our theater is sometimes like a boiling pot . . ."

She broke off and then added in a tone of ardent supplication: "Only please don't tell anyone else. 'Cause you know we're not allowed to carry out of the theater what happens inside. That's the way it's been for a long long time!"

He was quick to assure her.

"Don't worry, don't worry! I won't tell a soul!"

"Your word?"

Szatkiewicz made immediate use of the subterfuge traditionally employed by all men when they have no intention of keeping their word. He threw out his chest and declared with a sense of superiority:

"My dear! I don't give in to such stupidities as 'word of honor.' If you don't believe me, then . . ."

He made a sweeping gesture with his hand, magnificent and striking. Irma felt intimidated and protested: "Oh come on . . . I was just talking, from habit." . . .

Around eight the next morning a timid knock on the door awakened Szatkiewicz. With a sleepy voice he shouted:

"*Herein!*"[10]

But no one entered; the same delicate and discreet scraping on the door was just repeated.

"*Entrez!*" groaned Szatkiewicz from beneath his soiled quilt.

He couldn't bring himself to utter the expression "Please come in!" He used the German or French simply from force of long habit and not out of a desire to ape the aristocracy.

The door opened and a female figure appeared on the threshold. A second

10. German for "Come in!"

shadow loomed behind her but quickly disappeared before Szatkiewicz could see who it was.

"Who's there?"

"It's me, Freiwilligowa, at your service, sir."

Szatkiewicz opened his sleepy eyes. A fairly fat but obviously asthmatic Jewess bowed to him sideways, stepping on her skirt, which was somewhat too long in front. She was attired in a long, unfashionable jacket and wore a wig of walnut-colored ribbons, which must have been satin when new. Her wig was topped by a hat that was a masterful combination of patches of different material, velvet ribbons, feathers, and two astonishing amaranth roses, fastened on both sides of the head like two flaming splintered horns. The woman's face was also a poem of composition, of a kind of contortion so painful as to drain her lips of blood, a covetous flickering of huge black magnificent eyes, and constant fright revealed in a certain twisting of one side of the face. In her hand she held a package wrapped in a rag. From under her jacket appeared a small pair of scissors hung on a ribbon.

Szatkiewicz propped himself up on an elbow and gazed at the Jewess standing in front of him with a certain wonder.

"What are you doing here?" he finally asked.

The Jewess smiled discretely. She raised herself oddly on her toes like a tenor getting ready to sing an aria and whispered with a mysterious expression on her face:

"I . . . came here . . . sir . . . because Panna Irma from the theater said you had some business . . ." She interrupted herself and added quickly: "Some orders for me." She spoke slowly, but pierced Szatkiewicz with her gaze. She didn't look in any corners. When she entered the room she grasped the entire situation with a single knowing glance. She saw before her a gentleman who was still not "something," but could become "something."

Szatkiewicz suddenly recalled his conversation of the day before with Irma and felt easier about everything. The satin-walnut hairdo of the Jewess struck him as a felicitous phenomenon permitting him to extricate himself from his daily cares. He sat down on his bed, pulled the quilt around him, and at once, like everyone who is forced to borrow money, became unusually polite.

"Please sit down, madam!"

"Thank you, but I'll stand if you don't mind, sir, I'm so used to walking and standing. I don't have any time for sitting. My husband and I we always walk and sit down for a longer time only on *shabas*."[11] She grew silent for a moment and, folding her hands over her stomach, seemed to be expecting the first word to come from Szatkiewicz's mouth.

But all of a sudden he felt inhibited and confused. Above all, he wanted a little

---

11. Yiddish for "Sabbath."

money, but was unsure that he wouldn't be met with a rebuff. It wasn't a matter of feeling humiliated; but he did feel that his joy would utterly disappear and that he would once again have to wallow in despair. So he prolonged the moment of delusion as much as possible. Freiwilligowa, on the other hand, was the first to lose patience and, without changing her position, asked:

"Do you need a little rug, sir? Curtains? Linen, maybe? Socks? Handkerchiefs? Some jewelry? Maybe a fine opera glass on a cord? How about some real Russian tea?"

She tossed all that out in a single breath then grew silent again like an unwound music box. For the sake of getting to the subject of money, Szatkiewicz would have taken not only the opera glass and the Russian tea but even the tower of the Church of Mary if Freiwilligowa considered it appropriate, something he "needed."

"I've got everything here . . . in the lobby. I'll call down!"

Without waiting for his permission, she opened the door and jabbered something softly. Like a shadow, a phantom, an apparition, an old Jew appeared, stooped and contrite. He had a huge bundle on his shoulder, an even larger one over his chest, and smaller ones in his hands from which chintz and calico stuck out. Despite his heavy burden, he entered quietly, or rather crept in, and just as quietly began to lay out his bundles on the floor. His hands trembled constantly and his head shook as if on a spring.

He was a very old Jew, maybe sixty years old, perhaps even seventy or more. He seemed to be as old as Cracow itself, this Ahasuerus in a gray, shiny gaberdine so threadbare it looked completely green. And he was so pale that there didn't seem to be a drop of blood beneath his skin. His long beard and sparse hair on his temples also lacked color and resembled sun-faded straw.

When he deposited his bundles on the floor, he retreated to the door and stood out against the white background like the silhouette of an anemic old man trembling from the blows of an invisible whip with which some mysterious and merciless hand was lashing his body.

The morning sun, similarly unsteady and pale, penetrated the depths of the room through the curtainless window. Falling short of the beggar's head, it suddenly illuminated his hands flickering with yellow patches of skin and skeletal lines. Lowered on both sides of his emaciated body, his hands brought to mind a pair of haggard Jewish jades awaiting a new, graver misery. . . .

He stood and looked straight ahead with the gaze of an expiring fish paying no heed either to Freiwilligowa, who had begun quickly untying the bundles, or to Szatkiewicz, who was observing the two Jews from beneath furrowed brows with a stupid and constrained smile.

And so began the display of shabby goods, cheap little rugs, cotton socks, and tasteless curtains made of a pinkish paper material. They were seconds, transported from shabby stalls in Kazimierz,[12] carried by the sweat of the brow through rain and mud with the thought, hope, and desire of making a little profit, which then had to be divided up among the "partners" of the whole deal hatched over a cup of coffee in a dark coffeehouse.

The outcome of Freiwilligowa's visit was a pair of curtains on the window, a small rug in the "Persian style," a pound of tea, a porcelain Chinaman with his tongue stuck out, and a dozen handkerchiefs.

"I'll give you a hundred on loan, sir, if someone reliable signs for you."

A reliable guarantor! The shadow of the editor himself crossed Szatkiewicz's mind. He knew that that editor often guaranteed loans not only for his colleagues, but also for other members of the literary community who happened to find themselves in financial straits. And afterward, like a fly caught in a trap, no matter how much he struggled the borrower couldn't refrain from relations with the person who had done him such a favor. He was a collaborator of the *Kurier* against his will and desire, but if asked why he permitted his name to be used to all sorts of devious ends, he answered in despair: "Just wait until I pay off that loan!" But the loan tended most of the time to be extended and dragged along after that journeyman of the pen like the ball and chain around the feet of a galley slave, weighing him down and enchaining him for years.

All this entered Szatkiewicz's mind in a flash. There was also the consideration that his pride would suffer no little if he asked for a guarantee for such a paltry loan at the beginning of his career. Were it a matter of thousands, that would be one thing; but a mere hundred! Feverishly he ran through all his connections and acquaintances in his mind, but not a single name he could come up with would serve as a guarantor; others he didn't want to ask, or couldn't bring himself to. There seemed to be no way out of his depressing situation.

Freiwilligowa, in the meantime, followed Szatkiewicz with her gaze. The skilled physiognomist knew the meaning of such an evasive look, forced smile, and fingers nervously scratching his head. Yes, she understood at once, this young gentleman sitting amid the litter of his bed had nobody who would back him up. Smiling ever so sweetly, she approached his bed: "You don't have anyone, sir, who'd cosign a loan?"

"I don't!"

"No matter. You're new in Cracow, you don't know a lot of people . . ."

Squinting, her hands folded across her belly, she added: "I'll loan you the money without a guarantor!"

Szatkiewicz experienced a revelation. He seemed to be drowning and someone on shore threw him a line.

"Only," the Jewess began, "you know I don't have money myself and will have

---

12. The historic Jewish quarter of Cracow.

to get it from others. They take kindly to profits, but can often be very hard-hearted; you'll probably have to pay a high interest."

Szatkiewicz would have agreed to a hundred for a hundred so long as he could get his hands on the money; but for appearances, he protested: "Oh! Oh! I won't let myself get fleeced!"

Freiwilligowa pretended to be insulted and pursed her lips.

"Right away 'fleeced'! Nobody's fleecing you. It's just that those people who lend you the money are taking a chance. You're getting the loan without a guarantee. That's a big risk! You may be a fine, upright person, sir, but maybe you won't be able to pay it back!"

She stopped, reflected for a moment, and added: "And I don't even know if I'll be able to get the money!"

Everything suddenly grew dark before Szatkiewicz's eyes. The rays of the sun disappeared. Emptiness and cold set in. But he still managed a heroic word. He threw himself against the pillows and exclaimed: "Well, no matter, I'll get by!"

Silence ensued. Freiwilligowa bound up the rest of the goods. The pale silent Jew was still standing at the door, his hands continuing to tremble. A cloud covered the sun and the light enveloping the threadbare tails of his dilapidated gaberdine in golden gauze was gone. Szatkiewicz was overcome by anxiety. It wasn't enough that any hope of obtaining the money he wanted disappeared; in addition, he now had the expense of the curtains and other trifles. He bit his lip in anger, but feigned good humor and absentmindedly kept striking the edge of the bed with his foot. Suddenly Freiwilligowa took a small box out of a pocket and, opening it, asked:

"Would you like to buy this ring with a green stone? Some woman is selling it but she doesn't want people to know about it . . ."

But Szatkiewicz interrupted her as he wrapped himself up in the quilt: "I don't want anything, since I can't come to terms with you!" Freiwilligowa wrung her hands. "What are you saying, sir? There's no merchant easier to get along with than me. Why, I did business with Pani Mondrzejewska,[13] and with other ladies, and never had any trouble. I'm still on good terms even with that Pani Zapolska who's supposed to be such a shrew and who ordered me thrown out only twice . . . I'll tell you what, sir: I'll let you have that hundred, and right away I'll take off twenty guldens in interest for three months and ten for the first month's installment. I'll give you seventy guldens and you'll let me have an I.O.U. for 140 guldens good for a year. I'm doing this just for you, sir, because I have a high regard for you. I'll take the chance and guarantee the loan myself!"

Szatkiewicz set his brain to work. But he couldn't figure out the interest the Jewess was proposing. He saw just the prospect of seventy guldens and that in-

---

13. Probably an allusion to the well-known Polish actress Helena Modrzejewska (1840–1909).

trigued him. Again for the sake of appearance he voiced his opposition to her proposal, although he trembled inwardly lest Freiwilligowa withdraw her offer.

"That's too much, I simply can't!"

But the Jewess began shouting: "Why too much? I wouldn't give my own brother an interest rate like that. I'll even throw in half a dozen pairs of socks for just five guldens, a count's socks, the count from the border—what's his name?—wears them."[14] She placed the socks on the quilt and drew a purse out of a pocket.

"I have the note. You want to sign it?"

Szatkiewicz extended his hand.

"All right, let me have it!"

She handed him a pen, groaning and sighing. He asked her to sit down in a very polite way and with a pale smile on his face, trembling slightly, signed his name and filled out the promissory note. The Jewess indicated the appropriate places and dictated the proper terms. She ran a coarse, thick finger, with blackened fingernail, along the paper right in front of Szatkiewicz's eyes. He wrote rapidly in order to rid himself of the sight of that finger, which irritated him and unnerved him in the worst possible way. But when Freiwilligowa withdrew seven ten-gulden bills from the same purse and laid them out on the quilt like a bright ribbon, Szatkiewicz was seized with happiness. He squeezed the hand of the Jewess, who wished him luck with "this money" and then stretched out in the bed with the look of a sovereign prince. He looked pleasantly at Freiwilligowa, who was bustling about her bundles and then turned his attention to the pale Jew standing by the door.

"Who's that," he asked, "your assistant?"

But Freiwilligowa replied, a bit condescendingly: "No, that's my husband!"

"How come he doesn't say anything?"

The Jewess shrugged her shoulders.

"What's he got to say? He just thinks, he's that kind, you know . . . religious!" Then she began to pile the various loads on the shoulders and chest of the "religious one."

"We're off now!"

But she was slow to leave. She still had to make out a separate bill for the things Szatkiewicz purchased; he had to pay the first installment on them; and there remained to be gathered up the gold-plated chain and the other porcelain Chinaman with his tongue sticking out. At long last, Freiwilligowa and her husband, their bundles, and even their shadows, disappeared, leaving behind that characteristic odor indicating the passage of Jews through a closed room or apartment. . . .

---

14. A reference to Stanisław Tarnowski (1837–1917), a well-known and influential historian of literature and professor at the Jagiellonian University in Cracow.

VI

Every few days now "notices" from the theatrical world appeared regularly in the *Kurier Narodowy*. They were unsubstantiated rumors, inserted in the hope, always, that "something would stick." Suddenly, like a rocket, news shot out about some scandal offstage on account of which a play was withdrawn, or that "Pani X is leaving the Cracow stage for reasons about which discretion commands us to remain silent." Without the slightest scruple, Szatkiewicz dragged out of Irma whatever he could and entered the paper puffed up and pregnant with the overheard rumor. Taking a seat at a table, he terrorized Binder with his silence and after an hour's anticipation Binder at last learned the "information" altered and filtered through the prism of Szatkiewicz's own imagination. They were frequently rumors harmful to the management of the theater, to one group of actors or another, and especially to actresses. Seasoned with poisonous envy and venom, the sole aim of these rumors was to destroy and crush everything so as to be able to raise a new edifice on these ashes on one's own hook.

Gratified and happy that Szatkiewicz had at last begun to take pleasure in talking to her more frequently than before, Irma now rummaged in her memory and was a faithful echo of everything that ran through the corridors of the theater like the ripple of a whole flock of mice. Often, when a copy of the *Kurier Narodowy* fell into her hands, she was astonished that "these gentlemen" were writing about the same things that she knew and heard, but she was far from guessing that she was seeing her own words printed in the paper's columns. After all, she made Szatkiewicz swear that he wouldn't repeat to a soul what he heard from her, and he promised her with the look on his face of an offended turkey.

"Do you take me for an old gossipmonger?"

She said nothing further, subdued and convinced. From that moment on, he felt entirely at ease. Often, possessed by an inexplicable need to lie common to all women, she even made up things, coloring some groundless rumor with her own conjectures and suppositions, desirous of making a still greater impression on her lover. In point of fact she knew very little since she didn't dare intrude on the circle of superior artists during rehearsals and performances. In the dressing rooms, on the other hand, people talked about "everything," although not many rumors were exchanged since each actress tended to be very cautious in front of the other.

Before long, however, Irma noticed that the actors, and especially the actresses, were giving her strange looks, and several of them made a point of avoiding her altogether. She now had more frequent occasion to meet the leading forces of the theater, since rehearsals were begun of that play in which she had the small part of a nun. Excited over her debut, preoccupied with the importance of the moment, she began arriving for rehearsals before the scheduled time and wandering about the stage curtains on which the golden rays of the sun fell through the huge windows to the rear.

She appeared only in the last act, but it seemed to her that she had an obligation to be present from the beginning and to pay close attention to the entire play. Day and night she dreamed about the nun's habit, the white cornet illuminating her face with a nimbus of gentleness, the long gray dress, and the rosary beads hanging down on the dark sapphire-blue apron. Once she ran across such a sister of mercy on the street. She immediately turned around and followed her, looking at her in rapture. The nun reached the opened doors of a church and went inside, bidding farewell on the threshold. Irma paused and stood for a long time gazing at the dark interior in which shone the gold of lit candles. The low, drawn-out tones of organs could be heard from within. The young woman listened to them and her heart began to melt. She had the impression that a cluster of peaceful, gentle impressions was flowing to her from that open church. And as if drawn by a magnetic force, she crossed the threshold of the porch and found herself on the inside.

The church was small and quite old. It had a primitive, even poor look with its three altars containing images turning dark with age and hemmed with garlands of paper roses. It struck Irma that from the outside the church seemed to her a dark abyss; but once she entered it, she found the pure whiteness of the walls strange and indeterminate. The altars were poor and simple, but one side altar had been braided by pious hands into a lace of apple blossoms so delicate and subtle that it was as if someone had hung snowflakes on invisible threads. Whole branches climbed upward, virginally white and pure, and the image of Mary seemed almost entirely hidden behind that screen of spring foliage, which seemed to blossom so early in order to bathe the figure of the Virgin in the cascade of its whiteness. Irma stopped before the altar and timidly raised her eyes. She met the eyes of Mary, which seemed to be saying: "I am love itself, nothing, just love."

And the chorus girl remained that way a long time, her gaze fixed on those gentle eyes which seemed to look at her from behind the flowers, drawing her to herself, to forgive . . . to convert.

Szatkiewicz, however, was still unsatisfied. He kept on supplying the freshest news, digging up long-forgotten insults, as if taking the part of the actors and actresses, sowing constant disharmony between the management and the personnel of the theater, attacking the leading ladies with the brutality of a drunkard; yet everything he did was via Binder, who had absolutely no desire to let the scepter of critic pass from his hands. Just as before, Szatkiewicz was used for "notices," but it wasn't really a matter of that; he wanted to assume the position of the well-known critic Z. in Warsaw. He wanted to terrorize, punish, slay with irony, prick the entire theatrical world with poisoned darts. But his editor was still content to entrust full authority to Binder, who went on taking his seat at every premiere with the air of a licensed critic.

This state of affairs had to end.

From the time he straightened himself out (as they say) with the help of Frei-willigowa, Szatkiewicz changed his way of life somewhat. He began spending more time at home and even bought paper, pen, and ink with which at last to write his play. But he still couldn't decide whether even to write a sketch. All he did was print out in capital letters the title "FIGHT TO THE FINISH, A Social Drama in Three Acts." But that was as far as it went.

He was always glad to talk about his work openly and at length. Strolling the streets with friends, he halted in front of every passerby who was dressed worse than himself and looked steadily at him. He claimed that he was collecting "material." That began to lend him a certain fame and surround him with the halo of future greatness. He even placed a notice about himself in the *Kurier Narodowy,* adding that his play was finished. When Binder asked him in a voice full of envy: "Where do you intend to stage it?" he replied nonchalantly: "I'm in touch with Warsaw!"

During this period he did his paper an important service. The sensational [Dreyfus] affair had begun in Paris and was reverberating throughout the entire world. A Parisian correspondent had to be invented in Cracow. With a strange agility, Szatkiewicz began plundering the French newspapers, throwing in such expressions as "in my opinion" and "as I see it" in order to convince his myopic readers of the authenticity of those "personal" letters in the *Kurier Narodowy.*

The editor himself paid the closest attention to this activity and began putting Szatkiewicz to more important use. And so, a carefully prepared *Judenheca* [anti-Jewish intrigue] was instigated in conjunction with an antisocialist demonstration. A trivial event was chosen—the trip of some delegate or other—but the actual basis was to be the later ovation conducted beneath the windows of the paper in celebration of its noble proclivities.

With a certain artfulness, cleverly, quietly, the basis for the demonstration had been prepared for a long time, going back several years in fact. Racial and religious hatred had been tenderly nurtured like a poisonous but exceptionally rare plant. In small but steady ways the masses were worked on; the base instincts of the throng were flattered. Heaps of commonplaces were poured from a mould and thrown into battle right and left.

And at this point Szatkiewicz began to shine in an unexpected way. The *Kurier* was gripped by a real revolution. He himself was surprised at his own "enterprise" in the campaign, but he knew that the lion's share of duty would fall on him. Binder and other colleagues were kept at a distance. Their articles were as effective as a glass of warm water. Only Szatkiewicz triumphed, and he became intoxicated on the foam of hatred. Everyone began recognizing in him something that would "get somewhere," provided he didn't look around. He himself well understood that such "looking around" would reveal to him the utter disgracefulness of his behavior. Therefore, he shut his eyes and threw himself into the fray.

His relations with Freiwilligowa in the meantime increased. He paid her two monthly installments of ten guldens each and then ordered more goods from her in the amount of fifty guldens. She brought everything to him tirelessly. Soap, nail trimmers, a cane, a fake emerald ring, a lamp, opera glasses, pomade; in short, everything. He suddenly became a great dandy and thanks to Freiwilligowa found a Jewish tailor who attired him on credit. His affair with Irma, however, he kept quiet about, since she was a mere chorus girl and that would have lowered him in the eyes of his fellow workers. Yet despite his efforts at concealment, they were sometimes met in each other's company and began attracting the attention of the theater crowd, who felt insulted by all the gossip about them in the *Kurier Narodowy*. No one as yet openly confessed their suspicions to Irma, but they were slowly reaching the conclusion that she had to be the one who was "carrying out" whatever was going on inside the theater. And those suspicions encircled her like a net, invisible but real. She kept away from them once she began intuiting their suspicions in her nerves, but she still had no idea what the basis of them was. It seemed to her that the very success of the play rested on her shoulders. And even though she made her appearance only in the last act, she was the first to show up for rehearsals. The most excited of anyone, her cheeks flushed, she wandered about the empty stage and curtains, going over her part and making meaningless gestures in the semidarkness out of sight of the stage hands sitting on a pile of rags or perched atop a pyramid of furniture.

Szatkiewicz visited her usually in the afternoon, and she did her best to treat him to coffee or tea with cakes, depending on the state of her kitchen. Often, however, she took some little piece of pastry out onto the stairway and disappeared for a few moments into the neighboring apartment. When she returned, her hair was often tussled and there were traces of someone else's tears on her cheeks. Szatkiewicz never took any notice of it. He sat sprawled out and haughty as he gave her some pointers about her part in the play; his tone was patronizing, and he preferred drinking coffee to tea. He rarely caressed her now but rather permitted himself to be loved like a great and kindly master who deigned to lower himself even to the level of a slave. Once he had collected a sufficient quantity of pleasures and theatrical gossip, he dashed away, preoccupied, as if he bore the fate of Europe on his shoulders.

It was not the fate of Europe, to be sure, but the fate, in part, of an issue of the *Kurier*. He had to rush and strike while the iron was still hot. The continuous incitement and agitation against Jews and socialists had begun to bear fruit. In small towns reached by that venomous hiss the flame of hatred grew in hearts that were dark and deaf to the voice of universal love. Disturbances began breaking out here and there; human animals began raging, restrained until then by the fetters of tolerance and understanding imposed by civilization. The *Kurier Naro-*

dowy began gathering the harvest of its bloody and disgusting seeds. Cab drivers in their coaches were reading pamphlets written by priests stirring hatred against their fellow men. Terrorized, Jews cheated in shops with the growing fury of their own hatred and desire for revenge. A fiery, burning breath now blew across the city, whispering satanic curses with which the white mantle of Christ had nothing in common. Oh, how distant from the rabble using His name was that radiant Jew who embodied such great love! How different were His words of forgiveness, groaned on the cross, from words inciting to constant disharmony, provocation, and . . . murder. And what was that "faction," which had usurped the name Christian, next to true Christians carrying words of peace, harmony, and love to the whole world!

And here and there, the mob was just a mob.

Words of love for one's fellow man reverberated in the air; the wings of the doves of peace fluttered. A throng raced after these words and itself became a white dove and attracted even criminals to itself.

Now bats flapped wings of hatred above Cracow. And the throng metamorphosed slowly from a dove into a savage, bloodthirsty beast. Base instincts stirred those black wings, slimy with mud and ill will. The intellectual proletariat devoured the scurrilous writings with delight. The specter of the Essene, barefooted and blameless in his coarse garb, paled on the horizon and the rainbow of concord dissolved in space.[15] Nothing remained of Christ's teachings. The sky instead took on the color of blood, more crimson and burning than any other, for it was fraternal blood, that of one's fellow man, human! The *Kurier Narodowy* triumphed, having achieved the figure of three thousand subscribers!

*   *   *

"Write that the one who was playing the part of the nun is a Jewess, and as such has no right to wear the habit and play the role of a sister of mercy . . . Don't forget. Oh, one other thing; add that the play is reprehensible and nothing more than a heap of mud!"

"Yes, sir!"

Szatkiewicz left the editor's office and began writing the review. It was a great, festive day for him. He took over Binder's job as theater critic, the true, official, confirmed critic of the *Kurier Narodowy* and not just a writer of "notices."

His chest swelled with pride. However, he passed by Binder—who at that moment wore the expression of a dethroned monarch—with considerable courtesy. He went into the office, sat down, and took pen in hand. Suddenly, he recalled the editor's words. Irma was the Jewess! It had never occurred to him. She spoke perfect Polish, her nose was, in truth, ever so slightly crooked, but that was barely

---

15. A reference to the Essenes, an ascetic Jewish sect, among whom Christ is believed to have lived for a time.

noticeable. Only now, sifting through old impressions, he came to the conclusion that she really could be Jewish in view of a certain characteristic twist to her mouth, especially in sunlight, her curly hair, and her prominent ears.

Yes, yes, the editor was right. The girl who never wanted to tell him anything about herself was a Jewess. And even if it weren't so, the editor ordered him to write that Irma was a Jewess and he wasn't going to argue the point. What would happen if in his first review he paid no heed to the editor's order? Binder, who most certainly heard what the editor told Szatkiewicz, wouldn't fail to take advantage of it.

So he began writing, his brows compulsively wrinkled, pretending to be a person exceptionally preoccupied with the importance of what he was doing. The vacuum of esteem was already filling about him. He was now being viewed as the editor's "right hand." Everyone knew that he was writing his "first review." They made way for him discreetly, but nevertheless carefully followed his every movement, every dip of his pen.

But Szatkiewicz suddenly grew thoughtful and stopped writing. He recalled with what joy, and hope, Irma approached the playing of the role of the nun. He felt sorry for the girl who had shown him so much kindness in his hard times. The feeling of masculine honor tugged at him. After all, she was a woman who was close to him, who was good, kind, and even loving . . .

But then his gaze fell on the figure of Binder sitting alongside him and he encountered the steely eyes of the handsome blond, and the look in those eyes struck him like the blow of a whip. Under the yellowish light of the lamp Szatkiewicz perceived in Binder's gaze an ocean of mockery and envy. He then straightened himself up, puffed out his lips contemptuously, and began writing hurriedly.

"The part of the nun has been entrusted most inappropriately to a Jewess, Irma Pasmantieri. Her Jewish origins profane the sanctity of the habit and evoke repugnance and indignation in Christian viewers . . ."

He reflected for a moment, and, carried away by the subject, added on his own even forgetting what he was writing about:

"Moreover, the actress in question cannot even speak Polish. The harsh sounds she produces recall instead the jargon used in Kazimierz rather than the sound of our native language. But the management of the theater, oblivious to the fact that the entrance to the sanctuary bears the inscription 'The Nation to Art,' changes the temple of national art into an exhibition of Jewish beauties and invites the profanation not only of the building but of the vestments dear to the heart of each and every Christian Pole." And with a great flourish, he signed: "Szatkiewicz."

The entire newspaper, meanwhile, bubbled with happiness.

Splendid news arrived from the provinces. A Judenheca had begun in towns and settlements; here and there arms were taken up.[16] In one place, the three corpses of peasants were cooling beneath a shed, the unconscious instruments of

---

16. An allusion to actual armed attacks on Jews in Galicia in the late 1890s.

the monetary desires of their leaders. Others who had been arrested were crowded together in foul common detention centers like a flock of sheep blind from the bloody desire for murder and conflagration.

The members of the editorial board, huddled around their big table beneath a large burning lamp, their faces lit up in smiles, were absorbed in this bloody "mail," which came from afar, redolent with the scent of fresh human blood and, it seemed, still breathing in the night with the curses of fraternal battle. Szatkiewicz arose from his table and slowly approached the group. Their satisfaction enveloped him as well. Tomorrow's issue was going to be stupendous!

The Judenhecas, further embellished by the paper, were in and of themselves capable of arousing all Cracow. The issue of the paper would be sold out and would circulate in thousands of copies. And then, the review! His review! In a bold move, he stretched out his hand to the letters and telegrams on the table.

"If you gentlemen allow me, I'll bring these papers to the editor!" he exclaimed, gathering up the papers.

No one opposed him.

Szatkiewicz collected the papers and his review, the ring he bought from Freiwilligowa on credit flashing, and headed to the doors of the editor's office. In a moment the anti-Semite from conviction disappeared behind them. Crossing the threshold of the office, the only thing he had on his mind was the determination, reached in advance, to ask for an increase in his monthly salary.

And he received it.

Part Three ■ From World War I to World War II

The Popular Anti-Semitic Press from 1915 to 1929: Four Treatises

J. Grabowski ■ Poles, Jews, Russians (1915)

[The devastation of Poland during World War I, the rebirth of an independent Polish state after the war, and the political and economic instability of the interwar period — combined with accelerated Jewish assimilation now perceived as a grave economic threat — gave rise to a zealous, nationalistic, and in some instances clerical popular anti-Semitic press. The four treatises from which the following excerpts have been drawn are typical of this literature. The first, *Poles, Jews, Russians*, was probably written by Julian Grabowski (1867–1926), a medical doctor and long-time member of the Polish Socialist Party (PPS). Although well-known as a political activist, there is little in the scant biographical information on him to indicate any strong anti-Jewish bias.]

The direction of special attention to the Kingdom of Poland as a territory where the Jewish question must be resolved one way or another is, as may be imagined, related to the conviction inculcated in the Russian masses that the Jews resident in the Kingdom of Poland represent the core, the *gros* of the Jewish population of the entire Russian state, and that on the land of the Kingdom of Poland they dwell in relatively greater density than in other areas.

Statistics demonstrate, however, that this is not the case. The Jews in the Kingdom of Poland represent barely 25.23 percent of the Jews of the entire Russian state whereas Jews constitute 70 percent of the population of the Pale of Settlement. The Jews living in the Kingdom of Poland make up 11.3 percent of the world Jewish population, whereas those living in the Pale constitute 31 percent of the Jews of the entire world. Thus if we take into consideration the possible unification of Polish lands, in accordance with the Proclamation of the Commander in Chief, then the numerical relationship of Jews to the rest of the population, amounting at present to less than 14 percent, would, with the addition of Galicia and the Poznań region, especially the latter with its small Jewish population (1.58 percent), fall to just several percent and become negligible with respect to the huge predominance of the non-Jewish population. Considering that in the entire so-called Western Region [of Russia] the density of the Jewish population is greater than in Palestine, for example, and that in the Minsk district, the numerical percentage of Jews is 17.5, and in the Grodno district 16.6, one would have to assume, say what you will, that it is precisely in such areas that the Jewish population could demand recognition of its rights as a significant minority population.

J. Grabowski, *Polacy, Żydzi, Rosjanie* (Warsaw: n.p., 1915).

Belorussia, Lithuania, and the Ukraine, it would seem, should be the area chosen by the Jews as the territorial basis for their national development insofar as they regard as indispensable the acquisition of such a base. They should also, logically, aspire to legislative changes guaranteeing them civic and national liberties where Jewish settlement is densest. Russian administrative bodies, particularly the Ministry of Internal Affairs, should resolve this primarily Russian internal problem. There is no place for its resolution on the territory of Poland, as the above-cited numerical data demonstrate.

Entirely unfathomable is the question why 11.3 percent of the general Jewish population demands exceptional privileges while acquiescing in the denial of the benefits of national rights to their fellow countrymen whose population is three times larger. It is as if the Poles of the entire world came forward with a demand for the granting of national autonomy to the Polish population settled in West-phalia while at the same time secretly encouraging expropriation in the Poznań district!

This anomaly becomes understandable if we consider the legal (juridical-state) character of Russian anti-Semitism. Demands for the enfranchisement of Jewish nationality in the Empire would be met with such resistance on the part of even the most sincere friends of Jewry in Russian liberal spheres that the very utterance of similarly utopian fantasies, with respect to the Pale of Settlement, concerning exceptional rights and so to say "privileges" for Russian Jewry would condemn the entire Jewish question to paralysis and would nip in the bud the handsomely developing Judeo-Russian understanding. Hence if the Jews demand the recognition of Jewry as a separate and distinct nation in Poland, then they would most evidently regard as advantageous the acquisition of the very best territory as the basis for national development, without taking into account at all the percentage of the population as a whole they would constitute in this territory at any given moment. *They want to take advantage of the tractability of a new political structure* [i.e., a new Polish state] *in order to put their stamp on it and turn it into a future refuge and haven for all Jews threatened anywhere with restrictions.*

*   *   *

The choice of the Jews has fallen at present on Poland. This is understandable for yet another reason, namely, that beyond Poland, Belorussia, and the Ukraine, nowhere do the Jews establish communities with the appearance of a separate national group and nowhere do they use a different language. The demands of Jewish nationalists are not limited to the utterly fair demand for civic equality; they encompass, besides that, the demand for the guarantee of their national rights.

How are the national rights of Jews to be understood? There have been so many arguments as to whether or not the Jews are a nation, and if there are objective conditions permitting Jewry to be recognized as a separate nationality, that the resolution of this question, which rests in fact on the recognition, or nonrecognition, of a certain definition of the concept of nation—a methodological argument, if you will—has no practical significance. The important thing is that the Jewish nationalists demand national rights, rights complementary to the general freedoms of citizenship and leading to national enfranchisement. What would this enfranchisement of Jewry be based on? On the recognition, in legal-political relations, of certain features of Jewish separateness not covered by general laws of religious tolerance, freedom of conscience, and so on.

Let us agree that the objective feature of cultural nationality, that is of a nationality not constituting a state but a separate autonomous entity, and possessing, relatively speaking, neither objective conditions for the achievement of a similar organization nor aspiring to achieve such, is a separate language. Since, in my judgment, the Jews can be considered only a cultural nationality, they might demand recognition of their separate language as a language equivalent to any other language recognized as an official language of the state.

Examples of the coexistence of two or even several official languages are easy to find. For example: quadrilingual Switzerland (counting the Rhaeto-Romanic [Romansh] language); bilingual Belgium, with the Flemish and French languages, and so on. Theoretically, then, in light of the existence of factual precedents, the Jewish demands are possible to fulfill.

The separate language of the Jews is their colloquial jargon, or rather jargons, bearing in mind that besides German, they also make use of a corrupted Spanish, that there exists a Hispanic-Jewish literature, completely distinct from the general German-jargon literature, and that a journal is published in Vienna intended for Sephardic (Spanish) jargon speakers. The existence of two separate jargons, as different from one another as Spanish and German, complicates and confuses the matter of the enfranchisement of a Jewish language. Preference for one Jewish national language discriminates against the other, and in this way "denationalizes" a part of Jewish society, or forces it into denationalization.

In effect, the Jews themselves have already resolved this issue. Based on the numerical relationship of those speaking a German dialect compared to those using Spanish, that is, of Ashkenazim to Sephardim, they have recognized the commonly called jargon, or German dialect, as the Jewish language. Thus, only the Germano-Jewish jargon, the speech of the Jews residing in Poland, can be enfranchised by us in satisfying the demands of Jewish nationalists.

Let us assert in advance that the Jewish jargon in Poland is truly a separate and distinct language. A Pole does not understand this jargon, just as a Jew who does not know the Polish language does not understand Polish. Let us agree further that the jargon is a folk language, that it dispenses with grammar, that it assimilates terms from its surroundings with exceptional facility, reworking them in its own fashion in accordance with the spirit of the language, or accepting them without any changes whatsoever. . . . But once the Jewish jargon is to become a bureaucratic language, a language of school, then it is self-evident that it must emerge from the swaddling-clothes of folkishness, that it must strive for unification, crystallization, and submission to certain constant grammatical forms, and that from a folk dialect it must become a language. It is not difficult to foresee the direction the jargon will follow if it becomes, or aspires to become, a real language.

In pressing their demands for the recognition of their jargon as a separate language, the Jews attempt, as much as possible, to obscure the irrefutable fact that the so-called Jewish jargon is a German language and nothing else, a true folk dialect of that language, adorned in borrowings from the languages of its surroundings, borrowings that are liquid in nature in that they fluctuate depending on circumstances and on the political influences of one nation or another. The very manner of reworking or assimilating foreign acquisitions is irrefutable evidence of the fact that the spirit of the [Jewish] language is German. Let us take for example the title of one of the plays performed in jargon theaters: *Ferblondzet* [Yiddish for confused, astray]. A superficial analysis of the term—fer-blondzet—suffices to convince one of the way this term, with its Slavic root *błąd* [Polish for error], has been Germanized. . . .

The German jargon, the folk speech of the Jews, differs from the literary language of the Germans much less than Plattdeutsch, for example. The unification of the German dialects, one of which the Jews speak, must lead to their merger with the German literary language. That is an irrevocable eventuality issuing from the direct influence of the German language, its vigor and strength acquired through cultural values gathered in the course of centuries. There is no need to have recourse to predictions; the facts themselves speak in favor of our assertion—above all, the fact that in Germany, notwithstanding the considerable number of Jews who have lived there from time immemorial, not a single publication in Yiddish appears. This does not at all mean that the Jews have assimilated in Germany to such an extent that they have ceased being Jews. The German Jews do not forget their Jewishness for a moment, and German anti-Semitism, which is a hundred percent more humiliating to the Jews than the Polish, does not permit them to forget their separateness. The German Jews have abandoned their dialect for the literary language. Since they know the German alphabet (Swabian) or the Latin, thanks to universal education, they prefer to write and publish in German in the appropriate letters rather than bend the Hebrew alphabet to the sounds of the German language. Yiddish signs, in Hebrew letters, the kind you can see in Königsberg, or even in Berlin, are primarily for the benefit of arrivals from Poland or Lithuania who in fact speak German but do not know any other alphabet than the Hebrew. Moreover, as is in fact asserted on the Jewish side, in plays presented in Yiddish-language theaters, the following phenomenon can be observed: characters drawn from the masses speak to the audience in dialect, in a Yiddish full of Polish or Russian borrowings depending on the location. But the more intelligent the figure being presented, the more the language he speaks approaches classical German. We see taking place before our eyes, therefore, an evolution from the popular dialect to a literary language, in this case German. It is impossible for us to delude ourselves as to the final effect of this development. *The German literary language is the end goal to which the German dialect called the Jewish jargon in Poland strives.*

II

. . . Moreover, an exclusively Yiddish-language culture, a German-jargon culture with its Hebrew signs, develops only where the Jewish masses, who are alien to general culture, are compelled to confine themselves to cultural values acquired in the *cheder,* that is, in a school of folkish, confessional, and separatist character. The best example of this phenomenon can be found in the United States where Yiddish newspapers draw their readers only from the ranks of new immigrants. The entire Yiddish culture of America is the culture of a single generation; second-generation Jewish immigrants are already Americanized. . . .

The demands of the Jewish nationalists with respect to the linguistic enfranchisement of the Jews can be clearly formulated as follows: (1) We demand the recognition of the German language as a co-official language of Poland; (2) We demand legal permission for the use of the Hebrew alphabet for the expression of the sounds of that language.

Can the demand for the recognition of the German language as a privileged language be reconciled with the slogans in whose name the present war is being waged? I judge not. As long as it is a matter now of liberating the world from beneath the oppression of German militarism, the German system of government, and "steel-plated" German culture, how can a state that is independent of Germany agree to grant special privileges to the German language? . . .

Hence the demand on the part of Jewish nationalists for the enfranchisement of Yiddish is a dangerous threat to the significance of the outcome of the war now in progress. It is also an attempt to create a German oasis outside the German state as well as to open a door to the intrusion into Polish affairs for the future defenders of the oppressed linguistic freedom of a German-speaking people.

Anonymous ■ *Jews during the War* (1918?)

[This is the second of the four selections from the popular anti-Semitic press of this period.]

The term "assimilation," taken abstractly, or detached from reality, sounds quite nice.

So, too, does the desire for cooperation for the purpose of advancing the country's economy.

But how does the matter seem when viewed from other angles?

To begin with, the process of assimilation always works to the advantage of the Jewish element and to the disadvantage of the Polish element. In the course of this process of "peace" and "harmony" the Polish population has gradually disappeared from the cities and towns of the Kingdom of Poland and its place has been taken by the Jewish population.

All commerce has passed into Jewish hands. Money has passed into Jewish hands. Land is also slowly passing into Jewish hands. Financial decisions often rest exclusively in Jewish hands.

Not only is the percentage of Jews increasing in Poland, but their influence is also on the increase. Their social position among us is assuming ever greater significance. We are being relegated more and more to a secondary position and have less and less to say.

Moreover, the assimilationist movement has in no way impeded the Polish Jews from maintaining close contacts with the Litvaks [Russian-speaking Jews] and always taking their side when conflict has arisen between us. It has also not stood in the way of their entering into shady deals with Petersburg behind our back and with Berlin during the war itself. . . .

As a result of assimilation, the Jews have entered our intelligentsia, taken part in our public opinion, and even tried to direct it.

As a result of assimilation, the Jews have entered our literature and press, debased our language, warped our Polish national thought and national spirit; with the help of the pen and word they are contributing to the perversion of our mores and have contributed greatly to the cosmopolitan outlook of various of our social spheres.

In critical moments, as, for example, during wars and revolutionary upheavals, these assimilated Jews, who at every moment join forces with unassimilated Jews,

---

Żydzi podczas wojny (n.d., n.p.; photocopy available at Harvard Deposit Library), 3–5, 20–24, 28–31.

are an uncertain element. They try to support policies of advantage to others, but not to us.

As a result of assimilation, organizations arise whose goal is to direct the Jews into agriculture and the trades. These organizations do not uphold the principle of equal rights, but by reason of their mandate support Jews everywhere and push Poles aside.

When the Russian revolution erupted, and a program for autonomy, with a parliament in Warsaw, emerged among us, the Jews, even assimilated ones, were very opposed to it. They wanted all our essential affairs to be decided in Petersburg. Although they branded the Russians as "pogromists" abroad, although they knew that pogroms were really happening in Russia and were even supported by the Russian authorities, they understood perfectly that where the Kingdom of Poland was concerned the regime would to a certain extent support the Jews in order to weaken the significance of the Polish element. This was of considerable importance during the Russification of Lithuania.

But now radical changes have taken place. Russia has withdrawn. Her place has been taken by the Germans. The Jews are always very consistent. Now it would be very much in their interest if, with their help, Berlin weakened us. A German policy aimed at restraining the immigration of Jews into Germany suits them greatly. In the German Jews they have, after all, powerful guardians, since these guardians also do not want Polish Jews flowing into Germany and creating competition for them. So they work toward an improvement of the conditions of Jews here, naturally at our expense.

The result of all of this is that, in the new scheme of things, that is, when the Kingdom of Poland is falling under German influence, the Jews in Poland represent a privileged element. German goals coincide with Jewish goals. And the slogan of increased assimilation, or the greater entry of Jews among us and the introduction in our ranks of dissension, similarly coincides with this policy. . . .

Whoever speaks of Jewish assimilation says nothing about the fact that assimilation should begin with the Jew taking on other mores, improving himself morally so that in matters of trade and commerce he would cease being a criminal, a swindler, and a forger.

But the Jews are so numerous among us that we cannot exert any influence on them whatsoever. Rather, it is they who infect us with their immorality; it is we who are becoming assimilated in our ways by the Jews.

It is possible to speak about the aesthetic assimilation of the Jews. But is that a behavioral assimilation? On the contrary. The leading Jewish spheres are undermining Christianity among us, and the influence of the clergy. They do everything they can [to ensure] that the Catholic chaplain ceases to be a social and political organizer of the Polish middle class and peasantry. . . .

Taking advantage of the turmoil of war and of the bizarre circumstances prevailing among us under the German occupation, Jewish members of the intelligentsia thrust themselves into chairs of universities and polytechnics, where they teach Polish history and literature and, in short, make sure that the Polish spirit remains constantly under their control.

The Jews invested large sums of money in the establishment of publishing houses that are superficially Polish but in actuality promote Jewish interests. Dispensing funds on all sides, they attracted various Polish men of letters and poets, essayists and journalists, and finally the naivest among us, who always let themselves be led around by the nose, namely, Polish scholars. Regrettably, the Polish scholar who would not let himself be taken into Jewish captivity is far more the exception than the rule. On the other hand, we can say with no small satisfaction that our Catholic clergy, disposing of the means still remaining to it, is perhaps the only body carrying out its responsibilities, Polish as well as Catholic, during this terrible war. . . .

In our battle with the Jews the Polish priest is perhaps the last worker who has not thrown up his hands or let the grass grow under his feet.

If our leading strata sin, if we're fed up with the fact that reform on the Jewish question will not come from the top down, but from the bottom up, this is a comforting development in that this bottom — which will play such an important role in the future — remains under the direction of the Catholic chaplain, who during the present war recalled his most illustrious traditions. . . .

Fr. Jan Gnatowski (1855–1925)   ■   *On the Jewish Question*

[The third selection, *On the Jewish Question,* is by a native of Lwów, the Roman Catholic priest and writer Jan Gnatowski, who sometimes used the pseudonym Jan Łada. Prolific, if lacking in originality, he wrote mostly on such emotional issues as Polish martyrology, the religious persecution of the Poles in the Prussian partition, and the social and economic problems represented by the Jews of Poland.]

I remember once, during a debate in my presence about accounts of the murder of Christian children, someone shouted out, annoyed at the opposition: "But Jews must want them murdered if they do things that cannot have any other consequence!"

At the time the argument seemed to me to be conclusive. I still do not believe

---

Ks. Jan Gnatowski, *W kwestji Żydowskiej* (Warsaw: Gebethner i Wolf, n. d.), 35–86. A reprint from the journal *Wiara.*

in the murder of children by Jews, but I have not ceased to believe in the value of the argument. Life has convinced me that the Jews sometimes do things that are worthy of amazement for the express purpose, it would seem, of leading the majority around them to hatred, revenge, and even, *proh dolor,* to murder!

V

What else is the role of the Jews in relation to Christianity, and especially in relation to Catholicism, if not a clear — but perhaps not unintentional — incitement to hatred? The worldwide Jewish press breathes with the same hatred against the Church with which the Jewish rabble once demanded Christ's blood of Pilate. There is not a single lie, or deception, from which the telegraph agencies and the best informed newspapers would shrink when it comes to the ridiculing, insulting, and compromising of the Church, the papacy, priests, and even the Sisters of Charity, whose honor and dedication even the Turks and pagans could recognize. . . . And this is done not by this or that Jew, but by the whole of Jewry, since, among others, the Jewish kings of the Stock Exchange dedicate a part of their millions to the domination and organization of the press in order to turn it into a battering ram against the Cross.

And yet, through the centuries, the Jews themselves were the object of many calumnies. What was not concocted against them by an ignorance strengthened by fanaticism in order to denigrate and destroy them? But ignorance is a greater misfortune than a sin; how less evil it is than a lie told in full consciousness! The little shoemaker who screams in good faith that Jews in a neighboring street drew the blood from a Christian child can be excused to some extent in light of his stupidity. But how much less deserving of forbearance is the highly educated editor of a prominent newspaper who twice daily, with the smile of an augur, feeds his readers tales of Jesuit millions, the secrets of cloisters and confessionals, even the illegitimate children of Pius IX and Leo XIII, the debauchery reigning at the court of these two popes as well as at that of Pius X, cardinals being poisoned by other cardinals, and still other cardinals operating houses of ill repute for the augmentation of their income! . . .

And in politics, what has been the role of contemporary Israel?

In Germany the Jewish press fell into convulsions in an excess of enthusiasm for Bismarck and Falk when with the brutality of spike-helmeted knights they aimed the lances of special laws against Catholics under the weight of which the German Jews themselves groaned a few decades before. Now among the Jews the government slogan "Ausrotten!" (Root Out!) has the most fervent admirers and allies.

In Austria, hardly did they attain power, when the Jews forged legislation touching the very depths of the holiest feelings of the Catholic population and aimed at debasing their faith, weakening it, and gradually destroying it. Between

1867 and 1878, Vienna was the seat of a veritable orgy of Jewish omnipotence. . . . The farsighted foresaw a reaction, but they were ridiculed among their coreligionists. And the reaction came. The father of it was not Lueger, but Jewish blindness. . . .[1]

In France, the Jews moved heaven and earth to rehabilitate Dreyfus. I don't know if Dreyfus was a scoundrel or a sacrifice; but I do know that if he was a sacrifice he wasn't the only sacrifice to injustice and force in the world. In the last quarter century, that is in the same period, there were, just as there are today, sacrifices worthier perhaps of the sympathy of the omnipotent Jewish press than Dreyfus, if only for the fact that they numbered in the thousands. People were deprived of a livelihood, of respect, of their homes; people shed blood for their faith and for their native language. A hundred thousand Armenians were uprooted in Turkey, whose laws concerning the Bosnian Slavs several of our progressive papers are making such a fuss about; there were mass murders of Christians in China; there was a law passed expropriating Polish land in the Poznań district and church property in France; there were children beaten for saying their prayers in Polish in Prussian schools. The latter event has been written about abroad, mostly in France, by Catholic newspapers; the Jewish papers preserved a discreet silence about the matter or made light of it. . . .

VI

We are not drawing up an indictment, but rather confirming phenomena that are the result of the history and psychology of the Jews. These phenomena are harmful to Christian societies and still more harmful to the Jewish.

The Jew is the way he is in part because of his unusual capabilities, in part because of centuries-old adversity. He is excessively effusive and grasping because he was unduly inhibited. He is arrogant because he was maltreated. He oppresses because for a long time he bore the burden of oppression. He is unable to stand alongside others and desires leadership and privilege because until now he himself has been beyond the law and wishes, when he has the strength, to counter centuries of exceptional discrimination.

He battles with the Cross of Christ and with the Church foremost in the bearing of the Cross because the Cross is the negation of his ideas and his aspirations, a judgment against his past and his future.

He is the embodiment of negation and disharmony. Like spreading rust, he eats away at the national and social traditions as well as the religious beliefs of the Christians surrounding him, for these traditions hold nothing for him except bad memories, and so long as these memories endure they must be a hindrance to his rule and influence. . . . Everything in Christian society is alien and hostile to

---

1. Karl Lueger, the anti-Semitic mayor of Vienna from 1897 to 1910.

him. Its cultural achievements, its ethical system, its political and social ideals—
everything—is not for him! . . .

Through capital, the Stock Exchange, the press, and Masonry, the Jews today
hold governments and peoples tightly in their hands. The fluctuation of opinion
and money depends on them, and if politics itself does not, rest assured that what
goes on behind the wings does, and in politics we know how important that is.
What more do the Jews want and why do they strive for upheaval where it would
be dangerous for them as well, for once the Red Banner triumphs it is hard to
imagine that the expropriators would make an exception for the Rothschilds. It
is true that during the Commune the offices and palaces of the Rothschilds were
defended effectively by federal guards, and socialist agitators and revolutionary
orators telling the ignorant tales about the treasuries of priests and nobility were
restrained in their remarks about Jewish businesses and bankers. . . . In the prepa-
ratory stage, a revolution spares Jewish capital because it regards it as a temporary
ally. But when the time comes for action, the Jews are drowned by the same wave
as others. And since this is so, what advantage is it to the Jews to support upheaval
not only where things are bad for them, but also where they have it best of all? . . .

VII

We have endeavored to present an impartial picture of the consequences of a new
era of Jewish existence in western societies. There remains for us now to view the
struggle for the equality of rights for the Jews and present efforts to achieve a
resolution of the Jewish problem among us.

Equality of rights on the basis of assimilation, or as the means effectively leading to it, was the watchword of elements supporting civic equality in Poland at
the end of the eighteenth and the beginning of the nineteenth centuries as well
as in the time of the Duchy of Warsaw [1807–15]. Less was heard about it in 1830,
whereas on the threshold of 1863 it began to reverberate on all sides and became,
as it were, a national dogma whose chief propagator was a person of such exceptional influence as J. I. Kraszewski.[2]

The dogma did not brook discussion; it even seemed at the time that it offered
no possibility of it. Indeed, what more appropriate outlet, what other outlet, in
fact, was there for a society ten percent of whose entire population consisted of
Jews and whose trade, exclusively, and industry, predominantly, rested in Jewish
hands? In addition, this society faced a host of inimicable elements, internal and
external, hence the necessity for it to seek allies and the elimination of every com-
plication in its way capable of being eliminated. Hands were extended sincerely
and without reservation to the "Poles of the Mosaic faith." And may God protect
us from the claim that harm was done. The effort had to be made, though there
were those who did not believe in its outcome. For our part, to tell the truth, we
believed a bit too hastily and too ardently. . . .

2. The author is referring here to the Polish Insurrections of November 1830 and January 1863.

Fairness compels us to assert that the Polish appeal to brotherhood did not remain without a response. There were individuals and entire groups among the Jews who responded favorably to it and stood beneath the banner of assimilation. In truth, the great majority of those who previously had no reservations and had no other outlooks and views went a step farther, a decisive step—and accepted the Cross. Be that as it may, however, that same fairness does not allow us to deny that the masses of Jews either did not accept the hand extended them or, in accepting it, were unable to give up egoistic aims or aims that were not always loyal to Polish society. This does not diminish the service of those who sincerely thought about assimilation and acted in its behalf; it does not even take away entirely from the service of those who assimilated out of personal considerations. In political and social compromises, self-interest always plays a greater role than emotion and nobody should be condemned for opportunism. Once having taken the position of self-interest and bilateral agreement, one must ask what advantages this self-interest brought to the two sides concluding the agreement?

To Polish society, assimilation brought an undeniable benefit insofar as a number of individuals entered it who sincerely and wholly united with it. . . . Baptized Jews have sunk roots in our society, obviously bringing it certain of their negative attributes, but alongside these many commendable traits and talents. And even among those who have not decided to take this decisive step, and one essential for a perfect union with it, there can be found not only good Poles but even pioneers of Polishness. . . .

It would be biased stubbornness to assume that all these people acted only out of self-interest. To begin with, for many of them it has been disadvantageous. Alongside theoretical philo-Semitism and practical submission to Jewish hands without the slightest opposition and consideration, Polish society has always harbored, down to the present, a considerable measure of a quite unsavory and boorish anti-Semitism. And curiously, instead of diminishing, this anti-Semitism has in fact grown after Jews have become baptized. The unbaptized Jew often emerges whole from the mills of our polished but not always clever malice; perhaps because we trust him less and regard him as an enemy. The neophyte, even though a tenth-generation neophyte descendant, is a favorite target of our animus. We avenge ourselves on him mercilessly for the fact that he wanted to become our brother, a Catholic and a Pole.

So what if that former Jew wants to serve his chosen fatherland as sincerely as possible, that he desires to tune his spirit to its feelings, its aspirations, its ideals? So what if Christian and Polish blood flows in his veins alongside the Jewish? Even were he Mickiewicz, they would still remind him that his mother had descended from a family that had once been Jewish . . . The eternal tragedy of the Israelite fate never strikes home as clearly as when a Jew stops being a Jew. . . .

More or less, this is how assimilation has looked among the Jews. It has been superficial and self-seeking. The benefit from it for the Poles has been more imaginary than real, and there have been a hundred times more harmful aspects and dangerous consequences. The Jews have proclaimed themselves Poles, but their Polishness has been limited to words pronounced somewhat too purely; it never penetrated to their deeds, never changed either their internal system or their attitude toward the Polish people. In villages and small towns, the Jew has continued to encourage the peasant's drinking the same as before, so long as the [spirits'] monopoly allows him to; he has continued to demoralize and exploit him with a vengeance, just as he used to. In his relations with the gentry, the Jew has played the same role of a leech and parasite, enriching himself on usury, acting as a go-between and helping young and old alike in debauchery and prodigality. And as to the intelligentsia, especially in the cities? From the time of assimilation, and thanks to assimilation, Jewish influence on this milieu has grown even worse; indeed it has become outright deadly.

We have mentioned that most Jews accepted assimilation out of self-interest. This self-interest represented, as it were, a kind of safety valve against any and all accusations and attempts at counteraction by Poles. Jewish solidarity, otherwise laudatory and worthy of emulation, has the negative trait of not being above concealing excesses and offenses. The "Polishness" of the Jewish masses revealed itself above all in the desire for impunity on the part of Polish society. "You can't touch us; we're Poles, after all!" The nervousness and touchiness, native to the Jewish character throughout the world, prompted the sounding of the alarm and complaints about the inflaming of racial and religious hatred, and about Jew-baiting, where all that was involved was an objective criticism of a particular fact, or a defense against a particular troublemaker. We do not at all deny that anti-Semitism, both informal and journalistic, has in large measure contributed to such an attitude. Nevertheless, thanks to cleverness, energy, and the influence of the press, the Jews and their friends succeeded in fashioning a kind of privilege of inviolability whereby it is impossible to make a charge against anyone, no matter what the pretext, without the risk of being charged in turn with anti-Semitism.

The following situation thus arose. The Polish press was able to write against usury and the inebriation of peasants, but on the condition that the usurer and tavern-keeper be identified as a Catholic and a Pole, or even a German, but never a Jew. So someone like Klemens Junosza could swear a hundred times over that he had no intention in his *Pająki* (*Spiders*) of singling out Jews, and that his only concern was branding usurers in general, but it was to no avail whatsoever; he became an anti-Semite. . . .

VIII

We have endeavored to point out something that is easy to assert because it is evident: that throughout the whole world the Jews have taken advantages of rights granted them, but among us, as a result of the assimilationist current, in a manner overwhelmingly harmful and even dangerous to society as a whole.

Official opinion, manipulated by a press subservient to Jewish influences, can ignore it. Liberal doctrinairism of the old school can shield it. But the testimony of the Jews themselves in a fit of impartiality or bad humor does not deny it.

There is thus no doubt that Jewry understands equality of rights as control and monopoly, and that it exploits this monopoly both for the subversion of the existing moral and social system and for the introduction into the life of nations of an element of disintegration.

Having lost its own faith, contemporary Israel has not ceased hating the faith of its former masters, nor has it ceased regarding these masters as enemies even though they are no longer masters. Having lost its own fatherland, it has been unable, at least not entirely, to attach itself in its heart to any other.

Wherever it finds itself, it is always a society within a society, a foreign body, and despite its exceptional attributes, talents, and energies, despite its multi-faceted and sometimes excessively prominent activity in one field or another, it is, nonetheless, taken in its entirety and in relation to the broad masses, a parasite.

In light of this, it is no wonder that the idea of equal rights, just as the idea of assimilation, quickly loses its footing both in the West and among us. . . .

IX

Whatever the Jewish problem may be elsewhere, there is no doubt that it appears grave among us.

On one hand, there is the mass of Jews—ignorant, fanatic, Christian-hating, and indiscriminate in the means of battle against Christians.

On the other hand, there is the Jewish intelligentsia, in part nationalistic and Zionistic, in part cosmopolitan, and, to the smallest degree, Polish. The last because the Polish language and Polish ways, used as a convenient cloak beneath which to smuggle in their own goals and influences, to shape the Polish community to their own model and to deflect it from its traditional values—are, in truth, excessively cheap commodities. Just as cheap a commodity is the acknowledgment of their joint partnership with us among so many, so very many educated Jews!

In view of this, what are we to do and what position should we take?

We have already indicated this. It cannot be the position of a theoretical doctrine, nor a position of sentiment. Doctrinairism and sentimentality have already caused us enough trouble; breaking with them is an obligation and necessity, especially when one is weak and holds neither many cards nor good ones in his hand. Besides, the time has past when the liberalism of the preceding generation was governed by doctrinairism and sentimentality; there are other slogans in the air these days. The Jews repeat them the loudest, so long as they don't concern them. Do we not have the right to apply these slogans to the Jews themselves?

Today's slogans are: the right of the stronger; strength before right; the ruthless terrorizing of the minority by the majority and of the majority by the minority. These are the slogans of the fist, the club, the Browning.

And these are the slogans — of the Jews!

The Jewish minority aspires, where possible, to the subjugation of the Christian majority. Is that not for us both an indicator and an example? And does not the Christian majority have the right to do the same with respect to the Jewish minority?

Obviously it would were it not Christian.

But it is Christian, and because it is, it cannot apply to anyone, hence not even the Jews, the principle: "An eye for an eye, a tooth for a tooth!" It cannot, because it is governed by another principle, an infinitely higher one, first revealed to the Jews but established only by Christ: "Love your neighbor as you do yourself!"

And everyone is a neighbor, the Jew as well, and in equal measure.

Hence it is forbidden to rise up against the Jew, as indeed against anyone else, inciting the rabble with the cry: "Let's get them!" It is forbidden to stir up people's passions and bad instincts against them; it is forbidden to deny them honor as Jews and just for the fact that they are Jews. . . .

From the Christian viewpoint, anti-Semitism is not only an error in principle and a grave sin in its practical application; it is, moreover, an absurdity, just as a-Semitism in and of itself is an absurdity.

That is because terms and the concepts indicated by them must be understood according to their constant meaning. If that is so, then anti-Semitism connotes the active opposition to everything related to the Semitic tribe, and a-Semitism — the peaceful boycott of it.

Now the Arabs are undeniably Semites, to say nothing of the Syrians, the Chaldeans, and perhaps also the Armenians. Therefore, in the name of logic, the Arabs, Syrians, Chaldeans, and so on must also be boycotted. But all of them, excepting the Arabs, are exclusively Christian; and even among the Arabs, there are over a million Christians, and among the Christians about 100,000 so-called Melchites and more than 30,000 Maronites confess Catholicism. Do anti-Semitic injunctions apply to them also? Presumably they do, since they are Semites.

And what if a Jew converts? The answer to that is easy: "Converts! A joke!" Fine, but if the convert happens to be Father Alphonse Ratisbonne, converted by a special miracle, or the blessed Libermann, raised onto the altar; does anti-Semitism apply to them as well?[3]

3. Marie Alphonse Ratisbonne (1814–84) was a French Jew who belonged to the most important Jewish family in Alsace. The turning point in his life was the vision of the Virgin Mary he claimed he had in the church of St. Andrea delle Fratte in Rome in January 1842. He converted almost immediately to Catholicism and subsequently entered the Society of Jesus (Jesuits). After his ordination in 1848, he requested permission to leave the Society in order to join his brother, Théodore — who had converted to Catholicism before him — in working for the conversion of the Jews. In 1855, he went to Palestine where he devoted the remainder of his life to the conversion of Jews and Muslims. The founder of the congregations of Notre Dame de Sion and the Fathers of Sion, Ratisbonne was also the author of *Elévations sur les Latanies de la Sainte Vierge* (1847).

François Marie Paul Libermann (1802–52) was a French Jew and rabbi's son who converted to Catholicism. He is remembered primarily as the founder in 1839 of the Society of the Immaculate Heart of Mary whose purpose was to evangelize former black slaves. Several of his missionaries were

Logic replies—yes!

When the consequences of an assertion lead to absurdity, obviously the assertion itself is absurd.

Perhaps we can then substitute anti-Jewishness for anti-Semitism?

But if a Jew becomes baptized and despite that remains a Jew in his political and social convictions? I don't know if such instances occur; I do know that they are possible, that in view of the growth of Zionistic currents they are inevitable. Every era has its neophytes; so too will this era in which Zionism is developing stronger than ever before. With what right, then, would a Christian Aryan proclaim battle against a Christian by faith and a Jew by nationality?

Should the battle cry be limited to creed? By what right, and why? Because the Talmud is hateful and harmful! Does the Koran overflow with tolerance? Have we such little knowledge of sects, even deviations of Christianity, which proclaim beliefs both evil and inimicable to the social order? Is it proper, therefore, to raise the banner of boycott, hatred, and extermination against their adherents? When the Mormons established in Utah a state within a state based on criminality and oppression, the Americans crushed their power and legally prosecuted those practices of theirs that are contrary to ethics and public security; but we have never heard anything about an anti-Mormon campaign in society. Opposing the errors of the Talmud and its fanatic spirit is the responsibility of the state, of society as well, just as it is the responsibility of both to oppose everything harmful to the majority in the internal structure and influence of Jewry. But does that necessitate a conflict with Jewishness as such?

We judge not.

But in such a case must we simply cross our arms and watch indifferently as the dishonest Jewish usurer, swindler, and exploiter goes about oppressing the peasant, the landlord, and the town "intelligent," while another Jew demoralizes each of them in his own sphere? Just because he is a Jew must he get off without punishment?

No. Opposition must be directed at one and the other not because they are Jews, but because they are malefactors. . . . It is entirely fair for society and the state—insofar as the state is the true expression of society—to protect their people by a series of defensive and, if necessary, even exceptional measures not so much against the Jews as against the malefactors, exploiters, leeches, fences, rabble rousers against faith and social harmony, and peddlers of revolutionary novelties and "progressive" fancies who are pouring into our villages. Highly cultured societies differ from less cultured ones in that they protect the child against deprivation and foolishness by means of special legislation. It is just as appropriate

---

among the first to penetrate the African interior. In 1848, the Society merged with the Holy Ghost Fathers, which was originally founded in 1703. Libermann became the eleventh superior general of the order.

in the same way to protect that great child, the folk, so long as it remains a child.

The moment experience demonstrates that the village Jew brings harm to the surrounding populace, one has the right and even the obligation to protect that populace from harm, even at the cost of expelling the Jew. Obviously, only as an extreme measure, just as in general every exceptional law should be applied only absent other means.

The same with young people. It is inappropriate to place them under the influence of teachers without faith. A Jew who is faithful to Judaism (if there be any among the educated) is a fundamental enemy of Christianity. The confessionless Jew is the enemy of all faith. Neither one nor the other should be permitted to fulfill his mission as an educator of the Christian child, not because of his origin, but because he is alien and hostile to Christian ideals. By the same token, a non-believer cannot fulfill such a mission though certified a Catholic. . . .

Through its own foresight and energy, society must counteract the pressure of corrupting elements of the Jewish spirit. Fully acknowledging the right of the Jews to the air and sun, guaranteeing their position, work, religious freedom, and civic inviolability, protecting them and even more itself against persecution, which is always more harmful to the wrongful than to the wronged, the Christian majority must vigilantly guard the Christian character of its social, intellectual, and political life. . . . In a Christian country, the schools must be Christian; the press, the lecture hall, literary and artistic productivity, the stage, and even the street must be Christian, or at least respectful of Christianity. . . . In the Christian, Catholic, and national consciousness, and in Christian, Catholic, and national self-help and solidarity lie the solution to the Jewish question in our country, the medicine for the Jewish sore spot.

Such consciousness and self-help have no need of hatred and repression. If the Jew is taken for what he is, without any illusions, and the effort undertaken to prevent him from becoming harmful, society will succeed in honoring him and in making appropriate use of him, sometimes changing him from what he is into a valuable presence, thereby raising the general level.

And at the same time there will develop more broadly than ever, and in a more fundamental way than ever, this one enduring bond and this one true and unfailing assimilation possible between Jewish society and our own — the bond of unity of spirit, conscience, and faith, assimilation through the Cross.

Stanisław Pieńkowski (1872–1944) ■ "On Values and Super-Values" (1929)

[The fourth selection, "On Values and Super-Values," is by a notorious anti-Semite, Stanisław Pieńkowski, a middling literary and theatrical critic, journalist, poet, and translator.]

. . . Let us first consider the matter of human language, or speech, an object of great importance and utility, an object that is the creation of all human communities and many generations, thus of entire nations. The character of every nation is reflected in its language. The German language is heavy, just like the German; it is composed in a convenient way of a small number of elements, and so is handy, frugal, and poor in imagination, just as the German, its creator, is bereft of flights of fancy and artistry. The Polish language is the opposite of the German. It is endowed with a huge number of native elements; it is rich and supple in syntax; and it surpasses in its quantity of sounds not only the German but other languages as well. This attests to the physical and spiritual superiority of the Pole. Omitting, however, the differences between various Aryan languages, and without citing more examples, one feature of them should be identified as common and distinctive: each nation is deeply and inseparably bound and attached to its language, except the Jew. How can this be explained?

Every Aryan puts his own creativity, hence a certain store of personal utilitarian values, which he constantly needs and employs, into his language. Another, foreign language does not offer him these utilitarian values; thus he remains almost religiously attached only to his own. Only in his own language can he express himself to the depths of his soul. The Jew, on the other hand, as a noncreative type who does not generate utilitarian values, is indifferent to language to the extent that he lost his own centuries ago and makes use of the first one that comes along as merely a commutative value. The Jews in Eastern Europe took the German language, a foreign tongue, and spoiled it even more. And that is also a commutative attribute of theirs: they accepted the most convenient and poorest language, a language possessing the fewest creative and artistic features, and the easiest to get around in. Not long ago the Jews invented and are cultivating an artificial language, Esperanto.[1] And in this they similarly revealed their alienness with respect to creativity and utilitarian value in general. They recognized human speech only as a commutative value, like a phony banknote that one values only

Stanisław Pieńkowski, "O wartościach i nadwartościach," in *W ogniu walki: Szkice w sprawie żydowskiej* (Warsaw: Skład Główny w Domu Książki Polskiej, 1929), 62–70, 197–99.
  1. Esperanto was the invention of a Polish Jew, L. I. Zamenhof (d. 1917).

from the viewpoint of its facility and circulatory universality in the world market.

As a completely different example, let us now take craftsmanship. It can be boldly stated that three quarters of human culture is contained in craftsmanship. Art, after all, contains craftsmanship, and all of today's industry is only mechanized craftsmanship. Craftsmanship also exists in science. Civilized and civilizing man (with the exception of the Jew) is a born craftsman, and a great one, an architect of life, its creator and inventor. . . . The work of the Jew is only—profiteering. When the Jew betakes himself to a craft, it is only of dire necessity, and it is well known the kind of artisan he was and is: a miserable maker of shoddy merchandise who works any old way since he sees nothing in an object beyond commutative value and because he possesses in himself no creative, utilitarian value. As for the Jew and any kind of agricultural work—the less said the better. The magnificent mastery of the land by the human spirit and hands—this is toil to which the Jew never put a hand. He merely sponges off this human labor and trades in it. . . .

When we finally consider science and art . . . even here, as elsewhere, the participation of the Jews either amounts to nothing, or is inconsequential and harmful. Their philosophy is primitive, mechanical, intellectual (the Bible), or purely mathematical and schematic (Spinoza). Their morality is that of the caveman or brigand (the Talmud, the Shulchan-Aruch), or insidiously destructive, specially "for export," intended for Aryans. Their participation in scientific creativity has been nil, whereas in art it is limited to the lyric, and even that is saturated with the venom of hatred, pessimism, skepticism, irony, or sarcasm (the Prophets, Heine). . . .

Conclusion

In the introduction, I appealed to the instinct of self-preservation of the Poles. In essence, each sketch here, and each sentence, appeal to it. Any analysis of the soul, behavior, and general policies of the Jews has no other goal in our country but the awakening of Polish life and its energies for the overthrow of the yoke imposed on Poland by its new partitioners. For this an accurate knowledge of the enemy, his strengths and methods, is necessary. The present book offers at least the general framework for this knowledge. I await from my readers a detailed filling in of the framework; this will be the introduction to action in the Jewish affair.

But what action are we talking about? Its aim is evident: the removal of the Jews from Poland.[2] But the means and methods? I have not addressed that issue here, since that is a separate and broad issue. I cannot, however, take my leave of the reader without at least defining it in one generalizing statement. The first step

2. Pieńkowski uses the Polish word *usunięcie* for "removal." It can also be translated "expulsion," "elimination" in the sense of removal, "ousting," "dismissal," "expurgation," and so on.

in the expulsion of the Jews from the country is such an increase in and energizing of the spiritual, physical, and material strengths of the Polish nation so that by placing Poles in all areas and positions of social life it would thereby push out each and every last Jew and crypto-Jew among us. It will be a driving of the Jews back into their ghetto, their total isolation, confinement, and concentration in a single, as it were, concentration camp.

This will be an enormous and difficult task in view of the fact that the Jews have wormed their way into the entire Polish social and state organism. The state and the government, our foreign delegations, ministries, state and local offices, police and army, judiciary and bar, journalism and literature, science and art, social and cultural institutions, trades, commerce, industry and finance, free unions, and even social life are, to various degrees, replete with Jews or dominated by Jews. Difficulties arise, moreover, as a result of the provocative method of the Jews whereby they assume Polish names, pretend to be Poles and patriots, and additionally employ all kinds of deceptions, some of them quite subtle. The number of them in any given sphere of Polish life is also no indicator of the extent of their domination of it, since wherever they are, they occupy above all managerial positions, positions of leadership, in which case one Jew suffices for hundreds. We know that it is enough to control one main screw in order to become master of an entire complex factory machine. The same thing happens with the state, society, and culture. And the Jews are helped in this by Poles infected with Masonry, socialism, communism, and various other trends and ideas. They serve as a screen for the Jews and hinder our work. Meanwhile, standing behind all this is international Jewish finance in the form of the most terrible terroristic monetary dictatorship. We already feel the results of this dictatorship. In a country as naturally rich as Poland, stagnation and poverty reign in Polish society. We are plundered and ruined in broad daylight.

The first step of our work of liberation will therefore encounter gigantic obstacles. But what can the will of a nation threatened with extinction not accomplish?

After accomplishing the first half of this task the rest is achieved swiftly. The Ghetto, isolated and separated from the Poles by such a void, will fly into the air as if blown up by dynamite. The Jews themselves will quit Poland in droves, no longer possessing here a field for dealing and exploitation. We should assist them in this exodus, not with the sword now but with olive branches in our hands, and it will come to pass with ease. Until that time, however, we shall have to exert all our energies and capabilities in the first immeasurably difficult and complex half of the task. It will be our great life's examination for the degree of freedom and independence. The young will accomplish it. The young generation of Poles is coming, coming with closed ranks, that will at last liberate their country and open the gates to its happy future.

▪ Antoni Słonimski (1895–1976)
Two Poems

[Although Antoni Słonimski's paternal grandfather, Chaim Zelig Słonimski, was a respected Hebrew author who wrote several books in that language on astronomy and geometry, his son Stanisław converted to Roman Catholicism and brought up his own son, Antoni, in that faith. A well-published poet and prose writer, admired for his craftsmanship, Słonimski was outspoken in his liberal views and a foe of extremism in any form. He spent the war years in France and England, serving for a time as director of the Polish Cultural Institute in London. He returned to Poland in 1951, eventually made his peace with the communist authorities, and enjoyed a productive career in the postwar period. The following two poems, "Rozmowa z rodakiem" ("Conversation with a Countryman," 1922) and "Jeruzalem" (1922), grew out of a trip Słonimski took to Palestine. As the poems make clear, Słonimski's Catholicism never entirely compromised his identification with, and compassion for, his fellow Jews.]

Conversation with a Countryman

An old Jew asked me near the Jaffa Gate:
"Is the Saxon Garden still there? The same as ever?

Is there a fountain? At the entrance from Czysta Street
In the old days confectioners had a shop there with water."

"Everything is the way it was: the fountain and kiosks.
And Prince Poniatowski is still standing there."

"Poniatowski! The Polish army, as they used to say . . .
I don't know how it is now; it used to be good before.

I'm a little weak. But when I'm better
I want to travel; I'd like to live in Warsaw.

I even have a buyer here. As soon as I sell everything,
Maybe I'll have enough. . . . But my son won't give me anything.

He's very educated; Levi's his name, too.
When I talk about Poland, he doesn't know a thing.

I talk to him, explain things as best I can:
'Warsaw's there after all!' He doesn't understand."

Antoni Słonimski, "Rozmowa z rodakiem," and "Jeruzalem," in *Poezje* (Warsaw: Czytelnik, 1955), 76, 73.

Jerusalem

See the Mount of Olives and the Greek monastery.
Minarets and cupolas abound,
Squares of yellow houses like honeycomb.

The valley of Josephat, white, dry fields —
There in the dell, where it is azure and quiet,
Immobile, deep in the very depths, lies
The dead and sultry sea, golden Jericho.

That tree you see, that's the tree of Judah.
And those huge stones there — are Roman.
And there, where a red juniper shrub appears on the road,
Christ revealed himself to holy Magdalene.

You see this line of carriages, cars, and coaches?
Like a white road amid swirling dust, pious tourists
Travel to where far among the palm leaves
Sleeps the tiny earthen town of Nazareth.

And in this wild garden — here it's best —
I often sit a while, and leave with sadness:
Grass smells at noon, when sleep glues the eyes together;
Like in a village in Poland, flies buzz in Jerusalem.

■ Maria Kuncewiczowa (1899–1989)
The Stranger (1936)

[Maria Kuncewiczowa was one of the more respected women writers in interwar Poland. Her best work of prose remains *Cudzoziemka* (*The Stranger*), for which she won the Warsaw Literary Award in 1937. At its core autobiographical, the novel is a psychological character study of a Polish woman violinist who must gradually confront the "otherness" of her Russian upbringing. The main character, Róża (Rose), was patently based on Kuncewiczowa's mother, a violinist named Róża, who was of Russian background. It would be fair to argue that this perception of Kuncewiczowa's own otherness, as reflected in *The Stranger*, heightened her sensitivity toward the situation of the Jews in Poland, especially in the 1930s. The small excerpt from the novel included here demonstrates her willingness to confront the anti-Jewish prejudice of her fellow Poles. Also much admired among Kuncewiczowa's writings is a collection of stories, *Dwa księżyce* (*Two Moons*, 1933), set in the picturesque town of Kazimierz on the Vistula, which was long a haven for artists. Kuncewiczowa left Poland after the German invasion, stopped for a while in France, and settled primarily in England from 1940 to 1955. After that, she emigrated to the United States where she became a professor of Polish literature at the University of Chicago. As political conditions improved in postwar Poland, she returned there on a number of occasions, eventually resettling in Kazimierz until her death. In 1939, before the outbreak of war, Kuncewiczowa was invited by the Hebrew P.E.N. Club to visit Palestine. The record of her visit, *Miasto Heroda: Notatki Palestyńskie* (*The City of Herod: Palestinian Notes*), is particularly interesting for the author's observations concerning the attitudes toward Palestine and Jewish resettlement there among Polish Jews she encountered in her travels.]

One autumn Sunday she and her aunt went for a walk to the Łazieńki Park. . . . Cabs and carriages rattled over the rough pavement. They were stacked with ladies and girls, rustling with starch, "liberty" silk, and coarse fake wool. Gentlemen in top hats and bowlers hunched together on the front seats.

From time to time the pace of the procession of carriages was interrupted by the clatter of trotters, and among the cabs, phaetons, and landaus a carriage appeared drawn by a pair of tightly collared stallions with long tails, driven by a coachman in a padded coat. The police at the street corners snapped to attention, a wave of hatred and dread swept over the passersby, while in the middle of the street, avoiding the drab vehicles, the wife of a Russian general or police official hurried past with jingling harness. *Tante* Louise pursed her lips, looked straight

Maria Kuncewiczowa, *Cudzoziemka*, 4th ed. (New York: Roy Publishers, 1945), 42–46. Originally published in book form in 1936. For a translation of the entire novel into English, see Maria Kuncewiczowa, *The Stranger* (New York: L. B. Fischer, 1945).

ahead of her, and hissed through her teeth: "Don't stare; there's no need to get distracted, *Rosalie*."[1]

However, *Rosalie,* with mixed fascination and longing, followed the joyful course of the trotters until they disappeared from view.

When they finally reached the Łazieński Park, they made for the gingerbread stall. A *marengo*-colored plush mantle with satin lining flowed from *Tante's* shoulders. The hem of her embroidered pantaloons peeped out from beneath her skirt. She rustled all over like a straw man, and her prunella shoes creaked.

Rose glanced sideways at *Tante* once or twice, and suddenly felt that her cheeks were quivering and that she was about to burst out laughing. Her aunt took such short steps and had such a respectable look on her face. Rose knew that she could never control her impulse to laugh, that she wouldn't succeed in controlling it now, and that her aunt would become irritated and at a loss to account for her laughter. What was she to do? Tapping the stones with the heels of her shoes, kicking up gravel, she raced down the hill into the busy, noisy avenue.

Tante was aghast, not knowing what had happened to her niece. She ran forward a few steps and began calling in panic: "Rose, Rose, my dear, what's the matter?" And then something happened that — in Louise's opinion — was utterly shameful, painful, and not to be forgotten.

Strollers turned their heads in the direction of the running child, caught sight of her raven plaits pulled taut in flight, heard the despairing cries "Rose, Rose!" and were greatly disturbed. What? On a Sunday morning in the Łazieński Park? Was the *rendezvous* of elegant Warsaw to be disturbed, Catholic society to be upset, by a black-haired Rose?

"Rosie, Rosie, stop, or you'll lose your drawers!" A fat fellow with a gold watch chain tried to make a joke of the matter. The other passersby, however, were not inclined to dismiss the intrusion as a childish prank. Voices called out: "What are things coming to? Is there no protection against kikes even here, in the Łazieński? Back to Nalewki, to the Krasiński Gardens![2] High Mass is still being celebrated at Holy Cross Church, and this Rosie with her curls has to disturb it!"

People stood still and someone growled: "Catch her and turn her over to the police! Let 'em take her in! This is illegal! Jews aren't allowed here!"

A Russian lieutenant who happened to be eyeing the girls, dragging his sword after him, slung low from its loop — pleased with an excuse for approaching the rancorous crowd of Poles — ran up, blocked Rose's way, and caught her in his arms. Rose — unconscious of the effect of her escapade and of her Jewish-

---

1. Because of the possibly confusing variants of the name Róża in Polish in the original text, I have translated the name as Rose, and Rosie, where appropriate. Róża's aunt calls her by the French name Rosalie; the narrator on occasion refers to her by the more familiar Rózia; a Pole makes fun of her by using the nickname Royza, to draw attention to the girl's Jewishness. Róża (Rose) was a common Jewish girl's name in Poland, and Rosie would be the English equivalent of the Polish Royza.

2. The main Jewish quarters of Warsaw.

sounding name — did not even resist when she felt a man's hand on her shoulder. The merry face of the lieutenant seemed familiar; he exuded a breath of Taganrog, of Yula's perfumes, nothing at all frightening. She looked trustingly and laughingly into his eyes. The lieutenant was taken aback.

"Is she really a Jewess?" he muttered in Russian, looking askance at the agitated bystanders.

But *Tante Louise* had now come up, in her rustling prunella shoes. She flared up in anger, struck the lieutenant on the arm with her long, thin parasol, and shouted: "Leave the girl alone at once! What is happening here, for heaven's sake? *Il y a encore des juges à Varsovie* (There are still judges in Warsaw). I'll see that you get your due." She looked commandingly at the people around her. "What is this, ladies and gentlemen? A Muscovite roughneck molests a Polish girl, and you remain silent? Has Poland fallen so low in her captivity?"

The lieutenant let go of Rose and went away quickly, muttering: "Damned Polacks, the hell with the lot of you!"

Rose pulled out a handkerchief, and her aunt took her by the arm. "Come, child, hold on to me. A Polish girl can no longer count on the honor of her countrymen."

The public retreated in confusion; only the fat fellow with the gold watch chain — who had been so amicable in the beginning — barked after her: "You pretend to be a Polish matron, my good woman, yet you give your granddaughter the name Rosie! 'Poland; Polish honor!' Then all of a sudden — Rosie. Some compatriot!" He looked suspiciously at Louise.

Oh, what a hard day it had been! Her aunt prayed the whole afternoon, wept, was given laurel drops on several occasions, and the Sunday coffee and cream remained untouched. Rose was forbidden to visit her girlfriends or say prayers and instead had to copy out five of Kochanowski's *Laments*. That evening *Tante* called her into her room, rose slowly from her pre-dieu, and issued instructions: "My child, give the canary its seed and go to bed. Starting tomorrow I'm going to call you *Éveline*. Rose . . . here in Warsaw all of Nalewki echoes with that vulgar name. I do not wish my brother's daughter — only an uncouth, shortsighted boor could take you for my granddaughter — I do not wish the granddaughter of a captain of the Napoleonic Legions to be taken for an Israelite! It really was quite thoughtless of *Sophie* to give a Polish child such a name."

■ Maria Kuncewiczowa
The City of Herod: Palestinian Notes (1939)

Rachel

I have a whole lot of small friends in Kazimierz. One day they brought a four-year-old girl to my garden. She made a great impression on everyone. Witold crawled down from the cherry tree; Karolina stopped beating egg whites; and we all followed her around, pushing aside the rest of the group, hissing whenever her incomprehensible Hebrew words were drowned out. She did not depend on comprehension and clearly spoke just to herself or to supernatural creatures such as Queen Saba, or to the proud butterfly that King Solomon had befriended. She sat down beside different plants, looked them over with an attentively wrinkled nose, as if disapproving of some and approving of others. On a footpath, where there were holes from heels, she grew sorrowful; but a moment later she caught sight of a small plank and used it to erase the marks. That done, she grabbed me by a leg and, without saying anything, explained to me that I had to get rid of the offending slippers immediately. While all this was going on, Witold attempted to attract the attention of the unusual visitor. Finally, he ran to the house and through a window fired five percussion shots one right after the other at the garden. The girl stopped, fluttered her eyelashes, and raising a finger whispered, "Arabim." Then she sang a long warlike song while tapping her feet and making a menacing gesture like a knight in a puppet play. After the conclusion of this lovely demonstration, I attempted to kiss her, but she wriggled out of my arms. She shot me a flashing, evasive glance of impenetrable strangeness, tossed her curls—and disappeared.

I soon learned that the little Hebrew girl was the niece of neighbors, that she was born in Tel Aviv, and that she had come to Poland for the first time to visit relatives. The child, whose name was Rachel, interested me greatly. She was absolutely different from her Kazimierz cousins. Her Levantine exaltation, impulsiveness, and standoffishness did not retreat in the slightest before anything threatening. Between thought and deed there wasn't a second's hesitation. Free of the hypocrisy of those Jewish children who are busy outsmarting the world, Rachel did not conform to the observations, malice, or admiration of others' judgment. She danced for the sparrows behind the hedge. She expressed her desires without attention to compromise. She disabused a portrait artist of the idea of immobilizing her by means of chocolate. She cared not a whit for the local powers, who were greeted with curtsies by "wise" children, or coins, which she tossed into the Vistula, to the distraction of her aunts.

Maria Kuncewicz, *Miasto Heroda: Notatki Palestyńskie* (Warsaw: Towarzystwo Wydawnicze "Rój," 1939).

After making the acquaintance of Rachel, I thought again of Palestine, over-come for the first time by interest. What magic was responsible for the fact that it sufficed a Jewish girl just to be born there so that in her fifth year of life she did not yet show off how smart she was, did not respect money, and avoided inti-macy with important people?

Some two years later, the poet Yehuda Warszawiak invited me, in the name of the Hebrew P.E.N. Club, to visit Palestine. The project seemed troublesome. Palestine, my God, the Holy Land. . . . The Hebrew P.E.N. Club. The new Pales-tine — the land of Rachel.

Jews on the Acropolis

In the meantime, the decks, the reading room, every passageway upstairs and downstairs were seething with Jews. People sat in their cabins, while outside the windows a constant promenade went on; heels tapped, women's voices shot out in shrill, aggressive questions; men's voices boomed defensively, but soon enough the men themselves were crowing, pecking each other to pieces, and killing each other with painful jabber. Old women croaked in a measured way, but even among them in the end a soloist always broke out — and roared for all the others. Just like in Kazimierz, when the sun sets, the Vistula changes color, something takes place, something moves on, something arises, while the Jews on the bul-wark, crowded together, shout their own things, their backs turned to the world.

Anyway, a fair crowd signed on for the visit to Athens. The expedition was efficiently organized: taxis were waiting in front of the maritime station in the Piraeus, and we set out under the direction of a Greek woman, a doctor of phi-losophy who was licensed as a guide by the Ministry of Education. She spoke flu-ent German, with an accent that would be taken among us for that of the eastern Polish borderland. She had a diminutive black head, classic features, and warm eyes. We rode through Faleron, a seaside spa known to antiquity. The Greek guide began to tell us its history in brief, but she was interrupted and asked feverishly if there were any hotels around. "It's not Athens, and besides even in Athens there won't be time for any hotels." "It's not the hotels we're interested in, just the stickers," shot back an energetic answer, "and I don't expect them for nothing, I'll pay for them. What good is a suitcase without stickers to a cultured person?" Before the question died down, the suburbs of Athens appeared, a new and poor district. Bedding was airing in the open, men in fezzes and women in galligaskins were tending to household chores, herding brown goats, or shouting at children. Refugees from Asia Minor, Turkicized Greeks, who after a five-hundred-year exodus were expelled by Kemal Pasha and were returning to the bosom of their fatherland, both to their own and to their fatherland's distress. The Jews forgot about the hotel stickers, and an old, well-to-do manufacturer of pasta from Łódź foamed: "Is this politics? Is this what's called the twentieth century? Why did they bother these people? Doesn't everyone have the right to die where he was born?"

And a bearded man and a woman in a wig—probably from Słonim, and neither one of them understanding a syllable of Polish—assented wistfully. . . .

The journalist-politician was putting his notes in order.

"An artificial creation, this whole Palestine," he said, "stillborn, with no prospects for the future. Would-be agricultural communes and would-be workers' unions, on the one hand, and on the other—nationalism, the Jabotinskys, fascism . . . What does it all amount to? The collective upbringing of children, progress, but kosher kitchens and old men in tsytses . . . Is this supposed to be a modern society? In my opinion, they're nothing but romantic experiments, nothing but a luxury—a luxury for elderly ladies and beautiful spirits. Just so that in the promised land a few score doctors of philosophy might indulge themselves in milking cows with their own hands while millions of beggars go starving and stuff the boxes of the Keren Kayemet.[1] The Arab worker is certainly right in protesting that it's a conspiracy of international capital."

"Come on now!" replied the student. "That business about milking cows by hand is just nonsense. They do it now electrically. I know it for a fact from a bookkeeper from Nieszawa who's working in a cow barn on a collective farm in Emek. In the final analysis, is that worse than keeping books? Every profession can be intelligent. But I'm concerned about something else. Why do I absolutely have to milk cows in Palestine? Why am I not free to milk cows in Poland? I don't happen to like Palestine; it's a foreign country, what do I have in common with it? Can you rationalize fatherland to yourself? Fatherland can just be a pretext. Fatherland is where a person's born. That's his right, and the rest is literature. I was born in Nieszawa; it stinks there—and how!—and oranges grow in Palestine. But I'm used to Nieszawa; that's where the best smell is for me, and the best life."

A young woman—obviously someone reticent, or lazy—who was sick aboard ship during both passages, was lovingly looked after by her husband, and never conversed with any of her travel companions, now spoke up: "The best life! Can you, a student, say that? Sitting on a bench reserved for pariahs is better, according to you?[2] I don't want my daughter sitting separately like some shabby wretch." Her face turned red and there were tears in her eyes. Her husband took her by the hand.

"Roma, don't upset yourself! I beg you, you're ruining your health! What's the use of getting all worked up now about Irenka's future studies? People will think you've got a grown-up daughter." Coquettishly embarrassed, he looked at the people present and began stroking his wife. "She's already worried about the numerous clausus, but our girl is just six. What can you do, sir? A woman." He shrugged his shoulders. She pushed him away.

"You don't need a woman for that; I'm sure everyone's had enough. The child

1. The Zionist movement's National Fund.
2. The speaker is referring to the so-called *numerus clausus*, which effectively segregated Jews from Poles in the universities by requiring the Jews to sit together in certain places in lecture halls.

is small? But she knows how to write. And I ask you, show this gentleman the letter!" and she pulled a small sheet from her husband's pocket. "Here, have a look at what a small child writes: 'Panna Halina is leaving on the first, because she can't work for Jews. I am very sad about it and I'm also going to go away somewhere on the first.' Well, what do you say to that? This Halina got a salary from us that more than a single official in Sosnowiec could envy. And I gave her a room with a balcony. The child got attached to her, and now she can't work for Jews. My sister's son, when he comes home from school sometimes, doesn't want supper; he's too depressed. Pretty soon we're going to have a bench ghetto . . . My husband earns a very good living; people have to respect him because they need him, because there isn't a better dentist in the whole town. But what can he do to stop people from calling his daughter 'Jew-girl' in the park?"

The dentist stopped his ears. "Quiet, quiet, Roma, what do you care what idiots call anyone? I told the child: 'You ought to be glad and you ought to be proud if they call you a Jewess.' Would you prefer, Roma, that they called her nothing just so she could get a bullet in the head from some Arab?" She clenched her fists; her husband continued:

"I know what I'm doing. You wanted to see Eretz Israel . . . Did I spare any money? You've seen it. You've seen blood in the street and blood in the field. Well, I think, you've seen enough." . . .

The Jews were silent. Finally, someone, rustling the pages of a newspaper, whispered: "They don't seem to write anything about the pogroms in Poland. . . ."

The dentist sighed. "Naturally! It's an exaggeration. They bang people around somewhere so right away it's a pogrom. I'm telling you, Roma, things are better. Last year they poured kvass on the fur coats of three Jewish women in Sosnowiec; but this year — did you notice? — on just one. . . ."

"Unavoidable paths" run and the weak return to endure. Jerusalem continuously remains the city of Herod, inimicable to the Savior, where the strong slay the weak. Of late, Arabs fall more thickly than Jews, since there are no weak Jews today in Palestine. They are Maccabees, athletic on European playing fields, wanting their own wars at the cost of their lives; they are girls who are "huge, and arrayed like an army," who want their own soldiers; they are people locked in dreams; they are poets yearning for the ecstasies of Job.

The city of Herod is Zion, where the Jewish nation seeks its own youth, which was lost at the dawn of history and perhaps no longer exists.

But what did Poles, Germans, and Americans seek in Palestine, and why are they returning crestfallen? There is as much angelic bread in the Holy Land as in every human country; there is as much poison in Eretz Israel as in every captured and defended fatherland.

But the sadness of Christians, the shame of Christians should not surprise. For nearly two thousand years our era has been flowing against Herod, in vain.

Stanisław Vincenz (1888–1971)
"The Bałaguła" (1936)

[Descended from a French family from Provence that had settled in Poland, Vincenz grew up in the Hucul (Hutzul) region of the Carpathian Mountains in eastern Galicia. The Huculs were a sheepherding Slavic people who spoke a dialect of Ukrainian. The region had been part of the Polish-Lithuanian Commonwealth; it fell under Austrian rule in the partitions and reverted to Poland between 1918 and 1939. Although he studied biology, Slavic philology, and Sanskrit, Vincenz took a doctorate in philosophy at the University of Vienna. He began his literary career as a translator of Dostoevsky and Walt Whitman. But it was his abiding fascination with the Huculs, and the Carpathians, that shaped Vincenz's major work, a fascinating, multifaceted collection of writings — valuable as both literature and anthropology — on virtually every aspect of the Hucul region and its people, including the mostly Hasidic Jews who lived there. It was, in fact, in the Hucul region that the founder of Hasidism, Baal-Shem-Tov, once lived and taught. The first volume of Vincenz's work, which he titled *Na wysokiej połoninie* (*On the High Uplands*), appeared in 1936; the second and third volumes were subsequently published only in fragments between 1939 and 1952. When World War II broke out, Vincenz fled to Hungary and remained there until 1946. In 1947 he moved to southeastern France, and in 1949 settled permanently in Grenoble. Of the many stories about the Hasidism in *On the High Uplands*, "Bałaguła" is perhaps the best known, in part because of its humorous yet well-informed theological element.]

In the path of the wind several extraordinary vehicles set forth one after another from the town of Kołomyja. They were well known to the people of those times and our parts, but to strangers they were no common marvel. They were known as *bałagułas*.

In its rather more solemn sense "bałaguła" means a master of horses; in more modern usage it means a horse dealer; in really contemporary usage, the driver of a nag. To people who have no connection with the Hucul region, "bałaguła" unfortunately means a sluggish laggard, and the verb "bałagulić" means to procrastinate endlessly.

The bałaguła is not a brisk four-in-hand ready to fly around the world, but a wagon bound strictly to the earth. In our region the owners, and also the drivers and conductors, are Jews from Kuty, from Kosów, Delatyn, and even Kołomyja, who have devoted all their lives, and the lives of several generations, to the task

Stanisław Vincenz, "Bałaguły," *On the High Uplands,* trans. H. C. Stevens (New York: Roy, 1955), 248–67. The work was originally included in the last, unpublished volume of Vincenz's collection of stories *Na wysokiej połoninie* (*On the High Uplands*). I have made some changes in the Stevens translation on the basis of the text as it appears in Stanisław Vincenz. *Tematy żydowskie* (London: Oficyna Poetów i Malarzy, 1977), 123–50.

of transport. The wagons themselves, high on the wheels, for they have to pass through fords, and sometimes covered, but more often open, are surmounted by a series of parallel seats held down with leather or hempen straps, and padded with stacks of hay. The passengers can face in any direction; they sit with faces, shoulders or backs to one another, according to taste and necessity.

The bałaguła has many marks of distinction, and all the features of a benevolent institution. Travel by it is very cheap. It is safe, because it is slow; but no one notices how slow it is, so interesting is the vitality of the drivers, so attractive the variety and above all the number of passengers. And yet it's never overloaded. It is always full, but nobody is ever refused a place. Its capacity is unlimited. And so it stops often and waits long. Despite its inherited or inherent gaiety, the bałaguła is not frivolous. It never turns off the road. Oh no! But neither does it abandon the countryside. People who are masters of the art of seeing and listening should never travel otherwise than by bałaguła.

In Kołomyja it stops at least three times—officially. When at last it sets out from the Hay Square, by the church, it goes only a few yards farther on for water, to the well called the Monastery Well, and continually gathers passengers in its travels. For a couple of groszy—or if it is a question of picking up some distinguished person such as the pottery master, or even some junior official of the town hall, not to mention state personages—it will drive up to a traveler's door. Thus by a circuitous route, jogging through many little streets, in Kołomyja alone it will have made no small journey. In addition, when it is quite certain of its passengers it visits various shops and attends to various matters on behalf of smaller towns or villages on its route, such as Jabłonowo, Utoropy, Kosów, or Kuty, and for their various environs. The bałaguła really departs from Kołomyja only when there is no hope of any further passengers. And so a violent crack of the whip is not meant for the horse at all, but serves only to encourage people; and this applies to the cries, enthusiastically repeated every minute or two, of "Now we're off!"

Sometimes, owing to its diligent gathering up of passengers, it sets out too late, and spends the night just beyond the bridge outside the town, or preferably a little farther on so that the passengers cannot slip away. During the night halt it collects more guests. Never yet has it been known—or at least I have never heard of it—for a bałaguła to break down or come to a halt through being overfilled. Nor have the horses ever been known to grow tired or refuse to obey. On the other hand, it never enters anybody's head to hurry. It shambles along at an unvaried jog-trot, while the horses take tiny step after tiny step; many a cart will overtake it, but none will travel more steadily or surely. . . .

That memorable night when the wind was unleashed, every honest Kołomyja inhabitant, every civilized Galician citizen, thought sleepily: "Oho! So not only the journey but the wedding is all over." But the sunny morning and the warm wind pouring triumphantly through the azure roused the youths for the departure.

Juliusz Kossak (1824–99), "Fair near Warsaw" (1866). Courtesy Muzeum Narodowe we Wrocławiu.

Five bałaguła wagons reserved for the journey as far as Krzyworównia, stuffed with hay in place of springs, and covered with canvas sheeting, had been waiting on Hay Square since dawn. At their head stood the official doyen of the Kołomyja bałaguła drivers, Byumen Petranker, with a long and heavy whip. He was wearing very high and ancient boots, flour-stained trousers, a jacket of indefinite color, and a ragged sheepskin cap. He was a tall, tough, gray-eyed man, with hanging bushy eyebrows, thick whiskers, and a small gray beard. Unlike his Jewish brethren, he had clear, unfaded eyes and features that radiated enthusiasm without a hint of doubt. For without enthusiasm who would be able to spend the whole of a long life without interruption, in all kinds of weather, traveling between Kołomyja and Kuty at least a hundred times a year? He had the capacity to spend a long time negotiating with every candidate for passenger. He mastered every kind of temperament, he disarmed the roughs, shouted down the stupid, gave assurance to the timid. During the journey and at halts he readily related reminiscences, petty histories, legends. In his everyday conversation he used a Slavic language that was completely eclectic, and based on the peculiar Kołomyja dialect. But it was known that he could pass easily from one to another of at least five languages: from Polish to Ruthenian, then to Yiddish, then to German and even Romanian. When he spoke Yiddish he borrowed the note of sincerity from the Ruthenian, of pedantry from the German, of elegance from the Polish, and of supreme wisdom from Hebrew. He wore a faintly derisive smile that never left his face. Whom he

Juliusz Kossak, "Fair near Warsaw," detail. The left foreground of the painting clearly shows Jewish horse traders trying to sell an emaciated nag with cataracts. The mounted figures to the rear left are Cossacks. Courtesy Muzeum Narodowe we Wrocławiu.

derided no one knew, whether his own lot as an everlasting driver, or the victims of fate, his bałaguła passengers. Certain it is that he did not sneer at his partner, the organizer and financier of the bałaguła owners, Pan Ajbigman.

Pan Ajbigman was still quite young, and was always neatly attired in a long town-coat and long trousers. By his bearing he gave one to understand that he was Byumen's boss rather than his partner, and he did not admit any of the bałaguła owners into his confidence. Day after day, before their departure, he passed with a measured step along the line of wagons, waving his hand systematically and regularly. He had very sharp features and thin lips, he often narrowed his eyes contemptuously, and when he put forward his arguments and talked with Byumen in a declamatory tone he wagged his head in a manner that perfectly described the sign for infinity.

Every day he drove with Byumen as far as the bridge over the Prut River. There he alighted and held a whispered conversation with one or another of the passengers, then returned to Kołomyja on foot, continually looking back at Byumen. And who knows, perhaps he had some other way also of disloyally checking up on Byumen? On the other hand, at times of activity and bustle Byumen treated him as a cavalryman treats an old-clothes peddler. When the wagon was full, when the horses looked round to see whether it really was so, Byumen pushed to the forefront, cracked his whip and cried in a resounding voice: "Now, now, now we're off!" He did not even glance at Pan Ajbigman, and the financier and organizer suddenly appeared quite unnecessary.

The other bałaguła drivers were named Abrum senior, Yudka, Chaim, and Abrum junior. Abrum senior had the light and soft beard of an artist, dreamy eyes, quiet movements, a facial expression not lacking in an unworldly benevolence. When the wagon started off his resigned look gave way to one of quiet satisfaction.

Abrum was said to be very devout, and he even enjoyed a certain respect in the Hasidic synagogue, called "Bojańska," where the faithful were rather exclusive. This synagogue was named after the little town of Bojan in the Bukovina, where a master rabbi had lived to whom both the faithful and also the unfaithful and curious traveled from far and wide for the Jewish Sabbaths and holidays. The master excelled in such rapture of the Lord, in such internal fire, that when he raised a glass of wine to his lips on the Sabbath those standing around him saw the wine boil. (Obviously the wine could not have been heated in any natural manner, as it is forbidden to light a fire on the Sabbath.) This sacred flame was extended to all the little Bojan communities and synagogues scattered over the whole Hucul region. In the course of time the name "Bojan" came to signify all those who feared God, through the association with the Polish "boją się" (they fear), and even something more. Byumen also attended the Bojan synagogue, though admittedly less often and less regularly than Abrum.

Yudka was an older, poorer Jew with a blind eye (the right) and a long twisted gray beard. He was not very sociable, in fact he was rather surly, and really a bad business man. On the other hand, he was regarded as honest.

Chaim, a little red-faced and red-haired Jew, with the appearance of youth and eyes veiled by a smile, had no concern whatever for other people's regard. It was openly said that he was afraid to tell the truth about anything. Evidently he did not trust truth as a patron of good business. When he was reproached for always lying, he confessed, veiling his eyes with a smile: "What of it? Is my business with the truth or with horses?" Public opinion had its way of dealing with him: he was called "Chaim the liar."

The younger Abrum had a swollen face and peaked nose, was still in his "teens," but was "rotten before he was ripe." He tried without success to imitate Byumen's cavalry shouts, croaking in a hoarse, grotesquely thin voice: "Now, now, now we're off." He sulked unnecessarily, and even opposed his passengers at any opportunity. And so he earned no good wishes, except perhaps from those who jeered at him.

On that memorable morning they were standing in a compact group, like horses in search of warmth. They waited quite a long time, bored and yawning, before the passengers who had booked places arrived. Only Pan Ajbigman, as neatly dressed as usual, walked up and down alone in the wind, uninterruptedly taking important strides alongside the vehicles. At last he halted, raised his eyes, and gazed long up at the sky. He lowered his head, half closed his eyes again, sighed, whispered, and smacked his lips as though in rapture. He seemed to be rejoicing in the powerful wind. But no; for in the end, apparently disgusted, he shook his head. In fact, Pan Ajbigman (as he admitted later) had been reckoning exactly how much income a bałaguła would bring in if it travelled at the same speed as this very wind.

Looking at his partner, Byumen reflected aloud: "Why, is Pan Ajbigman worried about the wind?"

Pan Ajbigman declaimed patiently and pedantically, describing the sign for infinity with his head: "I'm not at all worried about the wind. I'm making calculations on account of the wind."

His partner, the driver Byumen, had few equals as an authority on the weather, and he reassured Ajbigman, smiling broadly: "Believe me, Pan Ajbigman, it's a good year when there's a wind like this, and a good year is exactly like this wind. The weather flies past merrily. It's more difficult to hold out through weather that slashes miserably and drags on and on."

Pan Ajbigman half closed his eyes haughtily: "That's nothing to do with it. All that matters is what it means for business."

"It means very much for our business," Byumen declared. "When there's a good wind like today's a man is at once where he's got to be, where the mountain and the sky meet."

Abrum junior asked in a squeal: "Why have I got to be at once where I've got to be, where the mountain and the sky meet?"

Byumen looked at him closely: "Wait another forty years, and you'll find out. Do you see the Jabłonowo beech woods, high above the church there? Where it's green? Fine! Look well, and you're there; they're closer already. And then, in less than no time, down the hill to the bottom, Utoropy, Stopczietów, and they're nearer already. Up the hill to the top, Ispas, Pistyń, and they're nearer already. Nearer to whom? What do I have to get to, that it should be nearer? To the beech wood, to where the mountain and the sky meet, to home, to my father. Good, but my father isn't in this world any longer, so I want to be where it is necessary for him to be nearer. To whom does he need to be nearer? He needs to be nearer to his father. Father after father, and that father after his father, homeward, always upward, always higher, always nearer. But where to? That we know. Always higher, always nearer — the wind."

"What's it got to do with the wind?"

"Movement! The wind is the chief bałaguła, he clatters and whistles, he sweeps away for everybody, he gathers in everybody, he overtakes everybody. Make way!"

Yudka groaned: "Oy, the bałaguła will overtake everybody."

Byumen shouted back: "The wind will!"

Chaim, nicknamed Pot-Belly, asked innocently: "So what kind of a bałaguła is it?"

Byumen shouted further: "When there's no wagon around, no legs, neither horse's, human's, or dog's, no movement, nothing, the wind will come."

"For whom?" asked Yudka.

Byumen refused to be driven off course: "What do you mean for whom? For the last trotter, the very last one."

"Then the wind is the slowest?" Chaim asked again.

"No, he's the same as me, he is where he was and because of that he's where he has to be. He's here, and now he's already there, already he's roaring through the beech groves continually nearer, now he's in Pistyń among the spruces, he's higher already, he's already roaring in Rybnyca, they're roaring together, he's in the springs, he's in Czarnohora, continually higher! Who will hold him back? He's already in the stars, in Leviathan,[1] always steadily higher, always nearer."

"But what's all this to do with you?"

"With me? Am I still the same little Byumen in knickers always open at the back? No, I'm not! Am I old Byumen, a lousy old driver? I'm not that either, yet I'm always the same Byumen, through the beech woods to home, to father, always nearer."

Chaim, nicknamed Pot-Belly, inquired, veiling his eyes with his lashes: "But do you drink sometimes, Byumen?"

"What d'you mean by drink?" Byumen asked in astonishment.

"I mean always nearer to the bottle, steadily nearer."

Byumen turned angry and shouted at Chaim, Abrum junior squealed with laughter, Yudka snorted at Chaim indignantly, they all started shouting, taking sides for and against Chaim. Interpreting the hubbub as the signal for departure, the young passengers ran up in a panic, desperately waving handkerchiefs and shouting: "Wait! Don't go without us!"

"We're not starting in any case," the drivers reassured them in chorus.

"Then what's all the shouting for?"

"Because of the wind," Byumen replied evasively. Giving no further explanations, he began to crack his whip. The bałaguła drivers calmed down and cracked their whips again and again. This was the first bell before the still distant moment of departure. . . .

Byumen turned back to the human beings. Pan Ajbigman continued to walk up and down in solitary state some distance away. Byumen and the young gentlemen went up to him.

"Well, Pan Ajbigman, when our Jews began to bawl they didn't let you answer why you're bothered on account of the wind."

---

1. Also the Jewish name for the Milky Way, which is of mystical significance.

Pan Ajbigman narrowed his eyes, and declaimed weightily:

"Now look, Byumen, that's not a matter for talk; I'm looking at it from the business viewpoint. How long does it take this wind to travel from here to Kosów? Half an hour. So if it returned to Kołomyja at once it would be back here again in just over an hour. How many journeys daily? Twelve. Now let's reckon that we'd harnessed it to a bałaguła, you understand? Well, I grant it's the wind, but you've got to allow for stops, fodder, adjustments. And what is the result? Say an hour to Kosów. There and back, two hours. How many journeys daily? Taking it easy, six. What does that mean? Twelve paid places, there and back at twenty kreutzers apiece, that produces two gulden forty kreutzers for a complete journey, or over fourteen gulden daily. Gross, of course. In the winter not so much, four times a day, that produces ten gulden. Now reckoning five winter months and seven summer months—it's a fortune."

They all pricked up their ears; Pan Ajbigman smiled seductively.

"Now that would be travel, movement, traffic!"

"Traffic!" Abrum junior whispered.

"A fortune!" Chaim smacked his lips.

"But wait!" Pan Ajbigman smiled contemptuously. "Where are you going to get all those passengers from? You see what you've got in your minds? No! In such times as these it wouldn't pay." He narrowed his eyes, and turned his back on the wind. He paced along sedately, waving his arms evenly, each step, each wave according to calculation.

The bałaguła drivers looked at one another reluctantly.

"Pan Ajbigman is a hundred percent right," Abrum junior flattered him.

"There's no such thing as a hundred percent right," Byumen barked.

"How's that? A hundred percent is the finest of all business," Abrum junior said with an air of wisdom.

"The chief commandment for all kinds of business," Byumen shouted him down, "is that there's no such thing as a hundred percent right."

"How d'you make that out, Byumen?" one of the young gentlemen asked. "In calculations any percentage is permissible."

"But not in right," Byumen said obstinately.

"I don't understand."

"There's nothing to understand. If two people quarrel and one is genuinely 55 percent right, that's very good, and there's no point in fighting. But who is ever 60 percent right? That's fine, that's a great happiness, and let him thank God. And what would you say of 70 percent right? Wise people say that that's very suspicious. Well, then what of 100 percent? Anyone who says he's 100 percent right is a filthy liar, a terrible robber, and the biggest of scoundrels."

"That isn't the chief commandment for business at all," Chaim declared.

"Then what is the chief commandment?"

"The chief commandment," Chaim announced with relish, "is to sell yourself to yourself, in other words to convince yourself in regard to the goods and the price."

"What for?"

"When I have to persuade the passengers that there isn't a better omnibus than mine, and that my journey is worth at least fifteen groszy in one direction, I must so completely convince myself that I shall weep, I shall be sorry for myself, my wife, and my horses; and then the passenger also begins to weep and pays up at once."

"But supposing you don't convince yourself?"

"Then I'm a merchant good for nothing! I'm saying it all with my tongue in my cheek, and the passenger sees at once that I'm lying."

"So first of all you must cheat yourself?"

"Why cheat? I never cheat anyone; I sell myself to myself, I cry."

"My Uncle Yankel," Abrum junior intervened, "has quite a different commandment for business. Business is not the Talmud, it's practice, exactly ten commandments. And Uncle Yankel . . ."

No one wanted to listen to Abrum junior. Byumen began to crack his whip again, the other drivers imitated him, until the echoes rolled round the church and down the hill to the stonewalled well called the Monastery Well.

As though they had been waiting for this sign, new guests slowly came up. All the Kołomyja musicians who had been booked for the wedding arrived in one group. At their head trotted their conductor, Pan Szpilbaum, a very small man, who cautiously carried an imposing belly in front of him and a violin case as cautiously in both hands. On his right strode the gigantic Muraszko, a master craftsman, an expert on flooring, parqueting, and French polish. He was going to the wedding in order to prepare the fundamental element, the floors, for dancing, and also simply as a wedding guest. This was an honor to both sides: Krzyworównia had never seen a parquet-floor expert before, and the expert Muraszko had never attended a wedding of the gentry before. Immediately behind him a youthful journeyman carried a heavy package containing instruments and parquet blocks.

Other guests were still waiting beyond the town hall, by the Turk's shop, which was thrust into a gloomy gateway opposite the local railway halt. The Turk's name was really Shloma, but he maintained that he was a Turk and he was generally called Turk. According to tradition, one of his forebears had acquired his exotic shop from a genuine Turk. The dainties sold there were Turkish; the youthful passengers were buying long colored sweets on sticks, baked honey and poppy seeds on sticks, honey and nut mixtures, Turkish honey, Rahat Lakoum, and pears in honey, and were drinking goblets of apple cider, raspberry juice, and other fruit drinks. Most of them were members of a choir, consisting of pupils and students, which was intending to honor the feasts at Krzyworównia. Sucking their Turkish dainties on sticks, or licking them from their fingers, they strode across the center of the market place, breaking into song as they came. They were dominated by an extraordinarily rumbling bass, which presaged unusual shivers. Its owner was a priest's son, Nykolcio Balicki, who was himself studying for the Greek Catholic Church. Slowly the choir surrounded the wagons. The wind now flowed past, now struck in cheerful gusts. The bałaguła drivers chatted away indefatigably but quietly.

"What a life!" Yudka groaned. "You say," Reb Petranker, "that the bałaguła's the wind. A fine wind I am, everybody passes me. Pan Klęski passes me, the young gentleman from Krzyworównia flashes past with his four-in-hand, the drozhki driver passes me, and the Kosów post van; even old Pan Torosiewicz, that old miser, passes me. Even Abrum junior passes me. My horses are old."

Abrum junior blew out his cheeks:

"They pass you? Good for them! I not only pass you; at present I'm a bałaguła driver, but later, oho! I may be a drozhki driver, and then I too shall go whistling under all your noses," he squealed.

"What of it?" Abrum senior turned on him. "The wind drives and sweeps away the rubbish."

"Serve him right!" Chaim confirmed.

"Wait!" Byumen said. "It's Satan that teaches: 'Don't be the last.' Satan says: 'The one who's last gets it in the neck.' "

They began to grow excited. Abrum junior stammered:

"And so he should; he shouldn't be the last. Let him either catch up or die."

"On the contrary," Byumen instructed him. "If you drive too fast you break your neck, but if you're left behind you're left. He's lower than the dust, and that's why he wins. Old Bercunio Wajzer of Kosów always tells — "

"He doesn't any longer, he's dead!" Chaim broke in.

"What d'you mean by dead?" Byumen asked impatiently. "He tells me. When the gate creaks on Kosów market square everybody sees Bercunio walking out through the gate, a white shade. What difference is there? He's just the same now as before. And he still carries a heavy jug of milk, so that everybody can have a drink."

"A great Rothschild, he wants to give everybody a drink!"

"Not a Rothschild at all; he's hospitable, he looks after his cow, feeds it, and cleans it; the cow doesn't stint the milk from him, and he doesn't regret giving it to others. 'Hospitality is more important than going early to the synagogue,' says that great . . . What's his name?" he turned to Abrum senior.

"Rabbi Dimi," Abrum senior hastened to reply. "Not only that, but Rabbi Yehudah says even more dangerously: 'To receive a guest is more important than to receive God for the Sabbath.' "

Byumen smiled, and drawled amiably:

"Exactly, exactly; when Bercunio comes out of his gate with the jug of milk he invites everyone quietly, very quietly, like a cat lapping up milk."

Chaim and Abrum junior both went for him simultaneously, as though by agreement.

"Now he is lapping even more softly," Abrum made the tasteless joke.

"What's milk to him?" said Chaim. "He's always going for fish."

"Don't talk rubbish!" Byumen roared. "You're lying! He never eats fish when I'm around."

Chaim tittered:

"What do I get by lying? I didn't say he eats fish, I say he goes for fish. He told me once: 'What is eating in this world to me? Maize polenta with milk, milk with maize polenta, water, and in the autumn apple cider. That's good enough for me. But up above, ho-ho, there will be special dishes there, I shall eat Leviathan day and night.' I heard him myself. I had such a longing for Leviathan that I fled."

"Get away, you stupid liar; do you know what Leviathan is?" Byumen demanded.

"It's only a great fish."

"To the stupid it's only a fish, but to the Hasid—"

"To the Hasid everything's the wrong way round," Abrum junior provoked him.

Abrum senior poured oil on the troubled waters.

"It isn't the wrong way round, it's the reverse, and that's something more. You go on, Reb Byumen; and you listen, Abrum!"

"Bercunio tells of a man who couldn't help being last," Byumen said. "We know already who's the last, the one all the others have overtaken. It's the bałaguła driver. So it seems to us, but it really isn't so.

"The man who was last had turned his hand to everything—to water-carrying, cobbling, tailoring, and glazing; and everything was bad. Not at all bad really, only he was hot and impatient, and so he was the greatest of warriors. He worried terribly: this one's thirsty, that one's naked, the other's barefoot, and the wind blows into another's room. He worried more and more; he worried over everything. Everything, you know that's not nothing. And so he became the most patient, and that made him the last.

"At first he was a water-carrier, he had to earn his living somehow. He walked stoutly, but he was the last, because he carried the water from a long way off, from the purest of springs right below Ihrec, so Bercunio says. He earned enough to live, for he ate as little as possible, and he was the last in that too. Nobody thought anything of him; the girls showed no interest in him, even illness had no appetite for him. He was tall, thin, and all bones.

"Finally he bought skins, some glass, and cloth. And what of it? He trusted people; they stole all the skins from him. He was polite, and he stepped out of the way; so he fell under a cart, and all his glass was broken. Lambs came down shivering with cold from the upland, and he made them jackets. What sort of tailor was he? For lambs. He was the very last.

"Now he didn't buy any more skins, cloth, or glass. Where could he get the money to buy them with? He walked stoutly, he went all the way back, very far into the mountains, to where there is material that you can make into skins and cloth and glass. Meanwhile his former playmates had grown up and become masters and he had gone ahead as far as Kołomyja and out into the world, but he had gone the other way. There in the mountains, out of sand, grass and clay he made such materials as he needed. He was inclined to go even farther along that high path, for farther on there's material from which you can make even more, and still farther on there's material from which you can make everything. But no! He turned back; once more he was quite the last on both the one and the other upland track. But he had his own material. And so he makes everything, not at all badly, in fact rather too well, for he wants it to be the best, and so he makes it not for the fashion, not for today, for he makes it perfectly. And meanwhile the fashion's changed. Everybody is hurrying along in order to be right on time, they chase after fashion, and tumble over. In the end they hurried along after Satan in accordance with his commandments, one trampled on another, and then they tumbled into Gehenna. All that generation perished, and only the Last was left.

"Then the Lord God made up the accounts, and looked: the Last was left, because he had made the best. He had stitched shoes, taking his measure from God; where are the people to make such shoes for? He painted the glass in heavenly azure, such as God needs; for Him everything is transparent, He alone is veiled. On the glass he paints fishes, birds, stars, to the design of the creator. Then he makes a cloak for God. Why for God? Because he didn't cut the cloth, or stitch it, or patch it, only made it broad and warm, so that it should last.

"God's antagonist, Satan, Samael, also had a look. He was upset. 'Everything's flown away and disappeared, and now new ones are rising from the earth to outvie one another; only this man is sticking in one place and making a cloak.' Thinks Samael: 'I know what I'll do, it's simple. In the Scriptures it says that the angel stands and the man walks. This man walks stoutly, we'll make him a runner, we'll entice him into outrunning others. But what is to be done with such as have no desire to outrun others? Send him to a school for runners, to learn.'

"As it happened it was Yom Kippur, the Day of Judgment. And Samael flew up into the Presence of the Judgment, where all the sons of God were presenting themselves to the Lord. 'Whence comest thou, Samael?' the Lord asks. 'From going to and fro on earth, and from walking up and down on it.' 'But did you see that just man from the Bojans?' Samael could not reply to the Lord as he once had in Job: 'Doth Job fear God for naught?' For the Last was not Job, he had nothing except what he had made himself. Samael knows the Scriptures, he wanted to test the Lord, and he answered quite differently, also from the Book of Job, 'Shall mortal man be more just than God? Shall a man be more pure than his Maker?' The Lord had the Last man's account ready on the table in front of him, and he laughed at Samael: 'But perhaps you'd like to take something from him, Samael, as was done to Job? Perhaps a couple of thousand camels, or a thousand sheep, or his servants, or his children perhaps?' Samael saw quite clearly what was afoot: 'Please, Illustrious Judgment, I could take from Job, for he was rich; but this is a poor man, he's the Last. Will the Illustrious Judgment allow me to give him something? There's no other way of testing a poor wretch.' 'Give him what you like, I allow it,' the Lord laughs. And Samael flew down on earth.

"Samael did not look down on the Last from above as though from a town hall, like the great gentlemen do, like our Pan Ajbigman, for instance; for his business is different. 'Good morning, Reb Last, and a good New Year,' he said politely. 'I'd like to give you something for the New Year.' 'Thank you, Rabbi Samael, and excuse me,' said the Last. 'I can't accept anything, for I've nothing to repay you with; I'm not ready with my work, I can't even get it done.'

'The greatest present you could have would be learning, you shall go to school,' said Samael. 'What school?' the Last asked. 'To a Hasid school,' Samael swiftly replied, 'the most humble of schools, so that you can learn to walk like a little child, so that you can walk properly, for man is intended to walk and not stick in one place. No offence meant, Reb Last.' 'To walk properly?' the Last says. 'Good, teacher, and thank you. I shall try to show my gratitude. There is no greater sign of gratitude to a teacher than a bright pupil.'

"Samael teaches him, the Last does everything properly, walks stoutly, marches as best he can, he had a better step than I have. One-two, one-two, he outstrips the others. 'Bravo!' Samael cries. 'Why, Reb Last, you're already the First now.' As soon as he had said this, the Last thought: 'On the contrary! Why have I always got to take steps forward? Who will go to the rear?' So he turns round and marches back. And he had a good step, he simply flew back, then he turned round again and overtook the others. Satan rejoiced continually. But then the Last remembered: 'This isn't quite right either; who's going to walk at the side?' And so he goes, one-two, one-two, to the right. Satan was a little discontented at that, for to go to the right is to go against him; but, growing impatient, he commanded his own people: 'To the devil! To the right!' Now it was obvious that the Last outstripped them all. But the Last says: 'No! Excuse me, but this isn't right; is the left side of the world a step-child? This can't be allowed.' And off he goes with all his might to the left. The antagonist of God was rather pleased that he'd gone to the left, for after all, he was Samael, the head of the left, and so he cried again: 'To the left! The left is on top!' The Last walked stoutly, but meanwhile the others had torn off to the right and, even though it was to the right, they flew straight into hell. Satan went after them to make sure that they too did not slip out of his hands somehow. And that was the second generation lost.

"The Last was of no use either to human beings or to Satan. But he was of use to God; he remained the Last, he lived long, he was quite the last on earth. He scattered like ripe seed when the wind blows. But when he fell asleep the Fish descended from heaven to carry him away. On the earth everything was made transparent, all the waters were quite transparent, and began to roar, all the fishes splashed terribly, and rejoiced that their breed was on top. Even the earth became transparent, you could see right down to hell. The people in hell took fright, for they were afraid that they would be transparent too; so they hid in dens, in the caves of hell. The Fish did not bother about them, only about the Last. 'Please, Reb the Last, sit down at me and have a taste.' And who is it that's eating the Fish high above, in heaven? It's the Last. But do you think he cuts the Fish with a knife, and bites it? No, he sucks at the Fish. But perhaps he stuffs himself, stuffs his belly like a sack with hay? No; Leviathan is transparent. Gaze up at heaven; you can't see in the daytime, only in the night.' And the Last also was transparent; only when man is completely transparent will he taste of Leviathan. Someone must be the last. The Hasid understands that, he wants that; but he isn't sure of himself, and many of them are fearful: 'But perhaps I want to surpass someone, perhaps I shall drive with the wind to Gehenna?' But that's absurd; the one who's really last is not afraid, the wind doesn't carry him away, the devil doesn't entice him, he's not rubbish. Such a man lies on his cart with his navel upward and gazes at Leviathan. So Bercunio says." Byumen sighed.

He turned abruptly to his horse. "Well, Prince, what do you make of that?" He questioned the old gray aloud, supplying the answers himself, while the horse looked at him mournfully. "Does the finest horse have to be the last? On the contrary! But why, Prince? Because other horses are not like human beings. And why else? Because a sincere horse doesn't have to be a worrier."

Satisfied with this examination, he turned back to the human beings. At once Abrum junior burst out in a croaking tone: "But what I say is that you've got everything crooked. First the wind's the best because it's at once where it has to be, and then the last is the best."

"You have to take that in the opposite sense," Abrum senior suggested. "He doesn't fly with the wind at all; his body is in dust in the earth, but that doesn't matter to him."

Balicki, the student at the theological college, took an interest in the talk: "And those others will all fly off to Gehenna, to break their necks?"

"To break their necks," Byumen repeated.

The youthful theologian was troubled at this. "Among us it's arranged so that one Righteous ransoms all . . . But you say they break their necks and nobody troubles about them?"

"No," Abrum senior protested energetically. "What's the Chubah for? Don't you know, sir?"

"I don't. What does it mean?"

"I can't talk like Byumen; perhaps Reb Byumen will explain," he excused himself.

"The Chubah, may it please your reverence, young sir," Byumen began to explain, "is just as if we were all riding from Kołomyja to Kosów, and we're already in the beech woods, on the hill at Jabłonowo; it's very nice there, and cheerful, we have a rest for food, the passengers talk, and wait, and pay. But then from the hill we see — terror, horror, Kołomyja is on fire! But I take command, I shout to my bałagułas, 'Hand the money back! Gallop to Kołomyja, carry water, save the town!' The Chubah is the return the Lord God gives to such people. The Scripture says: "The Lord says, I am Hasid, I shall not be angry for ever.' And when the Last sucks Leviathan a great breath will blow, everybody will return from Gehenna and then there will be a movement back upward."

"But will that one let them go?" the student asked.

"Which one?"

"The evil power, the head of the left, as you put it."

"Samael? What say has he in it? He'll fly up with them?"

"Satan will fly off to God?" Pan Ajbigman laughed loudly and provocatively.

"He's no longer Satan then," Byumen continued. "After all, he's Samael. Pan Ajbigman will allow me, but we shall see who laughs last. The Last will be the greatest *zaddik*[2] of all, the greatest of all worriers. And so from Leviathan he will laugh heartily, and at Samael too, for after all he's the teacher. And he will draw him up. A great wind! Samael's poison will melt, the venom in his words will drop away, and that which is divine will remain."

"So the Great Rabbi of Safed writes, that's certain," Abrum senior added quietly.

Looking down on them from his height, Muraszko, the tallest of them all, laughed sourly and muttered: "Pah! It would be a fine thing, me dear sir, if I should be the last and arrived to attend to the floors in Krzyworównia after the wedding was over. A good excuse for the negligent who have no sense of honor. Let's be going."

Abrum senior again intervened vivaciously: "Honor, master? But what has just been said? It has to be taken contrarily and from the other side."

"From the other side?" the craftsman snorted. "And then gather the whole band of hell's brood to your heart from that side—and even the devil too? Pah! Each has his own place and rank."

"A fine place, to sit forever in dung at the bottom of hell," Byumen laughed.

Muraszko retained his gravity. "If I were the devil, pah! I wouldn't allow myself to be gathered up by that Jew, that Last Fellow; each has his own honor."

"Well, and it will be to each according to his honor." Byumen consoled him. "But please, master, please take your place."

The master had been assigned the place of honor, beside Byumen. His seat was tightly packed with hay, so that it should not sink. The master musician, Szpilbaum, had his place just behind him, to one side. He sat down quickly, with his back to the others; he did not take up much room, but he had plenty of space for his belly. Muraszko clambered carefully on to the wagon, and Byumen spoke to his gray:

---

2. The Hebrew word for "righteous one." It was used primarily with reference to the Hasid rabbis. According to Hebrew mythology there are only thirty-six zaddikim in the world. No one knows who they are, but their mission in life is to save the world from perdition.

"Well, Prince, it can't be helped; we've had our rest, now we move!" Prince neighed and set off prematurely; the master overbalanced, and jumped down. Byumen soothed the nag: "Wait, Prince; don't be so impatient!"

Abrum senior dared to speak up yet again:

"That Last *zaddik,* he needn't be a Jew at all."

At that an indescribable hubbub broke out. They all talked, shouted, bawled at once.

"The greatest worrier of all, and not a Jew?" Yudka snorted.

"The last bałaguła, and not a Jew?" Abrum junior croaked.

"Righteous, and not a Jew?" Chaim tittered venomously.

"A *zaddik,* and not a Jew?" the students shouted one above another.

"Let me speak!" Byumen out-shouted them all.

"But you're telling us about your own Jewish faith," the youthful theologian said, very much to the point.

"Not at all," Byumen laughed. "The last *zaddik* is only the greatest of worriers. He's impatient, he's hot; Bercunio says that when someone is hurt, he's hurt doubly. All the worries of the world flood over him. And so he is patient."

"That's worse than worries," Abrum senior intervened. " 'Sighs even before eating, but the groans roar like water,' so it is written."

Chaim tittered.

"May God grant that all our competitors and enemies be *zaddikím!* "

Byumen agreed with Abrum senior.

"It's much worse than worry, that's true; but today there's a wedding, so we don't talk about that. All the same, he doesn't have to be a Jew. Abrum, tell us what the Great One of Spain[3] writes about the Hasidim of other nations."

Abrum senior recited the passage without hesitation:

"Not only He; Moshe Ben Maimon says the same. It says quite clearly in the Tosefta Sanhedrin[4] 'The Hasidim among the goyim will also occupy a place in the future world.' They will be partners."

"Exactly, exactly; take your place, please, master, for it's late," Byumen urged them on.

"What's the hurry for? The Last doesn't hurry," Chaim sneered.

"It's just the reverse," Abrum junior agreed, growing insolent.

As he seated himself on his hummock-like seat, Master Muraszko roared through his laughter: "Jewish twisting, my dear sir; but all the same, without you life would be very sad." He seated himself higher than the others, and laughed with satisfaction.

"Well, Prince, this time we're really off." Prince gave his master a searching

---

3. A reference to Maimonides.

4. The Tosefta is a collection of tannaic teaching related to the Mishnah, or legal codification of Jewish Oral Law. The Tannaim were sages of the first and second centuries A.D. Sanhedrin here refers to the fourth tractate in the Mishnah order of *Nezikim* ("damages"), which deals mostly with legal and judicial matters.

look. "You see him." Byumen pointed to the gray. "When he's alone with me he talks. I mean, he doesn't talk yet," Byumen corrected himself, "but one word from him will be wiser than all that Abrum junior says day and night for a whole year."

A general laugh drowned Abrum junior's retort.

"Well, Wołoch, excuse me." Byumen squinted at the other horse. "You can sleep after dinner in Jaworowo, but now, get a move on."

Once more there was a surge of movement round the vehicles, and without any lengthy ceremony, without shouting or driving round the town, the wagons set off; it was just before six. This time Pan Ajbigman did not accompany the bałagułas to the bridge. Having collected the money, he said goodbye with a contemptuous stare at the people who had to travel on bałagułas. . . .

The rattling pace at once put the company into a joyful mood. However, it must be remembered that they consisted of various groups of people who were unknown to one another: craftsmen, members of the choir, temporary servants, and the Jewish wedding band — people who had been invited to the wedding individually by name, people invited in groups, and people not invited at all. At first they hardly knew what to talk about to one another, but the spirit of the bałagułas and the wind, too, brought them together. As soon as they crossed the River Prut caps and hats began to fly off; the flying headgear had to be watched patiently, and then, when it landed, one had to shoot after it like an arrow before the wind began to play about again. This called for attention and cooperation.

At last one of the students, with the wind for accompaniment, began to sing the old steppe song:

> Oy, in the field the grave talked with the wind:
> Breathe, stormy wind, that I may not turn black.

The chorus was taken up by all the wagons:

> That I may not turn black, that I may not be spoilt,
> That on me the grass may grow and be green.

As soon as the steeds moderated their pace, Pan Szpilbaum opened his violin case. Without saying much of anything, he tuned the instrument, whistled, roused the other musicians one after another with his finger, and all the band took up the chorus:

> Neither sun will warm nor wind will blow,
> But in the field, by the roadside, the green grass will show.

"Uva! Uva!" Byumen shouted powerfully. "Uva!" the other drivers repeated. They cracked their whips to the rhythm of the song. And so, with whips cracking, the wagons clattering, the wind brawling, the bałagułas moved off through the azure October dawn, through the mountain villages, slowly, like Venetian gondolas laden with song.

Only Abrum senior did not crack his whip, did not shout. He just whirled his whip above his head as if it were a standard, and smiled pleasantly toward the mountain through a window of wind. He smiled and sighed, as though he had taken to heart the saying of Master Nachman of Bracław, from whose yellowing books the praying Bojans drew their happiness: "Sighing is a good, sorrow an evil." Abrum's full beard flapped constantly so that more than one spectator, or ironist, would say: "There's some artist in the bałaguła coach-box!"

In Jabłonowo, at the steps of the first pass, the first halt was made. Hardly were the feed bags hung on the horses when Abrum junior, chuckling shrilly, fired a readied arrow at Byumen:

"Reb Petranker! A hundred percent right exists, that's evident."

"Who says?" Byumen retorted casually.

"It's true, for the Last is a hundred percent right against Samael, isn't that so? Or don't you think so?"

Byumen shook his head negatively, replying patiently: "No, he doesn't; he has to give him the rest."

"What rest?"

"Go to the Bojans, and if you don't make too much commotion you'll find out."

In Jabłonowo, in Pistyń, in Kosów more guests took their seats. By the time they had reached the halting-places they all knew one another: the Kołomyja people, the masters, the musicians, the students, the servants, and those identifiable as "wedding travelers generally."

In the track of the wind, they rode into the mountains.

■ Czesław Miłosz
Native Realm: A Search for Self-Definition (1959)

[The best-known Polish poet of the twentieth century, Czesław Miłosz was awarded the Nobel Prize for Literature in 1980. Apart from his many volumes of poetry, he is also the author of several books of prose, including novels, critical essays, and a book of reminiscences about growing up in Lithuania titled *Rodzinna Europa* ("Native Europe," literally, but translated into English under the title *Native Realm*, 1959). Czesław Miłosz has lived in the United States since 1961, when he accepted a professorship in the Department of Slavic Languages at the University of California at Berkeley.

Native Realm is the closest Miłosz has come to writing his autobiography. The pages in it devoted to Polish-Jewish relations in his native city of Wilno (now Vilnius, the capital of Lithuania) in the interwar period, and his remarks on Polish attitudes toward Jews in general, are an objective yet poignant record of the author's understanding of the tragic dimension of the Polish-Jewish relationship.]

European Jews used to call Wilno the Northern Jerusalem, and rightly considered it their cultural capital. Here were institutions of learning (subsequently transferred to New York); here the Zionist movement developed a strong center; and here the pupils of the local Hebrew schools contributed, perhaps more than anyone else, to the rebirth of the Biblical language in Israel. In the tiny stores where I used to buy stamps, there was always a collection box with a Star of David on it for Zionist causes. A whole community with multiple currents, orientations, and strivings had grown up within this city, famous for its exegetes of the Talmud and its vehement disputes between rabbis and Hasidim — in other words, it was an old abode for the Jews, whom it would have been difficult to call newcomers. . . .

The Catholic and Jewish communities (some districts were almost entirely Jewish) lived within the same walls, yet as if on separate planets. Contact was limited to everyday business matters; at home different customs were observed, different newspapers were read, different words were used to communicate — the vast majority of Jews spoke Yiddish, an emancipated minority spoke Russian, and a very small percentage used Polish. . . .

The isolation of the Jews in this area was an old story. The reasons must be sought in differences of occupation (the Jews were merchants amid a rural population) and of religion (the rhythms of Catholic and Jewish customs did not coincide). Political anti-Semitism appeared, however, very late. It was devised by Tsarist officials, when the monarchy was already deteriorating, as an instrument of *divide et impera*. Before that, there were rare cases of crowds getting out of

Czesław Miłosz, *Native Realm: A Search for Self-Definition,* trans. Catherine S. Leach (Garden City, N.Y.: Doubleday, 1968), 91–95, 99, 103–6.

hand in a context of religious fanaticism, but the quarrels among Christians — for example the battles with stones and clubs between Catholics and Calvinists, which filled the seventeenth century in our city — attracted more attention. . . .

Politics changed that. The Catholic population, in its furious resistance to Russia, gradually began to look upon Jews as a separate nationality that was not even an ally, because the game they were playing with the authorities was not the Polish game. Thus the old image of the Jews as the enemies of Christ was replaced by a new one: young men in high-necked Russian shirts, rallying to a foreign civilization. The Socialist movement, which was becoming stronger and stronger, split into two currents: anti-Russian (independence for those countries seized by the Empire) and pro-Russian (one revolutionary state formed from all the lands of the monarchy). Russian-speaking Jews (called Litvaks) were the mainstay of the second current, only to become, in revolutionary Russia, fomenters of all kinds of heresies.

The emotional attitude of Christians in that part of the world bore traces of various stratifications. From the old *Respublica*, with its rural and patriarchal customs, there had remained the idea of "our Jews" without whom life was unimaginable, who comprised an integral part of the human landscape, and whom it would never have entered anyone's head to disturb in the exercise of their age-old commercial functions or in the ordering of their internal affairs. A relatively recent acquisition was the idea of a Jew as a man who dresses, eats, and lives like everyone else but who uses a different language. The hostility toward him doubtless involved a resentment at the breaking of caste barriers: he violated the code that everyone ought to "know his place." But mainly it involved a conflict the past had not known, which after the First World War gave impetus to racial or economic arguments imported mostly from Warsaw, where the situation was different. Poles of Jewish extraction were fairly numerous in ethnic Poland, but in Wilno such individuals were still treated as exceptions . . .

The psychological portraits of anti-Semites that writers are fond of drawing rarely get to the heart of the matter because they overlook those peculiar traits that belong to geography and history rather than to psychology. The Age of Enlightenment made itself felt among the Jewish masses inhabiting the Polish-Lithuanian *Respublica* in a movement to oppose religious taboos and the ghetto. This drive appeared just at the time the *Respublica* was losing its independence. Three capitals became the new centers of attraction: St. Petersburg, Vienna, and Berlin. . . . But the flight from the medieval community also took another direction, provided by Polish schools and universities, which gave Polish literature and science many eminent representatives. This split among the enlightened was as wide as the distance that separated them both from the little closed cells of the diaspora. The Zionist movement stirred up a new ferment, and perhaps it is not accidental that its leader came from the eastern part of the former *Respublica*, where ethnic diversity inhibited fusion with any one collectivity.

It would be a mistake to draw analogies with France or Germany; it would also be hard to count any group whose numbers in the cities varied from thirty to seventy percent a minority. The complex distinctions within each community and the existence of an ill-defined middle stratum (where exactly did the professor, the doctor, the actor, the writer of Jewish extraction belong?) were reflected in the many types of relationships between people, which also changed, of course, according to the region. In general, Poles were unusually aware of Jews and anti-Semitic. Yet if ever the object of their oddly ambivalent feelings were somehow missing, they would be overcome by melancholy: "Without the Jews it's *boring.*" Many political movements and periodicals found their reason for existence in anti-Semitism because they appreciated the blessing of such a convenient theme—without which life would be empty—for demagoguery. No cabaret could get by without Jewish jokes, and the pungent gallows humor peculiar to cities like Warsaw bears the clear stamp of Jewish popular humor. This symbiosis prevented indifference. At the opposite pole it produced specimens of philo-Semites for whom even non-Jewish women had no appeal because they were regarded as intellectually inferior.

The Jews helped to form a complex in me thanks to which, at an early age, I was already lost for the Right. The nationalist party—the party of the "right-thinking people"; that is, of the newly arrived petty bourgeoisie—came into being at the end of the last century and was active mainly in the Vistula River basin, where it combated the Socialists. Its principal appeal was the vague but positive aura that surrounds the word *nation*. This was to be a linguistic, cultural, religious (meaning Catholic), and soon racial unity, although more than one descendant of a rabbi could be found among its most energetic propagandists. . . .

The whole country was in any case permeated by an unhealthy atmosphere. Christians, when they said that someone was a Jew, lowered their voices as if a shameful disease were being mentioned, or added, "He's a jew, but he's decent." Worse still, the same scale of values was more or less adopted by "assimilated" Jews who were diligently erasing their traces. In such conditions every personal contact evaded the laws of friendship and brotherhood, only to fall captive to a situation. One: "He thinks that I am a Jew." The other: "He thinks that I think that he is a Jew." Or the pyramid grows. One: "He thinks that I suspect him of thinking that I am a Jew." The other: "He thinks that I think that he suspects me of thinking that he is a Jew." There is simply no way out of such a situation. . . .

I present the period between the two wars in condensed form. Perhaps this is unfair, since everything was in motion. At first, the Right stressed democratic legality, but gradually, under the influence of a hopeless economic depression and notions borrowed from Germany, it acquired a totalitarian hue. People shouted about a "national revolution," and the political scene swarmed with petty tyrants whose ambitions, it must be admitted, resembled those of the later Arabian dictators more than they did those of Hitler or Mussolini. Demagoguery turned its sharp edge against foreign capital and "Judeo-plutocrats," which students as well as the small-town *Lumpenproletariat* took as a signal for assaults on peddlers' stands. Wretches battled against wretches.

In Wilno during the spring of 1934, disorders of this sort lasted for three days. They were touched off by a quarrel over cadavers. The "Radical-Nationalist" cell at the university had scored an important victory because the students who worked in the anatomical laboratory declared a strike, demanding that the supply of Jewish cadavers for dissection be proportional to the number of Jews in the Department of Medicine. The strike became a street demonstration, which headed toward the former ghetto district, breaking windows along the way and beating up pedestrians. However, it ran up against the resistance of strong Jewish butchers and freight loaders. A cobblestone torn from the paving struck one of the students on the head, and he died several hours later. The city found itself at the mercy of mob fury. Shops were bolted up, and people went into hiding, keeping an eye on the danger through cracks in their shutters, while the rabble surged down the middle of the street in search of victims. The police were indecisive. They tried to break into the student dormitory where the leaders lived, but the besieged used fire hoses to pour water on the police from upstairs, and finally they dispersed. Their hesitancy was the result of inner frictions within the government of "the Colonels," where elements in favor of flattering not the Leftist but the Rightist opposition were steadily gaining prominence. To these elements, "Radical-Nationalism" appeared as the wave of the future, which should not be obstructed.

In defense of the Poles it must be said that despite the hooliganism in that part of Europe, they betrayed less of an urge to strike at the life or health of their neighbors than one might have expected. Anti-Semitic incidents usually stopped at material damages. Though excitable and anarchic, the people of this nationality seem not to lose moral restraints, even in a crowd, and an impulse of hatred rather quickly gives way to shame. They submit to discipline with difficulty, and only discipline can justify cruelties committed in cold blood. Thus the foreigner who tries to understand Polish politics constantly runs into the unexpected. Party divisions are not very clear; they are held together more by spiritual kinship between individuals than by an agreement on platforms. Assassination of one's adversaries, that most acceptable of twentieth-century tactics, is applied unwillingly because it compromises the perpetrators in the eyes of public opinion. Almost every Polish system eludes outside definitions. Under the dictatorship of "the Colonels," the parliament was a fiction and one concentration camp was opened (so that Poland would not lag behind its neighbors), yet outright Fascists, though the government wooed them, were an opposition force. The Communist Party was illegal, yet a number of journals propounded its ideas, and dignitaries of the regime hobnobbed with revolutionary poets who were protected from jail by a telephone call from above. . . .

It is hard for me to write about the Jews, because no small effort is demanded

if one is to distinguish these prewar tensions from one of the greatest tragedies of
history: the slaughter of some three million "non-Aryan" Polish citizens by the
Nazis. As an eyewitness to the crime of genocide, and therefore deprived of the
luxury of innocence, I am prone to agree with the accusations brought against
myself and others. In reality, however, it is not easy to judge, because the price of
aiding the victims of terror was the death penalty. Individual behavior depended
upon too many circumstances and motives to be able to establish for certain the
connection with prewar anti-Semitic tendencies. Religious motives (convents particularly distinguished themselves in rescue missions), personal courage, neigh-
borly ties, or greed for money clashed with physical impossibility, fear, or apathy.
Blackmailers, recruited from the scum of the citizenry, constituted a grave danger for refugees from the ghetto, which presented an opportunity for easy plunder. If some political organizations in Poland had openly collaborated, as they
did in other countries Hitler conquered, the picture would be clearer. But Polish
collaborationists were simply killed. So any Nazi sympathizers (and there were
some) had at least to keep up the appearances of noncollaboration. The extreme
Right had not, of course, disappeared; it fed the ranks of the underground Home
Army and the National Armed Forces (a not very numerous Fascist group). If
the Home Army permitted more than one furtive slaying of Jews who had taken
cover in the forests, it was a decision made by individual officers or soldiers, and it
depended on personal attitudes. The National Armed Forces, on the other hand,
officially planned many of their raids. As for the Left, both Socialist and Communist parties entered the war either weak or divided, and it was not they who set
the tone for the Resistance movement.

The responsibility for the Jews being regarded as a *different nationality* by
most of the population lay, above all, with nationalist writers and journalists. At
a hypothetical court trial, however, they could appeal to the schools, the text-
books, and historical conditions, since it was, after all, historical conditions that
had prevented the two "nations" in Polish cities from merging into a single whole.
Nevertheless one must still charge these writers with irresponsibility in submit-
ting to irrational impulses and with stupidity. Similarly, the Home Army leaders
acted like Molière's Monsieur Jourdain, who did not know that he was speaking
prose. They condemned the whole ideology of Nazism, but at the same time refused to admit Jews into their forest units; this seemed to them quite natural. If
any of them are alive today, they would doubtless be astonished to hear themselves accused of racial discrimination.

A country or a state should endure longer than an individual. At least this
seems to be in keeping with the order of things. Today, however, one is constantly
running across survivors of various Atlantises. Their lands in the course of time
are transformed in memory and take on outlines that are no longer verifiable.
Similarly, between-the-wars Poland has sunk beneath the surface. In her place a

new organism has appeared on the map, with the same name but within different borders, an ironic fulfilment of the nationalist dream, now clear of its minorities, or at least with a very negligible number. Flames consumed the old synagogues; the foot of some passerby in the city suburbs trips over the remains of a grave-stone with Hebrew letters—all that is left of the old cemeteries.

■ Leon Kruczkowski (1900–1962)
"Cultural Anti-Semitism" (1937)

[Leon Kruczkowski's literary fame in the interwar period rested chiefly on the controversy stirred up by his novel *Kordian i cham* (*Kordian and the Boor,* 1932), a Marxist interpretation of the class aspect of the November Insurrection of 1830. After returning to Poland in 1945, after five years in a German prisoner-of-war camp, Kruczkowski switched from the novel to the drama. His most popular play, *Niemcy* (*The Germans,* 1949), which also enjoyed a certain international renown, deals with the moral dimension of the behavior of a German professor and his family toward the Nazi regime.]

"Cultural anti-Semitism?" And what may that be? you ask surprised. "Cultural anti-Semitism" — why it sounds paradoxical, more or less as if someone said "benevolent cannibalism," or "intelligent stupidity." What can anti-Semitism, that boorish weapon of every obscurantism, of nationalistic fraudulence, of the militant church of social reaction, have in common with culture? *Cultural* anti-Semitism? The Black Hundreds and "pogromists," the shatterers of Jewish shops — the avant-garde of civilization?

Obviously, nothing!

In giving my present remarks the title "Cultural Anti-Semitism," I am far from ascribing cultural features to the phenomenon under discussion. In this case, "cultural anti-Semitism" means anti-Semitism in culture, anti-Semitic currents in cultural life — in learning, in art, in literature; in short, everything the German would characterize as "Kultur-antisemitismus."

Although anti-Semitism has always been, and still is, an "ideology" of the mob (and also, even today above all, of the "educated" mob), it is not limited exclusively to the material spheres of life (chiefly the economic spheres) that are most important to it; it encroaches as well, with its dull and primitive club, onto the steeper levels of so-called spiritual creativity. Perhaps you think it does so for creative purposes? So as to enrich the achievements of human thought and noble beauty? What pretense! Cultural-creative ambitions are organically opposed to anti-Semitism (as, in general, to any nationalism), despite the weighty phrases about "national" culture, "national" art, and "national" literature. No, the tribal "ideologists" and adherents of hatred are not concerned with constructive enterprises.

Then with what?

The answer to this question comes rather easily.

In its principal, socioeconomic source, anti-Semitism develops under the

Leon Kruczkowki, "Antysemityzm kulturalny," in *Polacy o żydach: Zbiór artykułów z przedruku* (Warsaw: Wydawnictwo Polskiej Unii Zgody Narodów, 1937), 27–35.

action of two driving forces. One is the conflict of economic interests, the competitive struggle of two factions of bourgeois society for participation in the squeezing out of profits (in the given instance, primarily profits from mercantile mediation). It is a fact that waves of anti-Semitism always gather and arise in periods of economic crisis, when in violently contracting economic life the competition of interests within the framework of *the same social class* assumes particularly fierce forms.

But another phenomenon inevitably arises in periods of economic crisis: the growth of social tensions, inter-class opposition, attitudes dangerous to the existing "order." Attempts to intercept these attitudes of radicalizing masses and direct them into channels of racist-nationalistic folly unharmful to the social order becomes the distinct second impetus to anti-Semitism, and the driving force for the stirring up of its waves.

Class anti-Semitism then clearly develops against the backdrop of socioeconomic crises. Amid these fires, the reigning bourgeoisie wants to kill two birds with the same stone: (1) It wants to get rid of Jewish bourgeois competition, or to limit and weaken it, in order to ferret out more grazing ground for itself; and (2) It wants to lead astray and disarm the growing social radicalism of the peasant, workers', and petty bourgeois masses. The pogrom anti-Semitism of Tsarist Russia after 1905 elaborated in this respect classical, and to this day, emulated "methods," which nevertheless — as we know — neither saved the tsardom, nor the Russian bourgeoisie, from a well-deserved fate.

The precise reflection of the above twofold sense of anti-Semitic currents can be demonstrated in "cultural" anti-Semitism. The laws governing the bases of the social order obtain as well in its cultural superstructure. Like every production in capitalism, so-called spiritual creativity similarly possesses, speaking in social terms, the character of a *commodity*. It has its own economics, its booms and crises, its "market," "demand," and "supply"; it is, in short, the plane of certain interests. This fact cannot be obscured by any lofty declamation; whoever knows official "cultural life" from the inside knows full well the kinds of often cynical battles, games, and operations of a decidedly economic character that swirl about there. What is more, the most brutal "knights of [cultural] industry" are usually those who are the fondest of discoursing most affectedly on, for example, "the writer's calling!" It is entirely understandable. In capitalism, cultural creators (writers, artists) are people who derive from their creativity — according to the laws of the market — the means of subsistence, revenues, and earnings. And precisely from this point of view, "cultural" anti-Semitism is, to a certain degree, an expression of a competitive economic conflict among certain groups of bourgeois producers of literature and art.[1]

1. How strangely in bourgeois cultural life does economics entwine with "ideology," as for example, the capital competitive conflict that occurred recently between the "national" weekly *Prosto z mostu* (*Straight from the Shoulder*) and the *Wiadomości Literackie* (*Literary News*), which the Endeks [from N. D., National Democrats, the right-wing party of Roman Dmowski] decried as a "Jewish"

In Polish circumstances, this is a relatively new phenomenon. Up until the immediate prewar [World War I] years, the cultural life of the proprietary classes remained under the overpowering influence of a filtered gentry mind-set. Although it yielded once—after [the insurrection of] the year 1863—to the growing bourgeoisie in the economic and political spheres, the landed gentry did, however, in the long run exert a decisive influence on the atmosphere and character of cultural creativity the leading representatives of which indeed came mostly from this social class. This circumstance, as well as the progressive-democratic tendencies of the elite of the Polish intelligentsia at the time, can be ascribed wholly to the near absence of anti-Semitic currents in the prewar cultural life of the country. Quite the contrary, in fact, as concerns literature, one can point to many writers whose relationship to the Jews had all the features of an indisputable and often, to be sure, zealous friendliness, from the notorious "Judeophile" Mickiewicz to Konopnicka, Orzeszkowa, Zapolska, Żeromski, and numerous lesser figures.

The *urbanization* of Polish life, simultaneous with the reconstruction of the country after independence, and related to processes of postwar change in the world, decisively shattered the hegemony of gentry influences in the culture of the Polish proprietary classes. Elements of "native" bourgeois origin are gaining the advantage. In Polish circumstances, in view of the mixed demographic structure of the cities, this has meant the appearance of a relatively significant number of creators, writers and artists, of Jewish origin. And the Jews are a gifted nation, with an unusually high percentage of talented people who play a leading role in the cultural life of all nations. When we take this circumstance into account, as well as recall what was said earlier about the economic character of cultural creativity in the capitalist system, we understand at once an important spring in the mechanism of "cultural" anti-Semitism—the competitive conflict simply of "professional" interests among certain groups of bourgeois producers of "spiritual" goods.

Out of fairness, it must be said that the advocates of "cultural" anti-Semitism among us (with very few exceptions) are predominantly mediocre, weak, and third-rate talents. They lament most vocally the would-be "Jewification" of Polish cultural life for the purpose of presenting their own talentlessness, or spiritual infirmity, as an oppressed virtue, as a sacrifice to hostile Jewish competition. But a considerable majority of the more or less outstanding, or of the most outstanding, creators, writers, and artists of bourgeois "Aryan" origin do not nurture, or

---

journal. The conflict was all the more piquant in that it concerned the well-known "national" and anti-Semitic writer, Adolf Nowaczyński. This author wrote a cycle of painfully "revisionistic" articles about Mickiewicz. The first two of them were printed in *Prosto z mostu*, but the third—the most interesting—went instead to *Wiadomości Literackie*. At that point, the Endek weekly "unmasked" the Endek writer on the grounds that he "moved" to the "Jewish-Masonic" competition because of the higher honorarium offered Nowaczyński by *Wiadomości Literackie*. It would be hard to find a pithier illustration of the "ideological"-economic links of "cultural" anti-Semitism. [Original note by Kruczkowski.]

at least do not manifest, anti-Semitic feelings. Perhaps this is because the "Judeo-philic" traditions of Polish literature of the period of servitude, about which we spoke above, are in some measure still active. However, the deciding role—speaking candidly—is played by economic considerations. It is difficult to deny that the Jewish intelligentsia represents a very serious base of consumers of cultural creativity, literature, and art, one disproportionately larger than would be assumed from demographic relations. This is less the result of the economic predominance of the Jewish intelligentsia, for that is often completely problematic, than of the (sometimes only snobbish) drive for culture peculiar to this group of people, as well as their vivacity, and the direction of their internal interests and needs. Against this background, the evident obscurantism of the Polish bourgeoisie and petty gentry stands out vividly. Even in their economically stronger and purportedly intelligent branches, these strata weakly manifest cultural interests and needs. Rather they enjoy the easy and mindless, though expensive, pleasures of "comradely"—and "tavernly"—life. Hence the following paradoxical situation: Jews, to a considerable extent, are rescuing the economic bases of today's progressively contracting Polish bourgeois cultural creativity. As purchasers of books, frequenters of theaters, lectures, concerts, and so on, they represent to a certain degree that element without which the spiritual production of the Polish proprietary classes—which even so is barely clinging to life—would experience its final crisis.

But the economic moment, the moment of competitive envy of the more mediocre bourgeois Aryan creators in relation to the more fortunately talented artists of Jewish origin, still does not exhaust the question of anti-Semitism in cultural life. Another factor comes into play, of even greater importance than the other.

Speaking about anti-Semitism in general, we stated that it always appears in periods of great class conflicts, like a diversionary current endeavoring to mislead and channel in a false direction the growing social radicalism of the masses. Hence the social tensions of the age always find their expression in cultural life, in writing, in literature, and in art. On the one hand, progressive-liberal tendencies, which in the past animated the ruling class, disappear in cultural life; on the other hand, socially revolutionary currents, corresponding to the aspirations of the exploited classes, emerge in it. These two factors merge into a broader, and important, strain of "cultural" anti-Semitism considerably more perfidious than the economic. The perfidy rests, *inter alia,* on the rather stupid attribution of these socially radical currents in literature, for example, to "destructive" Jewish-Masonic influences. And it is at this point that an orgy of nonsense and fraudulence begins. Various dullards, "specialists" on "national" culture, phrase-mongers, Savonarolas of intellectuality from "Saxon" times, mobilize their quills in order to strike with their concealed points at the creative work of radicalizing peasant, worker, and petty bourgeois writers—and all beneath the cloak of anti-

Semitism. Their national-racist "criteria" lead to an obscurantistically understood "national" culture, and this "postulate" in turn to a campaign against worker-peasant, class, and international cultural currents.

The competitive bourgeois struggle, not so much of creators as of producers of culture, stirred up by mercenary journalistic-publicistic troublemakers, and the class diversion against progressive or revolutionary currents in culture are the two springs in the mechanism of anti-Semitism and, in general, of "cultural" nationalism. There are no lofty, no truly creative conflicts in all of this. Not a single great work of the human spirit has ever arisen amid the empty and clamorous uproar of national or racial egoisms, in the gloomy trenches of obscurantism, or in the marketplace of small, narrow interests of competitive cliques. The climate in which true and fruitful creativity grows is an atmosphere of struggles truly worthy of the name—struggles against violence, against injury and oppression, against political and social captivity, against the barbarity of primitive instincts, against systems of ignorance, meanness, and crime. It was in such an atmosphere that there arose the works of Shelley and Byron, Schiller and Mickiewicz, the works of Ibsen and Zola, Heine and Rimbaud, Tolstoy and Gorky, Romain Rolland and Barbusse—creators to whom the nationalists have no one to compare. . . .

■ Zygmunt Szymanowski (1873–1956)
"The Anti-Semitism of Academic Youth" (1937)

[Zygmunt Szymanowski was a professor of bacteriology at the University of Warsaw and a strong supporter of socialism in Poland.]

Anti-Semitism in our institutions of higher learning is no special discovery of academic youth, but simply the reflection, and a constituent part, of a current permeating our entire society. We will not linger here over its genesis. . . .

Young people, by nature susceptible and unprepared by school to deal with essential problems of social life, cling to simplistic anti-Semitic propaganda, beat up their Jewish colleagues, demonstrate noisily in lecture halls, and out on the street smash the windows of Jewish shops, and rough up Jews or those suspected of being Jewish.

Since last summer, slogans of anti-Semitism have been reverberating with a previously unheard-of ferocity. They recall the fraternal conflicts of 1905 and subsequent years.

The National Democratic Party has always willingly grazed in the field of youth. In comparison with the pre-independence period, the mass of academic youth has taken a decisive turn to the right. The socialists have become the minority.

In independent Poland, the National Democrats have prevailed in institutions of higher learning from the very beginning. This is true both for professors as well as students. Among the former, the "sanacja" has made certain inroads, though less than would seem to be the case. Among young people, socialists, communists, and in part peasant youth decisively oppose the Endeks. The "sanacja" youth, cocky because of the regime's moral and material support, turned out, in the beginning, in large numbers; but they failed to pull off a victory for the Endeks. Such a disposition of forces guarantees that even the riskiest undertakings of the Endeks can often count on success, and almost always on impunity, the more so since the young Endek enters a university already molded in advance by Endek teachers and instructors in Catholicism. State education in no way weakens the influence of Endek ideology. In such conditions anti-Semitic slogans can only spread like wildfire.

In the fall of last year the anti-Semitic storm raged with particular ferocity. It was accompanied by an unheard-of brutality. Collective attacks on individuals,

Zygmunt Szymanowski, "Antysemityzm młodzieży akademickiej," in *Polacy o Żydach: Zbiór artykułów z przedruku* (Warsaw: Wydawnictwo Polskiej Unii Zgody Narodów, 1937), 60–65. The article originally appeared in the weekly *Epoka* on October 5, 1936.

with even women not being spared, forcing people to run the gauntlet, expulsion not only from lecture halls but even from the grounds of a university, are common occurrences. The campaign is as a rule planned in advance. An armed band acts under the leadership of a command, assumes previously assigned positions, and is armed with clubs and brass knuckles concealed in briefcases. The most violent scenes took place last November in the Lwów Polytechnic. Of the sixty people who were beaten, fifteen had to be taken to clinics. The disturbances continued until the holidays, but in January calm had still not completely returned.

At the present the Endek campaign has entered a new phase, not previously experienced. The continuous boycott of Jewish students has been called for. The external expression of this is the designation of separate places for them in lecture halls and class rooms. The boycott is extended equally to Christians who dare defend their Jewish colleagues. In this way the anti-Semitic campaign is transformed into a chronic civil war on the grounds of universities. It is undoubtedly planned politics, dictated from above, since the incidence of brutal anti-Semitic excesses increases simultaneously in different parts of the country, organizations of professional intelligentsia, especially lawyers, vote in favor of the expulsion of Jews from the respective union, and so on. At the same time Endek newspapers openly call for the introduction in Poland of Hitlerite practices and sedulously note all anti-Jewish manifestations. Small but obediently organized groups carry out special anti-Semitic actions in academic institutions. Armed bands are recruited from them, and candidates emerge from them who dominate mutual aid organizations and scholarly circles. These groups hold the entire initiative in their hands. The unorganized mass truly wants to study but willingly listens to anti-Semitic appeals and, most important, remains passive.

In this state of affairs the behavior of the academic authorities assumes a more special significance. The decisive condemnation of excesses, and above all the stern punishment of proven culprits, might restrain the aggressive impulses of the armed bands and their friends and lend courage to the broad majority who undoubtedly want to study and make their way as soon as possible through the materially hard years of study. Unfortunately, and stereotypically, only one means has been employed until now—the suspension of lectures and the issuance of appeals for peace. Individual punishments occur infrequently and are astonishingly mild. Cold-blooded planned adventures are treated with odd obstinacy like elemental disturbances or childish games. Attempts at demasking the organizers are distinguished by shocking inefficiency.

The present phase of the academic anti-Semitic campaign merits separate discussion. The principle of separate benches for Jews, usually at the end of the hall, is enforced with utter ruthlessness. Whoever opposes it, is expelled. Polish students who sit alongside Jews are subject to the same boycott. This modern academic ghetto is probably the invention of the Lwów Polytechnic, but it is being accepted in other institutions. One must confess with mixed astonishment and sadness that none of this was met with solid opposition on the part of the professors and deans. Some, to the contrary, even sanctioned this blameworthy idiocy by designating separate places as well as art studios for Jewish students. Anyone opposing such a measure was, I understand, threatened with expulsion. . . .

Such is the general balance of the situation that has created such an unusually tense atmosphere in the university. The university cannot be the grounds of a basic showdown with anti-Semitism. Political factions—socialists, communists, various democratic groupings—wage battle with it. It is a difficult battle, but it must end with the victory of social justice. In the university, the final goal of Endek politics is the complete expulsion of the Jews and their elimination from those professions requiring academic preparation. The issue of Jewish professors is treated the same way. Following the example of the Hitlerites, Endek barbarity respects neither scholarship, nor merit, nor old age. Those who by responsibility and position stand in defense of culture must struggle against these manifestations of hooliganism, physical violence, and moral pressure that are terrorizing everything that we value in cultural life. Professors should carry high the banner of the dignity of scholarship; they should courageously and sincerely extend their hand to those young people who want peace in the academy; they should condemn those who conduct strife with their colleagues and by their behavior stain the honor of the repository of learning. They should oppose their own civil courage to the clamorous demagoguery of a deluded youth and the Endek press.

Part Four ■ World War II and the Holocaust

■ Czesław Miłosz
"A Poor Christian Looks at the Ghetto" (1943)

[Two well-known poems by Miłosz, "Campo dei Fiori" and "Biedny chrześcijanin patrzy na ghetto" ("A Poor Christian Looks at the Ghetto")—which is quoted below—were written in 1943 and reflect the poet's experiences in occupied Poland where he was active in the literary underground.]

Bees build around red liver,
Ants build around black bone.
It has begun: the tearing, the trampling on silks,
It has begun: the breaking of glass, wood, copper, nickel, silver, foam
Of gypsum, iron sheets, violin strings, trumpets, leaves, balls, crystals.
Poof! Phosphorescent fire from yellow walls
Engulfs animal and human hair.

Bees build around the honeycomb of lungs,
Ants build around white bone.
Torn is paper, rubber, linen, leather, flax,
Fiber, fabrics, cellulose, snakeskin, wire.
The roof and the wall collapse in flame and heat seizes the foundations.
Now there is only the earth, sandy, trodden down,
With one leafless tree.

Slowly, boring a tunnel, a guardian mole makes his way,
With a small red lamp fastened to his forehead.
He touches buried bodies, counts them, pushes on,
He distinguishes human ashes by their luminous vapor,
The ashes of each man by a different part of the spectrum.
Bees build around a red trace.
Ants build around the place left by my body.

I am afraid, so afraid of the guardian mole.
He has swollen eyelids, like a Patriarch
Who has sat much in the light of candles
Reading the great book of the species.

———
Czeslaw Milosz, "A Poor Christian Looks at the Ghetto," in *The Collected Poems, 1931–1987* (New York: The Ecco Press, 1988), 64–65. The original text is available in Czesław Miłosz, *Utwory poetyckie: Poems* (Ann Arbor: Michigan Slavic Publications, 1976), 100–101.

What will I tell him, I, a Jew of the New Testament,
Waiting two thousand years for the second coming of Jesus?
My broken body will deliver me to his sight
And he will count me among the helpers of death:
The uncircumcised.

■ Jerzy Andrzejewski (1909–83)
Holy Week (1943)

[Jerzy Andrzejewski's most famous novel remains *Popiół i diament* (*Ashes and Diamonds*, 1948), about the political conflict in immediate postwar Poland between the new communist regime and loyalists of the wartime London government in exile. As in other works by Andrzejewski, the moral element is strong. In this case, it concerns a former judge who has survived a German concentration camp but is exposed as having been responsible for the mistreatment of his fellow prisoners. Andrzejewski raises the question, so relevant in the postwar period, of the degree of accountability for morally reprehensible behavior during the occupation of otherwise decent citizens. Andrzejewski's interest in moral issues is reflected in his first novel, *Ład serca* (*Mode of the Heart*, 1938), for which he was awarded a prize in 1939 by the Polish Academy of Literature. Although he joined the Communist Party in 1949, and actively propagated socialist realism, his eventual disillusionment with its rigid dogma inspired the novels *Ciemności kryją ziemię* (*Darkness Covers the Earth*, 1957; translated into English under the title *The Inquisitors*), and *Bramy raju* (*The Gates of Paradise*, 1961). Both use historical settings as Aesopian camouflage. The first novel is set in Spain during the Inquisition; the second, in medieval France in the time of the so-called Children's Crusade. *Wielki tydzień* (*Holy Week*, 1943), a short novel set in occupied Warsaw, explores the complexity of Polish-Jewish relations against the background of the Warsaw Ghetto Uprising of 1943. The main focus of the work is on the experiences of a young Jewish woman, Irena Lilien, who is hidden by friends on the "Aryan side" of the city. While candid in his portrayal of Poles indifferent and unsympathetic to the plight of the Jews, Andrzejewski also presents common negative attitudes toward Jews even among those Poles willing to help them.]

Malecki had not seen Irena Lilien in a long time. In the summer of '41 they still got together quite often. To be sure, the Liliens had already been removed from Smug, but during that period the German occupation forces had not yet applied any harsher measures against the Jews. The Liliens had also made payoffs where necessary, thereby avoiding being locked up in the Warsaw ghetto. They even managed to save a few of their things and with this remainder of their estate, which was still considerable and valuable, the entire family settled near Warsaw.

The Liliens, who for several generations had been very well off before the war, had such a strongly developed sense of security that in the new critical situation in which they found themselves it never occurred to them to settle in another suburban district. Zalesinek, where they rented an apartment, was situated a quarter of the way to Smug, and along the route followed by the electric railway there

Jerzy Andrzejewski, *Wielki tydzień* (1943; Warsaw: Czytelnik, 1993), 5–7, 15–17, 18, 28–31, 34–37, 73–76, 78–87, 109–10, 129–30, 137–42, 162–66, 176–83, 204–9, 210–17.

were many people who knew the Liliens both personally and from sight. They themselves were so strongly assimilated into Polish culture and ways they had absolutely no idea that their appearance might in any way arouse suspicion. . . . Professor Lilien and his wife, together with Irena, traveled into Warsaw no less often than before. The professor's wife was relatively the safest. Petite, thin, and on the quiet side, she could pass for an Aryan with her irregular but pleasant features. With the professor and Irena, however, it was a lot worse.

Irena was in Warsaw at least several times a week. She visited friends and acquaintances, and also made a number of additional trips to see Malecki. Because she was fond of social life and merriment, she freely made dates with people in the coffeehouses and bars that were fashionable during the war. Irena Lilien was very pretty: tall, dark, and swarthy. Yet her coarse, thick hair and eastern eyes were strikingly Semitic. When Malecki explained to her that she had to be more cautious, Irena laughed and declared that the Germans didn't know about such things. It was true, of course, that at this time there were incidents of Jews being blackmailed by Poles, but Irena did not take seriously the possibility of something similar happening either to her or those closest to her. The comfort and social position in which she had been raised and to which she had become accustomed, shielded her from the perception of any danger. . . .

[The complacency of Irena and the Liliens is soon shattered when they are taken into custody by the Gestapo. But they are released after paying a high ransom. Although they secure Aryan papers, their situation becomes more precarious and they are forced to keep on the move. Malecki, in the meantime, marries Anna and loses touch with Irena. When they meet again, by chance, it is only in the spring of the next year, just before Easter and the outbreak of the Warsaw Ghetto Uprising.]

Holy Week was sad for Warsaw. Precisely the day before the meeting between Malecki and Irena Lilien, on Monday the nineteenth of April, part of the Jews who remained in the ghetto began defending themselves against new repression. Early in the morning, when SS units crossed the walls, the first shots fell on Stawki and Leszno. Not anticipating opposition, the Germans withdrew. The battle had begun.

News about this first collective opposition of Jews in centuries did not immediately spread throughout the city. Different versions made the rounds of Warsaw. In the first few hours the only thing that was certain was that the Germans were determined this time to liquidate the ghetto completely and to kill off all those Jews who had survived the massacres of the preceding year.

The districts nearest the walls filled with people. That is where one could find out fastest what was going on. Shots were falling one after the other from the windows of the buildings adjoining the walls. The Germans assembled military police just outside the ghetto. From hour to hour the shelling intensified. The defense, initially chaotic and random, quickly began to transform itself into a regular, planned battle. Machine guns could be heard in many places. Hand grenades were thrown.

Street movement still continued normally and in a number of locales the battle took place amid a crowd of spectators and the rumble of passing tramcars. In the meantime, where no resistance was offered, the remaining Jews were carted away. But even then there was hardly a soul who believed that the destruction of the ghetto would drag on for several weeks. Yet the Jews were to defend themselves for many days; and for many more the ghetto was to burn. And so in the midst of spring and the mood of Holy Week, in the heart of Warsaw, which four years of terror could not vanquish, a battle of Jewish insurgents had begun. It was the loneliest and most painful battle undertaken in that period in defense of life and freedom.

Malecki lived on the edge of Bielany, a distant residential quarter in the northern part of the city. He first encountered the battle on his way home from work on Friday evening. As he was riding in a tramcar along the walls of the ghetto, just behind Krasiński Square, he could sense the excitement all around him. People began rushing to windows, but nothing could be seen. Behind the walls stretched the tops of high gray walls slashed here and there with windows as narrow as peep-holes. Suddenly, on Bonifraterska Street, directly across from the Hospital of John the Divine, the tram came to an abrupt halt. At the same time, short, dull rifle shots hailed from above. A machine gun answered from the street.

Panic broke out in the tram. People hurriedly scattered from the windows, some hugging the floor, others rushing for the exit. In the meantime, shots were falling all the more thickly from the narrow crevice-like little windows of the Jewish buildings. A machine gun, placed in the middle of the street at the intersection of Bonifraterska and Konwiktorska, answered back with an intense clatter. An ambulance raced along the narrow strip of street between the tramway track and the walls of the ghetto. . . .

After the nightlong firing there was a short pause in the fighting toward daybreak. Then the shelling began again, more furious than the day before. Vehicles were no longer allowed to enter Krasiński Square. The unruly, noisy, and agitated throng therefore began filling Długa and Nowiniarska Streets. Like all greater events in Warsaw, this too, when viewed from the outside, had something of the spectacle to it. Varsovians are fond of fighting and just as fond of watching fights.

A swarm of young boys and nicely dressed girls with waved hair came running from the nearby streets of the Old Town. The more curious thrust as far as they could into Nowiniarska Street from where they had the widest view of the walls of the ghetto. In general, there was hardly anyone who felt sorry for the Jews. The people were glad that the hated Germans were having new troubles. From the point of view of the average man in the street, the very fact that they were forced to fight a handful of isolated Jews made the victorious occupiers look foolish. . . .

Malecki vacantly observed the movements of Irena's parasol. More keenly than usual he experienced that same knot of feelings which, without the participation of her will, instinctively and intrusively always formed in him whenever he came in contact with the tragedies of the Jews that had become so frequent in recent times. These feelings were different from those which arose in him under the influence of the sufferings of his own countrymen as well as of people of other nations. They were gloomy, more complex and vexing. In moments of the greatest intensity, they were also entangled with a particularly painful and humiliating awareness of a nebulous and indeterminate mutual responsibility for the boundless cruelties and crimes to which the Jewish people had been subjected for a few years with the silent consent of the entire world. This awareness, which was stronger than any rational arguments, was probably the most bitter experience he carried away from the war. There were periods, for example toward the end of the previous summer, when the Germans began their first mass slaughter of Jews and the Warsaw ghetto resounded for many days and nights with the echoes of shooting, when the feeling of complicity flared up in him exceptionally strongly. He bore it within him then like a wound in which all the evil of the world seemed to fester. He realized, however, that there was more uneasiness and dread in it than real love toward these defenseless, besieged people, who were alone in the world and whom fate deprived of a brotherhood that had in truth become debased but nevertheless existed. . . .

[After emerging from their temporary shelter during a lull in the shelling of the ghetto, Malecki notices that Irena is faint and asks a woman from a nearby basement to give her some water. While Irena recovers, the woman, a Pole, recounts her own losses during the war. Convinced that the woman is still better off than she and other Jews are, Irena takes leave of her brusquely and in a resentful mood.]

In the meantime the antitank gun stopped firing. The strong voice of a male tenor could be heard from a gramophone in the courtyard next door. The rounded and sonorous Italian words echoed loudly and clearly among the walls. In the rear of the square machine guns rattled obstinately. People who had withdrawn into the courtyard again returned to the gate. The small boy named Rysiek, whose mother was calling him, slipped out of there and ran up to the woman who had been standing all the while near the steps to the basement.

"Mama! The Germans are smashing Jewish houses! Oh, what gigantic holes they've already made!" he exclaimed, pointing them out.

"Go home, Rysiek!" the woman whispered.

He shook an unruly mop of hair.

"I'll be right back!" he said, then turning on his heel ran back.

"Maybe it'll now be possible to go out on the street?" declared Malecki, and he left Irena in order to see what was happening at the gate. He noticed a cannon standing in front of a house and several German soldiers alongside it. At the far end of the square a machine gun was firing continuously. The gate was half open and a crowd of people were negotiating with a tall, broad-shouldered soldier to let them leave. At first he refused. Then he moved aside and beckoned with his hand. Immediately a dozen or so people raced to the exit.

Malecki hurried back to Irena.

"Listen, we can go, but we have to hurry; any moment now for sure . . ." He broke off when he looked at Irena. She was pale, and the look on her face had changed. She leaned with one hand against a wall.

"What's the matter with you?" He was alarmed. "Are you weak?"

"No," she denied. But she turned paler. Malecki looked all around and went over quickly to the woman from the basement.

"Can you give me a little water? The woman over there feels faint."

The woman glanced at Irena. She hesitated for a moment. Finally she nodded her head: "Come on." . . .

Malecki looked at Irena. She had recovered completely except for the fact that she was somewhat paler than usual. She sat artificially, in an unnaturally upright position, her dark eyes following the woman in an attentive but unfriendly way. . . .

"Let's go!" Malecki said, leaning over to Irena.

She rose heavily, and in an indifferent and slightly contemptuous tone, thanked the woman for her hospitality.

Malecki prodded her.

"Irena!" he said reproachfully when they reached the top of the stairs. "How could you say goodbye to those unfortunate people in such a tone?"

She looked at him with the same mocking coldness as when they had first met.

"You didn't like my tone?"

"No."

But the hard edge to his voice didn't take her aback.

"I'm sorry if I seem that way."

"Irena!"

"Why are you surprised?" she interrupted him, displeasure in her voice. "That woman is still not the most unfortunate. She doesn't have to die of fear that any moment her sons can be shot to death just because they are who they are and not someone else. She has them, do you understand? She is free to live. But we?"

"We?" He didn't understand her at first.

"We. Jews." she replied.

A machine gun sounded very near this time. The cannon, though, was firing from the farther gate.

"You never used to say 'we'!" Malecki said softly.

"No, I didn't. But I learned. You taught me."

"We?"

"You, the Poles, the Germans . . ."

"You lump us together?"

"You're all Aryans, aren't you?"

"Irena!"

"You taught me that. Only recently did I finally come to understand that all the people on earth hated us and still hate us."

"An exaggeration!" he muttered.

"Not at all! And even if they don't hate us, then at the very most they barely tolerate us. Don't tell me that we have friends; it just seems that way, but the truth of the matter is nobody likes us. Even when they help us, it's just not the same as when they help others . . ."

"Not the same?"

"When it comes to us, you have to talk yourselves into self-sacrifice and compassion, everything that's human, good, and just. Oh, I assure you that if I could dislike Jews the way you do, then I'd never say 'we and you.' But I can't feel that way and so I have to be one of them. A Jewess! For who else can I be; tell me!"

"Yourself!" he replied, but without any greater conviction.

She did not answer immediately. She inclined her head and remained that way a long time, again tracing invisible signs above the floor with her parasol. Then suddenly she raised her lovely eastern eyes to Malecki and said in the same soft tone that often used to echo in her voice: "I am myself. But Panna Lilien of Smug no longer exists. I have been ordered to forget about her. So I forgot." . . .

[Malecki proposes that Irena stay with him and his wife when he learns that she has nowhere to go. The following conversation takes place when Irena meets Anna and Malecki's brother, Julek.]

"Good people saw to it that I didn't stay too long in one place."

Anna set out cups of tea and then took her place between her husband and Julek. No one spoke. Piotrowski played some prewar song, standing this time it seemed in the very window.

For no reason, Jan [Malecki] felt personally touched by Irena's words. Extinguishing his unfinished cigarette in an ashtray, he said: "I imagine you must have met not only such good people?"

"No, not only!" she replied calmly. "But do you believe that the truly good people excuse those others?"

Before he answered, Julek leaned across the table to him.

"You know, Janek, what I was reminded of? The old days, when we lived together on Poznańska, remember? You were going to the Polytechnic, while I was still a schoolboy. You had a lot of buddies hanging around you all the time . . . your corporation, you called it . . . Arconia, right? I remember once in the lobby counting five beanies and the same number of heavy clubs. Was I impressed! Only later, though, I found out the gentlemen of the corporation were on their way to beat Jews with those clubs and smash the windows of stores in Nalewki . . ."

Irena looked very attentively at the speaker.

"They also beat their own Jewish classmates!" she interjected softly.

Malecki pushed his cup away rather too forcefully.

"As concerns me, I never walked around with any corporate club, nor did I ever go along with such methods of conflict . . ."

Julek smiled as if in contradiction. "What methods did you go along with, then?" he asked.

"What do you mean 'what methods'?"

"Methods of anti-Semitism, fascism, or whatever you want to call it?"

"Me?" replied Jan indignantly.

Julek's unexpected words took Irena by surprise. "I have to take your brother's side," she said.

"Please!" Jan interrupted her brusquely.

Julek energetically pushed away from his forehead his blond, never completely dried hair.

"Hold on," he said, "you don't understand anything! After all, I'm not accusing him," he pointed to his brother, "of anything. But what does it mean 'not to go along with such methods of conflict'? You constantly hear that among us; all the so-called respectable Poles who condemn violence and criminal acts against Jews keep on repeating it. But what do they have in mind? Are they really enemies of anti-Semitism? Not at all! In their view, there is indeed a conflict, except that the methods of conflict should be different . . . Isn't that so? The issue here is one's own attitude toward the matter. I know full well what it means to qualify anti-Semitism according to the methods of conflict! Methods always worsen. Methods of conflict! But basically, isn't it a question of such a conflict never existing in the first place? Otherwise, it's always going to end in something like that!" he gestured behind himself in the direction of the distant ghetto. . . .

Irena had been living at the Makowskis for a few weeks. Since she almost never left the house, she felt that she was safe. But someone must have found out about her. For just that very morning, and when the Makowskis happened to be out, two young men arrived. One of them was a Gestapo agent. Besides her Aryan papers, they also took Irena with them to a car waiting in front of the house. They were very polite, but they did not conceal the fact that they were taking her in for questioning. Along the way, she ransomed herself with her last gold five-ruble piece. She got out just before they reached Szucha Avenue, but she was still afraid to return to Mokotów.

"The Makowskis know nothing?" he asked.

"No!"

Jan proposed going to them the following day and telling them everything and collecting Irena's most important things.

"There's obviously no sense in your going back there now!" he decided. "Better not run the risk."

She agreed, rather indifferently, that that would be best.

"But then what?" she lowered her head. "Then what? How am I to live? After all, I'm never going to be a normal human being again. You know, whenever I meet someone new now, the first thing I think when I look at his face is: can he betray me or not? It's a terrible feeling; you don't know what it's like . . ."

At just that moment Anna entered the studio. She paused for a moment at the door, then quietly sat down on the couch.

Irena raised her head and looked at Jan: "You know, when I first met you, I asked myself the same question?" He said nothing in reply.

"I just want to endure it to the end," she said.

"Everything will change then," he interjected.

"People won't change!" she contradicted him. "Or just to the extent that they won't have a right to kill me. But you'll see; those two young people who took me away in the car today will then look at me with contempt and will regret that they can no longer make a stupid five gold rubles off me."

"What are you saying?" he huffed.

"You'll see! We'll be hated even more because we'll be walking the streets freely, going back to our own homes, regaining our rights. Don't contradict me, I know that's how it's going to be, and you know it too. For the moment, ordinary shame doesn't allow many people to show their dislike of us. We are accepted out of necessity; they hide us out of a sense of obligation. But later on they won't be under any such obligation! But we, for our part, will forget nothing. You know that Jews are unable to forget wrongs. Just the opposite of you people. You forget everything. And when you're mistreated, and when you mistreat others . . ."

He couldn't contradict her, because he thought the same way. Besides, he himself wanted, and needed, to forget with all his heart and soul. He wanted to defend at least his weakness, to justify it somehow and ennoble it.

"Isn't that really a hope though?" he reflected.

"What is?" She did not understand his meaning.

"To forget!" And he pressed further: "The hope that it will be better. Must we drag these horrible years behind us the rest of our lives and never tear free of them?"

"I don't know," she answered. "In the course of these years I've become an entirely different person; I was compelled to become someone other than I was. It seems that that was accomplished. So how can I forget this entire period?"

"These years have changed everyone," asserted Jan.

"But not everyone was deprived of his dignity!"

Anna, who was sitting the whole time on the edge of the couch, motionless, with her legs tucked up under her, suddenly raised her head.

"Is it really possible to deprive a person of his dignity?" she asked softly.

Irena turned around to her.

"Is it possible? Oh yes! Believe me, it is possible. It's possible to strip a person of everything — will, pride, desire, hope, everything! Even fear . . . I've seen it with my own eyes. . . . Do you know how my father died?"

At the time the first mass murders of Jews began, that is in the summer of '43, the professor was staying together with Irena on someone's estate in Miechowski. Pani Lilienowna was living for the time being in Cracow, but soon she too had to leave for the country. The presence of the Liliens in a new place was quite well concealed. Irena was a clerk in a local distillery, while the professor pretended to be on the estate in the capacity of a teacher of the owners' sons. The first months of their stay went by peacefully and it might have seemed that finally, after all the trials and tribulations of the past year, they would be able to come to and survive. But there still remained the matter of getting Pani Lilienowa there. However, just when her arrival had been finally decided on, the anti-Jewish repressions began. Soon they even reached the area where Irena and her father were hiding. One day, toward evening, a specially trained Gestapo team drove up to Obwarów and began killing the local Jews. While this was going on, the owner of the estate received an anonymous phone call from which he gathered that the Germans knew about the Liliens and their origins. Only flight remained.

On none of the nearby estates was it possible then to hide the Liliens. Their departure for Cracow was also out of the question for the time being in view of the dangers along the way. Moreover, the professor was feeling quite ill; he had still not recovered from a bad case of the flu, and his heart continued to give him trouble. In such circumstances hiding out in the surrounding forests seemed the only possibility of salvation. This is what their host advised the Liliens, and the professor and Irena agreed. The plan was for them to hide for the time being in a forester's cottage some eight kilometers from the estate and there await a time when the danger would be the least. The professor was opposed to the plan, but someone from the estate or the farm began leading them to the place. But the professor no longer trusted people, and confided in almost no one. They went, therefore, by themselves. . . .

"It was a terrible night!" Irena went on. "Dark . . . we didn't know the area very well. At the outset the trees still looked familiar to us, but when we had to leave the road, or go along paths, we got completely confused. I was really the one who only later discovered that we were going in the wrong direction, just when it began to get light. Father could hardly walk — his heart was giving him a lot of trouble — so we were constantly having to rest along the way. He was now an entirely different person. He looked like an old, sick Jew, a frightened little Jew afraid of death. He was terribly afraid of falling into the hands of the Germans. Hardly did we sit down for a little while, when he jumped up right away, convinced that the forester's cottage wasn't far away. I could see already that we weren't going to make it, but he kept on deluding himself.

"When dawn came up, we came out onto some kind of a road. It still wasn't completely light, but rather gray . . . Father didn't want to go on the road. So I went alone and it was then that I saw some huge, dark crowd coming in our direction. Can you imagine what I was going through at the time? I wanted for us to flee at once into the depths of the forest, but father couldn't go on. He had become frightfully pale and began shaking . . . I thought it was the end. We hid instead in the bushes by the side of the road; there were thick bushes below, alderwood, I think. We lay down on the ground. Father was breathing heavily and constantly shivering like someone cold. It seemed an eternity before the crowd got near us. I pressed my face to the ground; there was dew on the grass. Had I lain there longer, I would surely have fallen asleep. I was so tired. But suddenly I heard my father's voice, greatly changed, trembling: 'Irena, they're Jews!' I raised my head and saw that the crowd wasn't very far at all. They really were all Jews . . . women, old men, and children; a mass of Jewish misery. I later learned that they were Jews from Obarów, people whom the Germans hadn't managed to shoot the night before. They were herded into some roundup area where there were supposed to be Jews from other towns and villages, from the entire region. You have no idea what a sight that was; I'll never forget it! A herd of people . . . jammed together, some of them barefooted, with bundles, all of them covered with dust, dirty, with pale, wearied faces . . . Many of them had bloodstained faces; women were carrying little children in their arms . . . One little girl—tiny, dark, and emaciated, in a pink, polka-dot, chintz dress—was carrying two babies, one in her hand, the other on her shoulders.

"At first I didn't even notice who was guarding them. A moment later, though, I caught sight of this German. He was walking off to one side, along the grass, no doubt to avoid getting his shiny boots dusty. He looked very innocent, just an ordinary young fellow, seventeen, maybe eighteen. He passed very near me, just a few steps away . . . I even heard the creaking of his boots. Suddenly I felt father getting up from the ground. I remember well that I wanted to shout at that moment, to stop him . . . but no, it's hard to say what was happening to me at the time. I saw that I had to do something, not to let him go, to run after him, but I did nothing . . . I lay without moving a muscle and just looked. I saw how father, crouching and stooped, stood on the edge of the road. A few people in the approaching crowd who were the closest suddenly stopped. I saw their eyes, which were almost as dead as the eyes of the blind. They came to a halt and gazed at father with their unseeing eyes. Then the young German looked around and, thinking for sure that father had separated from the crowd, shouted to him, leaped up to him, struck him a few times on the head and face with a whip and pushed him so hard that father fell. The German then went over to him and kicked him a few times. Some old Jewess wanted to help father get up, but she too was struck with the whip; finally, father got up on his own. He first stood on all fours, straightened up . . . I remember I closed my eyes, and when I opened them again, I could no longer find father in the crowd . . . everyone looked alike."

No one spoke for the longest time.

"Perhaps they didn't die?" said Jan. "They could have sent them to a camp."

"Oh, come on!" Julek muttered, stirring beneath the wall. "Don't you know how things were at the time? They set up a so-called roundup point in one place somewhere on a highway and herded Jews there from the entire district. First, a selection was conducted. The young, healthy, and strong were taken off to work, but the remaining were finished off on the spot. As they were going along . . . children, women, the elderly. . . ."

[As the fighting in the ghetto intensifies, Anna encounters Pani Piotrowska, a bigoted and nosy neighbor who is soon to suspect that Irena is a Jew being hidden by the Maleckis.]

On the steps of Banasiak's small shop located in the basement, Anna ran into the stout Pani Piotrowska. She was clambering up the stairs with a huge bag loaded with provisions.

"Oh, Pani Malecka, I see you're buying for the holidays too!" Piotrowska said, stopping as soon as she caught sight of Anna.

Anna replied that she was not celebrating any holidays that year. Piotrowska smiled sympathetically.

"People always say that! But when you have guests . . ."

"My brother-in-law came for a few days," explained Anna a bit too hurriedly. From Piotrowska's indulgent glance, she realized that she had made a mistake not freely acknowledging Irena's presence. "Besides, an old friend of mine is with us. But I still don't know if she's staying for the holidays; probably not."

Piotrowska shook her head as if in sympathy. Then she changed the subject.

"You know, I just heard that . . . what a tragedy! The Germans found a Jew in a house on Saska Kępa. He was hiding, like they do . . . And can you imagine that for one of them, five of ours were shot. What a tragedy, you agree?"

Anna remained silent for a moment.

"Yes," she said finally.

"So much innocent blood!" Piotrowska moved to higher ground. "In my opinion, my dear, any Pole who hides a Jew is a pig, if you don't mind my saying so! Yes indeed!" She thumped her chest. "I am a Pole, if you please, and that's how I think! It's just un-Christian—good Catholics dying for one Jew. That shouldn't be!"

She stood shaking her bag, overcome by her own indignation.

"That shouldn't be!" she repeated again with emphasis. "Everyone's life is dear to him. A person doesn't bear that burden just to die for Jews for nothing!"

Anna decided not to tell Jan about this conversation. She wanted to spare him further upset. She couldn't imagine that Piotrowska might go so far as to report them. Nevertheless, she returned home with a heavy heart. . . .

Since Anna wanted to take advantage of a good supply of gas in the evening in order to do some laundry in the tub, Jan went downstairs to breathe a little fresh air. Stefcio Osipowicz was still hopping up and down in front of the house, but as soon as his father began calling him from the second floor, the boy loped up-stairs like a kangaroo. In the small garden next door, an old, grayhaired man had just finished watering his flower beds, and, stooped a little in the shoulders, was slowly returning home with his green watering can. His grandson wasn't with him that day. Suddenly, Malecki caught Pan Piotrowski's low, drawling voice coming from an open window on the first floor.

"Who's the woman living at the Maleckis?"

"Some Jew-girl!" his wife called contemptuously from below.

"How do you know?"

"How do I know? Just have a look at her. And where did you see her? She wouldn't be hanging around, I'm sure."

"She wasn't hanging around at all," he replied indifferently. "She just came out on the balcony. Nice-looking woman!"

"But a Jew-girl!"

"So what?" laughed Piotrowski. "You think Jewesses don't have what it takes?"

"Pig!"

"You've got the right stuff too . . . don't get upset!"

"Pig!" repeated Pani Piotrowska, but in a softer voice. "I know myself what I've got, you don't have to tell me." . . .

Malecki left in the morning for the city at his usual hour. Only Good Friday was he supposed to have off from work in the office. However, when he arrived at the small, two-room premises of the company, it appeared that after yesterday's quite feverish confusion, there wasn't too much work for him. Furthermore, what there was, was easily disposed of. The owner of the company, Wolański, who was also an architect and a friend of Malecki's from before the war, didn't put in an appearance at all. However, in one of the two rooms, the so-called commons (the other one, where Malecki and Wolański worked, was known as Management), a lively conversation had been going on for some time. When Malecki dropped in, intrigued by the raised voices, he arrived at the peak of the heated discussion.

There were four people in the "commons." . . . The only member of the group not belonging to the company was a young man. He was a tall blond with an elongated face and deep-set eyes in a rather rapacious, bird-like face.

Malecki knew him, since Zalewski, or Zygmunt, as the secretary, Stefa, called him, came by very often during that period. He had studied law before the war; now, among other things, he traded in gold and currency. When Malecki entered the "commons," Zalewski was sitting on a table and gesticulating energetically as he spoke:

"I tell you, in this one instance we can be grateful to Hitler. They spared us this burdensome, and admittedly even unfortunate, dirty work. Now in general there won't be any more Jewish question! If Hitler hadn't done it, we ourselves would have to see to the liquidation of the Jews after the war. One worry less, that's clear! And all so-called humanitarian considerations" — he tossed a glance at Panna Marta sitting at her typewriter — "have absolutely no application here! Poland must be free of Jews; that is our reason of state. That's the first thing! The second is that we have no cause to pity the Jews . . . They don't have any pity for us! Every last one of them, if he could, would shoot the first Pole he came across right in the head. If the Jews ever came to power, rest assured, they'd show us what they're capable of!" . . .

Catching sight of Malecki, Zalewski turned in his direction: "Am I not right, sir?"

Malecki found himself in an unpleasant situation. He had not the slightest desire to intrude on the discussion. However, after Zalewski's question, all eyes were fixed on him. Even Panna Marta raised her head. She was very pale and her lips were quivering. He had to say something.

"Of course, I didn't hear the entire conversation," he began slowly, "but what you're saying doesn't strike me as new."

"Certainly!" Zalewski agreed with satisfaction. "The Polish nation has for some time now begun to understand what the Jews are."

"Before the war, such ideas were quite popular among our fascists," asserted Malecki.

Zalewski frowned.

"You mean 'nationalists,' don't you?"

"Aren't they the same?"

"No!" Zalewski retorted sharply. He eyed Malecki aggressively, his eyes blinking.

"We know full well in what circles the attempt is made to discredit us with the label 'fascists.' But once the war is over, we'll show those gentlemen the difference!"

"In concentration camps?" Marta asked suddenly.

Zalewski was confused for a moment. However, he quickly gained control of himself.

"If necessary, then yes!" he replied sharply. "Especially there — nowhere else — we'll teach the Jews and communists who we are."

Everyone in the room was silent. A bit unsure whether Zalewski had gone too far, Panna Stefa took out her compact and, eyelashes fluttering, began powdering her pretty face. Panna Marta, on the other hand, turned even paler. As for Malecki, he would have been happiest to extricate himself from that unpleasant situation. Suddenly Panna Marta got up.

"How long the war is going to last no one knows," she declared, her voice trembling somewhat. "But right now I'll tell you what you are!"

Zalewski smiled ironically.

"By all means; I'm all ears."

"Bandits!" she said straight to his face.

He made a motion as if to interrupt her; instead, he measured her with such a contemptuous gaze that he had no need to reply.

"You're all bandits!" she repeated still louder. "You'd deserve nothing but contempt, were it not for the shame that you're Poles . . . You disgrace us, you animals!" she shouted suddenly with a passion unexpected of someone always so calm and in control of herself.

When she left the room, Malecki ran after her into the lobby.

"Marta!" he called.

She was hurriedly putting on her coat.

"What is it?" she looked at him coldly.

"I wanted . . ."

"I can well imagine!" she interrupted him. "No doubt you wanted to communicate to me the fact that I was right?"

"Of course!"

The young woman smiled ironically.

"Too bad you didn't say that in there!" she said, pointing to the room they had just left. . . .

[Convinced that the Maleckis are hiding a Jew, Pani Piotrowska tells her husband that she intends to reveal this to Pan Zamojski, the landlord of the apartment house the Maleckis and Piotrowskis live in.]

"What is it?" she met him, all excited, at the door. "Where were you so long? What's happened?"

"How do I know?" he tossed his hat on the bed. "There's just talk . . ."

"What do you mean 'just talk'? What talk?"

"That the Gestapo arrived somewhere on Liswoska Street . . ."

"What are you saying?" she became alarmed. "When, now? And what, they picked up someone?"

"Maybe some Jews," he replied indifferently.

Piotrowska turned red and did not immediately reply, so struck was she by the news. In a little while she came to.

"Józek!" she called energetically. "Watch the cake; I'll be right back."

She opened a closet, took out a dress, and began hurriedly dressing. Piotrowski made a wry face.

"Where you off to?"

"To Zamojski's," she answered briefly, pulling on a stocking.

He shrugged his shoulders.

"What is it now?"

"What do you mean, 'what is it now'?" she straightened up, flushed and sweating. "Don't you see what's happening? Am I supposed to wait with hands folded until they finish us all off on account of one Jew-girl? Not on your life! I won't run to the Gestapo; I don't want any blood on my conscience, but someone else will run to them." . . .

Zamojski happened to be reading *Pan Tadeusz* at the time, and Pani Piotrowska's visit was most inopportune. He knew from experience that a landlord never got anything good out of tenants' visits. However, his good upbringing caused him to rise immediately and to brighten his rabbit's face with a pleasant smile. Only the councillor's big nose betrayed his dissatisfaction.

Piotrowska sank into an armchair and, wiping her sweaty brow with a kerchief, got right down to business.

"You know, sir," she began, "that I'm an honorable person and that it would be hard to find a tenant who pays his rent more regularly."

Zamojski bowed politely. Piotrowska sighed deeply and again reached for her kerchief.

"Quite so!" she confirmed her previous statement. "So I do have the right to inform you that everything isn't as it should be in the building?"

Zamojski's face fell slightly.

"Yes, sir, I know what I'm saying, I'm not making things up! Do some people have the right, in such times, to endanger others because of their foolishness? Are people free to do that, to behave, so to say, unsocially?

"But . . . ," he mumbled.

"Oh yes!" Piotrowska attacked him. "What would you say, sir, I ask you, if you knew, for example, that here, in your house, under your roof, sir, people are hiding Jews, begging your pardon?"

Zamojski winced and his face fell more obviously.

"I know nothing about it," he declared in a rather weak voice.

"But I know!" exclaimed Piotrowska, fanning herself with her kerchief. "And the Maleckis also know."

Zamojski recovered from the first unpleasant impression.

"A moment, please," he said, assuming a business-like tone. "From what I understand, you're trying to say that there are other people living at the Maleckis'."

"Not people, but a Jew-girl!" she declared, cutting short any and all doubts.

"I see, I see . . . But how do you know that this woman . . ."

Zamojski wiped the tip of his nose with the back of his hand.

"I've got eyes after all!" she exploded. "I know about these things, sir. I just have to take one look."

Since the soft leather chair warmed her, she thrust herself to the very edge of it.

"If you please, sir, I'm a Pole," she wiped her sweaty brow, "and I'm not running to the Germans with this, have no fear."

"Why of course!" said Zamojski, spreading his hands, in this way wishing to make a point of how far he was from such an assumption.

"Well, naturally! But we can't live here as if on a volcano. Are there only a few children here, I ask you?"

"Yes, yes," Zamojski interrupted her. "I'll have a talk with the Maleckis; we've got to straighten the whole thing out. Perhaps there's some misunderstanding?"

"There's no misunderstanding, sir," she replied, indignant. "I'm a responsible person." . . .

[After Pani Piotrowska's visit, Zamojski decides to discuss with Malecki the matter of Irena's presence in his apartment.]

Malecki guessed what Zamojski had on his mind and had no intention on his part of making things any easier for him. He was just annoyed at Irena, convinced that she had been incautious again and must have gone out onto the balcony. Both men remained silent for a good few minutes. Zamojski's face fell even more. Finally the councillor collected his scattered thoughts.

"I wanted to have a little talk with you, my dear Pan Malecki, about a certain matter," he began. "Naturally in complete confidence. The matter is perhaps a bit serious . . ."

He broke off and with slightly reddened eyes sought some friendly help from Malecki.

"I'm listening," replied Malecki, refusing the kindness.

Zamojski sighed inside himself. Nothing for it, he had to get over his feelings.

"If I am not mistaken, a certain lady. . . . I'm sorry, I don't know her name . . . is living with you now."

"Pani Grabowska," Malecki explained calmly. "She's spending a few days with us. Concerned, are you, about her being registered?"

"Yes, and no," said Zamojski, skillfully extricating himself from the trap. "Registration? Yes, by all means. These days, you understand, I'm not the only one concerned . . ."

"I understand," Malecki allowed, in agreement.

"Only . . ."

"Only?"

"Forgive me," said Zamojski, pulling himself together, "but I have certain grounds to assume, more even, to be almost certain, yes, almost certain," he said with emphasis, "that the origin of Pani Grabowska . . . Please forgive me," he anticipated Malecki's reply, "but is that the lady's real name?"

As he asked this question, which he extracted with difficulty from misgivings, his face grew even longer, and his reddened eyes seemed to fly out as if each one individually wanted to bore right into Malecki. The latter answered nothing immediately, taken aback not so much by the question itself, as he expected it, as by the councillor's appearance. At first he couldn't completely fathom why the expression on Zamojski's face suddenly seemed so new. But then it struck him: it was a Semitic face, a face which at that moment was given away by the eyes, which were beyond all doubt Jewish. His gaze instinctively glided over the dark, solemn looking portraits on the walls. And suddenly he lost interest in carrying on a false game with Zamojski.

"Councillor," Malecki began, leaning toward Zamojski in a friendly way, "let's say that I gave a negative answer to your question. Let's say that Pani Grabowska's real name is something else. What then, in your opinion, am I to do?"

Zamojski sank into the depths of his armchair in panic.

"I don't want to know about anything!"

Malecki felt himself strengthened.

"Excuse me, but you yourself mentioned that our conversation was to take place in absolute confidence. In so doing, you encouraged my sincerity. Isn't that so? That is the sole reason I felt justified in asking what, in your opinion, am I to do?"

Zamojski ruefully stared at the speaker. His look clearly conveyed the reproach that he was being entangled in dark matters that were none of his concern.

"Forgive me," he mumbled finally, "but how can I know? I'm sick about everything that's going on . . . But there's a whole house here to be considered, you understand . . . So many people, women, children . . . If something happened, there'd be a search or, God help us, an accusation, you understand?" . . .

"I understand it all very well, believe me. But a person's life is at stake here."

Zamojski said nothing. He sank into himself, cringing.

"I know, I know," he finally muttered, shaking his head. "Human life must be respected."

Malecki suddenly launched another attack.

"I can assure you in any case that Pani Grabowska will not remain here more than a few days. You understand that from the point of view of my wife's position it would be in my interest. It is literally a matter of a few days. But now, an indiscrete question. Forgive me, but I'd like there to be no more vague hints and such. In what way did you learn that someone was living with us? Did you see Pani Grabowska?"

Zamojski denied this by a movement of his head.

"Then you were informed? May I know by whom? Was it someone from our house?"

The councillor hesitated.

"Piotrowska?" suggested Malecki.

Zamojski confirmed it by his silence.

"In that case, she has to be calmed," decided Malecki. "Explain to her that she was mistaken, that Pani Grabowska certainly does have a suspicious appearance, but that . . . and so on."

Zamojski created the impression of someone now utterly exhausted. He assented without saying a word. In the end, Malecki agreed to personally talk to Piotrowska and explain everything appropriately. Malecki himself offered to do it for the sake of helping out Zamojski. Indeed, a moment later he regretted his too hasty action, but it didn't enter his mind to get out of it. Besides, everything went a lot better than expected.

On leaving, he wanted in some way to express to Zamojski his appreciation and gratitude.

"Not everyone in your place would act as you have!"

Zamojski turned red like a young boy. He suddenly straightened himself out, his face flushed in embarrassment, and said with unexpected strength:

"With one reservation, sir! Every 'honorable Pole,' as the poet says, would behave no differently in my place."

His small face, encumbered with too large a nose, seemed to Malecki at that moment almost like the old-fashioned portraits turning dark at the rear of the room.

But he no longer had the strength to go downstairs to talk to Piotrowska. He decided to put it off until the next day.

And then it was Good Friday. The resistance of the insurgents continued a fifth day. Fires penetrated deeper into the ghetto. Amid the fire and smoke, shots clapped incessantly and the dry clacking of automatics and machine guns resounded. Raids on Jews in the city also began. From different places and at different times, individual Jews succeeded in fleeing beyond the walls and now beefed-up patrols of German MPs as well as blue-uniformed Polish and Ukrainian police were hunting the fugitives through the streets. Sentries were also stationed at the outlets of underground sewers, since it was by this route that Jews tried most often to make their way to freedom. These people were killed on the spot. For an entire day the echoes of short bursts of gunfire resounded from time to time in different districts of Warsaw. Panic then swept through the streets, and passersby sought the shelter of gateways. Sometimes a crouching, lone individual ran across a deserted square or depopulated street. Rifle salvos soon caught up with him. He fell onto the sidewalk. Military police on bicycles rode up to the person on the ground, followed by Ukrainian militiamen in green uniforms. Anyone still alive was finished off. In a little while, normal traffic animated the streets again. In front of churches, crowds of people gathered hurrying to Good Friday Sepulchers. It was the loveliest spring in the world. . . .

[Alone in the apartment, Irena is visited by Pan Piotrowski who has admired her since catching sight of her on the Maleckis' balcony.]

Piotrowski hesitated for a moment. However, he then felt the vodka he had consumed and whistled through his teeth. A short while later, he rang at the Maleckis' apartment. As soon as she heard the bell, Irena was convinced that it was Jan returning. She put down her book and got up from the couch. She was so sure it was Jan that she stepped back instinctively, almost in panic, when she opened the door and saw Piotrowski.

He did not enter, however.

"Is Pan Malecki in?" he asked.

Startled, she said that he wasn't. At that, Piotrowski revealed strong, white teeth in his smile. And before she could collect her senses, he crept inside with a nimble movement, almost like a cat's. He closed the door quietly after him and turned the key in the lock.

"Then we're alone!" He turned to her, and after removing his hat, placed his arms akimbo. In that brief moment, Irena succeeded in overcoming her initial impulse of fear.

"What does this mean?" she asked in a superior way.

Piotrowski narrowed his eyes.

"Whoah! Take it easy!" he drawled. "We've got time. Perhaps you'll invite a guest into your room."

"A guest?" she repeated in a contemptuous tone.

Piotrowski drew closer. His eyes flashed and his swarthy face darkened.

"For several days now I've wanted to make your acquaintance," he said in a lowered, slightly hoarse voice. "I only saw you on the balcony. There wasn't any chance."

He thrust his hands into the pockets of his trousers and took Irena in with a burning, somewhat awry gaze.

"Well, now here's a chance!" Again he showed his teeth as he smiled.

He stood so close she could smell his hot breath saturated with alcohol. But she did not draw back.

"I don't know what you mean," she said cooly. "What chance are you talking about? What is this all about?"

"You don't know?" he smiled roguishly.

"What is it you want?" she repeated. "Who are you really?"

And she suddenly lost control over herself. "Please leave this instant! Do you hear me?" she said, raising her voice when she saw that he was not moving. "Must I call the doorkeeper?"

Piotrowski stepped back.

"By all means!" he drawled in his own way. "Please, do as you like! Call him, go on."

He yanked up his trousers and hung his hat on a hook.

"Well, why aren't you calling? I'm not stopping you . . . Do as you like."

She remained silent. Piotrowski looked at her attentively.

"You're not calling?" he asked, teeth flashing. Well, in that case, maybe you'll ask me into your room?"

She hesitated for a moment, but then turned away, straightened her hair in a casual motion, and went into her room. She took out a cigarette from a pack lying on the table, lit it, and as she drew on it looked at Piotrowski leaning against the door.

"I'm sorry to upset you," she began, carelessly shaking ashes into a vase, "but . . ."

"But?" he chimed in.

"I don't have any money," she finished saying, looking him in the face. "Your predecessors or, better said, professional colleagues, saw to that quite expertly."

Piotrowski turned slightly red.

"What have I got to do with it?" he shrugged his shoulders. "You think I want money?"

He said that so convincingly that Irena was confused.

"Then what is it you want?" she asked uncertainly.

He laughed at that briefly. Then he came closer, but since an armchair separated him from Irena, he pushed it aside.

"Such a pretty woman like you, and you still ask?" he looked at her awry.

Now she knew what he was after. But before she could move away, he grabbed her by the arms and pulled her to him. He evidently expected no resistance, since she managed to free herself from his embrace with one jerk and repel him. He reeled and would surely have fallen had he not grabbed hold of the edge of the table at the last moment. Blood rushed to his head. He remained bent over for a moment, breathing hard, supporting himself against the table with a tightened fist, gazing at Irena with blinking eyes. . . .

He reached her in one leap. She defended herself ferociously and for a moment they struggled in silence. Finally he succeeded in turning her over onto the couch and pinning her down with his body. She stifled a groan. However, her strength left her and she was less able to defend herself. Piotrowski, on the other hand, immobilized both her hands with one adroit grab, raised himself up, and as he kept on kneading Irena's breasts while hurriedly and impatiently tugging at his belt, he began pulling down his trousers with his other, free hand. Even through her dress she suddenly felt on herself his hot nakedness taught with desire. She cringed. And when he was sure of himself, his knees tangled in his lowered trousers, he drew himself over her in order to rip off her underwear. But she resisted with her last remaining strength. While he was momentarily thrown off balance, she managed to slip sideways out of his grasp. In a second, she found herself on the floor.

She noticed that the door to the balcony was half open. She leaped to it, pushed it wide open, and came to a halt on the balcony. The voices of children reached her from below as if coming from out of a fog or from behind a thick curtain. She breathed deeply, then mechanically began straightening her rolled-up skirt and rumpled blouse.

Piotrowski, meanwhile, holding up his falling trousers with one hand, crawled awkwardly off the couch. He reeled slightly at first and stood for a moment with his shirt comically sticking out from under his crumpled jacket, dazed, half consciously casting his bleary, swollen eyes all around. He finally pulled up his trousers, and as he observed Irena motionless on the balcony, slowly began getting his clothes in order. He straightened himself up and with both hands smoothed his messed hair. However, hardly did he advance in the direction of the balcony when Irena stepped across the threshhold. . . .

Piotrowski did not try to come any closer. He stopped in the middle of the room, his hands thrust into the pockets of his trousers; his mouth was twisted into an ugly little smile. He observed Irena for the longest time, suddenly burst out in mocking laughter, and turning on his heel, left the room. . . .

Irena did not return to the room. The few minutes that went by before Piotrowski left the apartment seemed endlessly long to her. She was uncertain that he wouldn't change his mind and return. Only the sound of doors being slammed dissipated the tension in her nerves. She grew weak and her legs began giving way under her so that she had to lean against a railing of the balcony.

Below, before the front doorway, little Piotrowski was lying on his back, his arms stretched out like a cross and his eyes closed. Stefanek Osipowicz leaned over him, concerned.

"Why are you lying like that, better get up."

"No!" replied Wacek firmly.

"But why?"

"Because I'm Jesus."

"You're Jesus?"

"And you're an angel! Lean over, since I'm hanging on a cross."

The thin voice of Tereska who was leaning out a window like a rose-colored ball of yarn, could be heard from the stoop.

"Boys, what are you up to?"

"I am Jesus!" shouted Wacek from below, opening one eye. "Come to us!"

Resting her arms against the metal edge of the moulding, Tereksa leaned out so far her dark crop of hair tumbled over her eyes. She wanted to catch it when all of a sudden her hand slipped on the ledge. She lost her balance and the weight of her body pulled her down. She let out a short, ear-shattering cry.

The first to run outside was Piotrowska. When she saw Tereska lying on the ground she took her by the head.

"God Almighty!" she shouted at the top of her lungs. "What happened here? Jesus Christ!"

Springing to his feet, Wacek also screamed as loud as he could. At that moment Osipowicz was so frozen with fear he was utterly speechless.

"Tereska killed herself, Tereska killed herself!" Wacek howled shrilly, jumping up and down and plugging his ears with his fingers.

Piotrowski, who had just then come outside, when over to the girl lying motionless in the sand and wanted to bend over her. But his wife pushed him aside.

"Away from her, you scoundrel!" she snarled. "A child is something holy."

He shrugged his shoulders and withdrew to one side.

Meanwhile almost all the tenants, alarmed by Wacek's shouting, began running downstairs. . . . Two teenagers, one with a scooter, the other with a wooden rifle, raced down the street to the place of the accident. They shoved their way in among the people standing closest.

"Look!" prodded the boy with the scooter. "She killed herself."

The other one was so taken aback, all he could do was nod. The childish eyes of the ten-year-old shone with an unhealthy luster. He stuck out his tongue in order to see everything better, while with his left hand he scratched his gashed calf.

"Be off with you!" Piotrowska shouted indignantly. "You're just what we need now!"

They jumped somewhat to one side. Władek and Osipowicz, meanwhile, were leaning beside Tereska. They turned her over on her back. Pale as a wafer, inert, her eyes closed, she indeed gave the impression of someone dead.

"Well?" Zamojski tiptoed over.

Osipowicz put his ear to the girl's heart. He listened for a moment.

"She's alive! It seems that nothing happened to her. She just fainted."

"We've got to send for a doctor," advised Zamojski. Piotrowska thrust her away between them.

"What, she's alive? Alive?"

Just then she caught sight of Irena standing on the balcony, leaning with both hands against the railing. Her swollen face flashed with anger.

"Jew-girl!" she shouted, raising her hand. "It's all her fault!"

Everyone turned their gaze toward the balcony. Zamojski paled and bit his lips. A ripple of unrest moved through the crowd. Only Piotrowski stood to a side smiling to himself.

"Pani Piotrowska . . . ," Osipowicz whispered.

"Jew-girl!" she shrieked hatefully.

Only then did Irena withdraw inside the apartment. But her disappearance just angered Piotrowska all the more. Pushing aside the people standing closest to her, the silk of her tight dress rustling, she dashed in a rage to the staircase. In a moment she was on the first floor.

"Open up!" she began pounding on the door with her fists. "Open up at once!"

For a moment Irena stood in the middle of the room, her hands covering her ears. She was trembling, and all the blood seemed to drain from her face. Instinctively, she looked around to see where she might hide. The pounding became all the more insistent.

"Open up!" Piotrowska barked hysterically.

Irena was unable to stand the shouting any longer. Trembling in every limb, her lips blanched, she ran out into the anteroom.

Piotrowska looked frightful: red, disheveled, her mouth foaming.

"What's wrong with you? What's the matter?" stammered Irena.

"You'll see!" yelled Piotrowska.

And seizing Irena by the hand, she dragged her down the stairs after her. Only when she was on the landing did Irena try to put up some resistance. But the other woman jerked her forcefully and shoved her outside, among the people still milling about.

Dazed, Irena looked around at all the people gathered there. Osipowicz was holding Tereska in his hands. Everyone was confused and turned their eyes away from her. At the very back, she caught sight of Piotrowski. He was standing with his hands in his pants pockets and looking at her through narrowed eyes, a mischievous, derisive little smile on his face.

Piotrowska was breathing heavily.

"Well!" she pointed toward Irena. "Get out of here! Off with you!"

The residents of a neighboring house gathered on the other side of the wire fence.

"Look!" the boy with the scooter prodded his friend. "They caught a Jew!"

The other boy nodded. He kept on scratching his leg. Nobody else said anything. Even Wacek stopped crying.

"Pani Piotrowska, how can you do that?" whispered Pani Osipowiczowa, holding the terrified Stefanka by the hand.

Piotrowska turned to her, her arms akimbo.

"What can't I do?" she replied aggressively. "Maybe she'll deny she's a Jew? Let her deny it, just let her deny it! Deny it" she attacked Irena who was standing motionless. "Just dare deny it!"

Irena thought she wanted to strike her.

"Please don't touch me!" she whispered.

Piotrowska burst out laughing contemptuously.

"And who'd be wanting to touch the likes of you?"

She looked all around her and, unable to contain her hatred, shouted peremptorily:

"Get out of here now! Go back to the ghetto; find yourself a Srul there! Come on, get going!"

"Pani Piotrowska . . . ," Osipowiczowa again whispered.

But Piotrowska was seething with rage.

"What are you waiting for? Didn't you understand? Hit the road!"

Just at that moment Tereska stirred in the arms of the thin Osipowicz. She opened her eyes.

"Where's mommy?" she whispered.

"She's coming." He bent down to her. "Mommy'll be here very soon."

"And Włodek?"

"He's coming too."

Irena stood all the while without moving amid the people who were avoiding looking at her; her heart was beating in her throat like a scrap of living meat. She suddenly felt possessed by blind, overpowering hatred. She straightened herself.

"Fine, I'll leave!" she said in an unnaturally loud voice. And sure now of her superiority, she looked Piotrowska straight in the eyes and said:

"Your kid can break both his hands and legs . . ."

Piotrowska paled, opened her mouth, and completely caved in. She just drew Wacek close to her and covered his face with her hands.

Irena looked at the confused and suddenly terrified faces surrounding her. She felt a burning and antagonistic pleasure.

"The lot of you can croak like dogs!" she shot out vindictively. "I hope you're burned the same as us! Shot to death, murdered . . ."

She then quickly turned about and amid the deathly silence that prevailed began slowly making her way toward the exit. She opened the wicket, crossed the street at an angle, and walked down the sidewalk at an even, calm pace. Only when she turned into a side street and nobody from the building could see her any longer, she hastened her step. She began running.

Before long she found herself near the trams and hopped aboard a car that was just pulling out. It was almost empty. Hardly anyone traveled to the city at that late hour and especially on Holy Friday. The distant sound of heavy cannon fire could be heard in the distance and a bloody moon burned above the ghetto amid the black clouds.

■ Antoni Słonimski
"Elegy of Jewish Towns" (1947)

There are no more Jewish towns in Poland, no more,
In Hrubieszów, Karczew, Brody, Falenica,
You'd look in vain for lit candles, or try to catch
The sounds of singing from a wooden temple.

The last remains disappeared, Jewish rags,
Blood scattered like sand, traces cleared away
And walls whitewashed clean with strong lime
As after some plague or for a high holy day.

One moon shines here, cool, pallid, alien,
Beyond the city, on the highway, when night catches fire,
My Jewish relatives, poetic fellows,
Will not find Chagall's two golden moons.

Those moons now course over another planet,
They fluttered away, frightened, in sad silence.
Those towns are no longer where a shoemaker was a poet,
A watchmaker a philosopher, and a barber a troubadour.

Those towns are no longer where the wind joined
Biblical airs with Polish song and Slavic sorrow,
Where old Jews in gardens beneath the shade of cherry trees
Mourned the holy walls of Jerusalem.

Those towns are no longer, they've passed like shadows,
And these shadows will fall between our words,
Before two nations, nourished by the suffering of centuries,
Will approach each other fraternally and again unite.

Antoni Słonimski, "Elegia miasteczek żydowskich," in *Poezje* (Warsaw: Czytelnik, 1955), 356.

Part Five ■ The Postwar Era:
War and Holocaust Revisited

■ Tadeusz Borowski (1922–51)
"The Man with the Package" (1948)

To Adolf Rudnicki

[Tadeusz Borowski's literary reputation rests principally on two collections of stories—*Pożegnanie z Marią* (*Farewell to Mary*, 1948) and *Kamienny świat* (*World of Stone*, 1948)—which were based on his own experiences in Auschwitz and Dachau during World War II. The stories aroused considerable controversy because of their stark realism, lack of sentimentality, and cold-blooded first-person narration. After the war, he returned to Poland, threw his lot in with the communists, wrote mostly pro-Party journalism, and propagated socialist realism. A troubled love life and misgivings about the ideological orientation of his postwar writing are the usual explanations for his suicide in July 1951.]

Our *Schreiber*[1] was a Jew from Lublin who came to Auschwitz an already experienced prisoner from Majdanek. Since he found a close friend in the *Sonderkommando*—which because of its riches acquired from the crematoria exercised considerable influence in the camp—he immediately started playing sick and without any difficulty got into *K. B. zwei*—the abbreviation (from *Krankenbau II*) for the separate section at Birkenau designated as a hospital. Once there he obtained the excellent position of *Schreiber* in our block. Instead of turning the ground all day with a spade, or carrying bags of cement on an empty stomach, the *Schreiber* did clerical work. He was the object of envy and intrigues on the part of other big shots similarly seeking to set up their friends with cushy jobs. A *Schreiber* escorted patients in and out of the hospital, took charge of the block's roll calls, kept patients' records, and took part indirectly in the selection of the Jews destined for the gas chamber, which in the autumn of '43 took place almost regularly every two weeks in all the sections of our camp. Assisted by the orderlies, the *Schreiber* was responsible for conducting patients to the *Waschraum*, from where cars drove them at night to one of the four crematoria, which at the time were still working in shifts. Then, some time in November, the *Schreiber* suddenly came down with a high fever, as far as I recall, from the flu, and, as the only sick Jew in the block, he was marked *zur besonderen Behandlung*, that is, for the gas, at the first selection.

Right after the selection, the senior orderly, called "blockmaster" out of politeness, went to Block 14, which consisted almost entirely of Jews, to negotiate for us to deliver our *Schreiber* to them earlier and this way spare us the unpleasant task of escorting him separately to the *Waschraum*.

"We're transferring him *auf vierzehn, Doktor, verstehen?*"[2] he said, upon his

---

Tadeusz Borowski, "Człowiek z paczką," in *Kamienny świat* (Warsaw: Czytelnik, 1948), 31–38.

    1. *Schreiber* is the German for "scribe."

    2. "To 14, Doctor, understand?"

return from 14, to the head doctor who was sitting at a table with a stethoscope in his ear. He was carefully checking the lungs of a newly arrived patient and was filling out his medical card with meticulous penmanship. The doctor shrugged without interrupting his work.

The *Schreiber* was squatting in the upper bunk and carefully tying a string around a cardboard box in which he kept his Czech boots laced to the knee, a spoon, a knife, a pencil, as well as some fat, rolls, and fruit that he had received from patients for various services rendered. Practically all the Jewish doctors and orderlies at the K. B. did the same; unlike the Poles, after all, they could not receive packages from anyone. In fact, the Poles at the K. B., who did get help from home, also took tobacco and food from the patients.

In the bunk opposite the *Schreiber*'s, an elderly Polish army major, who had been held in the block for months for no apparent reason, was playing a solitary game of chess, his thumbs over his ears. Below him, the nightwatchman lazily urinated into a bedpan and immediately burrowed under the blanket. Coughing and wheezing could be heard from the farther rooms; bacon sizzled loudly on the little stove; it was stuffy and sultry, as always toward evening.

The *Schreiber* descended from the bunk and took his package. The blockmaster brusquely tossed him a blanket and told him to put on his sandals. They left the block. From out our window we could see that in front of 14 the blockmaster pulled the blanket from the *Schreiber*'s shoulders, took away his sandals, and patted him on the back. Then the *Schreiber*, now dressed only in a nightshirt that billowed in the wind, walked into Block 14 in the company of another orderly.

It was just before evening, after rations, tea, and packages had been distributed in the rooms, when the orderlies started leading the Muslims[3] out of the blocks, lining them up in front of the door, five in a row, and pulling off their blankets and sandals. The SS man on duty appeared and told the orderlies to form a chain in front of the *Waschraum* so that nobody could escape. In the meantime, all the others in the blocks were busy downing supper and fumbling about their new packages.

From out our window we saw the *Schreiber* come out of 14, his package in hand; he took his place in line and, urged on by the shouts of the orderlies, shuffled with the others to the lavatory.

"*Schauen Sie mal, Doktor!*"[4] I called. The doctor removed his stethoscope, walked heavily to the window, and put his hand on my shoulder. "He could show a little more good sense, don't you think?" I asked.

3. In *History of the Holocaust: A Handbook and Dictionary,* ed. Abraham J. Edelheit and Hershel Edelheit (Boulder, Colo.: Westview Press, 1994), 337, "Muslim" is defined thus: "An inmate on the verge of death from starvation, exhaustion, and despair. It appears that the term originated with the similarities between a concentration camp victim and the image of a Moslem prostrating himself in prayer."
4. "Have a look, Doctor!"

It was already getting dark out, but you could see white nightshirts moving in front of the blocks. People's faces were indistinct. They went to a side and disappeared from view. I noticed that the lamps over the barbed-wire fence were on.

"He knows perfectly well, the old timer," I continued, "that in an hour or two he'll go to the gas naked, without his shirt, and without his package. What a weird attachment to the last of his belongings! After all, he could give it to someone else. I don't think that I'd ever . . ."

"You really think so?" said the doctor indifferently. He removed his hand from my shoulder, his jaw moving as if sucking at a cavity in a tooth.

"Forgive me, *Doktor,* but I don't think that you would . . ." I said casually.

The doctor came from Berlin, had a daughter and a wife in Argentina,[5] and sometimes spoke of himself as *wir Preussen,*[6] with a smile that combined the painful bitterness of a Jew with the pride of a former Prussian officer.

"I don't know. I don't know what I'd do if I were going to the gas. I'd probably also take my package with me."

He turned toward me and smiled playfully. I noticed that he was very tired and in need of sleep.

"I think that even if I was on my way to the oven, I would surely believe that something would happen along the way. I'd hold the package like somebody's hand, you know?"

He left the window, sat down at the table, and ordered another patient yanked from bed. He was preparing the return of a group of "recovereds" to the camp the next day.

The sick Jews filled the *Waschraum* with shrieks and moans and wanted to set fire to the building, but not one of them dared to lay a hand on the SS sanitation officer seated in the corner with his eyes closed, either pretending to be asleep or actually sleeping. Late in the evening, heavy crematorium trucks drove up to the camp; several SS men entered and ordered the Jews to leave everything in the *Waschraum.* The orderlies then began shoving them naked into the vehicles until the trucks were stacked with huge heaps of people. Crying and cursing, floodlights shining at them, they then rode away from the camp, desperately holding on to each other to keep from falling to the ground.

I don't know why, but it was said later in the camp that on their way to the gas chamber the Jews sang some heart-rending Hebrew song that nobody could understand.

5. "Argentina" was the name given the part of the concentration camp reserved for women.
6. "We Prussians."

▪ Jarosław Iwaszkiewicz (1894–1980)
"The Mendelssohn Quartet" (1953)

To Adolf Rudnicki

[Although a prolific poet of bold technique and imagination, Jarosław Iwaszkiewicz became best known for his novels, the most intriguing of which is *Czerwone tarcze* (*Red Shields,* 1934), a kind of fantasy built around the far-flung adventures of a medieval Polish crusader. The three-volume novel *Sława i chwała* (*Fame and Glory,* 1956–62), Iwaszkiewicz's major postwar work, is a broad picture of the Polish intelligentsia from the outbreak of World War I to the end of World War II; the novel was honored by the Polish Ministry of Culture and Art in 1963.

In addition to his poetry and novels, Iwaszkiewicz wrote many stories and plays. Among his stories, the most engrossing is "Matka Joanna od Aniołów" ("Mother Joan of the Angels"), which he wrote during World War II in occupied Poland. It is based on accounts of demonic possession among the nuns of a seventeenth-century convent in Loudun, France, the same material Aldous Huxley later used for *The Devils of Loudun.* Iwaszkiewicz's best-known plays are *Lato w Nohant* (*Summer in Nohant,* 1936), based on the Chopin–George Sand relationship, and *Maskarada* (*Masquerade,* 1938), which was inspired by the Russian poet Pushkin's last days.

Iwaszkiewicz's interest in music, which he studied in his younger days in Kiev, remained with him throughout his life. In addition to writing music, he also supplied librettos to the Polish composer Karol Szymanowski. This interest in music is reflected in his postwar story "Kwartet Mendelssohna" ("The Mendelssohn Quartet"), about émigré Jews in South America.

Iwaszkiewicz's long and distinguished literary career was paralleled in public service. He held several diplomatic posts in the interwar period, was actively engaged in clandestine cultural activity during the German occupation in World War II, and became prominent in politics and professional literary organizations after the war. He also edited one of the major postwar Polish literary reviews, *Twórczość* (*Creativity*).]

On the first day after my arrival in Santiago, I was invited to the Sholom Aleichem Club for the commemoration of the tenth anniversary of the Warsaw Ghetto Uprising. The festivities took place in a remote neighborhood of the huge city, one recalling the colonial period. We arrived there, quite late, in the fog of a March evening. The moon, which broke through the mists rising from the ring of the Andes surrounding the city, illuminated an old church. Its icing-like filigree decorations were characteristic of the Portuguese-Spanish style of the colonial epoch. The street consisted of ordinary little one-storied houses forming a closed border. Each of these houses had a door in the middle with two large windows on either

---

Jarosław Iwaszkiewicz, "Kwartet Mendelssohna," in *Opowiadania, 1918–1953* (Warsaw: Czytelnik, 1956), 558–74.

side, the edges of which were usually also surrounded with icing-like decoration and cornices painted a chocolate or cream color. You entered through such doors into a wide entrance hall or even onto an exotic patio—nowadays most of the time in disrepair and dirty. The population moved from this elegant old neighborhood into charming little homes with gardens full of figs, grapes, oranges, and peaches extending to the north and east of the city up to the very mountains. Now the poor live here, the medium well-off, or those used to the old nineteenth-century ways of the residents of Santiago.

The Club was quartered in one of these old houses where we were headed. Its old patio had been turned into a lecture hall.

We arrived rather late. The applause that greeted us interrupted a lecture by a young, thickset Jew who gave us an unfriendly look. Even reckoning the customary Chilean delay—la hora chillena—we had gone a bit too far. They had begun without us. We took our places in the first row. The young fellow continued. He spoke in a heavily Germanized Yiddish so that I could understand every word. His lecture was full of hate, directed, unfortunately, not at the organizers and executioners of the ghetto—the German Nazis—but at the Poles on whose soil the massacre took place. If his words were to be believed, had it not been for the anti-Semitism of the Polish population, Hitler and Himmler would never have hit on the idea of exterminating the Jews. I felt uncomfortable. Fortunately, the speech of the primitive hothead didn't last long. He concluded on several strong notes.

Immediately afterward, a thin blond strode to the stage and in the tone of a confided secret announced that the Chilean poet Antoni Fajgenbaum would read two of his poems. The poems were not bad at all—as far as I could judge—but very melancholic in mood and hopeless in content. The young, tall, frail fellow sang his poems—all of them sing them there in the manner of Pablo Neruda— from time to time casting at his audience through large glasses in black frames a glance full of the sadness and contempt of his not entirely even looking, dark, shining eyes. He compared his far-flung compatriots to "mad dogs" and this refrain was repeated every few verses:

Perros hambrientes,
Perros errantes . . .
[Starving dogs,
Mad dogs]

I looked around the hall. People were listening to the poet silently and respectfully. A heavy blond woman not far from me shook her head in a kind of religious devotion. She seemed to be in agreement with what she heard, though she didn't look like someone starving.

The poetry didn't last long either. It was rewarded with abundant applause. Afterward, the young fellow with the intimate confidences appeared again and told us in Spanish, and then, evidently in deference to my presence, in Polish, that so and so (he mentioned names) were going to play the Mendelssohn Quartet "for two violins, viola, and cello."

Four musicians then appeared on the stage behind him. The first violin was handsome, young, and elegant; the second, dry, with a huge nose, perhaps a pharmacist; the viola player, a heavyset, bulging, grayish Jew, the butcher type. The one who interested me the most was the cellist. Since it took rather a long time to set up the music stands and lay out the music, I could observe him at my leisure. He was already a quite old man, with a gray beard, in gold-rimmed glasses, with an unusually sharp gaze with which he first took in the entire hall, then those of us sitting up front, and finally his colleagues on stage. He was the fastest to manage the chair, music stand, and music. Then he took his place and devoted himself entirely to the music. One could see that the festive expectation of the beginning of the quartet excited him. With a quiet whisper he hurried along the second violinist who was bothered by the height of the music stand and for whom everyone was waiting.

Finally they began playing. Contrary to custom, it wasn't the first violin but the cellist who gave the signal to begin. It was he who also set the tempo, tapped with his foot, shook his head until his gray mane fell over his forehead. He was absorbed in his own playing, tenderly stroking the strings of the cello. It soon became obvious that the ear of his imagination was tuned to some other ideal performance of the quartet, distant, alas, from the one to which the audience in the hall was listening.

The other performers barely kept up with the cellist and that caused a number of discordant notes. Moreover, the first violin must have known another conception of the entire work, for he tried to play "elegantly," lifting the bow from the strings with an exaggerated, round movement. It came out emphatically in the imitations. The phrase began seriously in the bass and as if inspired, strode indifferently past the viola and the second violin, and took new life in the first violin, elegant, accelerated, and executed with Viennese style, like a pair of fashionable shoes.

When the "intermezzo"—adagio—was reached, the cellist was in his own element. I looked at him the whole time. His hands extended themselves with the bow and along the strings, as if he were caressing some precious being. He didn't look at the music, played from memory, and with his eyes shut shook his head left and right. It even seemed that he was softly humming the Mendelssohn melody. When the adagio was finished, and there was a pause, in which the instruments were put aside, my cellist seemed to awaken and gazed directly at me with a certain dread. A good Jewish soul looked at me through his eyes behind a pair of gold-rimmed glasses with a kind of sincere trust into which the original expression of fear had transformed itself. He obviously perceived that I was listening to the quartet with great pleasure. But it wasn't the mediocre performance that was affording me the pleasure so much as the recollection associated with this particular work, which my wife and I used to play together as a piano duet a long time ago.

In the finale, unfortunately, it was the first violinist who triumphed. Paying no heed to the old man, he decided to present himself in the most favorable light. He raced ahead or added unnecessary fermatas, and played all melodious phrases with a gypsy schmalziness, which was very much out of place in this piece. The cellist did not hide his dissatisfaction, shrugged his shoulders, grumbled, hurriedly caught up with the high-flying leader and once even threw me a glance as if seeking help or understanding. I smiled.

Enthusiastic appeal greeted the conclusion of the performance. The members of the quartet bowed pleasantly to the audience. The sole exception was the old cellist. He made a contemptuous gesture with a hand, and while his colleagues were acknowledging the applause, started to leave the stage. Thoroughly pleased with himself, the first violinist bowed with the charm of an experienced virtuoso. While he was preoccupied with himself, he noticed the old man bolting from the stage, detained him by the hand, and forced him to bow.

"It was Pan Friedenssohn who really organized the quartet," my neighbor whispered into my ear.

The further course of the festivity was more complicated. We were invited to the chairman's table and a round of speeches and recollections then ensued. It all lasted a fairly long time. Then my turn came to say a few words. As I began, I noticed that old Friedenssohn was sitting in the hall attentively listening to my words. There were ordinary. I recounted what I had seen.

"I saw those columns of fire above the houses . . . I saw those curtains flapping in dead windows . . . I saw . . ."

My eye involuntarily returned to the figure of the old Jew with the white beard. Each time I began "I saw," he moved uncomfortably in his seat. When I finished these few poor sentences, disillusionment was painted on the face of the old cellist. As I was leaving the podium I noticed him making the same gesture of distaste and disappointment as he had after the performance. This began to intrigue me a bit.

When the commemorative meeting had come to an end, we went behind the curtains, to an adjacent narrow room, in order to congratulate the "artists." My Chilean friend bitterly reproached the young poet for his "stray dogs." Friedenssohn listened attentively. I introduced myself to him.

"Pan Friedenssohn, do you speak Polish?"

"Why shouldn't I?" He looked me over carefully.

"You left Poland a long time ago?" I asked.

"What do you think!"

His answer didn't sound encouraging. But suddenly the old man seemed to overcome something in himself. He turned to me with a different expression on his face.

"You are a writer, Pan Iwaszkiewicz? I'd like to have a little chat with you . . ."

"By all means. With pleasure; but when?"

"When, when? Right now. Tomorrow I won't want to talk."

I was taken aback.

"But where? Here?"

"There's a small bar on the corner here; not a bar really, but a coffee shop— something like that. Would you like to join me? Will you accept my invitation?"

I turned to my companions.

"Señor Friedenssohn is inviting me," I said. "There's a coffee shop somewhere nearby."

"An awful dump."

"Dump, no dump," interjected Friedenssohn in Spanish, "but it's near."

"Fine," said my friend. "But it so happens there's too many of us; we've got just the one car. We'll ride over and then send the car back."

"Splendid."

In a little while, we were sitting in the bar. It really was a dingy hole-in-the-wall, but unusually busy for this peaceful neighborhood. It wasn't a coffee shop or a bar, just an ordinary run-of-the-mill restaurant specializing in earthenware pots of national dishes: giblets in black sauce and kidneys with rice, along with pitchers of turbid "chicha," or grape juice, a splendid thirst quencher after the sharp local pepper but it went straight to the head. This was indeed right after the grape harvest.

The dive was full of people, for the most part simple, tired, eating greedily. Behind the cash register stood a handsome, arrogant gentleman dressed in white who was waiting on customers at the bar with a mild contempt. He evidently knew his way around people because he immediately shot us a glance full of considerable curiosity; people like us didn't come here as a rule.

Pan Friedenssohn—his first name was Nathan—and I sat down in a corner, behind a pillar, his thick body separating us from the barroom and the young men hanging around there who were already well in their cups. We ordered coffee and a little red wine. The whole time Friedenssohn avoided my gaze, rubbed his hands together, and examined with interest the design of the dirty paper napkin. He posed no questions to me, and in general had nothing to say. I began to regret accepting his invitation. In order to break the silence which was heaving heavily on me, I said:

"A lovely piece, that Mendelssohn quartet . . ."

The old man looked at me a bit from the side, inquisitively, and for a while, as if weighing the words he wanted to say.

Then he suddenly raised a finger and smacked his lips.

"What a quartet! Do you understand, the Men-dels-sohn quartet. What is the Mendelssohn quartet? And what do they understand of it, those poor excuses for musicians," he added contemptuously. "You heard how the first violin, Cohen's his name, how he played the finale? He didn't have the slightest idea, not the slightest. You know, he plays in an orchestra, a jazz orchestra, in the Hotel Carrera. Know what he plays? Rumbas, sambas, the "Persian Fair"! At the very most, the Hungarian dance . . . How can he play such a quartet? How do you say it in Polish? Such 'peaks of music' [szczyty muzyki]? A real feast, Pan Iwaszkiewicz. There can't be anything lovelier . . . so truly Jewish! So how can somebody like that play it, somebody who plays sambas every night and hums along with that cat's voice of his."

"Yet it was nice of him to take part in the quartet."

"Humph, don't believe him." Nathan said forcefully. "He plays here, he plays there . . ."

"What do you mean, "plays there?""

"What do I mean? You know, there . . . at the Zionists. He plays there as well . . . All he has to do is show how he lifts his bow. You saw it, didn't you? Ah, some big deal! They wave their bows around like that in every Viennese coffeehouse . . . What a misfortune . . . They never heard Cohen."

"Well, but you got by all right."

"Got by, got by . . . With Mendelssohn it's not a question of getting by, but of playing. It is music, Pan Iwaszkiewicz . . ."

"Have you been playing a long time?" I said, for the sake of saying something.

"What do you mean, a long time? I was born with a violin in my hands. And the cello my father put in my cradle." He burst out laughing all of a sudden and the laugh smoothed out his entire face with a kind of childish and good expression. His eyes, too, were laughing and he grew almost attractive. "I'm just telling it this way," he laughed again, "since a cello, after all, won't fit into a cradle. When I was ten years old, I used to sleep in the cello's case. There were a lot of us in the family and we didn't have enough beds . . . Even Barcewicz listened to me play when he visited Tarnów. 'Well, Nathan,' he said, 'you'll make something of yourself!' "

"And you see," I interjected thoughtlessly, "you have made something of yourself!"

Friedenssohn looked at me sadly. There was no longer a trace of laughter on his face, his white beard rose up, and it was obvious that he was gritting his teeth. "God," I thought to myself, "how I still somehow don't know how to talk to people!" Friedenssohn, before saying anything else, again began curiously examining the design of the paper napkin, and then with a slender, dry hand with long fingers shredded it into invisible fragments.

"Oh, you're joking, joking," he said finally, sighing, "but one has to joke somehow . . . somehow . . . differently . . ." As he sought the last word my flesh began crawling. "What have I made of myself? What am I? What has become of me? I never amounted to much . . . and now?"

"Do you live alone here? In Santiago?"

"Whom am I supposed to live with? I don't have anyone . . ."

"And what do you do?" I asked hurriedly. Our conversation resembled a walk through a huge hall containing many doors. Opening each door revealed an occupied room, and the doors had to be slammed shut so as not to complicate matters.

"A woman I know runs a business in the mall. She sells bracelets. Indian, Araucanian . . . Our Jews here make these Araucanian bracelets . . . and I keep accounts for her evenings. The balance, things like that. I'm an old bookkeeper, so I know how to balance everything so it comes out right, tip-top!"

"Pretty bad if the books didn't balance," I laughed.

"You said it," he laughed back, revealing long yellow teeth, "you said it. But somehow my life's never balanced out . . ."

"You're lonely," I said.

"Lonely, lonely," Friedenssohn flared up suddenly and rubbed his hand roughly along the table. "That's not what it's about. There are plenty of lonely people now. What I lost, I put down to losses . . ."

"Did you lose a lot?" I said.

"A lot? Depends. If Rockefeller loses a million dollars, that's not a lot for him. But if I lose a thousand pesos, that's a lot for me." He thought for a moment and then added more quietly and much more calmly: "I lost a lot: my wife, my son . . . in the ovens, over there, everyone."

He became silent. I looked at him, observing the play of expressions on his face, which changed greatly. After a while, he began speaking again: "Well what, Pan Iwaszkiewicz? I wanted to tell you a great deal, and nothing. You said you saw how the ghetto burned. So what if it burned? The way I see it, not much."

"How do you mean that, Nathan? The Jews took up arms!"

"Because it seemed to them that they had a country. You know, my Moritz thought the same. He went off to war, to Israel. When we were still in Tarnów people kept coming to us who were gathering Jews for the new fatherland, for Israel. My father didn't leave for Israel; he went instead to Argentina. And I thought that I had a country. My Moritz never mixed into politics; he was neither a Zionist nor a communist. But as soon as he heard that there was a war going on there, he left behind his violin."

"He played the violin?"

"How he played? Pan Iwaszkiewicz, that was playing . . . not like that phony Cohen from the Hotel Carrera. He abandoned his violin and said: 'Dad . . . daddy, there's a war over there, so I'm going.' And so, he went. As soon as he arrived, he died right away. On the Egyptian border . . . I ask you, what did he go for?"

"He evidently regarded it as his duty."

"My dear, we were all so stupid." He flared up suddenly, striking the table with both hands. "We were such idiots! Not only he, but I, Nathan Friedenssohn, also regarded it as a duty. Well, as you can see, I didn't succeed in balancing it correctly."

"What do you mean, Nathan?"

"Fatherland, fatherland . . . every person has his fatherland. Why is it that the Jews don't have their own fatherland? Well, you tell me."

"But you just said you consider Israel . . ."

"Israel?" He was so astonished that he even got up in his chair, looking at me without a pause. "Israel?" he repeated.

I was somewhat ashamed. I should have guessed.

But Nathan erupted in a torrent of words:

"You're right. I thought it would be our fatherland, mine, Moritz's, my wife's. I didn't need a fatherland in Tarnów, I didn't need a fatherland in Santiago, because I already had a fatherland. Do you understand? A Jewish state . . . a Jewish army, a Jewish press, Jewish education. The kind even Orzeszkowa didn't imagine. Well, what came of it? What? Why did we need a fatherland — just to spit on the Arab? Why did we need a fatherland — just to sell it to the Americans? Why did we need a fatherland — just to . . . Did you hear what they worked out with that Adenauer? For them to pay! For the gas, for the ashes, for the gold teeth — for them to pay. Did you ever hear of anything like it? Did you ever hear? I know what it's called. Thirty pieces of silver . . . imagine, money, for blood. Did anyone ever see the likes of it? Take what money? From whom? From those who murdered, who threw children into ovens . . . Did you ever hear of it? My entire family was sent to them, the whole of Tarnów. My wife didn't hold out. Her heart . . . ," he pointed to his heart, "one-two."

He stared at me for a while, and then again at his hands stretched out on the table. He was breathing hard, and I was afraid that he was going to burst out crying. But no, he calmed down, and a few minutes later began in an entirely different tone.

"Pan Iwaszkiewicz," he said, "that's all I wanted to say. I saw at once that you're a kindhearted man; I could tell from your eyes" — he was obviously using the word "kindhearted" in the meaning of "polite" — "and I thought to myself: Nathan, tell it to that man . . ."

I was a little surprised that that was all. But I remained silent.

He raised his eyes to me again.

"Well, so what can I do?"

I didn't understand the question. The old homeless man, standing over his grave. What was he asking me about? What did it mean? I still said nothing.

"You're surprised," Friedenssohn said, suddenly raising his eyes to me, "you're quite surprised. What is the old man asking? What can he do? He's got to die. Yes. But where is he to die?"

"What do you mean, where? We don't choose our place of death . . . or the time of death."

"That's not what it's about, Pan Iwaszkiewicz. But which side to die on? Where to stop? I'd like to die peacefully . . . but it seems I won't succeed."

"On the side of truth, Pan Friedenssohn. Truth is the best fatherland."

"That's a difficult fatherland," he sighed, "the road to it is far."

"Perhaps not."

"It's not so much that it's far, but it's so hard . . . I would like to die in Poland," he added a moment later in a whisper, "that's a country!"

"The same as others, Pan Friedenssohn. We're all human beings."

"But you . . . you want the truth, don't you? Well, no?"

"Yes, of course," I was a bit confused, "but I repeat: we are all human beings. Human work is sometimes fallible."

"If only I were there!" sighed the old Nathan, and after a while he added: "Why did that Moritz of mine go to Palestine? He should have gone to you . . ."

I looked at him, moved. We were silent a long while.

Rather it was just I who was silent. Nathan Friedenssohn whispered, as if to himself. That gave me somewhat of a fright. The dive was beginning to get lively and his whisper was drowned in the general hubbub. He repeated the words of the poem: "Perros hambrientes, / perros errantes."

Then he grew completely silent.

"They're making noise," he motioned with his head uncertainly in the direction of the bar.

I observed that it was now my turn. I realized that everything I'd say could only be banal. What could I say to that lonely, embittered old man?

"Dear Pan Friedenssohn," I began, "we all have a single fatherland: the struggle for peace and progress. In that land, we are all brothers."

To my surprise, Nathan perked up when he heard this trite generality. He strained his ear. Was it that he needed consolation and was willing to find it anywhere, or was it more likely that what seemed to me to be a trite phrase was still full of fresh content for him? Rarely had he met such a sentiment.

"Do you think so," he kept on asking, "do you really think so?"

And then suddenly opening his hands:

"And how is it with this peace, Pan Iwaszkiewicz?"

"No one on earth, and especially simple people, wants war. And because they don't want war, they join together as one. And so they are also like brothers, in peace."

I was somewhat embarrassed by these simplifications, but old Friedenssohn was listening with satisfaction.

"Oh, that's it, that's it!" he repeated. "I wouldn't want to be alone, you understand, Pan Iwaszkiewicz. Old—alone; that's not good."

I smiled gently.

"Old age, unfortunately, is always lonely," I observed.

Friedenssohn stirred.

"But what do you know about it? You're a Pole, from Poland, you're doing things there. You're not alone, Pan Iwaszkiewicz."

"You are not alone, Pan Friedenssohn," I repeated like an echo.

The old man again grew pensive. Then he suddenly raised his head and again looked at me. That same childlike smile as of a while before suddenly lit up and smoothed out his old man's face. I would say that some inner happiness changed his expression, and he looked the way he did at the beginning of the quartet.

"I had the feeling at once that you'd comfort me, Jarosław." This was the first time that he called me by my first name. "You are an intelligent man. And you like Jews."

"I would correct that perhaps to 'you like people,'" I interjected.

"It's good to talk to you," sighed Friedenssohn, looking at his watch.

I, too, glanced in the direction of the window through which I glimpsed the car waiting for me.

"But you nevertheless gestured after my talk," I said. "I displeased you, just like Cohen in the last part of the quartet."

"No, no, not at all," mused Nathan, "I gestured because I wasn't there. I'd have liked to see that."

"Why?" I asked surprised. "It was terrible!"

The waiter came over to us at that moment. I wanted to pay the small bill, but Friedenssohn wouldn't allow me to.

We got up and headed toward the exit, threading our way past thickly occupied tables. On the sidewalk, we were greeted by complete silence and a foggy, windless fall night, as customary here. Friedenssohn took me by the hand.

"Pan Iwaszkiewicz," he said. "I didn't gesture because of anything bad you said. I gestured because I was unable to see everything that was going on, because I wasn't able to fight."

He pronounced the word "fight" as if with difficulty, distaste, and surprise. One could see that the word was alien to him and that he was well aware how very strange it sounded coming from his lips.

On the street, I noticed for the first time that Nathan Friedenssohn was quite short, or rather that he was very thin and stooped. I hadn't realized it. Now he straightened himself up, with effort, and in a somehow sad yet at the same alert way, glanced down the street where a thick, white fog was rolling in. The light of the moon shone through the fog.

"Every upright person has to fight now. I always wanted to, but couldn't," a melancholy whisper sounded next to me. "Who ever saw a fighting Jew among us? In those days? I regret that I didn't see what you have. Moritz also wanted to fight. He managed to, but not on your side."

And again Nathan Friedenssohn made his usual gesture. As if wiping clean his whole wretched life, as if asking for forgiveness for being the way he was. He again fell to stooping as he gestured.

"I'll give you a lift, Pan Friedenssohn," I said as we drew near the automobile.

"No, no thank you," he begged off, looking at me sadly through his gold-rimmed glasses. I don't live far from here, and I still have to pick up my cello at the Club."

And as if the mention of the instrument reminded him of something else, he reached for my hand as I was about to open the door handle of the car and holding me by the arm, looking me in the eye, again cheered up, he said:

"There are those, Pan Iwaszkiewicz, who have one other fatherland—music. You know, I could play that Mendelssohn quartet from morning till evening . . ."

Was it the moon that was shining so? No, not really. In Nathan Friedenssohn's good, dark eyes tears were shining as he said to me:

"Farewell, Pan Iwaszkiewicz."

I opened the car door.

■ Marian Piechal (1905–89)
"Yankel's Last Concert" (1954)

[Marian Piechal was a prolific poet, satirist, and essayist. Between 1928 and 1930 he was a member of the "Meteor" group of poets in his native Łódź; in 1929, he also became affiliated with the "Kwadryga" group. He was a prisoner of war for a time during World War II and later served in the Polish Home Army. After the war, he served as editor-in-chief of the Łódź literary journal *Osnowa* (*The Foundation*), assistant editor-in-chief of the journal *Poezja* (*Poetry*), and finally editor of the poetry section of *Miesięcznik Literacki* (*Literary Monthly*). In 1954, he was awarded the literary prize of the city of Łódź, and in 1968 a State Award Second Class for the whole of his literary work. The Yankel of Piechal's poem refers to Yankel the dulcimer player in Mickiewicz's *Pan Tadeusz*.]

Yankel's Last Concert

In the ghetto old Yankel, a widower, who had buried
His own sons, daughters, and grandchildren, used to play the zither.
Dozing for days on end he was silent as a stone, grim,
At times speaking only on this instrument.
He was like an oak tree, struck suddenly by a bolt of misfortune,
With cut-off branches and burned half through.
A naked trunk! Sometimes the wind whistles through the shafts.
So it was that Yankel sometimes played on his zither.

When Yankel was taken from his camp to the gas
They let him take his zither so long as he played it.
The tattered throng was gathered in the Umschlagplatz.
Yankel was called forth. He was ordered to begin.
The bemedaled uniforms dazzled the eye.
"Play merrily, Yankel! You enjoy yourself too!"

Yankel strode to the middle with wavering steps.
He paused for a moment. He anxiously stroked his beard.
He was silent. He pressed the zither to his chest like a child,
The way a father does who senses that the child's death is near.
He fondled the zither a while, the child's living body,
The last that still bound him to life. And finally
He touched the zither's strings, stroking them like hair,
And from this hair he slowly brought forth a melody.

Marian Piechal "Ostatni koncert Jankiela," in *Moje imperium* (Łódź: Wydawnictwo Lodzkie, 1975), 28–32.

He played. He played as they wanted. He raised his spirits
When he recalled how an SS-man shot his son, and how,
Before he died, he ordered him to strike his father in the face
For having produced him, a Jewish brat,
And afterward ordered the father to strike his son in the face
For the fact that by beating his father, he forgot who he was.
And he ordered them to beat each other in the face
Until they fell to the ground in tears, blood, and spittle.
Then the *shaulis*,[1] in order to relieve the son's dying,
Pumped a bullet into his temple—like a period after a sentence.
Thus perished his first son, then a second one after him,
Then a third, next his daughters, and after his daughters,
The grandchildren. The stings of bullets hurled them into a
Bottomless pit where neither sun nor moon ever peer.

When he thus strayed in memory over his vanished family
A clear streamlet of melody flowed from beneath his fingers:
Waves play on the moon, stars twinkle in it,
Silver streaks flash, modulated by the night,
Strings lightly undulate, tone accompanies tone,
Constantly growing, like the downpour of a gathering storm.
One sound can be heard in it, like the bell of an alarm.
Yankel stifles it in vain, muffles it futilely,
Until at last he struck his auditors in the face with this sound
Then broke it off. As if suddenly the bell burst and fell from the tower.

Silence. Children huddle close to their elders like sheep.
Everything is hostile and foreign to the elders, wherever they look.
Even the sky is German. And the earth is German.
Only the soul of each of their children is Jewish.
And Yankel? Although his children were asleep in the ground,
Their living eyes continued to gaze at him.

Music can be heard. But what kind? He pays heed to no one.
It binds the rhythm of his heart with the staccato of the music.
Are those stars on the strings shining amid his fingers?
Are the tears running from his eyes flowing over his fingers?
Although the melody is mixed with stars and tears,
Its chords grow ever more stronger
And each chord is different, differently colored,
Clear on the surface, yet screamingly red down below.

1. Lithuanian Nazi collaborators.

From beneath his fingers, instead of sounds, blood begins to spurt,
To swell with blazing fire, to fling lightning bolts,
To thunder with anger, which, wrapped in a fog of grief,
Rumbles silently beneath the hand as if thrust into the ground.

"From my mother's womb, I came here, to the shores of the Vistula,
My sons and grandsons issued from my bones,
The pride of generations grew continually from father to son,
Like a forest of Lebanese cypress trees in Slavic lands.
What crime did we commit, of what sin were we guilty?
Did we break laws, violate statutes,
For which we are being burned alive today in crematoria,
For which one Goliath is beating thousands of Davids?
The hands of our enemies are strong, organized,
While ours are like leaves scattered by the wind.
Peace sleeps in a golden bed in a safe,
While war grazes on the blood and tears of the wretched.
They call us "tynef," nickname us "tsoa;"[2]
The yellow patch on our backs cries "Kill the Jew!"
Fate has united and equalized us in the face of death,
Those in gold and rags, those in roses and feces.
Jahweh, Jahweh, O Jahweh, O Emmanuel,
If you exist, hasten from the Sinai, Tabor, and Carmel!
A day passes not without Crime transgressing Your borders,
And separating us from the light like water from fire.
There is no Moses among us to nudge the rocks of hearts
With his stick and open a white stream of mercy.
The precipice has spoken, the abyss has raised its hands,
We are like oars tossed overboard,
We are like fusible snow in the sun atop a cliff,
We disappear suddenly from life like smoke after a shot."

Yankel stills the strings, unwraps them from the fog of grief,
And bares all the fires burning in the strings.
A hand suddenly chokes them, bends the strings down,
Extinguishes one string after another till they all vanish in smoke.

It seemed that he had paused. But with his right hand
He controls the strings like a gull the sea
In which an elusive prey suddenly shone.
But what is it? A groan or a sneer? A curse or a prayer?

---

2. Yiddish terms meaning "good-for-nothing" and "nuisance," respectively.

He raises up the zither and though shaken by weeping,
Begins intoning the "El mole rachmim" with full voice . . .

"Thou who art billion! Who art multiplied
By a billion billions, infinite Jahweh!
Who counteth Thy stars from dusk to dawn,
And by day wrappeth Thyself in silken azure!
Who hath brows of clouds and a head of storm,
And pupils of lightning bolts and speech of thunder!
Who raiseth the seas and openeth dawns—
What canst Thou mean on earth if Thou canst do naught?
If a people who until now believes only in Thy name
Counts for less than an echo and dies out like an echo?'

He grew silent, put down the zither, stifled by despair,
Beneath the Wailing Wall erected from all his tears.

His auditors stirred, like frightened sheep.
Everything their gaze rested on was hostile and foreign to them.
The bemedaled uniforms dazzled the eye:
"Play some more, Yankel! Rejoice after your tears!"
Then, suppressing tears and despair, he again took up the zither
And pointed it, like a shield, in the direction of the uniforms,
Saying: "The fool declared: I am master of the earth!—
And under his feet boils a volcano of fire,
A volcano of human anger that swells beneath the earth,
That will open its maw unto you and will blow as if at dust.
Ordinary people are arising against evil, the ordinary people of every nation.
People, hurry, attire yourself against the winds and storm!
By their anger will the people overthrow evil, the vile order of the world.
People, hurry, arm yourselves in thunder and fire!
The people will raise a million weapons forged from anger
And will move against you, enemies! And this people will triumph!"

Now Yankel takes his leave of the living forever
And thus draws forth those deeper tones, from below,
From the main current of despair, from the dark stream,
Changing the melodious song of grievance into a groan of pain.
He then reaches the clouds, takes his place among the whirlwinds,
And gathers the scampering clouds into a herd of thunderheads.
He clenches black balls of thick clouds all the tighter
And with lightning bolts opens sudden abysses in them
And hurls his enemies into them, and from the zither as if from a slingshot
Fires projectiles of anger at them with all his might:

"You beheld the heights, and the heights are crumbling;
You beheld cities, and the cities are aflame.
Everything you touch a fierce fire will reduce to ashes;
Your eyes and hands and feet are cursed!
Our torment will blossom in future generations;
Time will repay us in fruit for the seeds it took away.
Everything our enemy undertakes, he undertakes senselessly,
Arranging one day after another like coffin on coffin.
Crime, violating nature, commits a serious error,
Itself breeding the embryo of its own destruction.
Behold! That cloud forming from the mists of our blood
Conceals the future thunderbolt that will kill you.
For it has been said: 'Lightning will incinerate you
For the terrible EVIL that you have sown here!' "

Having said this, he touched the strings, as if stroking hair,
And suddenly evoked a song of triumph from them.
He played. He played as they wanted. He himself rejoiced.
But he did not finish . . .
                        the SS-man shot him straight in the heart.

Yankel flung his arms wide. He fell chest down on the zither.
It was a lovely April day. Easter. Sunday.
Just then the uprising began in the ghetto.
The beginning of it was Yankel's last concert.

■ Tadeusz Różewicz (1921–   )
"The Branch" (1973)

[Tadeusz Różewicz is one of Poland's most prominent contemporary writers. He began his career as a poet in the immediate aftermath of World War II, in which he fought as a member of the underground Home Army. His first books — *Niepokój* (*Anxiety*, 1947) and *Czerwona rękawiczka* (*The Red Glove*, 1948) — reflect the profound impact of the war on his consciousness and his repudiation of traditional poetics. Shaped by his wartime experiences, and by postwar political tensions, his outlook on the human condition has been bleak and depressing. This is true not only of his poetry, but of his prose and plays. Beginning with such works as *Kartoteka* (*The Card File*, 1961), *Świadkowie czyli nasza mała stabilizacja* (*The Witnesses, or Our Small Stabilization*, 1962), *Akt przerywany* (*The Interrupted Act*, 1966), and *Stara kobieta wysiaduje* (*An Old Woman Broods*, 1968), Różewicz soon established himself as one of the leading postwar Polish dramatists and a principal architect of the postwar Polish "theater of the absurd." The short story "The Branch" is from the collection *Przerwany egzamin* (*The Interrupted Examination*).]

The boy opened his eyes. It was night. He heard loud breathing and a groan. It was dark. Auntie had not shut the clothes closet for the night, even though uncle shouted at her and ordered her always to shut it. There was a wind. It ran across the roof and around the house and, out of breath, stuck its pointy mouth into all corners. The boy raised his head and looked through the door that had not been completely closed. On the bed beneath the wall, a large clump was tossing about. Somewhere a motor growled. A rectangle of light fell through the window; it moved along the wall. The boy saw in this light two big, white legs raised up, without black shoes and stockings; motionless like strange animals. Laughter, sobbing, and later clapping resounded in the darkness. Uncle and auntie were fighting in bed again.

The boy hid beneath the blanket, made a tent over his head, and tucked up his legs. Tears, warm and salty, flowed onto his lips.

Auntie was the nicest to him. Once when she came back from town, she told him to get out of the clothes closet and gave him a cookie, a sugar-sprinkled star. For a long time afterward he had sweet crumbs in his pocket. He liked scraping them out and tasting them with his tongue.

He felt stuffy and poked his head out. Now he heard snoring and faint whistling in the midst of the darkness that has no face and seems to be everywhere. The wind strolled over the roof and knocked against the tiles.

Again he heard something rapping on the window and the panes ring. "It's

Tadeusz Różewicz, *Proza* (Wrocław: Zakład Narodowy im. Ossolińskich, Wydawnictwo, 1973), 11–13.

probably mama come," he thought, "and she's standing outside the window." If it was mama, then he would kiss her and immediately ask her to comb out his hair. Sometimes he would grab a louse that crawled out of his head and walked about his ear; it was like a grain, big and soft like an unripe grain of wheat. The skin on his head burned a lot. When he again heard rapping on the window, he opened the clothes closet. The room was dark. Something moved on the other side of the window. He thrust a leg out of the clothes closet and touched the floor with his toes. Sudden snoring resounded and the boy slowly closed the clothes closet. He wrapped himself up in his blanket and did not breathe. It seemed to him that the clothes closet creaked and squeaked piercingly. He heard a monotonous rapping that grew softer and softer, and finally the knocks turned into a grating and rustling, as if someone was strewing sand against the window.

He got up, since there was no one at home. He carefully parted the door of the clothes closet and went out. He sat down in the armchair in the middle of the room. His legs felt artificial and as brittle as straw. His knees gave way. His uncle told him he would kill him the moment he left the clothes closet.

A mortar stood in the kitchen. It shone like a star. Something moved on the other side of the window. He heard rustling; a shadow swayed on the wall. Someone was rapping now on the pane. The boy escaped into the clothes closet. It was silent and dark like a bag. He never looked out through the window, even when he was alone; he turned his shoulders to it. He knew he was not allowed to. Mama had cried when she told him he was not permitted to look out the window. He said that he would not. Uncle told him that as soon as he looked out the window, the Germans would shoot him. The Germans wore huge black boots and everyone was afraid of them. They had red faces and fired golden bullets. The Germans carried these bullets in their teeth and you could see them shining. Once a German came up to uncle and fired at the ceiling with bullets like fire. But he could no longer recall it. It was the same as with the sun. He shut his eyes in order to see the sun; he pressed his eyelids with his fingers and then a small white circle without rays became visible in the darkness. The circle was not like the sun in the sky, and it was cold.

He put his small hand into a pocket. He had several stones in it that he played with. They were round and sharp. He knew all the stones and their colors. The smallest one, which was round, was pink; the triangular and sharp one was blue, like a flower. Others were gray and yellow. One was white and looked like a small egg. When you strike one stone against another, a small red spark that smells like rain leaps out. He collected the stones along the road, when mama took him to uncle's, to the clothes closet. He made himself a rattle out of them and softly rattled it near an ear. Sometimes he spoke to the stones and put them in his mouth.

He heard shouts, which came to him from the street, and again the rattling of the window panes, banging, and rustling, as if someone was scuffling outside the window. "It's mama," he thought, "she's been standing the whole night under the window, and now she's rapping and waiting for me." He opened the clothes closet and tip-toed to the window.

Across the way, beneath a red wall, boys were playing buttons. A branch struck the window. Wet leaves stuck to the pane and then flew off after the escaping branch; the wind blew at the trees and whispered something. One of the boys knelt down over a puddle and put a little white boat into the water. There was no sun in the sky. The boy who floated the boat raised his head up; he suddenly grabbed the little boat and ran up to the window. He pressed his face against the pane; he had a flattened nose and two big holes in his nose. The boy from the clothes closet stood by the window, unable to move. His legs were so light he did not feel them, and yet as heavy as a house. The eyes of the boy with the little boat were motionless, and of yellow glass. Suddenly he winked and shouted something. The crowd of boys from beneath the red wall came running up to the window. They stood on their toes and pressed their faces against the pane. The one who stood behind the others, like a pole, stuck out a big tongue, and then shrieked:

"Jew!"

The boys began jumping up and down and shouting:

"Jew, Jew-boy, Jew-boy!" After that they again pressed their foreheads, lips, noses, eyes, and tongues like wide, pink shovels against the pane. The boy who resembled a pole grabbed a stone and flung it at the window. He then began brandishing a stick. The boys scattered on all sides, shouting:

"Jew, Jew-boy, Jew-boy!"

The boy slowly turned away from the window. Beneath the table lay a gray, old stone. The boy looked at the stone and said:

"What did I do?"

He repeated these words several times, and then fled to the clothes closet and covered his head with the blanket.

■ Andrzej Szczypiorski (1924–)
The Beautiful Mrs. Seidenman (1986)

[A native of Warsaw, Andrzej Szczypiorski studied at the Academy of Political Science, and saw action during World War II as a member of the communist-led Armia Ludowa (People's Army). He began his literary career as a journalist after the war. His first fictional writing dates from 1955, the year he moved back to Warsaw after serving as editor of Polish Radio in Katowice. Although he has published several novels, including detective fiction under the pseudonym Maurice S. Andrews, his international reputation is based primarily on the novel *Początek* (Beginning, 1986; translated into English under the title *The Beautiful Mrs. Seidenman*). Like Andrzejewski's *Holy Week*, *The Beautiful Mrs. Seidenman* is the story of a Jewish woman who survives the war by living on the "Aryan" side of the Warsaw ghetto. This she manages to do because of her "Aryan" good looks, her estrangement from Judaism and Jewishness, and the false identity papers of a Polish officer's widow. Szczypiorski's novel is engrossing above all for the range of Polish and Jewish types presented, and the author's manifest desire to be evenhanded in his treatment of both groups. And at the end of the novel, in a curious twist, the scene shifts to the new state of Israel where Jewish soldiers lord it over Palestinian fedayeen. By drawing attention to what he regards as universal patterns of human behavior, Szczypiorski insinuates a curious moral relativism.

[The following excerpt introduces the phenomenon of the wartime bounty hunter of Jews.]

Not far from the wall, on the Aryan side, a certain elegant young man was circling about, known among the *szmalcowniks* as Beautiful Lolo.[1] He was slender as a poplar, fair as a spring morning, fast as the wind, bright as the Danube. He also had a real nose for Jews, zeroing in on them unerringly in the streets, and once he caught the scent, he followed it doggedly. Sometimes the prey would attempt to dodge him, for certain little Jews knew the passageways in the city, the connecting courtyards, the stores with back exits. But Beautiful Lolo knew the city even better. Truth be told, he didn't like the little Jews from the countryside, lost in Warsaw as in a strange forest, those cowed and terrified little Jews who surrendered immediately, struck by Beautiful Lolo's first, dead-accurate glance. He took from them everything they had, and sometimes it was a downright paltry penny. But a paltry penny disappointed him, and so Beautiful Lolo would then take the little Jew by the arm, lead him to the nearest precinct, or hand him over to the next military policeman, and his last words, directed at the little Jew, sounded

Andrzej Szczypiorski, *The Beautiful Mrs. Seidenman*, trans. Klara Glowczewska (New York: Grove Weidenfeld, 1989), 77–78, 184–86, 194–99.

1. *Szmalcownik* ("greaser"; from Polish *szmalec*, "grease") was the Polish slang term for a person who made money during the occupation either by blackmailing Jews in hiding or by turning them in to the German authorities.

bitter and melancholy: "Next time, kike, you should carry more cash on you. But there won't be any next time. *Adieu!*"

Saying "*Adieu!*" he felt a kind of solidarity with greater Europe, which was his motherland.

Lolo found joy in hunting. When he came upon a Jew more worthy of attention slinking through the streets, frightened but full of determination, he would tail him, letting the Jew understand that the game was up, that he was being followed, that he wouldn't get far. Then the Jew would try to dodge about cunningly, so as to put distance between himself and the hiding place where his family was. But this maneuver would never succeed under Beautiful Lolo's watchful eye. Because at the end he would catch up with the little Jew, persuade him without any trouble at all to take a walk with him and disclose the hiding place. Then they would cinch the deal. Lolo took money, jewelry, even clothing. He knew that right after he left the Jew would switch hiding places, perhaps even squat in some basement, or try to flee the city. While he was at it Lolo would also fleece the Jew's Aryan hosts, who in their panic would give him whatever he wanted. But he didn't do this often. He was never sure of being able to strike a deal with his Aryan countrymen. This kind of Polish "Sabbath goy," who hid and fed Jews, could be doing it for profit but also for lofty and humane reasons, and that always made Beautiful Lolo anxious, for the devil alone knew if a Pole like that, molded from such noble clay, wouldn't inform the underground of Lolo's visit, if he wasn't himself up to his ears in the underground, if he wouldn't bring trouble down on Beautiful Lolo's head. After all, now and then a *szmalcownik* had been known to die in a Warsaw street from the bullets of the underground, so it wasn't a good idea to take risks. For this reason also Lolo rarely turned up near the ghetto, for not only was the competition quite stiff there, but an unwelcome eye might also come to rest on his pretty face. . . .

[After her release by the Gestapo as a Polish woman named Gostomska who was mistakenly arrested as a Jew, Irma Seidenman revels in her Polishness and reflects on the alienness to her of everything Jewish. This proves bitterly ironic in view of her later forced emigration from Poland, as a Jew, in the anti-Semitic campaign of 1968. The man in knickerbockers referred to is Dr. Adam Korda, a classical philologist who befriends her.]

Never before had she felt so deeply and painfully the sense of belonging in Poland, never had she thought with such bitter joy and devotion about her Polishness. Poland, she thought, my Poland. It is these people who are Poland. This decent, unintelligent man in knickerbockers is Poland, the most sacred thing that I possess in the whole world. Her heart welled up with gratitude to fate for having made her a Pole; for it was here — in this city, among these people — that she had to suffer and endure. Never in the past had she felt connections with her Jewishness, having been brought up in the milieu of an old intelligentsia, assimilated decades ago. Her father, admittedly, was an ophthalmologist serving the Jewish poor and went around tirelessly among the rickety, foul-smelling courtyards; clambered up the damp, dark stairs of Jewish outbuildings; tended to snot-covered, dirty Jewish children in the neighborhoods of poverty and abasement. But he was himself an enlightened, educated, and prosperous man, who knew so clearly where he himself belonged that he never gave the mother even one uncertain or worried thought. And her husband, Dr. Ignacy Seidenman, felt similarly, being an accomplished radiologist with scholarly ambitions, the product of exclusive schools, an alumnus of Montpellier and Paris, a man of the world, the truest European she had ever met. And it was these two men—her father and her husband—who shaped her, who molded her into a girl, a marriageable young lady, and finally a woman, free of all doubts and anxieties resulting from questions of religion or race, removed from Jewishness, with which she was linked only by a very distant memory of a bearded old man talking to her when she was still a small child in an incomprehensible language and caressing her face with a gnarled hand; the memory of her grandfather, who died when she was five years old, maybe six, a Jew from an era long past, who linked her impassively and painlessly with those mysterious origins, with the exotic aura of Jewishness that, it is true, was all around her on the street, made itself felt sometimes in a jarring note of anti-Semitism, but generally speaking took place on the peripheries of her life because she was a blue-eyed blonde, a pretty woman with an enchanting smile and a slender figure. So Jewishness had no connections with her, existed separately—without her and beyond her—outside the sphere of her immediate experience, present, to be sure, and yet alien. Never in the past had she felt connections with Jewishness, that much she knew with absolute certainty! But perhaps for this very reason she also didn't feel any connections with Polishness, because Polishness to her was like the air she breathed—simply the self-evident. And only now, drinking milk under the watchful gaze of this comical man in knickerbockers and lace-up boots did she begin to realize that Polishness was the thing of greatest value in her life, that she was a Pole and belonged in Poland. . . .

[The following scene is from the last chapter of the novel. The wise aristocrat, Judge Romnicki, delivers the Jewish girl, Joasia, to the nun, Sister Weronika, for safekeeping for the duration of the war. Aware of the nun's thinly veiled anti-Semitism, and her desire to raise her Jewish wards as good Catholics, Romnicki tries to convince her of the futility of her intention to turn Joasia into a Catholic.]

Judge Romnicki smiled and said, "How pleasantly cool it is here."

Sister Weronika replied that the side of the building facing the vegetable garden is sometimes quite hot, but the cloister walls are thick, they go back to very distant times, and that is why it is usually cool inside.

"I brought the child," the judge said and stroked Joasia lightly on her dark head. "As we agreed."

"I understand, Judge," the nun said and looked at the little girl.

"She is a little too dark," she added after a moment.

"One cannot pick and choose these days, Sister."

"I'm not insisting on anything, but you do understand."

"Today man understands more than he should," the judge pronounced sententiously and again caressed Joasia's hair. "This is a charming little girl."

"One must always have hope, Judge."

"In accordance with what was settled upon, Mother Superior has already received certain funds," the judge said. "The war will not last forever. Besides, should the need arise, I am always at your disposal."

"It's not that," Sister Weronika replied. "We know our responsibilities, Judge." Now she caressed the child's hair.

"So her name is Joasia," she said. "We'll teach her her prayers today still."

"That might come in handy," said the judge.

Sister Weronika looked at him attentively.

"This will be a Catholic child, Judge. You brought us not only her body, in danger of terrible suffering, but also her strayed soul."

"Do you believe, Sister, that she has had the time to stray? She's only four years old, after all. Who is straying here, Sister?"

"I think it's understood that we will bring her up Catholic. It is our duty toward this child. You are a Catholic yourself, Judge, and so I don't have to prove . . ."

"Well, yes," said Judge Romnicki and wanted to end the conversation, when suddenly he felt a twofold pain. That he would have to part with this sweet, silent child. And that there was something seriously wrong with him, a feeling of deep anxiety, bitterness, or even disappointment.

So he said, "You should do what you consider right, Sister. But nothing will come of it."

"What will nothing come of?"

"This Catholicism, Sister," the judge said, and was himself surprised at the anger, perhaps even the vindictiveness, that resounded in his voice.

"What are you talking about, Judge?" Sister Weronika said harshly.

"Let me tell you something, Sister! Just try to think for a minute. Are there different gods? Or is there one and ineffable Almighty God, who has led us out of Egypt, out of the house of slavery? The same one, Sister, our merciful God, the one who revealed Himself to Moses in the burning bush, called to Jacob, stopped Abraham's knife as it was poised above Isaac's neck. That is our God, the Creator of all people . . ."

"Judge, please, remember the Savior!" Sister Weronika exclaimed.

"Let me tell you something, Sister, let me tell you something! I am a Catholic, a Roman Catholic down the generations, a Polish nobleman. I believe in Jesus Christ, in the protection of the Holy Virgin Mary. I believe in everything that religion and my beloved Poland have given me. And be so kind as not to interrupt me, Sister, because no one interrupts me when I am speaking—even President Mościcki didn't interrupt although I am certain he did not enjoy listening to cer-

tain things I said. So, what what are we talking about, Sister?! After all it's God
who led this child through five thousand years, it was God who led her by the
hand from the city of Ur to the land of Canaan, and then to Egypt, and then to
Jerusalem, and then into Babylonian captivity, and then once again into the Holy
Land, and then out over the entire vast world, to Rome and to Alexandria, to
Toledo and to Mainz—all the way here, to the shores of the Vistula. It was, after
all, God Himself who ordered this child to wander across the whole world from
one extreme to the other so that in the end she would find herself here, among
us, in this conflagration, in this end of all ends, where there is no choice anymore,
from which there is no escape other than into this cave of our Catholicism, our
Polishness, because that is the only chance of saving this child's life. So how is it to
be with the will of God, Sister? For all those thousands of years He led her so that
others might come to know Him, might understand Him, so that the Savior could
come, our Lord Jesus, in Whom we believe and Whom we adore on the Holy
Cross because He died for us, for our salvation He died under Pontius Pilate, so
for all those thousands of years the Lord led her, so that now, at the very end, she
should transform herself, should deny herself, because that's the way Adolf Hitler
wants it? Go ahead, Sister, baptize her, teach her prayers and the catechism, let
her name be Joasia Bogucka, or Joasia Kowalczykówna, I'll of course arrange it, in
two or at the most three days there will be a certificate of baptism ready, one proof
against any suspicion. Against any suspicion, in the name of a deceased Catholic
girl. So everything will be in the best possible order. Go ahead. Work on this child,
Sister. In a Christian way, in a Catholic way, in a Polish way too! I believe that
one must. It is necessary for her future, for her survival. But I will tell you, Sister,
what I think of this. We here are one thing. And God is something else. And God
will not permit it!I believe in this strongly, Sister, that He will not permit such an
ending. And she will be a Jewish woman, one day a Jewish woman will awaken in
her and she will shake the foreign dust from herself, to return to where she came
from. And her womb will be fertile, and she will bring forth new Maccabees into
the world. Because God will not forsake His own people! I am telling you this,
Sister. And now take her, Sister, and let her believe in our Lord, Jesus Christ, because that is, as you know very well, Sister, the bread of life. But one day Judith
will awaken in her, will draw a sword, and will cut off the head of Holofernes."

"Don't cry, Judge," said Sister Weronika.

And just as he said, a Jewish woman did awaken in Joasia, but not like the one
he had foreseen. Perhaps the judge did not fully understand God's designs, or
perhaps it was for a trivial reason. Joasia survived the war as Marysia Wiewóra, a
Catholic girl, an orphan from near Sanok, whose parents, poor farmers, had left
her behind in this world. After the war, she lived like the great majority of her
contemporaries, studied diligently, and considered a stomatological career, because she had agile hands and her presence had a calming influence on people.
But when she turned twenty she heard a voice calling her. And she followed it,

Bronisław Wojciech Linke (1906–62), "El Mole-Rachmim" (1946). From the cycle "The Stones Cry Out." Courtesy Muzeum Narodowe w Warszawie.

humbly and obediently. She emigrated to Israel, where she was no longer called Marysia Wiewióra but Miriam Wewer.

And she did not become a dentist. Some time after arriving in her new country, where the chosen nation was building its own state so as never again to experience persecution and humiliation, she saw strange Jews, who perhaps issued from her dreams and presentiments, or maybe appeared for quite earthbound reasons, just like others, who resembled them, had appeared before. These Jews wore berets, camouflage fatigues, and tall boots. Almost as a rule they carried loaded submachine guns under their arms. They had sunburned faces and used the spare vocabulary of armed men. Miriam saw how with one kick they would break down the doors of Palestinian houses, and then at gunpoint lead out into the blinding desert sun the bewildered fedayeen, their women and children. A kind of wild, shrill joy then awoke in her heart, as if something was finally being fulfilled, something that had been awaited for millennia, as if a dream that had been kept smothered in the generations of Israel was being realized, a dream that had burned through to the core of the tormented bodies of millions of European and Asian Jews, given life for entire centuries to these groups of eternal wanderers, gloomy, dark, frightened, cursed, and at the same time chosen. . . .

But the rapture did not last long. Miriam was a sensitive girl, and she also had a good deal of common sense. But perhaps neither her sensitivity nor her common sense would have sufficed had she not seen the subsequent scene, quite banal in fact, the most ordinary in the world and yet always educational. The Israeli soldiers, as soldiers are wont to do, stood facing the fedayeen, but the fedayeen were stooped, they held their hands behind their heads, their children screamed, although nothing was going on, their women shrieked, although no one took any interest in them, and all the while the soldiers stood there with their legs wide apart, their faces stony, looking rather stupid and boastful in this stoniness, and they held their fingers on the triggers of their guns. They stood that way, immobile, awaiting further orders from the officer, who with a swagger stick was drawing circles and lines in the desert sand, so concentrated on the historic decision he was about to make that he looked like a brainless buffoon, something in which he did not differ from all other officers in the world.

But for Miriam this was a deeply affecting scene, for she realized that she was participating in an absurdity, that no kick dealt a Palestinian fedayeen will erase centuries of history or constitute reparation. She was not educated enough to see at that moment that she was participating in an immemorial act of imitation, and that these soldiers did not invent even their imperious stance, because that is the way a man armed and conscious of his power has always stood before an unarmed and defeated one.

■ Jarosław Marek Rymkiewicz (1935–   )
The Final Station: Umschlagplatz (1988)

[Before the publication of *Umschlagplatz*—the original title of his work—Jarosław Rymkiewicz was known primarily as a poet, the genre in which he began his career as a writer in 1956. He has also written plays and essays on literary topics. Fluent in English, Rymkiewicz has published translations of Shakespeare and T. S. Eliot and wrote the introduction to a Polish collection of Wallace Stevens's poetry published in 1969.

"Umschlagplatz" refers to that area of the Warsaw ghetto where Jews were brought for deportation to the concentration camps. Since he was a child at the time, Rymkiewicz has no personal recollection of the events that make up the core of his book. Yet his obsession with the plight of the Jews during the occupation led him to explore the intricate web of Polish-Jewish relations during the Holocaust and in the immediate postwar period. His probing, unsettling work—narrated in the first person—moves from present to past and is intensely personal. Particularly noteworthy in it is the candid assessment of communist policy toward the Jews in the postwar period and the renewal of Polish-Jewish tensions attributable to it.]

"You remember Danka's story?" I ask. "The one about the woman at the corner of Grzybowska Street and Żelazna Street?"

"At the time"—this is Danka's story verbatim—"we were living on Grzybowska Street, between Wronia Street and Żelazna Street. The windows of our apartment overlooked the small ghetto and barbed wire. I used to walk past several times a day; it was the only way to the city center. We used the other side of the street. I often saw Jewish children in rags scrambling under the wire to the Aryan side, ragged little skeletons aged about five to seven. Once they had slipped through, they would start begging in the street or go from house to house knocking on the doors. The Germans—well, not actually Germans in this case; they had black uniforms, so they must have been Latvians or Ukrainians—fired shots at the small fugitives.

"One boy, he must have been about eight, called on us several times on Grzybowska Street. His name was Gecelek. It's not a name I know, but that is what we called him: 'Gecelek, we know some ladies who could hide you.' 'But I must go back, ma'am, my dad is sick and I have a little brother and I can't leave them alone. Someone has to work.' So eight-year-old Gecelek worked on the Aryan side knocking on the doors of Christian apartments. The last time he came to us—I think it was in May—he told us his dad had died, but his little brother was still alive, so he had to go back to the ghetto to look after him.

"But I want to tell you about that woman. I was nineteen at the time, and

Jarosław M. Rymkiewicz, *The Final Station: Umschlagplatz*, trans. Nina Taylor (New York: Farrar, Straus & Giroux, 1994), 41–45, 99–103.

everything that happened, everything that was done to them—how can I put it?—has made me what I am today. I was a witness, and nothing will ever change my nature now, because it was the most decisive thing in my life: I witnessed it. To come back to that woman, we were both walking down Grzybowska Street, just a few yards apart. Suddenly she began to scream. I don't recall exactly how it happened, I mean I don't remember who first noticed the child crawling under the barbed wire. I think she did. But I don't remember the child; all I remember is the woman shouting. She screamed: *Jude! Jude!*—urging the Germans or Ukrainians or Latvians to perform their duty and shoot a Jewish child. Listen, Jarek, that was not the only incident of its kind, I swear. No one knows how often it happened. But I was not the only one who heard it. It went on and on. That scream: *Jude! Jude!*"

"That woman," I asked. "Do you remember what she looked like?"

"Quite ordinary," said Danka. "Between thirty and forty years old. Anyway, she was unlucky; no one heard her prayer. Most likely there was no German or Latvian within earshot. So it all ended happily, if one can talk of a happy ending in such a context. There was a man walking ahead of me. He went up to the woman and slapped her in the face. Then he dragged her into a doorway and I don't know what happened next. He probably just continued to hit her in the face. Not that it matters. What matters is that woman. There's something about it I couldn't understand at the time, and I still can't understand it now. It's easy enough to grasp why the extortionists did what they did: they make a living from it. I can also understand the Germans: they were out to murder all Jews. But why was that woman so anxious for the Germans to capture and kill a Jewish child? Did she want to watch a small child die? What was she after?"

"From Danka's story," says Hania, "we can only infer that some people remain totally incomprehensible to others, as though they had an inexplicable mechanism inside them. If it is both incomprehensible and inexplicable, it defies description. Though who knows. Anyway it is not a topic for you. What can you be expected to know about it? You were only ten when the war ended, a small boy from Nowogródzka Street, from Koszykowa Street. When did you see your first Jew? Probably in 1945?"

"If I'm not to explore this topic," I say, "then I'd like to know who is. Do you know anyone willing to take it on? And I don't mean just what occurred here between Poles and Jews. Ultimately it may not even be the most important issue. The historians can deal with that; it's their job to document and judge our treatment of the Jewish nation, faults committed, services rendered, how many trees we have earned on Har Hazikaron, how many blackmailers we executed during the war. I'm interested in an aspect of Polish Jewish and Polish Christian relations that has not been fully thought over yet. How shall I put it? We do not know why the woman on Grzybowska Street screamed: *Jude! Jude!* It's no use calling them bastards, scoundrels, anti-Semitic scum, because that explains nothing. Though maybe I'm wrong; perhaps many an honest, pious Christian and many an honest, pious Jew has thought it all over, but is too frightened or ashamed to discuss it."

"But it is not a topic for you," Hania repeats, and tiny sparks light up, then fade and light up again in her red hair. There is something quite mysterious about this phenomenon: either her red hair catches and reflects the ambient light, trapping and entangling it, or else a secret tension is generated between the red locks, so the hair itself is a source of light. The sparks that flare up and then fade are a sort of electrical discharge, minute flashes of lightning that fly through billowing clouds, in a tempest of red hair. "That is a topic for the Jews, so let them get on with it. You just drop it."

"Even if the Jews haven't exhausted the topic yet," I say, "nothing they might still have to say can replace what the Christians can and ought to say on the subject. I sympathize with the Jews, with their wartime history and their contemporary history. I don't mean sympathy as a kind of pity, I mean it in the etymological sense of shared suffering, though not being a Jew, I feel like a Christian, I sym-pathize as a Christian. It is only as a Christian that I can address the problem. And a Christian testimony, to my mind, is what we need."

"You can't possibly write a thing like that," says Hania. "It's an absolutely impossible task. And even if you did, they'd give you such a thrashing you'd never live it down."

"Who would?"

"The Jews," says Hania, "and the Poles too. And frankly they'd both be right."

"Well, let them," I say. "In writing what it is my duty to write I am not trying to please the Poles or the Jews. It was all a highly disagreeable business, I don't think even God particularly enjoyed it, so there is no reason why anyone should enjoy it now."

"But remember, I warned you," Hania says. "As a Jew and as a Pole." . . .

"Listen, Hania. If I were a Jew, I'd have left Poland at the latest in 1950. And if I'd never left, or else left it a later date, I'd feel I had basically made a mess of my life. By 'Jew' I don't mean an assimilated or Polonized or communist convert Jew, or one who is a mixture of everything. I mean a decent, pious Orthodox Jew, because if I were a Jew that is the kind of Jew I'd want to be, lighting the candles, reading the Books, speaking Yiddish and Hebrew, with only a smattering of Polish or even no Polish at all. At least that is how I would like to imagine myself. Now, if I were a Jew I could of course be an assimilated Jew, say if my grandparents and parents, in spite of being Jews, had attended a Polish grammar school or secondary school. In that case I'd probably have no option but to continue the assimilation process. I don't know what I'd do then. The problem of assimilated Jews is too intricate for me, unlike the problem of communist Jews, which is too simple to be worth discussing. But the problem of assimilated Jews is too complex for my stupid Polish brain, and if I were a religious Jew, I'd probably conclude it was no problem for my stupid Jewish head.

"Isaac Singer once said in an interview—it was a long time ago and I can't remember where I read it, so I may have garbled or distorted it—that an assimilated Jew ceases to be a Jew and should therefore stop plaguing and pestering the Jews until he rediscovers his Jewish roots and returns to his Jewish nature. I may be exaggerating. I love Singer and all he has written for us Poles and Jews, but here I think he's going slightly over the top. As though he'd solved this thorny issue just a bit too easily, dismissively.

"But as I said, this problem surpasses my skills, because a goy like me is quite incapable of understanding the agony and torment of assimilated Jews who continue to be Jews even though they don't want to be. So I don't know, I cannot say who I'd have been and what I'd have done with myself if I'd been an assimilated Jew. I guess I'd have tried to build my Jewish-Polish, Polish-Jewish nature, my duality and dilemma, into the shifting, mobile foundations of my existence, so as to derive some spiritual benefit or existential advantage, if one can put it that way, from my duality and ambiguity. I'd exploit my dual identity as a means of enjoying a double existence. I'd use the ambiguity of my existence as a means of discovering my ambiguous self. But what can I hope to know about these things? If I had the option, I'd still choose the life of a pious Jew: tallith, mezuzah, tefillin, Torah, Talmud.

"I grant you, I might well have ceased to be the pious religious Jew from Jadów or Radzymin after all that happened to me during the war. I'd quite probably conclude that the cruel jokes of my Jewish God make it impossible for me to continue believing in Him. I might even concede that my own pious person is one of His jokes. But despite all that I'd not stop being a Jew, a Jew who wants to be a Jew and nothing but a Jew.

"To return to my earlier point: that is why I'd have left Poland in 1950 at the latest. I might have left even earlier, right after the pogrom in Kielce, in the summer or fall of 1946. Why on earth should I live in a country where Jews are constantly beaten up, and not only beaten but murdered—forty killed in the Kielce pogrom? It can hardly be pleasant for a Jew to live in a country that is one great Jewish cemetery, an overheated cemetery where the smoke from three million bodies drifts between sky and earth. And why should I have left in 1950 at the latest? Because persecutions of Jews started up afresh in 1949.

"Compared with wartime events this was mere child's play, no bastinadoes, no murders, no torturing. At the time, the Poles were torturing and murdering fellow Poles with far greater gusto. But in this case communists were settling scores with Poles who didn't want them, and if I'd been a Jew I doubt if I'd have got very involved. Why should I feel pity for Poles who during the war had shown no mercy for Jews? At least that is how I would have argued as a Jew.

"How should I define this new wave of persecutions? Persecution may be too strong a word. No one was harmed. For the umpteenth time since the world began the Jews were simply denied the right to their Jewish separateness, Jewish autonomy, and Jewish dignity. In December 1949 the communists, who had already assumed control of existing Jewish organizations in Poland, delegalized all

Jewish political parties. The Jews were given the option of continuing to live and function in communist Poland, to flourish and prosper even, on the condition that they obeyed the communists, collaborated with them, and helped them in the pleasurable pastime of tormenting the Poles.

"Many Jews accepted the proposal. If I'd been a Jew at the time I'd feel bitterly ashamed to reflect back on it now. But I am a goy—on that score my conscience is clear—so let the Jews feel guilty when they remember the Jews who behaved like non-Jews. If I'd been a Jew at that time I guess I'd have felt persecuted. For the communist proposal to collaborate contained a perverse and carefully veiled threat: either you renounce your Jewish separateness or you can pack up and go to your Palestine and Israel, we don't mind. So if I'd been a Jew at that time I'd have been forced to acknowledge that the only real option was to stop being a Jew or else get out. A sickening choice. What would I have decided if faced with this option? As I've already told you, I'd have chosen the second alternative as more palatable and dignified.

"Under the circumstances it is hardly surprising that a Jew who wanted to re- main a Jew, and felt disinclined to build socialism in Poland for the Poles, packed his bags and left. One could obviously argue that the Jews were solicited, not by Poles, but by the very Jews who many Poles seem to think were governing Poland in those days, like Hilary Minc or Jakub Berman or Roman Zambrowski.

"One might also claim that the Jews were placed in this predicament, not by Poles or by Jews, but by communists—in other words, by people who were neither Poles nor Jews. A wise old Jew reckons that a Jew who converts to communism ceases to be a Jew, as he no longer deserves to be one. The fact that he has joined the party proves he is either terribly stupid or stark raving mad. That's supposed to be a joke. When telling this joke, wise old Jews with communist pasts smile ambiguously to intimate that they were once rather foolish too, but that they have now outgrown their folly. So if it's a joke, it's meant provocatively, as it's not without relevance to some Poles.

"Yet even if we concede from the hindsight of forty years that it was not the Jews or the Poles but strange mutants who seized power in Poland and wanted to deprive the Jews of their Jewish separateness, it seems very unlikely that forty years ago Polish Jews should have seen and understood it that way. They were living in Poland. The government that wanted to turn them by means of some new and unprecedented form of assimilation into the builders of Polish commu- nism claimed to be the government of Poland. Whatever befell them was inspired and instigated by Poles. I imagine that's how they saw it. Even if they were acting on Stalin's orders, Stalin was a long way off, the Poles were around the corner. And whatever the Poles kept wanting of the Jews, it was never what the Jews wanted for themselves."

Selected Bibliography of Works in English on the Jews of Poland and Polish-Jewish Relations

Abramsky, Chimen, Maciej Jachimczyk, and Antony Polonsky, eds. *The Jews in Poland.* Oxford: Basil Blackwell, 1986.

Banas, Josef. *The Scapegoats: The Exodus of the Remnants of Polish Jewry.* Trans. Tadeusz Szafar. Ed. Lionel Kochan. London: Weidenfeld & Nicholson, 1979.

Bartoszewski, Władysław. *The Bloodshed Unites Us: Pages from the History of Help to the Jews in Occupied Poland.* Warsaw: Interpress, 1970.

———. *The Warsaw Ghetto: A Christian Testimony.* Boston: Beacon Press, 1987.

Bartoszewski, Władysław, and Zofia Lewin, eds. *Righteous among Nations: How Poles Helped the Jews, 1939–1945.* London: Earlscourt, 1969.

Bartoszewski, Władysław, and Antony Polonsky, eds. *The Jews in Warsaw: A History.* Oxford: Basil Blackwell, 1991.

Checinski, Michael. *Poland: Communism, Nationalism, Anti-Semitism.* Trans. in part by Tadeusz Szafar. New York: Karz-Cohl, 1982.

Davies, Norman, and Antony Polonsky. *Jews in Eastern Europe and the USSR, 1939–46.* Houndmills, Basingstoke, Hampshire: Macmillan, 1991.

Eisenbach, Artur. *The Emancipation of the Jews in Poland.* Trans. Janina Dorosz. Ed. Antony Polonsky. Oxford: Basil Blackwell, 1991.

Fuks, Marian, Zygmunt Hoffman, Maurycy Horn, and Jerzy Tomaszewski. *Polish Jewry: History and Culture.* Trans. Bogna Piotrowska and Lech Petrowicz. Warsaw: Interpress, 1982.

Heller, Celia Stopnicka. *On the Edge of Destruction: Jews of Poland between the Two World Wars.* Detroit: Wayne State University Press, 1994.

Hertz, Aleksander. *The Jews in Polish Culture.* Trans. Richard Lourie. Ed. Lucjan Dobroszycki. Evanston, Ill.: Northwestern University Press, 1985.

Hundert, Gershon David. *The Jews in a Polish Private Town: The Case of Opatów in the Eighteenth Century.* Baltimore: Johns Hopkins University Press, 1992.

Irwin-Zarecka, Iwona. *Neutralizing Memory: The Jew in Contemporary Poland.* New Brunswick, N.J.: Transaction, 1989.

Korboński, Stefan. *The Jews and the Poles in World War II.* New York: Hippocrene Books, 1989.

Levine, Hillel. *Economic Origins of Antisemitism: Poland and Its Jews in the Early Modern Period.* New Haven: Yale University Press, 1991.

Lewin, Abraham. *A Cup of Tears: A Diary of the Warsaw Ghetto.* Ed. Antony Polonsky. Trans. Christopher Hutton. Oxford: Basil Blackwell, 1988.

Lewin, Isaac. *A History of Polish Jewry during the Revival of Poland.* New York: Shengold, 1990.

Lewin, Isaac, and Nahum Michael Gelber. *The Jewish Community in Poland: Historical Essays.* New York: Philosophical Library, 1985.

Marcus, Joseph. *Social and Political History of the Jews in Poland, 1919–1939.* Berlin: Mouton, 1983.

Mendelsohn, Ezra. *The Jews of East Central Europe between the World Wars.* Bloomington: Indiana University Press, 1983.

———. *Zionism in Poland: The Formative Years, 1915–1926.* New Haven: Yale University Press, 1981.

Mushkat, Marion. *Philo-Semitic and Anti-Jewish Attitudes in Post-Holocaust Poland.* Lewiston: Edwin Mellen Press, 1992.

Niezabitowska, Małgorzata. *Remnants: The Last Jews of Poland.* Trans. William Brand and Hanna Dobosiewicz. New York: Friendly Press, 1986.

Opalski, Magdalena. *The Jewish Tavern-Keeper and His Tavern in Nineteenth-Century Polish Literature.* Jerusalem: Zalman Shazar Center, 1986.

Opalski, Magdalena, and Israel Bartal. *Poles and Jews: A Failed Brotherhood.* Hanover: University Press of New England, 1992.

Pogonowski, Iwo Cyprian. *Jews in Poland: A Documentary History.* New York: Hippocrene Books, 1993.

Polonsky, Antony. *Politics in Independent Poland, 1921–1939.* Oxford: Clarendon Press, 1972.

———, ed. *"My Brothers' Keeper?": Recent Polish Debates on the Holocaust.* London: Routledge, 1990.

Polonsky, Antony, Jakub Basista, and Andrzej Link-Lenczowski, eds. *The Jews in Old Poland, 1000–1795.* London: I. B. Tauris, 1991.

Ringelbaum, Emmanuel. *Polish-Jewish Relations during the Second World War.* Trans. Dafna Allon, Danuta Dabrowska, and Dana Keren. Ed. Joseph Kermish and Shmuel Krakowski. New York: Howard Fertig, 1976.

Rosman, Murray Jay. *The Lords' Jews: Magnate-Jewish Relations in the Polish-Lithuanian Commonwealth during the Eighteenth Century.* Cambridge: Harvard University Press, 1990.

Schatz, Jaff. *The Generation: The Rise and Fall of the Jewish Communists of Poland.* Berkeley and Los Angeles: University of California Press, 1991.